RELUCTANT IMPERIALIST

TIM HARDY

An adventurous life in

COLONIAL MALAYA,

AFRICA, FIJI and HONG KONG

Marshall Cavendish
Editions

To my grandchildren and great grandchildren.

Cover design: Opalworks
© 2009 Marshall Cavendish International (Asia) Pte Ltd
Published by Marshall Cavendish Editions
An imprint of Marshall Cavendish International
1 New Industrial Road, Singapore 536196

Other Marshall Cavendish Offices
Marshall Cavendish Ltd. 5th Floor, 32–38 Saffron Hill, London RC1N 8FH, UK • Marshall Cavendish Corporation. 99 White Plains Road, Tarrytown NY 10591-9001, USA • Marshall Cavendish International (Thailand) Co Ltd. 253 Asoke, 12th Flr, Sukhumvit 21 Road, Klongtoey Nua, Wattana, Bangkok 10110, Thailand • Marshall Cavendish (Malaysia) Sdn Bhd, Times Subang, Lot 46, Subang Hi-Tech Industrial Park, Batu Tiga, 40000 Shah Alam, Selangor Darul Ehsan, Malaysia

Marshall Cavendish is a trademark of Times Publishing Limited

National Library Board Singapore Cataloguing in Publication Data
Hardy, Tim, 1922-
The reluctant imperialist : an adventurous life in colonial Malaya, Africa, Fiji and Hong Kong / Tim Hardy. – Singapore : Marshall Cavendish Editions, c2009.
p. cm.
ISBN-13 : 978-981-261-768-2 (pbk.)

1. Hardy, Tim, 1922- 2. Police chiefs – Great Britain – Biography. 3. Colonial administrators – Great Britain – Biography. 4. Great Britain – Colonies – History – 20th century. 5. Great Britain – Colonies – Biography. I. Title.

HV7911
363.2092—dc22   OCN308973490

Printed in Singapore by Utopia Press Pte Ltd

Contents

Foreword

Tim was born in Nottingham in 1922 into a large and poor family of miners. He left school at 14, went to work, joined the Labour Party, educated himself, especially in literature and left-wing politics, fought in the Parachute Regiment during WW2, was dropped into occupied France on the night before DDay, got married and ended the war in Java – where he saw the South Asian world he came to love for the first time. After the war he joined the Special Branch of the British Colonial Police and was sent to live in the jungles of Malaya during the Communist insurgency of the 1940's – 1950's. Here Tim made life-long friendships with all types of people, '*The leaders of the Thai and Malay communities, and sweepers, ticket collectors, clerks, porters, shop assistants, businessmen...*' a habit he was to continue all over the world, and much of the tone of these memoirs is captured in a related sentence, '*The only intelligence I managed to collect in Perlis was how to play tennis and I was not much good at that either*'.

His career, specialising in the field of counter-terrorism, continued in Penang (Malaysia/Malaya), Tanganyika (Tanzania), Sarawak (Malaysia), Fiji and Hong Kong. Typically however Tim insists, '*I virtually never wore a uniform, and I became an Assistant Commissioner of Police without ever attending a training course*'. In Sarawak he was made Head of Special Branch during the confrontation with Indonesia, the memoirs describe this significant period in South Asian history in great detail. After this Tim was Head of Special Branch in Fiji: he lived through and describes the decline of Empire during the Cold War period and the creation of new Commonwealth democracies, and he writes warmly and perceptively about the important figures in this historic process that he knew and worked with, such as Julius Nyerere.

Tim writes vividly about his extraordinary life, his journey from the hard work and poverty of the coal mining towns around Nottingham to the beautiful islands of the Pacific, becoming an important figure, advising Ministers and Presidents in new Nations. All the time, though mixing with and working for the establishment, he retains the perspective of egalitarian socialism that he learned before the war: a man who left school while still a boy, to go straight to work, mixing with public school, University-educated people who were raised to rule people like him and his family. He writes knowledgeably, and in many places very critically but always readably, of the British Colonial Military and Security services in, for example, Hong Kong prior to the takeover by China. Throughout, his love of the places and peoples he lived among is conveyed by a humorous and lively descriptive style.

In 1982, Tim and his wife Doreen retired to a small hamlet in Shropshire, in England, on the Welsh border. After 35 years in the tropics the long, cold English winters were a new and unwelcome test of endurance. So Tim sat down, '*At a little desk, in a little room, in our little place*' and began writing his memoirs, in pen in large manuscript books. They took three winters to complete. But this work was not done just to deal with the winter: '*I knew very little of my grandparents and great grandparents, nothing was written down about them, we never had a letter in the post or even a letter box when I was a boy*'. So Tim's memoirs were initially written as a record of his life for his descendants (hence the dedication). But he also says '*I wanted to leave something, my history was so unusual I thought it ought to be written down... very few people went to five colonies and saw so many flag-lowering ceremonies, especially from my background.*'

It has taken many years but now everyone will be able to enjoy, learn from, and maybe marvel at, my father's amazing life story.

Chris Hardy
London, February 2009

Editor's Note: Although named Stanley at birth, the author was dubbed 'Tim' by Doreen (see page 83) who later became his wife. And Tim was the name he used subsequently, burying Stanley forever.

Above: Tim at age 11 in a photograph taken for school.

Right: Tim's parents Harry and Harriet Hardy in the 1950's

Below: Padang Besar, Malaya, 1951 — Tim (front second from left) with local officials, School Master, Station Master, Customs Officers.

Above: A highlight of Tim's Malaya posting was playing in the police football team, Pasir Mas 1953.

Above: Tim and Doreen Hong Kong 1983

Left: Tim and Roy Henry, Fiji 1971

Right: Tim, Doreen and children Jane and Christopher, Dar es Salaam 1960/61.

Aboce: Tim and his father Harry 1963

Above: Tim and Doreen relaxing on the beach, Sarawak 1965.

Left: Highgate Cemetery 1980

Above: Captain Chalong and Tim, Songkla, Thailand, 1965

Right: Bakiong, the Hardy's house-keeper and family, Kuching, 1963.

Above: Penang 1956: Tim was aide for a day to the Duke of Edinburgh ('I loathed wearing uniform').

- TICKET TAULIAH   S.C. 2

Ada-lah .... S. HARDY ....

No. .... ini telah dijadikan
dia saorang ASSISTANT COMMISSIONER
Sarawak Constabulary serta djberi akan
dia sachukup-chukup-nesa bagi kaadilan
menjadi saorang Pegawai Aman.

For .... Commissioner
Sarawak Constabulary.

Tarikh .... 8TH FEBRUARY 19.66

Tanda tangan Pemgang; Hardy

Chap Ibu Jari Kiri.

Above: Tim's Police Identity Card in Kuching, 1966.

1922–1939
The Deformative Years

St. Michael's Street

Lying in a heat-induced stupor on a Hong Kong beach, idly flipping through the May 1972 issue of a local journal *The Catholic Post-Secondary*, my eye caught a headline on page 6: 'A Solipsist Monogatory', a mini-autobiography, its author, one 'Tim-tim', opened with the momentous line: 'I was born on the day of my birth.'

The coincidence vulcanised me to my hot rock; not only was the biographer my binary namesake but, just like me, he'd been born on the day of his birth! Thus was I prompted to write my own 'Solipsist Monogatory'.

I, Tim Hardy, slithered out of Harriet Hardy, nee Scott, on 18 June 1922, sliding out into a world that only fours years earlier had been hoodwinked into believing that with the close of the 'war to end all wars', it could settle into eternal peace and plenty. My moving spirit, 'Tim-tim', failed to disclose the whereabouts of his birthplace (we can only assume it to have been somewhere within the vastness of Cathay) but I'll be more open and above board and tell you straight out that I first saw light in a little room in a little house in a mean street in a mean town. The address? No.63, St. Michael's Street, Sutton-in-Ashfield, Nottinghamshire, England.

I was a nobody born to nobodies. A few somebodies also lived in Sutton but we came across them only when they hired and fired us; lanced our boils; mended our broken limbs; pulled our teeth; turfed us out for not paying the rent; declared us to be 'consumptive', fit only to be shoved away in the 'San'; dubbed us 'indigent', to be locked away in workhouses and prisons; and, finally, they intoned to their gods over our corpses.

No.63 was one of many houses that faced each other on either side of St. Michael's Street. Apart from a 'jennel' at intervals the identical brick fronts ran unbroken from the top of the long street to the bottom, sharing one elongated roof on either side. Jennels were dark, slummy tunnels, which penetrated the rows of houses in order to give the inhabitants access to the courtyards that ran down the backs of the houses. If you were lucky, as we Hardys were, to rent a place immediately on either side of a jennel, you'd certainly be tormented by the noise of the ceaseless to-and-fro of people, animals and wheelbarrows but that nuisance would be more than compensated for by your having an extra – albeit miniscule – bedroom above it.

Like the houses in every other street for miles around, ours were built of the cheapest materials, constructed by and belonging to skin-flint mine-owners for the sole purpose of providing just enough shelter to keep colliers in good enough physical condition to enable them to hew coal from 'Faces' deep in the earth below their feet. Comforts didn't come into it; the houses furnished the barest minimum of what would nowadays be called 'services'. There were in fact just four of these; one cold faucet (the sole source of water) positioned above an earthenware sink in the scullery; a cast-iron 'range', and 'the boiler'. The latter, thoughtfully seated immediately beside the sink, was a big metal cistern set in cement above a small firebox. Unlike Quasimodo's great cauldron, this crucible – a central feature of the household – was used, not for boiling oil to pour over opponents but for boiling the dirt out of clothing and linen and for cooking up broths, pig-swill and illicit brews. Next to the boiler there came the heart of the dwelling: 'the hearth', a cast-iron 'range' set in the wall beneath the main chimney flue. Its centrepiece was an open fireplace that, besides warming the scullery, heated two 'hobs' (hot plates) on either side of the fire and each above a small oven. They were our only 'services'. But wait – a gas lamp hung from each of the ceilings of the two downstairs rooms (being sparsely furnished the front room or parlour was hardly ever used), for illumination upstairs we used candles.

The scullery at No.63, about six metres square, was the combination of living room, kitchen, bathroom, wash-house, dining-room, study, nursery, box-room, cloak-room, vestibule and games room for a family of six plus a dog. It was dominated by the fireplace, which all the year round, at times augmented by the boiler, pumped out heat. Its flames roared up the chimney and its coals blazed hot enough to boil kettles, bake bread in the ovens and heat saucepans and flat-irons on the hobs. In times of big freeze or heat wave alike, the bread still had to be baked, the water boiled and the clothes dried and ironed. On cold winter days, the scullery would be nice and snug – the Englishman in his castle beside his hearth sort of thing – but on warm June days the atmosphere wasn't anywhere near as romantic.

We St. Michael's Street Hardys were seldom really clean. How could we have been? With coal dust raining down from the skies every minute, even had we never moved from the scullery for the whole week, come the Saturday bath night and we'd still have been grubby. Over and above that, at least as far as the three males in the family were concerned (I can't speak for the three females), we wore neither underwear nor sleeping garments. Instead of underpants we tucked our shirt tails between our legs, while at bedtime all we did was remove our outer clothing and turn in wearing the shirt we'd wear for seven days at a time. Then again, all petty ablutions performed between one Saturday and the next – I mean all the washing, shaving, teeth-cleaning, hair-combing and nit-picking – was done under the one and only tap at the one and only sink before the one and only flyblown looking-glass.

Clean? Look at our old man, George Henry Hardy. Straight from having lain on his belly hacking away at coal for several hours he'd come home at about four o'clock of an afternoon looking like a miniature slag heap on two legs; his eyes and mouth the only visible parts of him that weren't sooty black. Right away he'd strip to the waist and bend over the sink to sluice water over the front of his torso while our mother, Harriet, scrubbed his back. His lower half couldn't have been much cleaner than the upper; even so it got washed only once a week. And given the fact that he didn't wear pyjamas over his legs when he went to bed, you can figure for yourselves how mucky the bedsheets were by the end of each week. No wonder Harriet rubbed her knuckles red on scrubbing boards every Monday morning.

Anyway, you can see that we were, well, unclean. Except, that is, for one night of the week – Saturday – when we took our weekly bath. Soon after high tea, a zinc tub (about half the size of a modern bath) that otherwise hung from a nail in the yard outside, was hauled into the scullery and with much banging about, plonked down on the rug in front of the hearth where it would be half-filled with water heated in as many kettles and saucepans as Harriet could fit on top of the 'range'. And then we were ready to bathe. The decencies, as always, were strictly observed. Not once in my life did I catch a glimpse of as much as an inch of flesh I wasn't supposed to see on any of the three women in our family. We bathed in separate male and female shifts, the water being changed at the changeover of the shift. We three males took turns, usually after tossing a coin. Inevitably, he who was last had to immerse himself in greyish, greasy, grizzly, lukewarm suds from which he emerged soon afterwards (there was no time for soaking) cleaner – but not by that much – than he'd been before he went in.

Another reason, apart from working-class prudishness, why I never got an eyeful of naughty female flesh was that for much of the time – when we were upstairs anyway, and that's where the undressing took place, we couldn't see ourselves clearly. Downstairs on dark nights we relied for illumination on the single gas mantle hanging from the scullery ceiling. It gave off a pleasant yellow light and a soothing hiss. Upstairs we had to make do with candles but only to see ourselves up the stairs and into bed; never, unless you were bedridden through illness, to brighten the room – candles cost money.

Standing about 20 paces from the house at the bottom of the backyard stood a brick shed the size of a sentry box – our lavatory. If taken short during the night, you were permitted to carry a candle to light your way but keeping it alight in a cross breeze prompted the better practice of following your nose. Once inside the door and having swept the seat of coal dust and, sometimes, snow, you settled down over a hole cut into rough wooden planks raised about two feet above the floor. You discharged into a big, hopefully well-positioned, double-handled, iron bucket. Provided always that some thoughtful soul had taken the trouble to tear them into 12-inch squares in the first place you wiped your arse on old newspapers that hung on a nail driven into the inside of the rickety wooden door. Being an iconoclast from a very early age, I found that the arrangement made for marvellously therapeutic movements. If, for instance, I discovered a royal likeness looking at me from one of the squares of newspaper, I'd evacuate gleefully and then perform one of the most exquisite, nigh-orgasmic, acts of gross lese-majesty in the book. These microseconds apart however the best that could be said for our privies was that they discouraged diarrhoea and constipation alike.

If urination was your early need you did it in the bedroom in a chamber pot that was emptied every day into the privy bucket which in its turn was emptied by 'night-soil' men once a week. A family of six would easily fill a latrine bucket to the brim in a week; hence twixt 'loo' at the bottom of the yard and 'perfume wagon' in the street there'd be many a slip; the spillover usually ending up in the jennel.

Neighbours hurled charge and counter-charge about whose turds fouled the passageway and who, accordingly, was responsible for clearing them away; nobody ever owned up.

Together with a rough coal-shed-cum-chicken-run-cum-pig-sty, the privy helped separate our stretch of the cobblestone backyard from our neighbours on either side. Some families tried to stamp their individualism on their space by putting up cheap fencing but it was so awful that it made the place look more God-forsaken than ever. The entire street-length of the backyard was crisscrossed with washing lines and cluttered with enough litter to make it look like an elongated rag-and-bone man's yard; home-made wheelbarrows (a 'barrer' for carting coal being essential to life; every house had one) bathtubs (not every house had one) botched-together push-chairs; rolls of old, rusted, ordure-clogged chicken-wire; heaps of kindling, dustbins; rabbit hutches; tubs of pig-swill; and all the other sorry detritus of poor living.

Thinking back, the only reason that St. Michael's Street wasn't a slum was because most folk who lived in it struggled mightily to keep it from becoming one. There were times when it was touch and go, when they nearly gave up and there were always those whom poverty overwhelmed but by and large communal self-esteem kept us just inside the line of civilisation. We all suffered the afflictions imposed by living barely above subsistence level: malnourishment, ignorance, self-depreciation, lice, fevers, sores, snuffles, rickets, pneumonia, bed-bugs and exhaustion but our women still pumiced the front-door steps and black-leaded their cooking ranges. For another thing, pertinent to this because of what I was to come to later, our tribe never shouted racial odds; for them the conflict was always between 'them' and 'us' – the 'thems' being the haves, be they Jews, Hottentots or Zulus; the 'us' being the have-nots, be they Muslims, Chinese or Yankees. They were neither heroic nor clever neither were they very engaging people but they were the only folk I knew at the time. And, of course, the ones I knew best and thought were the best were family.

The Paternal Side: the Hardys
Abe and Sarah

My paternal grandparents, Abraham and Sarah Anne Hardy, lived just across the street in a house identical to ours in every respect except that theirs wasn't next to a jennel. Abe was a slightly built, sinewy, cheeky moustached fellow with dark, merry, intelligent eyes and a sharpness about him that set him apart from the rest of the St. Michael's Street males, the difference being confirmed by his not being a collier. Not that he was all that much higher in the social class then his coal-pocked neighbour for he was nothing more than a pick-and-shovel labourer for the gas company (Abe never knew it of course but, forever digging holes and then filling them in again, he was your quintessential, empirical Keynesian) but his bearing, his cockiness made him stick out like a Papuan among Eskimos.

Abe was most different because of working above ground, not below it, and also in daylight in the open air, not in suffocating darkness. To cap it all, he was never 'laid off', never experienced the desolate feeling that came to men who had nothing to take home of a Friday evening. Almost alone among his peers in St. Michael's Street, Abe could count on collecting a wage – albeit a measly one – every Friday, meaning that he could meet every single weekly rent demand, a blessing others could only dream of. He could even afford a nightly jug of ale; I know that much because for a time one of my fixed 'errands' (each of us under 14 years had routine family chores) was at six sharp every evening to fetch Abe's pint and a half of mild and bitter which I carried across a large swathe of derelict land behind St. Michael's Street in a big jug that had been filled at the off-licence (a.k.a 'beer-off').

The uninterrupted flow of beer was in itself enough to confirm my grandfather's superior status but he had impressive family connections as well; his brother-in-law, Isaac Caunt, was a man of distinctive, if severe, even foreign, features. Isaac, who ran a pub in Hucknall, was given to wearing wing collars, bow ties, cravats, trilbies and spats and also to keeping his distance from the rest of us.

My grandma, Sarah Anne Hardy, nee Barker, was a short, dumpy woman with the face of an angry Manchester terrier and the voice of an anti-personnel mine. She was perpetually bad-tempered but she wasn't as jaundiced as she had a right to be after a lifetime of bearing umpteen children in a four-room house and neither was she so subdued as to be unable to seize the poker and chase her tormentor upstairs when he came home drunk, as Abe often did. There were few secrets in the street; at one time or another, most of its inhabitants had heard Sarah Anne's foghorn as, poker in hand and bellowing epithets, she charged up the stairs, always a step or two behind Abraham. It was in a little room at the top of these stairs that I was taken to witness the last moments of Sarah's father, my great-grandfather. Only about four then, I still remember being plonked at the foot of the bed in which there lay a person of whom only a head was visible: a large head it was, framed in thin white hair and a bushy white beard that flowed over the sheet. And the head croaked dryly like a worn out frog and then it stopped and I was told that my great-granddad was dead. That's how nobodies died in those days – in their own beds watched over by their own kind; old folk, middle-aged people, youngsters and babies – that's how they all went in those days.

Abe and Sarah were to finish their days in a pokey bungalow, one of a row built along the Sheepwash by the local council in a brave, commendable effort to give pensioners a place of their own to end their lives in and, as some people said, unkindly, to get them out of sight. Their last home was hardly big enough for Abe to lift his beer mug in, let alone to accommodate Sarah's wide as a church-door hips. Totally submissive because they had divined in their bones that their time was upon them, they took with them from St. Michael's Street only one bed, a little table, a few pots and pans, a coal shovel and two, just two, chairs. They settled themselves on either side of the mantelpiece, Abe to mourn the passing of the evenings when he could afford to sink his pint and a half of mild and bitter (his pension came to ten shillings and sixpence a week) and Sarah Anne, perhaps, to regret not having a staircase up which to drive her Abe. Forewarned or not they went quite slowly – though not unhappily – downhill, Sarah faster than Abe. They died as they'd lived, numbed by their environment without ever raising their eyes to horizons further distant than Skegness where during their entire life-span they'd spent no more than one or two seven-day holidays. Beyond gossiping about the people they lived amongst, they'd nothing to say to a visitor and yet to be with them was always to be at ease, to be quiet and harmonious.

Their offspring were, to put it mildly, unglamorous (they were short and runty, characteristics inherited by your chronicler) but they were a good deal more gumptious that the physically better-favoured in-laws on my maternal grandparents' side. Here's who they were:

Wilfred

Wilfred, the eldest, had bad teeth, but then so had almost everybody else. What made his look so much worse was that the few good molars he'd kept were so haphazardly positioned that they threw his jaw askew. Thus, what little speech he ever bothered to utter came out as a clobbering growl. It was a joke in the family that when visiting Wilfred you should carry an umbrella. He married Charlotte, a rather indecorous lady who nonetheless deserved better than 'Wilf'. Poor Wilf, the only colour he brought into anybody's life was the black of the coal dust that covered him every day he was at work.

Phoebe

Then came Phoebe, taller than other Hardys, raw-boned, short-sighted and bossy; a Thatcherite long before Margaret Hilda Roberts marked her own baleful creed of selfishness. Phoebe was every bit as raucous and as unfeeling as the daughter of the Grantham grocer ever was. She got no more than she deserved when she married John ('Jack') Pilsworth for he was a thin, humourless, dry-as-dust, miserly factory-hand employed in what had become the town's second industry – hosiery knitting. Both as stingy as they come, Phoebe and Jack scraped enough money between them to rent an off-licence. Any other Hardy would have drunk the profits as fast as they made them but the Pilsworths confounded both family and customers by going on the wagon. They ran the business with all the charm of an abattoir; even so, it prospered. Hard as it is to imagine the act being performed by so sour-spirited a pair, Phoebe (always the dominant partner) and Jack must have coupled at least once for they begat a Phoebe clone – Connie. Connie, however, was a clone only in her nature, by physique she came to resemble her chubby little Grandma Hardy. She was no sooner out of school at 14 than she 'went into business' as a hairdresser. A few years on and she hitched her star to that of a fellow barber together with whom she opened a *salon de beaute* which they ran as joylessly but not as profitably as Connie's parents ran their dram shop.

Winifred

Winnie, as brassy as a pawnbroker's knocker, was a regular Hardy female: a stocky micro morph with glassy eyes and a tocsin for a voice. She married Ernest Smith, a 'ganger'. (Half a dozen colliers would hire themselves out as a team; they'd nominate a ganger who'd cut deals with one of a coal-mine's 'deputies' (foremen), direct the digging operations and 'divvy up' the collective wage.) Being childless and with Ernest's status as a 'Ganger' affording him first go at his gang's communal pay-packet, the Smiths were relatively well-to-do. They were forever showing off to their more threadbare relatives like us.

They even purchased on the never-never, one of the first automatic-feed gramophones to come on the market. As eager to gawp at it as they were to flaunt it, we'd go round to Winnie's just to stare; mesmerised at the shiny monster, big as a sideboard. Displaying all the muscle-power of a ganger, Uncle Ernest would lift 12 heavy wax 78 rpm discs all at once, stack them one on top of the other inside the great machine, switch it on and then move the needle box until it fell into the sound groove of the bottom record. As each disc was spent – about every three minutes or so – the one immediately above it would fall upon it with a dust-raising thump, the needle arm would move automatically into its new position and off we'd go again until all 12 discs had been played. The rattling and banging of the moving parts was much more attention grabbing than the music. Indeed, the operation caused such havoc to the discs' surfaces that the Smiths all too soon cared only for the miracle of the automation, the novelty of which faded fast.

It was a blessing then when, even before Ernest had paid the final hire-purchase instalment, the automatic system packed in for good; the machine would now play only one record at a time. Both Winnie and Ernest were "buggered if they were going to get off their arses every three minutes"; they chucked the discs and the mechanical innards away and turned the gutted cabinet into an odds-and-ends repository whose contents were easily as interesting as the discs had been. The external, fake veneer hid things like shoe-polish, grate-blacking, broken clothes pegs, bits of old clothes lines (always useful for tying round Ernest's pit trousers just below the knee) empty tins, odd socks, bald scrubbing brushes, broken dentures (just about everyone who lived beyond 40 wore cheap, ill-fitting false-teeth), cracked spectacles and so on.

Abe died at Winnie's place (Sarah had gone before in the bungalow). He'd only been sick a day or two. One day he'd been in the pub, the next he was discovered standing over the fireplace in Winnie's 'front-room' holding fast to the mantlepiece and shaking one failing leg after another while swearing that he'd "mek the buggers werk". Winnie always had it that the woman next door called to see him on the night he died to ask if there was anything she could do for him. "Aye there is an' all," he's said to have responded, "bring a bottle a' gin and get in 'ere wi' me."

Annie

A pint-sized, chain-smoking, hard-faced, heavy-drinking harridan and a soccer hooligan to boot (she'd have been over the fence at the 'Eyeties' in the Heysel Stadium) Annie married Arthur Denby, a handsome, mild-mannered, non-smoking, teetotalling ganger who couldn't have cared less about football. Arthur, who'd been in the army in Salonika during World War I (1914–18), never stopped talking about Greece. He'd nothing to say about Hellenic furies but plenty about fevers, flies, bedbugs, dysentery, bad food, mosquitoes, military incompetence and "them thievin' Griks". Arthur and Annie begat Ronnie, a plump, rosy-cheeked, much-pampered fellow upon whom they lavished bounty, which to the rest of us was in the realm of treasure: such marvels as comics and even a real football. The football, the envy of youths for miles around, was a round leather casement with a three-inch slit through which you inserted a pig's bladder and which was laced up with a leather thong, an operation that frayed finger ends and tempers equally. Ronnie, who was the closest friend I had as a youth, might well have made something of himself had he not been killed at Anzio during the World War II (1939–45). "Anzio or Salonika," moaned Arthur, for whom geography wasn't a strong point, "wot's difference? Bluddy Griks."

Hilda

Scrawny, large-headed and vinegary as she was, Hilda still set her cap at and hooked one Harry Heppenstall, a dapper, thick-set chap off whom she begat Wilfred. Wilf grew into a nice, even-tempered young man who astounded all of us by breaking through the class barrier, albeit at its very lowest level. He became a post-office clerk no less and thus blackened his fingers with ink, not coal dust. Maybe even such a modest leap was too much for him though for he became unhinged, some said because he'd been shell-shocked during World War II, others because after his dad's early death he spent his last good many years in the sole company of his increasingly acidic, tobacco-addicted mother. Whichever way it was, the fact remained that for the last 40 years of his life the harmless, gentle Wilfred lived within a mindscape into which only he had access.

George Henry (Harry I)
My father, called 'Harry I', to whom we'll return later.

The Maternal Side: the Scotts
Charles and Maria
My maternal grandparents, Charles (never 'Charlie') and Maria Scott, lived in a colliers' row in Morley Street, a thoroughfare not far from St. Michael's Street that had lost so many of its sons in 'the war to end all wars' that it put up its very own roll of honour. Charles Scott was a good-looking man, Mexican-moustached, hirsute, large-eyed, heavy-browed, soft-voiced and gentle, a man seemingly unvulgarised by spending a third of a lifetime underground at the coalface. Maria, nee Armstrong, was a perpetually black-robed bulk whose grossness was but the outward sign of the damage brought about by having dropped, assembly-line style, no fewer than ten children – and that's not counting the two boys who died at birth or any of the miscarriages that were so common to working-class women at the time. Her offspring came in the following order:

Harriet Armstrong Scott
Harriet, my mother and the eldest of the Scott tribe, was born out of wedlock – hence the middle name, Armstrong being that of Maria; the Scott being added only when Charles did the right thing by Maria. But more of Harriet later.

Nellie

Nellie was a roly-poly, hubbly-bubbly, warm lady who, for better or worse (more of the worse I'd think) married Albert Troth, a tall, lean, jowly, blue-chinned, as often as not pickled collier under whose powerful frame she conceived and then safely delivered three young Troths. Marian, who came first was lucky enough to take after her mother but Jack, the next in line, was truly a chip off the Troth block: a strapping great numbskull who didn't know his arse from a pit shaft. Lastly came Bill, an equally gigantic, equally dumb Albertian who, playing cricket for the Co-op team, developed to be a tear-away fast bowler who terrorised the local cricket circuit and stirred just a little passing interest at Trent Bridge.

The Troths lived about two miles away from us in Huthwaite, a rough little mining settlement dominated by pit tips and a colossal Co-operative Wholesale Society factory. Their house, at the end of a colliers' row, was forever grubby, forever a shambles (their table never seemed to be clear of the debris from the last meal), forever smelling of the greasy effluent that oozed from flocks of fowl and geese who ran free in a large, squalid pound that covered most of the Troth's backyard, and, forever too, warm and welcoming: "Eh up! Lewk wot wind's blown in! If it in't our Stan! Tha's just in time for tea!"

Alice

Alice, as big as, nay, bigger than Nellie, was a much more restrained character. She was luckier too for she married Harold Allsopp, a good, teetotal collier who'd worked his way up (if one can use that expression about subterranean colliers) from face-worker to First Deputy at the coal face, a job that called for a voice fit to shake the pit props and the physique to go with it; a job that secured that most elusive, hence revered, of all benefactions: a guaranteed income – as the Chinese say, an iron rice bowl. As became a 'gaffer's man', Harold Alsopp wore black three-piece suits, wing collars, plain ties, bowler hats and, across his vast stomach, a silver watch chain. Given the bulk of both of them (Harold would have tipped the scales at 20 stones, Alice at about 18) they could have copulated only with difficulty and with an athleticism that I'd say was beyond either of them; hence it wasn't surprising that the Allsopps remained, as they said in those days, without issue.

Blessed by a regular and relatively munificent pay packet and by their not having to fork out money on rearing progeny, Alice and Harold gradually put together enough money – wonder upon wonders – to build their very own home. It was a large house, architecturally so undistinguished as to make it easy to believe Harold's boast that he'd designed it himself; from the landing window they had a panoramic view of Harold's coal mine. Sadly, the corpulent First Deputy wasn't to enjoy his vista for very long before he began to complain about a loss of vision. He blamed the pit but, First Deputy or not, the owners wouldn't wear it and he failed to prove it. Suddenly, almost in the time it would have taken him, thinking it was going dark, to reach for a light switch, he was blind. And on the bread line as far as the coal-owners were concerned.

Poor chap, in my early teens I was deputed to read to him on Sunday afternoons. It turned out that I read to his mother as well: an ancient illiterate crone who lived in a pretty one-room cottage nearby (in Huthwaite) and who took to the readings with at least as much interest as her sightless son. Unhappily, she had the habit of rewarding the reader with great dabs of bone-dry caraway-seed cake, a confectionery I've choked on ever since.

Polly

Just as Phoebe and Hilda proved the exception to the rule that all the Hardy women were avoirdupois, so Polly, together with Harriet, gave the lie to the assumption that all Scott females were leviathans. Polly was angular, not to say skinny. She was also unbelievably docile, so much so that some thought her simple-minded. But let her be called upon, as she frequently was, to defend her old man, Wilfred Shore, a man who God knows needed all the defending he could get, and she was a spitfire. A silver-tongued smart aleck, Wilfred Shore was far too clever a rogue ever to have given even a passing thought to digging coal for a living. And he was also far too vain ever to have risked disfiguring himself with coal-shards. Instead he devised and promoted his own religion.

To anybody with but an ounce of grey matter he was a four-flusher who messed about with the occult yet he found it easy to wheedle money out of the nobodies, not enough to keep him in the style he reckoned was his by divine right but enough, when supplemented by a bit of legitimate business, to keep him and Polly going. To create a front as a merchant he rented a one-room shop on Mansfield Road, a cheerless emporium furnished only with a trestle-table behind which, as his 'store supervisor' he pushed the ever-willing, ever-supine, Polly. Standing behind her insubstantial counter, Polly tried her best to flog its sad-looking merchandise – damaged crockery; oddments that Wilfred had coaxed out of market-place spivs who, but for Wilfred's pleas, would have thrown the stuff away as unsaleable. It was no use going into Shore's shop looking for any sort of matching cup and saucer let alone a pair made in Dresden. Even so, there were plenty of folk poor enough to be thankful that they need spend no more than a halfpenny for a single, flawed cup, a chipped pudding basin or, in the hope of coming across a lid somewhere else, a lidless teapot. They paid their pennies over to Polly who handed every single one to her Wilf.

While Polly, loyal to her clairvoyant husband through thick and thin and deaf to the endless, pestiferous gossip against him, while she froze in the little, unheated shop trying to sell a cracked saucer here, a fractured dish there, Wilfred practised his working-class freemasonry; he read palms and tea-leaves, dealt the tarot cards, mouthed mumbo-jumbo, span the crystal ball, thumped bibles, conducted séances and deciphered the innards of small, dead animals. And all the while he was squeezing three-penny bits out of nobodies whose miseries he laid down, together with those twin curses of the working class, drink and tobacco, to evil spirits. He was a good-looking man in the manner of a Bombay film star: broad-shouldered, fleshy, swarthy, large-headed, bushy-haired, thick-lipped and vibrantly voiced. Paired up with the waif-like Polly (one wonders how such an ill-adapted pair could ever have felt mutual attraction) he fathered

Christine – 'Chrissie' – a truly beautiful, magnificently proportioned girl with corn-coloured hair.

Jack

Jack was a slim, handsome, doe-eyed, boyish-looking, quiet man who displayed the courtliness, which by untruthful legend belonged only to the gentry. If you'd seen him in his Sunday-best suit, a reduced-price 'Thirty Shillings Tailors' three-piece job bought for half-a-crown down and a bob a week for 17 weeks, and you hadn't observed the tell-tale blue scars of the collier that pocked the backs of his hands, you'd have put him down as an insurance man or even a bank clerk. He married Rachel, a tiny, very pretty lady who, despite the dismal nature of their habitat on a miners' row in Alfreton Road, complemented Jack by presenting always a sedate, almost aristocratic, frontage. During the 1914–18 war Jack had 'gone for a soldier'; luckily he'd come home unscathed – outwardly unscathed that is – but he always gave the impression that he'd been grievously wounded internally. The only thing he'd ever say about that glorious defence of King and country was that it had been "tew soddin' daft to talk abart". Jack and Rachel Scott were very, very nice people and they begat a very nice, quiet boy, Leslie.

Elizabeth

Then there was Lizzie, a small, peppy young woman who twinkled like one of the sparklers we used to light up at Guy Fawkes and Christmas; she was everybody's favourite child/sister/aunt/neighbour. Her coupling to a mountainous coal-merchant (well, since he owned a great dray horse to pull a cart full of coal which he sold by the ton, the hundredweight, or the bag, he could be said to have been a merchant) a thoroughly appealing fellow in a rough-cut, Romany sort of way; her liason with him was as near to a romance as the rest of us were ever likely to get this side of the cinema screen. According to the nobodies' praxis it was acceptable – even laudable – for grown-ups outwardly to display affection and tenderness towards children and for human beings to be sentimental towards animals but any sign of ardour shown between two adult human beings was reviled as being 'sloppy', 'luvvy-duvvy', 'mushy' and 'mad-arseness'. But once you'd seen Lizzie and Baille Goddard together, he twice as tall and three times as heavy as she, you'd sense the magic that was theirs and you'd understand that even nobodies could ring each other's bells just as sweetly as film-stars could pretend to.

The Goddards lived in that God-forsaken place, Huthwaite, in a terraced box so miniscule that it would have made the Black Hole of Calcutta seem commodious. Its pokiness was good for one thing though – its acoustics radiated wonderfully Lizzie's non-stop laughter. Which pleasing resonance didn't however ring around the walls for very long because, without warning, the dreaded consumption came and galloped off with her at a clop never equalled by Baille's great mare. Before he'd time to weep the coal-merchant was left with only his horse to exult in.

Kate

Kate, rosy-cheeked and nearly as bulky as Alice and Nellie, married Bert Rose who was distinguished from the rest of us not only because he came from Mansfield, a town three miles away and not because he was unconnected with the coal mines, but because he was no mere factory hand but a foreman at the Metal Box Company to one of whose zillions of tin cans he was to lose a thumb. "Nobody," he used to say when talking of his small mutilation and leaving one thinking of Sweeney Todd, "nobody ever complained about finding a piece of Bert Rose floating among their tinned sausages; but then, that particular bit would have looked like a banger wouldn't it?" Bert was a tall, thin, serious-minded, pious man who neither smoked (a rarity in those days) nor drank (ditto) nor snored (ditto plus). To the rest of the men in the family he was 'a clever bugger'. They took the piss out of Bert for his "bein loony enuff to lissen t'news on t'wireless, to buy bewks and put 'em on t'sideboard", and, battiest of all things, "to borrer 'bewks' from t'library, daft sod".

Talking of books, one of the world's great writers, D.H. Lawrence, was born in a mining village just down the road from, and in the same miserable state as, ours. Lawrence had written immortal classics about colliers – *Sons and Lovers* for a start. In his *Lady Chatterley's Lover* he'd laid down a coal-owner's wanton wife lewdly to fornicate with a rude nobody in, of all places, Teversall. Teversall, a place next door, a place of whose pit most of our men had worked at one time or another. Yet I never once heard Lawrence's name mentioned by anybody, not even by Uncle Bert Rose, and I never met anybody who'd read anything he'd ever written.

Harry

Harry, the youngest Scott male (maybe 15 to 20 years Harriet's junior) looked lean and hungry but gave no cause for wariness. A stockinger (a stocking knitter), not a collier, he was the family favourite, or at least he was until he betrothed himself to the unhealthy, sorry-looking daughter of an even more ill-favoured railway clerk, one Mr. Elliot. The trouble began when Elliot proclaimed his opposition to the match on the grounds of social incompatibility – in other words, Meg Elliot was too good for Harry Scott. Taking this pronouncement as a slur on the whole tribe, the Scotts – all 30 of them (counting spouses and offspring) declared that the Elliots and, because he'd gone ahead and married Meg anyway, Harry himself, were untouchables. They boycotted the London & North Eastern Railway.

Amos

I don't know much about Amos except that he wasn't all that much luckier than his twin brother who'd died at birth. As a newly married youth, before my time, he'd 'gone for a soldier' early in World War I and he'd got himself killed. Like many other young lads, he'd not lived to enjoy life in the 'world fit for heroes' that they'd been promised by their King. Things went badly for the little family he'd left at home. Amos's King and Emperor doled out honours, awards and widows' pensions in accordance with what badges of rank each particular 'hero' was wearing when the King's enemies killed or maimed him; poor Amos, in his last,

I hope not too painful moments, was but a private solder. Thus his lack of ornamental livery on the killing fields meant that his gentle widow, Mary, and his meek little boy, Maurice, had to eke out a living on a pension that, supplemented by charity handouts (viz. – a couple of bags of coal, courtesy of the British Legion, at Xmas) was just big enough to keep them alive. Incredibly, but well in keeping with the ways of the nobodies, instead of reviling a monarch who'd broken his promises so badly that many of his 'heroes' and widows of his 'heroes' were being thrown into workhouses, Mary and Maurice still sported their poppies on Armistice Day and still prayed to a God to save their King.

Kathleen

Finally, there was Kathleen, a lean and lovely young woman who wore the pink bloom of 'consumption' across her otherwise marble pale cheeks. Still in her early glow she yet lay dying in Morley Street, her signs of life being eye movement and hand signals every now and then to raise her up so that she might spit gobs of yellow gumbo into a tumbler. The Scott tribe adored her; to them, with her black-as-Chinese hair spread like a fan around her pearl-white forehead and her glass-clear, bulging brown eyes shining like torch beams burning through a pitch-dark night, to them she was pure, virginal, untouched, innocent, a saint. They mounted a round-the-clock vigil at her bedside and they clubbed their pennies together to provide her with treats one of which was, astonishingly, a wireless set, the very first I ever saw or heard. The sick room being too small to accommodate the whopping great loudspeakers of those early days, Kathleen's radio came with headphones that she wore like a halo. These she'd clamp over my three- or four-year-old ears, then, lying back again, she'd fix me with those great orbs of hers, waiting to catch my look of wonderment over the miracle of broadcast sound. All I heard in fact was scratchy music and 'la-de-da' folk jabbering away, it seemed to me, against a background noise of the goings-on in a torture chamber: clattering, banging, moaning and sawing. My enchantment, all the same, was real enough.

Kathleen was taken away to 'the San' (Sanatorium) a sort of hospice for consumptives at Mansfield Woodhouse. There, like just about everybody else who was despatched to the place, she quickly ebbed away. The radio, whose stuck-up announcers were forever going on about how Princess so-and-so was unable to attend her engagements because of a cold or how the Duchess of such-and-such place had turned her ankle during a hunt, never said a word about Kathleen's consumption.

The Merger: Harry and Harriet

I don't know what became of it but always hanging on the wall in our front room there hung a great big, ornately framed, sepia photo taken on the wedding day of George Henry (Harry I) Hardy and Harriet Armstrong Scott, a merger that brought the Hardy and Scott families together. Harriet, I remember, stood there with her hair piled up high and wearing a severe, dark dress with a big lace collar. She wore a fair-sized brooch at her throat. The photographer had captured her at her best: looking high-born and zestful but he'd caught Harry I on an off-day, wearing a high-buttoned jacket over a high-buttoned waistcoat and looking uncharacteristically vacant and gumboilish (unable to afford dentifrice, nobodies were prone to gumboils).

George Henry – Harry I – was a shortish, robust fellow with lots of good hair to cover a fair share of grey matter. He was literate – just – but he kept his reading to a painful, word-by-word, almost letter-by-letter, deciphering of the sports pages of the local rag and he confined his writing to those times when, with a tanner to spare, he'd take up a pencil stub (he'd never dream of buying a whole pencil) and, wetting it sloppily and noisily with his tongue every few seconds, he'd fill in a football-pools coupon. (Our lot, who'd plead illiteracy when called upon to complete any official form, even marking an 'X' on a voting slip, would nevertheless breeze through complicated pools coupons as if they were playing OXO). Harry was neither simple nor inexpressive; he'd plenty of savvy when minded to use it and he'd the wit to clothe it in words too. One thing for certain: never for a moment was he too thick-skulled to stop foraging around for a way out of mining coal for a living. And, bless him; he brought it off in the end. True, he was well into his 50s by then and, true, he exchanged the coal face only for a dirty, noisy metal-bashing workshop in which he worked as a drudge but it was still a great achievement: he'd climbed his mountain.

Always on the look out for ways of getting hold of money without having to go down a mineshaft for it, he developed a shiftiness that sometimes worked for the good, often not. I always counted it greatly to his credit for example that by resisting the call of the trumpets, and by weathering jibes about his manhood; he managed to stay out of uniform during the first Great War. It wasn't that he'd had to wangle it (colliers were anyway exempt from the call-up) and it wasn't that he was a pacifist but, for my money, for him to have stayed out of the war was evidence of a higher IQ than those of his contemporaries who'd been block-headed enough to march for King and country when they hadn't had to and who came home, if they came home at all, much the worse for the experience. While they'd been getting themselves shot, shelled, gassed, snuffed-out or, like Arthur Denby and Jack Scott, mentally wounded for life, Harry I had spent the war safe and sound, impregnating Harriet.

On the other hand there were times when he used his nous corruptly; on scams for example like the 'Death and Divide' clubs he ran in one pub or another all his life. The way this worked was that once a week he'd collect his members' threepences, which he'd record on the spot in a halfpenny notebook that only he ever perused. The money, kept in a tin under the stairs, was held in readiness to cover the funeral expenses of any member who kicked the bucket (and in those days the sound of nobodies' buckets being kicked rang through the air like gunfire). I fear though that more than a few three-penny pieces stuck to Harry I's palm.

Fish and Chips, Meat Pies and Ice-Cream

He was a freethinker owing loyally to no one but his family, most certainly not to any class, religion or trade union. During the epic coal-strike of 1926, for instance, he defected from the National Union of Mineworkers to become, not to mince words, a blackleg, a 'Spencer Man' (named after one Spencer who, corrupted by the coal-owners, set up a rival 'scab' union). Indeed, it may well have been Judas's gold, in the nature of a backhander from a grateful coal-owner, that financed Harry I's initial and most ambitious attempt to break into what he believed was his natural setting – the world of business and high finance. It was 1927 (I'm clear on that because it coincided with my entry into primary school) when he rented a live-in shop on Mansfield Road. We moved from our near-slum in St. Michael's Street into rooms above and behind the behemoth stainless steel, oil-spitting vats in which Harry I and Harriet were going to fry fish and chips. And, of course, sell them. But it began to go wrong as soon as we unpacked our meagre belongings. Despite our knowing little more about the fish and chip business than that the fish came from the sea and the potatoes from the earth, Harry I was convinced that in no time at all gourmets from all over the country would be queuing up by the mile outside his estaminet.

In those days, at least at our level of subsistence, there was no such thing as market research and Harry I couldn't go to a bank for advice because never in his life did he once step inside a bank. It was enough for him that the location looked promising: there was a pub on one opposite corner, Dr. Durance's surgery stood on another and trams to and from Mansfield stopped to debus and pick up passengers right outside the shop's entrance. He never stopped to think however that most trams were clattering by empty because the entire locality was still groaning from the aftermath of the great strike, meaning that not only could his hoped-for customers not afford the tram fares but they were having a hard time feeding their families on bread-and-dripping, never mind about fish and chips. To cut a short story shorter, we never looked like making enough money to keep the fires burning under the frying pans, still less to allow the restaurateur himself to realise his dreams of spending carefree days at the races.

Far from being able to take off for Doncaster with a fob-pocket bursting with cigars and his trouser pockets a-jingle with sovereigns, Harry I was landed with the worst of all worlds. Business was so slow that he had to go back to digging coal for a living, leaving Harriet to run both shop and household. She hired a live-in help, Mabel. We were able to employ Mabel only because of her unsightly disfigurement; like a surprising number of nobodies she'd been born with a cleft-palate and a monstrous hare-lip, deformities that taken together forced her to communicate in a tortuous, feature-straining gibberish. Not surprisingly then, she was a quiet soul; not surprisingly also she was, cruelly, a public laughing stock. Anyway, in return for nothing more than bed and board, a few pennies of pocket money and a lot of affection, Mabel did most of the housework (one of her duties was to escort me to school) while Harriet stood over the frying pans and baked meat pies that she tried to sell at three-pence apiece. Having no means of refrigeration a great many fish and potatoes quietly decomposed while we ate meat pies for breakfast, dinner and tea.

Aware of the popular belief that men idolise their mothers, I'm determined to bend over backwards to be objective about Harriet Armstrong Hardy, nee Scott. Objectively then, she was indeed a thing of beauty. Her hair may never have been dressed, bobbed or shampooed in a shop, yet when it was undone to fall like a black velvet curtain down her back, it was of a fashion no coiffeur in the world could have improved upon. She carried a figure that denied all the years of child-bearing, raising a family, kneading dough, scrubbing privy seats, pumicing front steps, sweeping backyards, black-leading, cooking ranges, bending double over scrubbing boards to drub mountains of soiled clothes and bedding, pressing sheets with heavy irons, cooking Sunday roasts, swabbing Harry I's coal-blackened spine over scullery sinks and salting and hanging his sides of pig.

She may never have dressed haute couture; her shapely legs never knew the caress of silk; she possessed no dainty undergarments, only long, woollen bloomers. Cosmetics were unknown to her; many a time, she looked uncombed but Harriet was never anything but graceful. Ah yes, her hands, well, her hands would have betrayed her anywhere. Roughened and reddened by scrubbing and scouring; scarred by innumerable burns inflicted by ill-placed irons, spitting coals, tipping saucepans and scalding suds; and bloodied where her needles slipped during the hours she spent on that most spirit-sagging of all her tasks – the patching of Harry I's pit clothes with calico; yes, her long, bony hands were those of a drudge.

Until life at the fish-shop found her out, we'd always thought her to be indestructible. The rest of us took to our beds with flu, flushes, cankers, bilious bouts, stomach aches, boils, broken bones (I broke my arm twice) and chilblains (my eldest sister, Lillian, was forever hacking at the resultant papules with razor blades and dousing them with methylated spirit). Apart from the occasional snuffle or fainting fit (the sight of female nobodies keeling over in the streets was almost as common, but less serene, as the sight of them bearing their breasts to suckle their infants) and frequent lamentations straight from the heart about "bein' fed up wi' yew lot", Harriet never wavered.

But the hot, rancid vapours that hissed from the fizzing frying pans acted upon her like a nerve gas. Coincidentally, the very same miasma was also blamed by some for triggering the madness that had until then lurked harmlessly in the brain of Harry I's Great Dane, a handsome beast kept mainly to stand guard over the potatoes, fish and fat stored in a backyard shed. Whatever the cause, possibly the odour of impending business failure as much as anything else, the lithe Dane went one day into a rabid fit. It frothed at the mouth, went crazy and had to be chained to a wire fence until a pharmacist was found to administer poison. Harriet, on the other hand, didn't go crazy; she just got the shivers awfully badly. The Hardy-Scott team of would-be Harley Street consultants (real doctors cost money) blamed her distemper on the foetid breath of the Great Dane; on deadly flatus wafting over from the good Dr. Durance's surgery across the road; on the avenging spirits of dead fish; and, inevitably because the mark of the hare-lip was said to bode bad luck, on poor Mabel. In the end, and to hell with the cost, we had to turn to the excellent Durance for a diagnosis of the affliction and he advised that we pack restauranting in.

That's how we quit Mansfield Road: skint, sick, flattened. But Harry

I wasn't yet quite done with the idea that shopkeeping would lead to easy street; he still fancied himself as Sutton's answer to F. H. Woolworth, investing the profits raked in over one counter to buy another counter and so on. And he coupled that daydream with a vision of himself as a man-about-town, decked out in tailored suiting, fedoras and black cigarettes – Balkan Sobranie. With that utopia in mind he moved us into a small, rented grocery shop just round the corner in Oak Tree Road not far from Harry and Meg Scott's place. All I recall about this undertaking is that we churned ice-cream by hand in a little wooden barrel from which we tried to sell it, presumably with other foodstuffs, to the nobodies who lived nearby. The product was delicious but Harriet's meat pies had been equally scrumptious and we couldn't sell them either. More to the point, while we'd kept body and soul together with meat pies, we couldn't live on ice-cream.

Harry I had learned economics the hardest way of all but to be fair even the smartest and best funded entrepreneur could never have made a killing through trading in a colliery town in 1927–28. Anyway, within a week or two, we were on the move again, this time with our tails tightly between our legs. Once again the horse and cart picked up our pitiable belongings and once again they were carried but a stone's throw from our last place. It was symptomatic of the nobodies' way of living that every one of our migrations took place within the limited circumference of a few, identical, dreary streets – in other words, within a ghetto.

Short on Luck in Short Street

Gone were the dreams of cash registers rattling away in a chain of Hardy-owned bazaars; we couldn't even dream of running an open stall on the market square. We had to forget all about Balkan Sobranies and about homes with bathrooms, electric light, indoor lavatories, and outside lawns. Indeed, we had to be thankful that we could rent one of Howard Bacon's terraced slums in Short Street, a bleak drag at the bottom of St. Michael's Street. We were worse off than ever before.

Having squandered the coal-owner's stingy bribe (if that's where the cash had come from), Harry I was back to tramping round the pits looking for whatever work at whatever coalface and for whatever wage he could get. Short Street meant short rations. Apart from the rare halcyon days when Harry I managed to poach a rabbit, they were days where a hard-boiled egg was divided four ways for breakfast, days of bread-and-dripping, pigs' trotters, bread-and-salted lard, watered milk and even bread-and-sugar. Xmas stockings bore one orange – the only we'd see in a year, a pomegranate (a freakish sort of Xmas present but one we always got) a handful of gob-stoppers and, perhaps, a crayon or two. We neither sent nor received Xmas cards; indeed, apart from pushing a football-pools coupon under our door once a week (and our not having a letter-box speaks for itself) the postman never called. Gone were the days, not long since, when (presumably on the strength of the back-handers paid to Harry I) we four children would be photographed in our Whitsuntide clothes: two little boys wearing brass-buttoned, warm-looking overcoats, polished boots and smart caps and two bigger girls in stylish dresses topped off by the latest in ribboned hats, all four of us obviously scrubbed ready for parading round the town in the annual 'Whitsuntide Walk'. Gone were the days of plenty; now was the time for making-do with hand-me-downs and rifling through the cast-offs on the rag-and-bone man's pushcart.

Most dispiriting of all: Harriet didn't get better. First it was her eyes; cataracts (a sentence to blindness in those days) were suspected but, praise-be, the chemist at the top of Chatsworth Street came up with a pair of second-hand glasses that allowed her to focus more or less properly again. Then she was sorely (and I mean sorely) afflicted with pyorrhoea, a painful ailment by which she seemed to be bleeding to death through her mouth, weakening her by the hour. In a brutish operation spread over agonising weeks during which she could eat only slops, every tooth was pulled from her head. Then, to cap it all and without any warning being whispered to us four children (procreation, menstruation and the genitalia associated with them were never spoken of in front of children, if at all), Harriet was taken to a hospital in Nottingham where they sliced of her right breast and sent her back, mutilated, to Short Street.

I've no idea how it was all paid for: the glasses, the dentistry, the false teeth and the surgeon's knife; a whip-round among families, friends and neighbours would be my guess. In any event there wasn't enough cash to give us children a chance of visiting her in hospital. We were left waiting in Short Street – ignorant, fearful and silent. The most admirable, rosy-cheeked Kate took care of us through those, our blackest days. Polly took the washing, somebody else did the ironing and old Sarah Ann sent round saucepans full of broth she'd cooked up in her boiler. We came through it, Harry I ending up dumbstruck, the rest of us scared, ruffled, and insecure. We learned what our mother had gone through only by deciphering the code-language habitually used by grown-up nobodies when talking in front of infant nobodies. From this we were able to confirm what our eyes had told us already: Harriet's chest was lop-sided.

Guns, and Butter too!

Harriet had shrunk, she wasn't slim but skinny, her hair had turned grey and she'd aged many a year. But once she'd had a bit of a rest, filled her mouth with false teeth and her blouse with a false breast and once Harry I was back to digging coal full-time again, she began to stand up straight, to look people in the eye and to laugh and joke again. There was a coal boom. Right-wingers (an endangered species in the coal-fields then) told us that the easing of the early 1930s depression proved that capitalism brought prosperity. But for that to have been the truth then at the same time, capitalism had to be charged with spawning such loathsome creatures as Mussolini, Franco and Hitler whose war-like actions prompted panic-stricken cries for tanks, guns, warplanes, warships and all the associated hardware needed to put them down. Everybody knows that to make weapons of war you need to consume lots of energy, which, in the 1930s, meant coal – coal that had to be hewn out of the ground by the likes of Harry I. Such was the demand for the stuff that Harry I was able to move from pit to pit searching for one whose coalface was near to the bottom of the shaft; the shorter the journey from shaft to face, the more time he could spend in bed of a morning, instead of getting up at 0330 he might be in until 0400.

His daily grind went something like this: he'd be up at 0330, scoff a quick breakfast, then walk to a truck or bus that'd deliver him to the pithead by 0500 or 0530. He'd go down in the 'cage' and at the bottom of the shaft he'd climb aboard a pony-drawn wagon on rails that'd dump him at the coalface by 0600. There he'd hew away at coal with pick and shovel until 1400 whereupon he'd reverse his morning trek, getting back home by about 1600 – some 12 hours after he left it. Besides seeking a face near to the shaft Harry I also looked out for one high enough for him to be able to kneel rather then lie on his belly while picking at coal. Or even a face whose 'roof' in places might be high enough for him at noon to ease his cramp by standing up to eat his 'Snap' (usually bread-and-dripping packed overnight in a tin and called 'Snap because the time it took to say the word was about the time the colliers claimed they were given to eat it).

His hunt for a subterranean El Dorado was vain: just as Solzynitsin's gulag prisoners never found a good prison, so for Harry I there was no such thing as a good coal-mine. But he never gave up searching. Shouldering his tools of trade he 'signed on' at Brierley, Bolsover, Mansfield, Annesley, Pinxton, Kirkby, Teversall, Pleasley, Shirebrook and Blidworth.

Things were looking up. For a start, as soon as Harry I was at work again, we'd overnight burn as much coal as we could (free 'loads' of coal, the collier's one and only perk, were dumped on demand in the street outside the house) and we could laugh at memories of those black days when we, who'd been used to having good supplies of coal if naught else, had been driven to picking over slag heaps grubbing for burnable dross. When your coal house was empty you were down as low as you could go because without coal you would freeze in winter and couldn't boil a potato in summer.

Now, with a full coal house we could afford to make jokes about scratching in the dirt for coal slag; about that goofy Great Dane who went doolali-tap at the chip shop; about opening up after devouring loads of unsold home-made ice-cream; and about having to split an egg four ways. Nowadays, Harry I having acquired a chicken or two, we had an egg apiece of a morning. And every now and then, without any warning, he'd chase one of the squawking creatures around the backyard, catch it, wring its neck in his blackened fists and we'd dine on roast fowl! It wasn't that Short Street had suddenly turned into Easy Street; an orange was still a Hardy annual and bananas remained exotic, yellow things imported from faraway lands for the somebodies' tables. No, it was simply that we were warm, our bellies were filled and our shoes watertight.

Sitting around the scullery table on wintry nights, the gas light fizzing away above our heads, Harriet would celebrate our new-found well-being by dishing up succulent, piping-hot chips straight from the solid-iron chip pan that seared away on the open fire; crowning the treat by dropping an egg into the seething oil and almost in the same movement serving it, edged crisply brown, plonk! On top of the still scalding hot chips. No Tsar, J.P. Morgan or Maharaja ever dined as well.

A Palace and a Chapel

To add icing to our newly-found cake my two big sisters, Lillian and Muriel, were taken on at 'Hibbert and Buckland', the nearby stocking factory. And to add candles as well, the new wage earners joined Harry I in placing their Friday evening wage packets on a spanking new mantelpiece (wage-packets on the mantelpiece was a time-honoured ritual). For a miracle had taken place! Our name had come up for a brand new council house: No.32, Garden Lane. 32, Garden Lane – that address is burned into my soul, not only because it symbolised our elevation to something approaching a civilised existence but because in later years I was to post hundreds of letters to it.

No.32, Garden Lane was a three-and-a-bit up, two-and-a-bit down house with – glory be! – a real bathroom upstairs; an indoor, water-flushed lavatory downstairs; electric light (you can't imagine what a godsend it was just to press a switch for there to be instant light without any fumbling about with matches and without a lingering smell of gas (O! Faraday, if only you could have seen us then!). And being a corner house there were gardens front and back. We even had our own front gate! My-oh-my, how pleased we were with 32, Garden Lane. No doubt about it, that council house transformed our lives. So, all honour to those who brought council housing about and all contempt for those who, led by the infamous Margaret Thatcher, tore it apart.

Branded with almost equal force on my memory is our Co-op membership No.74806, which tripped off my tongue lightly and spun my heart to quote it to the man at the Co-op counter. For the first time in my life I enjoyed running errands. Instead of sidling up to his shop counter shamefully to beg for pennyworths of salt ("me mam sez we'll pay yer first thing Sat'dy morning") from Mr. Stokes, our short-tempered grocer on Short Street (but with customers like us who wouldn't have been grumpy?), I was able to stand up straight and to pay cash for my packets of sugar and tea, matches, pats of butter, slices of bacon and slabs of carbolic soap; I could stand tall to sing out loud and clear (so as to register our future claim to miniscule dividends – 'divvies'), "74806!"

Somewhat restored physically, with money in her purse and with Lillian and Muriel giving a hand about the house while brother Harry II and I hauled coal, shined shoes and ran errands, Harriet was able to turn to her two favourite pastimes. One was the 'laying out' of the dead; a ghoulish divertissement you might think, but remember (sublime as 32, Garden Lane was, we still lived within spitting distance of St. Michael's Street) the nobodies in our ghetto had little or no money for doctors, even less for undertakers. And remember too that at that time of poverty and want all sorts of 'distempers' and 'flukes' were felling the nobodies like flies.

For example, when their lungs finally filled up with coal-dust colliers cocked their toes to resemble egg timers filled with slag instead of sand. Then again, they and their womenfolk burned like furnaces with 'flushes'. They keeled over with 'the pip'; were stopped in their tracks with 'colic'; went 'dotty'; lost sleep through piles and erysipelas; were scourged by ringworm, bunions, eczema, abscesses, bronchitis and carbuncles; got lock-jawed (to hear Harriet on about it half the ghetto went around with their chops in fetters); and, all too frequently, they were knocked so far sideways by the whole sodding business of just staying alive that they did away with themselves. Hanging was the favourite way of escape; Harriet often wished out loud that she'd as many pound notes as the number of times she'd straightened out poor slobs who'd snuffed it on the end of a rope.

She'd come home, take her hat off, make a pot of tea and sit down at the scullery table and tell us all about it, never missing a single, macabre detail yet never offending the proprieties and never slighting the wretched suicide. There we'd be sitting perhaps over high tea (five o'clock, bread and butter and maybe some corned beef or sardines) listening spellbound while this fragile, wounded matron told us how she'd just laid out 'Mister X or Missus Y'.

"They found 'im 'anging under t'stairs" (stairwells were much preferred places for suicide by noose). "Poor sod, 'is neck lewked as if it were all crooked an all. 'is breeches were full – pooh. But as soon as we 'ad 'im stripped an' washed an' straightened out a bit an' as soon as we'd stuffed 'is tongue back as far as it'd go – eh it were all black an' that – and after we'd shaved 'im, well 'e lewked a treat. A lot better than 'e did the last time I clapped eyes on 'im wen 'e were alive, any road up. 'is eyeballs stick out tew far for us to get pennies in but we'll 'ave another go at that in t'mornin'. We got a clean shirt on 'im, did it up to 'is poor old chin, an' wi a bit o' trouble we got 'is arms crossed, in a fashion any road up; 'e'll dew. 'is folks were ivver so grateful. Eh lewk is that t'right time? No rest for the wicked is there?"

Many a widow, widower or parent became Harriet's friends for life after she'd performed her ministrations over their dead but she never took a penny for her 'laying out' services; maybe half-a-dozen eggs now and then but nothing more.

Her other abiding passion was for the Congregational Chapel in Chatsworth Street, another grim thoroughfare running between two rows of blackened bricks and jennels paralleled with St. Michael's Street, hence well within the ghetto. The chapel was a cheap-jack place externally lacking the least decorative touch. It could easily have been taken for a warehouse (which indeed it was turned into later on) or, had it had a higher roof, a tram-shed. The only outside indication that it was a minor basilica was a notice board declaring it to be a 'House of Worship'.

Inside, ecclesiastical décor was limited to the far-end wall, the other three sides being dressed only in damp-ravaged, greenish distemper. From each side of the central aisle there ran lines of dime-a-dozen chairs bolted together to imitate pews. The sole Episcopal feature – and the focus of Harriet's adoration – was a semi-circular stage (sorry, Harriet, altar) covered in electric-blue carpeting that could well have been a cheap cut-off from the floor covering the new Odeon cinema in Mansfield. In the middle of the altar stood a heavy little table, a pedestal for a plywood lectern draped in a velvet cloth and topped with a large Bible. A little old upright piano, made wheezy by the damp and seldom either tuned or, indeed, played, sat plaintively to one side (oh how Harriet envied the Methodists up the road who'd just installed a Wurlitzer organ). On the back wall, above the shrine, there was painted a rainbow proclaiming the cause 'O worship the Lord in the spirit of Holiness'. That iridescent mantra formed a halo around a framed roll of honour in remembrance of those Chatsworth Street heroes whom God had forsaken during the Great War and never mind their repeated declarations that they had been fighting on His side.

It was neither church-like, nor monasterial, nor hallowed: tin-pot and cheap more like it. All the same, it was Harriet's very own Notre Dame. The 'preachers' (laymen who circulated round the local chapels) were hot – some hotter then others – gospellers. Harriet's favourite was a sparky pulpit basher named Arthur Maddox. Young for the job (about 35 at the time) always sporting a severe suit; slim and wavy-haired, he had a fog-horn of a voice that, when he was in full cry, must have been heard by the Anglican somebodies in their church several streets away, Arthur could have come straight out of a Goldwyn-Meyer casting agency which had been asked to come up with a hick-town, Bible-bashing heart-throb.

To Harriet's delight Maddox would sometimes (on Sundays when he was to appear at her chapel) grace No.32, Garden Lane with his presence and take tea with us. On those red-letter days Harriet was in seventh heaven. The rest of the family found Arthur's visits congenial too because out came the best 'pots' and the tin of salmon! All dolled up in our Sunday best, for an hour or so we'd pretend to be somebodies, marvelling all the while at the way in which every single hair on Maddox's curly head was held in place by a glue that shone like black-lead. By half-past six, he'd be finished with railing from the lectern-under-the-rainbow, done with bawling out us 20 nobodies (he packed 'em in, Arthur did, no other circuit-rider drew more than half-a-dozen) for being gross sinners (at which the saintly Harriet would nod her head in agreement) then we'd all be good and ready to belt out the hymns. Released from his tongue-lashing we'd let rip, ending up with the haunting motet that had even Uncle Bert going: "The day thou gavest Lord is ended." Atheist that I am, that hymn still turns me on.

The chapel's caretaker was a deformed, illiterate, fleshless widow who lived in the house right opposite and whose only remuneration was to be fed scraps from the already lean tables of the worshippers themselves. The place otherwise was in the keep of the Scott women helped by (Treasurer) Bert Rose and a posse of housewives from Chatsworth Street. The Hardy clan, including Harry I, stayed well clear. With the passing of the Scott women the signboard was altered to offer, not a cloister for Christian nobodies but 'Best Prices' for discarded furniture. I wonder if the new owners started business by selling off the lectern, the tinny little piano and the rows of chairs? The day thou gavest Lord was ended.

Lillian, Clarence and a Bicycle Made For Two

I was the 'babby', according to my brother and two sisters, Harriet's favourite. All four of us agreed however that Harry I was even handed, giving each of us an equal – meaning very limited – amount of his time. Lillian, the eldest and by a long chalk the nicest of the four children, was in her early 20s when we moved into Garden Lane. Her feminine roundedness (not yet overweight she was, let's say, curvaceous) were the first to stir my curiosity about the different construction of male and female bodies. She wasn't much of a thinker, never read a line of anything and, like the rest of the run-of-mill ghetto youngsters, when the time came she couldn't flee school fast enough. It was with the greatest glee that she'd taken her place on a factory assembly line. Then, after a few years, her joy having long since been replaced by crushing boredom, she took us by surprise by making her own bid to escape the ghetto; she joined a cycle club. But she had a problem: relatively well-to-do as we were, we still couldn't run to buying bicycles. Ergo, she paired up with one Clarence Trigg, a collier from Clipstone who, glory be, owned a tandem. The question, never answered, was: who did Lillian fall for? Clarence or his bicycle made for two?

Clarence had a tongue like a chainsaw. Well attuned as we were to hearing what is called 'local dialect' but which in reality is a pitiful, diabolical misuse of the national language, we were still outraged by what came out of Clarence's mouth. The local vernacular had long since begun to set my own teeth on edge; I squirmed, and I still do squirm, when my ear-drums are assaulted by such off-pitch yowls as "Gerronwiyer!" (You don't say?), "Initt?" (Isn't it?), "Yo" (You), "Th'art" (You are), "Watter" (Water), "Ark!" (Listen!) and "Shurrup!" (Shut up!). I associated that sort of phonic abuse with dirty fingernails, snotty noses, ratty hair, crippled feet, rickets and witlessness. As I saw things, it was the well-spoken folk – the ones our lot ridiculed as 'stuck-up' and 'la-de-da' – it was they who read books, had more than one pair of shoes and who went on holidays. It was they, who carried wallets with money in them, fancy cigarette cases with fags in them and mouths with their own teeth in them. I'd worked it out that good locution helped mightily to open the ghetto gates.

Clarence would sit back in his chair and spit in the fire (a sure sign of bad breeding that, especially if your aim wasn't too good) he plastered his hair with lard (a common, if smelly and unhygienic, practice in a community which couldn't afford hair-cream) and he cursed a lot. "Buggers" and "bloodies" came out with every other word; degraded as our society of nobodies was, that habit, particularly when employed in mixed company or in front of the children, was deplored.

But fair's fair; he suited Lillian, or seemed to. He was bold enough to carry her off from Garden Lane wearing shorts – a daredevil thing to do at a time when girls wearing shorts were seen only on cinema screens or lantern slides. Away they'd go on Sunday mornings seated on his bicycle-made-for-two, Clarence in front, Lillian behind him, headed for the Derbyshire hills. To a 12-year-old like me who'd hardly been outside Sutton, place names like Matlock, Bakewell, Ambergate and Crich spelled exotic, far distant terrain. The two of them made for clean air, dry stonewalls, breathtaking views and sparkling streams and they'd return five or six hours and 30–40 miles later, red-faced, laughing and looking healthy, enriched. For all his faults then Clarence had to be credited with giving us a glimpse of what glories lay beyond our mean streets.

They married and moved to Clipstone, a scabrous, grey little mining village overshadowed and polluted by an Everest of a slagheap whose occasionally combustible effluent came almost to their unhappy front door. Clipstone was a mere seven miles from Garden Lane but it seemed a hundred for us to get there. You had to take a tram to Mansfield, a bus to Woodhouse and shanks' pony for the last mile – and then only to end up in a place even lousier than Sutton. Lillian and Clarence lived in a dreadful hole-and-corner terraced house, a big comedown for Lillian after 32, Garden Lane; indeed in most respects it was even lower down the scale than Short Street. The tandem, now unexercised, rusted swiftly away by the side of the coal-shed while those daring shorts were turned into cleaning rags. Lillian produced two fine boys in quick succession: Gary and Roger Trigg. She'd moved only from one ghetto into another.

Muriel, Oz and Mabel Avenue

Muriel was different. She herself would admit that she was no scholar but she'd also say that far from being a shortcoming her lack of education was an asset; she always had it in for "know-alls" and "big 'eads". She had no need of formal tuition for she was naturally sharp as a whip. No

beauty either, yet she made the most of what she'd got: good features, a
fine figure, clear skin ("like a 'trew' English rose untouched by t'sun")
splendid carriage and appealing perkiness. She steered well clear of the
Hardys, including, whenever she could, Harry I, writing them off as
"uncivilised 'ooligans". Come to think of it, apart from Harriet whom
she worshipped she didn't think much of the Scotts either. Much as she
wanted out of the ghetto she'd never have dreamed of riding out of it on
a bicycle; cycling was much too 'common' a divertissement for Muriel.
The surest escape route for her, she figured, was on the arms of a man
who'd whisk her out of it in an automobile or at least in the side-car of a
motor bike.

Thus did she set out her stall. But she failed to meet any catchable
motorists (in those days automobiles were as rare in Sutton as were snow-
ploughs on Madagascar) while whatever motorbike freaks were thrown
up by her reconnaissance turned out on inspection to be only slightly
better off versions of Clarence Trigg. Nonetheless, her ferreting around
eventually paid off; she came home one evening to announce that she was
"goin' courtin'" with one Oswald Atkin. From the way she talked about
her unseen suitor, 'Oz' (a diminutive even she had to concede to calling
him in the end), we expected nothing less than a Rudolph Valentino: tall,
dark, strong – a masher.

What she eventually brought home was a pint-sized, dapper chap with
jug ears and the look of a startled frog. But Muriel protested saying that
she'd never claimed that he was much to look at, neither had she tried to
hide the fact that he was no but an ordinary stockinger who worked, as
she did, at Hibbert and Buckland's. But, she drilled the news into us, he
happened to be a son of the Atkins, top-of-the-street business-folk who
owned a shop right across from the Portland Cinema in the centre of
town. What was more, though you'd never have guessed it, he'd been to
grammar school! In a word, he had potential. So there!

Oz didn't wear cloth caps. Oz smoked Players, not Woodbines. Oz
carried cigarettes not fags and he carried them in a fancy silver-plated case
not in an old shag tin. Oz, on his days off, wore a dark suit, collar and tie,

cuff-links even, black patent leather shoes, a wrist not a fob watch and, sometimes, spats. Oz shined his less than abundant hair with a green, greasy, sickly scented substance that went under the name 'Brilliantine'. Oz shaved every single day, carried a comb in his top pocket (imagine! the Atkins had more than one comb) and money in a purse. Oz claimed to have taken the train to Nottingham where he'd eaten egg and chips at the Trocadero! Oz didn't think much of football. Oz despised the coal-mining fraternity and most of his fellow stockingers as well; he steadfastly refused to join a trade union and he cursed those who did (though not of course with cuss-words) accusing them of "Rockin' t'boat, bitin' t'and as feeds 'em". Oz idolised the establishment. Oz read the *Daily Express*. Oz stood up when he heard the national anthem.

Muriel wouldn't have been human (which she was in spades) had she not recognised that "Ee's no oil paintin', I'll gi' 'yo that, but lewks i'nt everythin'. All right then, 'ees more Buster Keaton than Clark Gable but 'eel dew; 'ees a catch an' 'alf 'ee is." Well, it transpired that he hadn't taken that much catching either because he admitted having been hooked as soon as he'd swapped a glance with the predatory Muriel. From the first eye contact to the end of his days, he was to be led, blissfully, by the nose.

And, without much time for reflection, by the nose he was led up the aisle. The aisle what's more of a Church of England church, and the big one as well; the one at the junction of Alfreton and Huthwaite roads, a temple which on that day hosted not only the ceremony of joining Muriel and Oz in holy wedlock but also the one and only meeting – confrontation really – of the Atkin and Hardy-Scott tribes. (Much to Muriel's dismay her lot turned up in force: "Nivver miss a chance o' getting; summat for nought.") The Atkins, nose-in-the-air moneybags, made an unspoken truce with the Hardys-Scotts, a pact that lasted only for that one single day never to be renewed thereafter, not even for half-an-hour. I personally, for instance, never exchanged a single word with an Atkin other than Oz, nor did I ever set foot in their shop or their home; indeed, I'd cross the road rather than pass by their shop window.

But let's go back to the church. Oz, in hired grey topper and tails which, him being so short, nearly swept the ground, looked as if he'd stepped right out of a Keystone Cops movie while Muriel, decked out in white, kept glancing nervously over her shoulder in our direction, her eyes pleading with us to behave ourselves, "Lewk," she appeared to be saying, "Mother Atkin's splashed out as much on this as'd keep t'chapel goin' for a 12 month, so watch it!" Here was no tinny, out-of-tune piano murdering Mendelssohn but a sodding great pipe organ belting it out as Harry I, looking all shrunken and out-of-place in his Co-op tailored suit, escorted his second daughter down the aisle. Here was no Arthur Maddox in his 30-bob jacket but a frocked parson; here were none of your street-clad Chatsworth Street urchins mewling away 'songs of praise' but a choir of scrubbed, surpliced, middle-class boys harmonising 'proper' hymns; here were trellised altars with fancy rails, pastoral staff, croziers and all the accoutrements of inherited clerical authority. The Hardys and the Scotts came away feeling uneasy; they hadn't somehow enjoyed it. The question was – had they been put in their place? They retreated to think about it but they never again tried to advance on that particular front.

A day or two later Oz was led (possibly carried) over the threshold of what was to be named 'Rosstrevor', a house on a stuffy road named after the builder's wife: Mabel Avenue. Rosstrevor was a brand new, semi-detached, bay-window place of a type much prized by the lower middle classes in the 1930s; houses built, like their owners' confidence in their entrenched class environs, to last forever. It stood within the latest in aspirant up-market housing estates in a pretentious area not far from the factory where Bert Rose lost his thumb to a tin can. As Muriel never tired of telling us, it cost all of £400 – an unimaginably big sum to the rest of us. It was a present from the Atkins, a gift that proved what she'd said all along, "Oz mightn't be much to look at but still…."

The 'trevor' in Rosstrevor came from the name they gave their first-born. I've no idea where the 'Ross' came from but it certainly wouldn't have been T.E. Lawrence's assumed name because Muriel and Oz would never have allowed that Lawrence of Arabia might have been less than Herculean; to them he was always the mighty, good and manly Englishman who'd "sorted out the dirty, skiving Arabs". Anyway, the move into Rosstrevor meant the achievement of Muriel's first goal: she'd escaped from the ghetto and with a vengeance.

That left four of us in Garden Lane. We'd go up to Mabel Avenue to gossip about the treasure within Rosstrevor, hardly believing our eyes. We thought we'd struck it rich in No.32 but in Muriel's palace we saw things we'd seen before only in pictures: a 'three-piece suite' whose chairs were big enough to have accommodated Farouk, the young King of Egypt whose bulk grew with every published photo; a scullery you didn't eat in and which had gas rings; carpeting on the stairs even; lamp shades; lights at the top of the stairs; different 'pots' for dinner and breakfast; funny-looking knives said to be for eating fish with; wardrobes with full-length mirrors (in which we'd steal glimpses of our own ill-favoured selves); pyjamas (we went to bed in our shirts); dressing gowns (we had to be told what they were for and to this very day I've been unable to bring myself to wear one); carpets that hadn't been hand-pegged at home; two lavatories, and, for Trevor, a canopied baby 'carriage' almost as big as a motor car. As long as we wiped our feet and minded where we sat, Muriel would allow us in to ooh and ah over her Aladdin's cave.

Clarence Trigg, of course, was non-persona grato absoluta. His exclusion, never voiced but clearly understood, meant that Lillian also never once crossed Rosstrevor's beatified portals. As for Harry I, the place fussed him so much that he was only too happy to give it a miss. At times like christenings and birthdays when he couldn't avoid putting in an appearance, he'd swiftly be undone by being capsized into the pulpy guts of the low-slung sofa under which handicap he'd be instructed to "stop slouching – sit up straight!". He'd be scolded for flicking fag-ash into the fireplace instead of into the ashtray ("Bloody daft," he'd say afterwards with undeniable logic, "She'll only tip t'soddin ash inta fireplace any road so why bother wi' ashtrays?"). "Like a soddin' kiddy", he'd complain, he'd been "learned" how to hold his knife properly and ordered to take his elbows off the table. As for his dog (Harry I always had one at his heels) he was given a stark choice: "Either t'garridge or t'coal-'ouse, I'm not 'avin' it in 'ere and its not runnin' round t'garden either."

Having dreamed of confirming her new class status by "goin' inta business" a few years after her marriage she managed it. She and Oz moved into a corner grocery, a small capitalist redoubt from within whose keep she waged a bitter, no-holds barred and eventually triumphant struggle against a nearby Co-op whose cultivation of the working class/council house tenant custom she wanted for herself. It was her part in the war against 'bolshevism'. Opening all hours, every day, all the year round, undercutting the Co-op, granting 'tick' and using her considerable charm to woo her customers, Muriel was soon turning a profit while the 'commie' next-door-but-one were going to the wall. I'm not saying that she had the Midas touch but she made her shop pay to the extent that she installed a telephone, an instrument as rare in those days as the red squirrel is today. And, would you believe it, she/they opened a Building Society account!

In the meantime Muriel and Oz produced their second, last offspring (their abstinence in this order of life was also offered as an example to the lower orders who "went at it like rabbits"), another son they named John, who rose to be a foreman at Uncle Bert's old company. Trevor fled, and not just around the corner either but, to Newfoundland! Upon which forever-wintry island he became a superior sort of engineer specialising in generating electricity. Muriel and Oz (it was never put the other way round which says a lot) were a lot like their idol Margaret Thatcher (what a tussle they must have waged inwardly over whom to worship the most: the Queen Mother or Thatcher?) called 'go-getters'. The shop was open from dawn to dusk. They never took a holiday that lasted more than 48 hours. They never saw a movie and, apart from Oz's couple of years with the army in North Africa during the war ("Dirty Ayrobs, they'd pinch t'wax from your ears if yo'd let 'em; they're no good for ought."), they seldom left Sutton. They once went on an overnight trip to London returning with Union Jacks shining from their eyes. Like the world travellers they afterwards considered themselves to be, they swooned, "Nought like in t'rest o'world. Teks your breath away it does. They can keep their Paris an' their Rome an' places like that, none of 'ems a patch on Lundun." Every Saturday morning, topped up with Oz's pay packet (for he never stopped working for Hibbert and Buckland who, in the end, after exploiting him for 40 years, rewarded him with a gold-plated fob watch which he drooled over as if it had been a Fauberge egg) they'd stash the week's takings into the Building Society.

Years after the end of the war (which, according to the Atkins we'd won all on our own; the Russians and the Yanks had done a lot of shouting "but bugger all else") they retired from shop-keeping to move into a duplicate of Rosstrevor and only spitting distance from it. Upon their new abode they bestowed the immodest appellation: 'Newstead' after the nearby abbey of that name that had once housed Lord Byron. And, just in case passers-by missed the nameplate, they splashed out on a hearse-sized automobile, a black Humber which, provided it wasn't raining, would be rolled out to stand gleaming and spotless in front of Newstead – a mobile shrine to bulldog capitalism.

Oz had the misfortune always to present himself as the humourless skinflint but behind that façade he had a warm, good side. As for Muriel, once you'd wrenched the flag out of her hand; talked her out of raving against 'rotten trade-unionists, filthy communists, welfare scroungers, work-shys, no-good blacks, social workers, colliers, foreigners, republicans and council house tenants', and calmed her down with a fag and got her talking family, she would turn into a more articulate, funnier – and fatter – Harriet. A marvellous mimic with almost total recall, her enormous sense of fun and a remarkably full vocabulary, she'd have done a lot better job relating all this than I'm doing.

Inside the steely salesperson there dwelled a kind, loveable woman. And it was to this inner being that I turned for solace during the miserable, homesick days I endured early in the war; and it was Muriel and Oz who offered me, and my new wife, shelter in Rosstrevor while we waited for the completion of our own house in Kirkby in 1946. It was Muriel – not without Oz's blessing and support – who nursed Harriet at her end in Garden Lane (Harriet had been sliced once more to be left with a totally flat chest but at the finish, which came while I was on the high seas between Malaya and England in 1956, it was her heart that attacked her). And it was Muriel who took Harry I into Newstead to die in 1964. What I'm saying is that Muriel's outward form was just for show; let any foreign, coloured, Marxist, paid-up member of the coal-miners' union approach Muriel seeking solicitude and he'd be smothered in kindness.

Harry II Turning Heels, The Burn Street Doldrums

Although George Henry, my elder brother by two years, whom we shall call Harry II, slept for 17 years in the same bed as myself, ate the same food and shared the same piss-pot and hair-comb, we were never as close as two, nor yet 200, years. We shared a common lineage, hence the common burden of underclass status, but thereafter we diverged as far as two aeroplanes flying from London, one to Lima the other to Luzon. For instance, while I became a bookworm, Harry II never voluntarily turned the pages of a single volume and while I took off for distant lands, never once (except for an enforced trip to North Africa as a soldier in the war) did Harry II lift his eyes further than camp sites or boarding houses in Skegness, Great Yarmouth and Blackpool. He loathed Hardwick Lane Elementary School. Released at the age of 14 from what he and most nobodies thought of as the bondage of learning, he went, in delirious delight, into a factory that made ladies' stockings, a living that wasn't all that much of an improvement on coal-mining but one which Harry II saw as offering life-enhancing promise. His initiation into it represented the honouring of the sole pledge ever sworn by Harry I to his sons: that they'd never go down a mineshaft.

The idea that higher education might lead his offspring into better lives never entered the old man's head ("learnin's not for uz") nor did he for one moment aspire on our behalf to white-collar jobs ("bobbies' jobs aren't for the likes of uz") or even to craft apprenticeships but, bless him, he drew the line at following him down the pits. "Ah don't know wots to 'appen to yer," he'd whine during the blackest of times, "but this much ah'll tell thee – tha'll not goo down t'pit." And he was true to his word. With a wink here, a greased palm there and the acceptance on our account of something less than the going wage rate, he somehow wangled first Harry II then me into 'stockinging'. Running a temperature over getting out of school for good, my brother would've marched into a pit cage quite cheerfully; instead he found himself working a machine that 'turned' the heels of stockings (the welts and legs were knitted on a different device) in a grubby little sweat-shop on Station Road. And of an evening he made his way into billiard saloons – scrubby, one-sex, nicotine-polluted – but dry – centres of so-called entertainment that took male working-class teenagers about as far as they could go into the high-life.

He also made his way into a good-looking female counterpart of Clarence Trigg named Nellie. She murdered the English language on the Trigg scale, a crime she committed through the weapon of a glass-shattering howl that was her conversational tone of voice. Muriel of course would have nothing to do with her. The rest of us merely recoiled but the fact remains that the coupling gave life to Joy, a sparkling, beautiful child who grew into a vivacious, self-confident, wide-visioned woman whom we all took to our bosoms with delight. But, Joy apart, Harry II and Nellie produced nothing but misery for each other and for everybody else. Forever at each other's throats, it was a relief all round when they called it a day and went their separate ways.

On Harriet's death he moved back to share 32, Garden Lane with Harry I. Visiting the two of them in 1963 I found the house little changed since I'd left it 24 years earlier. Gladioli, the only non-edible plant Harry I would ever grow, still bloomed in the front garden, the same old rag rug lay in the hearth while still in its old place ("Blockin' everybody's road") there stood the truly hideous 'cabinet' that Harry I had once cobbled together out of plywood, pieces of two-by-four and lengths of beading, a varnished box built to house the unwieldy wet batteries that had once powered the Murphy wireless set that stood proudly on its lace covered top. That same old wood-encased radio still stood there in 1963 but its pride had long gone for, deprived of its batteries, it had been mute for years. Harrys I and II made a sad but companionable pair, degenerating in good fellowship nurtured by their sharing the self-inflicted abuses of consuming fry-ups and 20 or 30 fags apiece every day. Father was now a pensioner; he topped up his miserly income by doing 'lollipop' work – seeing school-kids safely across the road – but otherwise (his much-loved allotments having been built over) he just sat by the fire at No.32. Harry II, having given up stockinging years before (and with it the obligatory exercise involved in running up and down the length of a heeling machine – half the length of a cricket pitch – umpteen times an hour) was a milkman, up at three in the morning to drive an electric-motored van to deliver milk to doorsteps. It was a vocation he'd chosen because it liberated him at noon every day, leaving him with oodles of spare time but he used the spare time very badly, spending most of it in nicotine-fugged poolrooms.

Being older by 30 years, Harry I was the first to go under. By the time Muriel took him into Newstead to die, the house had no fireplace for him to flick his ash into but by then anyway he wasn't making a lot of ash.

The local council moved Harry II out of 32, Garden Lane into a two-room apartment in an austere, unwelcoming estate on Alfreton Road right opposite the house in which the admirable Uncle Jack, Aunt Rachel and Leslie used to live. Suffering from gout, arthritis, emphysema, high-blood pressure and depression, he'd been given the sack by the Co-op's milk delivery department, but ever his own man, he'd hire himself out on hourly-wage labouring terms to garages. Garages? In the ghetto? Well yes and plenty of them because by the 1960s Nottinghamshire's rich coal seams proved to be well suited to the new mechanical coal-rippers. Local collieries – particularly Clarence Trigg's pit at Clipstone – boomed and colliers were driving motorcars to the pitheads and to resorts in Spain and France as well.

Harry II, never a bad-looking chap, could still put on a bit of a show. Well-built, dark (Hardys and Scotts alike tanned easily; Harry I had only to spend a day in the sun at Trent Bridge and he looked as if he'd been in Morocco for a month) hook-nosed, brown-eyed and usually tidily groomed, as long as he kept his trap shut and as long as he didn't blubber, he could still turn a woman's head. But he remained a frying pan and nicotine addict and, though it didn't show around his waistline, he began to seize-up. He complained of being unable to turn his head without blacking-out from pain and he began to limp.

They found him lying unconscious in his flat. The doctors saved him but only at the cost of being wheelchaired, an impairment that meant moving him from Alfreton Road into a dark, miniscule ground-floor bed-sit at 17, Burn Street. It was 1983 and Harry had come full circle; he laid his head in a place built almost precisely above the spot where Abe and Harry I had once tilled their allotments, right there at the junction of Short Street and Garden Lane, not more than a few hundred yards from Chatsworth and St. Michael's streets. He'd returned to the centre of the ghetto and it was there that I found him being minded by his erstwhile doxy, Joan, a large-boned, scruffy, grim-visaged troll who spoke with a high-pitched wail that by comparison made Nellie sound like Maria Callas.

Harry II had always been a weeper and the tears flowed freely. He'd been known to bawl at hellos, goodbyes, Land of Hope and Glory, either winning or losing a game of lawn-bowls, being teased, shouted at or praised, an armistice day poppy, a wag of a dog's tail, the blare of a brass band and the voice of Gracie Fields. I always thought his tendency to pipe the eye to be his very best feature but, conditioned to the machismo of billiard saloons, Harry II himself was ashamed of it. So ashamed that he wept because he wept. Back there in Burn Street he'd plenty to weep about.

The Bobby Dazzler, Huckleberry Finn and Emil Ludwig

Then there was me, Stanley. Like most nobody-kids in the street I had my own treasured playthings, sometimes home-made, sometimes hand-me-downs. Things like a whip and top, a bowling hoop, and most precious of all, a cloth bag full of multi-coloured glass marbles, the most brilliant of which was called, by tradition, 'the bobby dazzler', Harriet used to say that of her own bag of 'little marvels' Stanley was her 'bobby dazzler'. Every day between our fish-and-chip shop and the Mansfield Road Primary School where, to the rest of the family's disbelief, if not disapprobation, I took to the learning process like a duck to water. For all my eagerness however, all I recall of primary school days is singing "There's a hole in my bucket dear Liza…" But there must have been a lot more to it than merely lamenting Georgie's ignorance of the art of the tinsmith because from the moment I first went through the school gate my hands were seldom without pencils, slate, paper and books.

"Leave 'im be," Harriet would say whenever Harry I remonstrated against what he saw as my perversion, "e'll grow out on it soon enuff." But she was wrong, I never did. I read, or tried to read, every printed word I laid eyes on: the *Nottingham Evening News*, the *Sutton Free Press*, labels on 'Camp Coffee' bottles, twists of newspaper which had wrapped around pennyworths of broken biscuits and, on Saturday nights, the pink *Football News*.

Had it been left to the citizens of places like Sutton every author that ever lived would have died of starvation; I doubt if one in a hundred ever read a book in their lives. For a certainty, the houses that sheltered the Hardy tribe and, apart from Kate's and Polly's all of the Scotts' as well, were never contaminated by a single volume. That was until in about 1930 when, by the hand of God himself, Huckleberry Finn came into our house in Short Street. It came about through the Sunday School, a cheerless gathering of half-a-dozen runny-nosed, rebellious kids, which assembled, unwillingly, every Sabbath afternoon in a pokey room at the back of Harriet's Chatsworth Street chapel. Keen on schooling I certainly was but the standard of tuition at that particular seminary was so low that even I had to be strong-armed into attending it. Our 'teacher' was a 17-year-old religious freak so unappealing and so dim that she couldn't have excited us had she recited from the Karma Sutra; what chance therefore did she have with the New Testament? You didn't have to be 'Brain of Britain' to top the class, all that was needed was sufficient guile to hide your boredom better than the others did. And that's how I came to be presented with the Congregational Church Sunday-School Prize:

a copy of Huckleberry Finn. Once started on Mark Twain, there was no going back to wasting Sunday afternoons in Chatsworth Street. From the moment I read the first page I'd spend my Sabbaths fighting off Harriet's pleas that I devote them to Jesus. Ignoring also Harry I's warnings that "my nose would drop off if I didn't take it out of bewks", I'd settle down to devour those I'd borrowed from the 'Free Library' in the centre of town. Apart from Uncle Bert, from whom I got the idea and who was forever blamed for my apostasy, nobody I knew had ever walked up the granite steps leading to the public library.

On the day I plucked up enough courage to do it myself I half expected to be thrown out for my insolence: "This i'nt the place for the likes of yew." Instead, I was welcomed, presented with a borrower's card and let loose in a treasure trove crammed with books, newspapers and journals. There and then I wanted to telegraph all the world's authors: 'Don't write any more until I've been through this lot."

Using an eeny-meeny-miney-moh system I started off with the works of Emil Ludwig, a biographer who, to judge by the number of his books on the shelves must have been related to the Chairman of the library's book selection committee. Ludwig may not figure in literature's hall of fame but it was he, together with Mark Twain, who without my setting a foot outside the ghetto, spirited me far, far away from it. Emil wrote about Napoleon, Bismark, Peter the Great and Garibaldi, taking me up mountains from whose peaks I saw things my folks would never gaze upon and pointing me towards other writers of greater merit than he, writers who electrified and often disturbed me at the same time. Zola, for example, whose coal-mine towns in northern France were a bit too close to home for my escapist longings.

The family's aversion to my obsession with the printed word increased at the same pace as I indulged it. But, hurtful as their deprecation of my habit was, it was also, in retrospect, understandable. The enjoyment of literature was simply beyond their comprehension; also, by making me the odd man out, it disrupted the even pattern of family life. The scullery for instance was the only place in the house that had continuous light and heat; hence all activity other than sleeping, bathing and defecation was performed, for most of the year anyway, within its space. Ergo, because the great scullery table occupied most of the room, your book-reader had no choice but to sit with his legs underneath it. The table was dining table, kitchen-table, workbench, ironing board, escritoire, saw-horse, garment cutting surface, rug-pegging base, card table and then some, all rolled into one. (A word about rug pegging. It was a most pleasant winter evening chore in which all six of us sat round the table pegging scraps of rags into a sheet of Hessian large enough to be the next hearth rug.) There were times when the table would be strewn with well-thumbed playing cards, draughts, dominoes, snakes-and-ladders, ludo boards and tiddly-winks. And all the time, whether they were eating, working or playing, they would rackety-yak and quarrel like mad while the Murphy wireless piped-away non-stop in the background.

Small wonder then that when one of the six persons round the table chose to bury his head in a book the other five were a bit miffed. They made no bones about it. While Fred Astaire droned on from the Murphy about "The folks who lived on the hill" or while Bing Crosby crooned some mindless ditty or other (I've loathed Astaire and Crosby ever since) the five non-literati would keep up a steady twitting: "We're not gud enuff for lord Muck 'ere"; "Git your elbows off t'table Shakespeare, it's rude an' some on uzz 'ave werk to dew onit an' all"; "Bewk lernin' nivver brung us sort a brass farthin'"; and "Smart Arse!" And, illogically – but not to them – "Thar'd be better off enjoyin' thissen." Only Harriet, in a miscued sort of way, stood up for me: "Leave 'im be; 'e's dewin no 'arm, it costs nought an' e'l grow out on it."

Looking back I can see that they were damned nearly proved right, because for all my 'bewk lernin', I landed up as nothing more than a trainee stockinger in a sweatshop. And it was neither Mark Twain nor Emil Ludwig who led me physically to escape: rather it was those philistines: Mussolini, Hitler, Franco and Tojo.

It wasn't true anyway that I was a heart-and-soul bibliomaniac; rug-making, cards, tiddly-winks and darts were lots of fun and I had my full share of them. I took particular delight in the après baths hour on wintry Saturday nights when we'd check the football results against Harry I's pools coupons. If he'd been flush enough to have laid a tanner on the pools so much the better because we'd then have real money to check over but even if he hadn't wagered a penny we'd still have made the coupons out on the previous Monday and pretended on the Saturday that we'd bought a postal order and sent it off with the coupons to Liverpool. In that way we made sure of getting our Saturday evening highs. No oil-fattened Emir from the Gulf playing the wheels for millions at Vegas could have been more hyped up than Harry I on those Saturdays. Sixpence at stake or not we'd settle down, sweet smelling, to study the afternoon's results in the *Football News*. It wasn't that, deep down, we really expected ever to win anything (and we never did) but that we cherished the adrenalin boost, Harry I had heard tales of nobodies "cumin up on t'pewls" but, never having met a big winner, he couldn't confirm the stories. Indeed, he had it worked out that, since colliers were never paid enough for them ever to be stung for income tax, the somebodies had hatched the idea of football pools as another way of fleecing them. He never explained though how, having seen through their diabolical plot, he nevertheless fell for it.

Other blissful moments were those spent on raw winter nights sitting across the hearth from Harriet in front of a blazing fire with Harry I snoozing nearby and holding a skein of wool at arms' length while she wound it into balls. She was a compulsive knitter. Her wooden needles stopped clicking only when she was asleep or while she was cooking, cleaning, laying-out her dead or rolling her wool into balls. We seldom bought a jersey and scarcely a pair of socks. Discarded woollens (some bought for pennies from the rag-and-bone man) were unpicked, the wool washed and recycled into balls ready for knitting up once more. Worn-out clothes were washed and stashed away in 'ragbags' to be opened in late autumn in preparation for the rug pegging. In later years her needles would go right ahead tap-tapping in the darkness of the cinema; neither Boris Karloff nor Charlie Chaplin could flurry her into dropping a stitch.

Harry I Revisited

Then there were hot summer days spent on Harry I's allotments; roasting spuds on a stick rammed into the heart of his smoking garden fire while he toiled steadily away, composed, at peace. Like most colliers, Harry I could never get enough fresh, open air. For next-to-nothing he rented two large allotments from the council, parcels of good land running alongside a third leased by his father, Abe, whose little potting shed, wheelbarrow and whatnots he shared and whose strawberries I plundered. Apart from gladioli to which blooms he devoted the whole of the small front garden in Garden Lane, he refused to grow flowers ("yer can't eat 'em") and he stood out against things like mint ("grow mint an' y'll soon 'ave nought else in t'garden") and strawberries ("same as mint"). Otherwise he was marvellously green fingered; we seldom bought vegetables, indeed he gave tons of greens away usually to folk who didn't need his benevolence, people, I suspect, to whom he might one day turn for favours. As I've already told you, he'd get up at half past three in the morning (at least when he was in work) and get back home at about four in the afternoon. A quick wash down at the sink, a big 'dinner', forty winks, and with his dog in happy tow, he'd be away to his allotments there to work until eight. A mug of cocoa with maybe a slice of bread-and-dripping and he'd be fast asleep by nine.

He was never without a hound of some sort. The one to whom he whispered his most passionate sweet-nothings was a wire-haired terrier who, apart from a black patch over one eye, was pristine white all over. Harry I named her, unpoetically of course, 'Dot'. He spent more time on her Sunday morning grooming than he spent on his own; brushing white powder into her coat, combing her with our one and only (steel) comb, clipping her ears and tail and teaching her simple new tricks. He loved parading her in front of his mates outside the pub; pointing out the sheen of her coat, the elegance of her carriage, the sparkle in her eyes and the lift of her tail: "Sign o' gud breedin' they are, pedigree she is." But she wasn't; Dot's finer points were attributable less to her progenitorship than to her need to return Harry I's adoration. Dot's death in 1938 cast a pall of gloom over 32, Garden Lane; Harriet laid her out in her very best laying-out style and she was interred, solemnly, beneath Harry I's allotment.

Despite his being short on words and despite his being, outwardly at least, unsentimental towards anything except dogs, Harry I brought me to a love of cricket in all its subtleties – subtleties that were much more prevalent in the game during the 1930s than they are now, but still. At least twice he scraped enough together to take me to Trent Bridge there to chide me for over-excitement: "Nay lad, don't meek such a fuss, shooting's not for cricket". I remember one Saturday morning in 1934 when we went together to Chesterfield to see the visiting Australians. Sitting on the top deck of a tram as we approached the ground we had a good view of the wicket and could see that play had already begun. Harry I grabbed my arm and said "Lewk down there, it's Bradman." Sure enough I caught a glimpse of the little wizard but by the time we got into the ground the Don was out. Fourteen years later – in 1948 – sitting side-by-side at Trent Bridge again, we saw Bradman once more. But it was almost a repetition of Chesterfield because, having hit a hundred the day before, the great man got out to the second ball of the day. Harry I observed: "T'English team ought to carry uz tew around wi' 'em all t'time; we're t'only English as can get 'im out early on."

And I well recall another, earlier, summer Saturday evening in St. Michael's Street when Harry I, having backed a winner at the races and having celebrated by getting plastered, came home in a syce-driven pony and trap. Pulling into the kerb outside the front door, the big spender lolled in the back seat steadying an ancient, upright piano he'd bought for a couple of quid (a lot of money in those days). Harriet nearly had a fit on her well-pumiced doorstep. Wiping her hands over and over again on her apron – a nervous habit of hers – she said "Yo daft sod, weer are we goin' to put a soddin' piano?" Well, the soddin piano was to stand in front rooms in St. Michael's Street, Mansfield Road, Oak Tree Road, Short Street and Garden Lane, its keyboard through all those years hardly ever fingered, none of us ever learned to play it – who on earth could have taught us? Using only two fingers Harry I taught himself to play a few bars of 'In a Monastery Garden'. When we had company he'd thump away his appalling masterpiece as though he were Rachmaninov performing at the Albert Hall. He remained totally unmoved by all entreaties to part with his piano; like the old Murphy wireless set he kept it by him, silent as a stone, until the very end.

The last time I was with Harry I was in the summer of 1963. The two of us sat watching England playing the West Indies at Trent Bridge. The hard bench didn't do his piles any good and he was also being needled by the behaviour of a few local rowdies who, unhappy at seeing their heroes taking a pasting at the hands of blacks, were hissing and booing. By late afternoon old Harry had had enough. "Nay, nay," he cried out "Give over, give over, weer dost thee think thart? Tha shuddna mek a row 'ere, not 'ere, not 'ere." I said my last goodbye to him when, at the close of that day's play I saw him on to a bus that was to take him back to Garden Lane.

The 'Head Boy' and the Butcher's Daughter

In 1932 I passed effortlessly into the Station Road Higher Standard Elementary School. The headmaster was one Mr. Conway, an enlightened young man who had the idea that some nobodies at least could be raised above the torpor of the masses through education. It was an idea shared by very few of the nobodies. Conway advanced the teaching of algebra, trigonometry, French, art and drama but for all the encouragement he received from most of the parents he might as well have promoted the teaching of Tagalog. Long conditioned to accepting their lot uncomplainingly, parent nobodies sought nothing more from a school than to keep their kids off the streets until at 14, they could be put to the grind. Nevertheless, the headmaster persisted. I thought the world of Conway; I scrubbed my knees for him, washed the back of my neck for him, and I played the lead in his annual tableaus. The admiration was reciprocated – he appointed me 'Head Boy'; even Harry I was impressed with the 'Head Boy' badge I wore all the time, even in bed.

There was a 'Head Girl' too; a redhead named Joyce Beastall to whom I took an unscholarly fancy. Inexperienced in the art of courtship, the only romantic approach I could think of was to pass her a note proposing that we held hands on our way to and from school. I was coldly rebuffed because Joyce was the daughter of a butcher while I was a collier's son. The class divide was wide as an ocean; her brother for instance was relatively so well set-up that he possessed his very own cricket bat and 'compo' ball, treasures way beyond Stanley Hardy's pocket or even dreams. Hence I got no nearer to my Head Girl than to fold my mitts not around her but around the handle of her brother's bat. Never mind, disappointment in love was the only painful episode in an otherwise long period of unbroken bliss at Station Road High. Except, that is, for what happened in the end.

As the day on which the authorities would lose their power to retain me in formal education – my 14th birthday – approached, Conway met my parents to try to persuade them to allow me to go forward into grammar school. He failed. Harry I wouldn't hear of it and Harriet didn't believe strongly enough in the advantages of higher education to oppose him. I was heartbroken but what could I say to them – to people who'd all along drilled me in the nobodies' canon: "Folks like us can't work our ticket threw beak learning." Neither could I fault their socio-economic reasoning. "Any road up," Harry I would say with a sigh of resignation, "'own kid we pay for it? Ah mean, ah know as it's a scholarship but what about t'bewks, uniforms, fancy 'ats an' tram fares? An' for years on end an' all. Ah mean lewk at it like this – it wouldna be fair on t'others wud it? Them there's already bringin munny in, see? It'd be the same as askin' 'em to pay for yo' not to werk. 'Tint right summow. Cum on ner – own up tew it; let's be right eh?" And so on with damnable logic and with never a whisper of support for the other side of the argument. Thus it was that my dreams of walking the corridors of ancient universities were snuffed out. It was a time for shedding a tear or two of my own.

Ragged Trousers and the Clothing Club

It wasn't the end of the world; I was young, I still had my books and I could still make-believe. I read the likes of Keir Hardie, James Maxton and the Webbs; they mayn't have been outstanding or impartial political philosophers but they were learned enough for me. I absorbed the anti-imperialism of 'The Ragged Trousered Philanthropist' while at the same time I listened to my geography and history teachers, as well as to plummy voices over the Murphy wireless, telling me how lucky I was to be British, the race that ruled the largest empire the world had ever known and so on. Well-nourished voices bade me rejoice in Britain's ownership of a third of the world and in my share of our empire's wealth and power. On Empire Days and on the King Emperor's birthdays we were invited to stand in front of maps of the world covered in large red areas and we were hyped-up to wave flags, to ask God to save our gracious King and to sing the praises of our Land of Hope and Glory.

Meanwhile, there was one particular Saturday afternoon in our scullery. Harry I was either out of work or on short time or else he was sick or perhaps injured (mining accidents were commonplace) or even suffering from a combination of all of these misfortunes. Anyhow, we were out at the elbows alright. I found Harriet sobbing her heart out because she hadn't a sixpence to pay Mr. Arnold, the clothing clubman. Arnold was a large, florid, intimidating man who, winter and summer alike, wore a heavy black overcoat. He called twice a month to collect a few pennies. He'd enter the payments in a red notebook that over the years acquired the aura of the scriptures. Every now and then, against our credit (and sometimes against the debt into which he'd calculatedly allowed us to dip so that he could whack us with swingeing interest payments) he'd supply us with items of clothing we couldn't do without – things like boots and pit clothes. Arnold and his kind knew bloody well that we didn't trust ourselves to take care of our own money; cash put aside in tins on the mantelpiece or under the bed would always be 'blued in' on things we could do without – thinks like beer, fags, gob-stoppers or broken biscuits. What it boiled down to was that we were so financially undisciplined that we actually paid creatures like Arnold to keep our hands off our own money!

But it wasn't being short of a sixpence that had reduced Harriet to blubbering as if her world had ended; we'd missed paying Arnold many a time. No, it wasn't that. It was being short of a sixpence on a Saturday that did it. Friday, you see, was payday. Ergo, to be skint on a Saturday meant having to get through six whole days on nought. Listening to Harriet wailing like she did, it came to me that no matter what anybody said or wrote about it, any empire that couldn't come up with a sixpence on a Saturday afternoon for a good woman like Harriet wasn't worth having. I made up my mind to change the world from Short Street.

I read about sugar-cane workers in the Caribbean who, having no need for heating, hot water, draught-proofing, heavy clothing or boots and, given that they'd only to stretch their arms to pick bread-fruit, bananas, mangoes and coconuts off the trees, were a darned sight better off than we, their rulers, were back in the imperial homeland. The Union Jack flew above poverty-stricken masses: black, brown, yellow and, at home, albeit beneath the coal dust, white.

All the claptrap about Britain's 'civilising mission' overseas was but dust thrown into our eyes to blind us from seeing that the true concerns of our colonisers were riches, authority and the panoply of power for the few. The truth was that the black cane-cutter in the tropics and the whitish collier in Sutton suffered a common misery brought upon them by a common exploiter: the British ruling class. The lesson sank deeply into my soul. But when it came to telling my fellow nobodies about my discovery, I might as well have recited the Upanishads in Uzbekistan.

H. & C.H. Blinkhorn, Hosiery Manufacturers, 'same as that'

Aged 14, I looked eleven. No matter, grown up or not, ready or not, I was on the labour market. Harry I had a word with Uncle Harry Scott (who looked none the worse for marrying Meg Elliot) who had a word with his employers. The outcome was an instruction to present myself for consideration for a job as an 'alley lad' with the firm of H &

C.H. Blinkhorn, Hosiery Manufacturers. Knees knocking as though I were a candidate for the directorship of a bank instead of for a job as a grease-monkey, on one Friday afternoon in the autumn of 1936 I duly appeared outside the Blinkhorn's factory, a small plant of such grim aspect that, put alongside it, the pithead at Rufford would have looked like the Taj Mahal.

Imagining that I'd be met by a door-keeper who'd usher me into a plush office there to be questioned gently by a smooth executive, I'd put on my Sunday suit, polished my shoes and water-slicked my hair. And I showed up a good half-an-hour before the appointed time. In my sweaty hand I clutched a 'testimonial' addressed to 'To whom it may concern' and signed by Headmaster Conway. Couched in language more suitable as an introduction to a board of college governors than to the hirers of factory labourers, the document commented Stanley Hardy for, I remember, 'excellent disposition and high scholastic promise'. There I stood, all of a dither, facing a dingy green door when who should turn up to compete with me for the job than two youths I'd known at school. All the more reason to clutch my testimonial much more tightly.

At the appointed time we rang the doorbell then stood back to await the arrival of the unctuous scrivener we expected to appear before us. Instead, in answer there appeared two men dressed in oily work clothes, one tall and straight, the other short and bent, both looking like toilworn machinists out for a breath of air and a smoke. Rude plebeians they looked and, as soon as they opened their mouths, rude plebeians they sounded. To our amazement however they announced themselves to be the oligarchs. They were the brothers H. (Harold) and C.H. (Charles) Blinkhorn, Hosiery Manufacturers. From the portals of their Dickensian – looking factory this unlikely pair of entrepreneurs looked down their noses at us as if we were turds. The ugly faces of capitalism never came uglier than those of H. & C.H. Blinkhorn, Hosiery Manufacturers. We weren't invited inside.

"Same as that," the lanky Charlie said, uttering the vacuous catch-phrase with which I was to learn over the next three years, he and brother Harold opened every single statement they ever uttered, "Same as that, which o' yo three's 'Ardy?" Still unable to believe that we stood in the presence of captains of industry and not a pair of down-on-their luck nobodies, I stuck out a hand proffering my priceless testimonial. Without as much as a glance at my offering, Charlie said "Same as that, yo'll dew. Cum 'ere Mundi 'arf seven sharp and bring yer own tewls wi' yer." Whereupon both hosiery manufacturers turned on their oil-fouled heels leaving me standing, my arm still outstretched offering my abjured certificate and feeling as if I'd been shat on. Never mind, I was to be a wage earner; the rest of our tribe would be pleased with me. On Monday morning at half-seven sharp, I went through the slimy green door of H. & C.H. Blinkhorn, Hosiery Manufacturers to begin what I expected to be my lifetime's work; not having read Fanon at that time I didn't register the scene that faced me as such but I look back upon it now as having been right out of 'The Wretched of the Earth'. I was in a kind of a small aeroplane hanger which housed not aircraft but half-a-dozen machines resembling the leviathans in Chaplin's *Modern Times*, each one half a cricket pitch long and a metre-and-a-half wide. Imported from Germany those behemoths were embedded in a foot or more of concrete. They stood in three rows, two facing each other on either side of three wood-flagged 'alleys', lanes which years of bearing human traffic for 138 hours a week and an incessant soaking in oil had turned into skating rinks which were so narrow that two skaters, one operating each machine, passed each other only with difficulty. Each passage prompted an exchange of raillery, which added to the already deafening noise level.

The machine knitted ladies' stockings either out of rayon or silk, both brittle fibres whose elasticity was maintained by keeping the whole plant hot and damp and by their being fed from bobbins to the machines' needles by way of baths of a foul-smelling liquid called 'lather'. One of the worst of my jobs was to keep my machines' 24 lather baths topped up. If one of them dried up the yarn would snap thus ruining a stocking whereupon one of the ever-hovering Blinkhorns would dock my wages on the spot: 'Same as that'. The uninterrupted evaporation of 150 baths of lather made a stink that must have been like that described by 19th century travellers who visited the lavatories in the public steam baths of the Ottoman Empire.

The machines were always more important than their operators. Each epitomised the supremacy of Teutonic efficiency and the industrial supremacy of Hitler's Germany; they testified that the Nazis were good at making things other than guns. Each was worked round the clock Mondays to Fridays and for 12 hours on Saturdays. The noise they made collectively resembled the soundtrack of a Hollywood war movie: booms, blasts, whines, shudders and screechings that were impossible to talk above. The silence that fell at noon on Saturdays always caught us nobodies shouting at each other as if we were miles not metres apart from one another.

Each mechanical beast shuttled hundreds of thousands of locked steel needles to knit 24 ladies' stockings (minus the heels which were knitted separately) every 75 minutes or so. Each was allotted a three-man team which worked three, one-man, eight-hour shifts: So, for all but 36 hours a week, there'd be six sweaty, aproned men tearing up and down three long, narrow oil slicks servicing six huge Rhine maidens made of steel. In between the skating up and down (usually the relatively peaceful 20 minutes it took the machine to knit that part of the stocking between thigh and knee) the operators would grab a bite to eat, a swig out of a thermos (the Blinkhorns would never have thought of providing a canteen – same as that), a smoke (allowed only in the toilet), a leak or, if they were desperate enough (and given the appalling state of the Hogarthian single-holer that passed as a lavatory bowl they had to be in extremis even to think of using it) a crap.

Uncle Harry was in one of the three-man teams. He and his mates, Ernie and Jack, had worked it out that with the help of a fleet-footed 'alley lad' working nine hours a day (0730–1730 with an hour off for 'dinner') they could boost their pay packets by a lot more than they'd have to pay the lad in wages. And that's how I came to be their 'alley lad'. In no time at all I was flying up and down my alley like a skier on a steep descent.

In a matter of weeks I was 'clipping ends', 'turning welts' (the cotton part at the top of the hose) and oiling bearings as speedily as Ernie and Jack and ahead of Uncle Harry who, bless him, was never one to rush. I was also a dab hand at the nauseating chore of mixing buckets of lather, a job that from the first day my seniors made over to me. In no time at all, at least during the hours I worked, we were turning out a dozen pairs of hose every 60, as opposed to every 75, minutes. Since the team paid me a mere half-a-crown apiece a week (seven shillings and sixpence all told from which Harold and Charlie took sixpence for national insurance) Harry, Ernie and Jack were soon showing a handsome profit from their 'alley lad' idea. The extra seven shillings on the mantelpiece (well, six and threepence after she'd given me ninepence pocket money) was a godsend to Harriet.

The role of 'alley lad' wasn't exactly mind-expanding but it could have been a lot worse. The hullabaloo created by the German mastodons for instance silenced idle chatter and vulgar badinage leaving me with nine hours a day for pipe dreaming. While mixing lather I'd imagine that I was stirring bean stew over an open fire in a camp outside Barcelona where the International Brigade was preparing for a victorious assault on Franco's army (the Spanish civil war brought me elation, hope and finally despair) the oil with which I filled my oil can became ghee for offering to Gandhi behind whom I'd walk through Rajastan; my pliers were the conductors through which I'd detonate the mines to blow up Mussolini; the log book I'd see as the constitutional document I'd drawn up to abolish the House of Lords and the monarchy; and, as I 'turned welts', I'd smooth them over the creamy thighs of Carole Lombard.

Cycles and Cinemas

Since we were a bit flush and since the Blinkhorn plant was a good three-quarters-of-an-hour's walk from Garden Lane, and since I was a good boy, the family lashed out on a never-never (a shilling a week) purchase of a Raleigh bicycle for me. It promptly skidded on ice and broke my left arm; nevertheless it became the Pegasus upon which at weekends I flew over Lillian's old tracks in Derbyshire and, less frequently, it carried me to her prison at Clipstone. So began my romance with bicycles.

To the extent to which my meagre spending money allowed I became a film addict as well. It's said that the 1930s were the golden age of films; that was true, certainly, in numbers. Picture houses ranging from gungy little fleapits to ornate palaces sprang up everywhere – even Huthwaite had one. I always went to the pictures alone because, while my workmates and others went to the same cinemas on the same nights as I did, from what they said afterwards they'd seen different movies. Take Uncle Harry for example. A cinema habitué like me, if we'd both seen a gangster movie he'd have registered only the excitement, the blood-letting, the cursing, the tinsel, the jazzy clothes, the smart cars and the flashes of the broads' flesh, whereas I'd have seen Paul Muni and Edward G. Robinson as Blinkhorns with guns – the message that got through to me, moralistic prig that I was, was social and political; mind you, those glimpses of rounded female bosoms didn't exactly leave me cold either.

1939–1946
Army Days

Wars and Talk of Wars

There were stories in the newspaper we could now afford to buy about black-clad Romans bombing the daylights out of black-skinned Abyssinians: about a short-arsed Spanish general leading Moors back to Spain not to revive the Moorish culture in his homeland but to kill indigenous socialists; about how a Chinese general, cashing in a Yankee promise of greenbacks for converting his soldiers to Christianity, lined his vast army before him and sprayed it from hose-pipes thus baptising entire divisions in a few moments; about a Nippon general who had the nerve to suggest that empires in Asia ought to be run by Asians; and about a former German corporal whose hair and moustache looked as if they'd been painted on but who now ran his country and hinted at slaughtering Jews in abattoirs.

Even in Sutton's soot-laden atmosphere you could smell cordite: a great war was in the air. We were called upon to 'gird loins', shown how to wear gas-masks and assured that hundreds of millions of people clear across the globe were keen, together with us, to die for love of the Windsors. In the parks, brass bands played 'Tipperary' and 'Pack Up Your Troubles'. Union Jacks were hoisted above national institutions such as H. & C.H. Blinkhorns, Hosiery Manufacturers – 'same as that'. There were air displays at Hucknall Torkard. Ordnance assembly lines switched on to overtime thus raising appeals for more coal to be mined by people who'd only the day before been treated as though they were lice but who today were being lauded as 'the empire's finest'. Women, ever conditioned to pleasing warriors on the eve of battle, craved more and more silk stockings the more exciting to make their pleasing ways. Thus, Harry I could take his pick and shovel and find work at any pit he liked while, as soon as it was lawful for them to order it, the Blinkhorns put me on a 12-hour day – same as that.

On the one hand the flag-waving and tub-thumping offended my Lansburyite pacifism, on the other some of the things being done in the world were enough to provoke saints to reach for guns. We were accustomed to the routine beatings-up of Africans, Asians and Latin Americans but when Europeans themselves were being killed by jack-booted sadists simply because they believed in the equality of all men or because they were short on foreskins or read the wrong books, then it was time for fear and anger. After much soul-searching I came down on the side of those who reasoned that maybe for the first time in history the interests of the masses and the rulers coincided to justify war.

The King's Shilling

Once I'd made up my mind it was a case of in for a shilling, in for a war; I joined the part-time Territorial Army. But to tell the truth it wasn't only my desire to get my hands on a gun that led me one late-August 1939 evening to the drill hall on Alfreton Road. No, a less noble incentive was behind it: in the Territorial Army I could spend two whole weeks a year away from Sutton in places as exotic as Yorkshire and as foreign as Wales. While away on those exercises-cum-holidays the state would pay my wages and a bit more besides while H. & C.H. Blinkhorn, Hosiery Manufacturers, were bound by law to both release me when the army so ordered and to welcome me back as a heroic defender of the realm. In other words by joining the army I was working the system nicely, or so I thought; by trebling my seven days annual holiday entitlement I was giving the finger to the Blinkhorns who didn't hold with holidays and I was being given a chance to see distant places for free and, as a bonus, I was to be taught how to kill people like Hitler, which I wanted, badly, to do. Anyway, the upshot was that I shamefacedly took part in one of the many childish rites that make up the ridiculous mummery by which the British establishment blinds its masses to their vassal status. I 'took the King's shilling' and so became a soldier, albeit only a spare-time one: 4977691 Private Stanley Hardy, 8th (T.A.) Battalion, Sherwood Foresters.

Another reason for joining the T.A. lay in my loins. I dreamed the same lecherous dreams as any 17-year-old but my chance of ever fulfilling them seemed remote. Maybe I brought my sexual starvation upon myself by not following the crowd. The vulgar banter exchanged by my workmates and the leering of the factory girls didn't turn me on at all. I was a romantic who imagined that dozens of educated, refined, hot-bloodied young females were lying on beds of sweet grass outside military encampments on the Yorkshire moors and in the Welsh valleys waiting, moist with desire, only for me.

Well, I never had the chance to find out whether carnality awaited me either on Ilkley Moor or in the Brecon Hills because no sooner had I taken the King's shilling (the bastard, I hoped it was his last one and that Mr. Arnold called on him that very day) than the T.A. was mobilised in readiness for war! "Nay lad, they'll nivver tek thee," Harriet swore with utter conviction, "tha's nobbut a yewth, tha's nivver seen a gun, tha's not strong enuff to carry one, nay, they don't mean yo.'" And Harry I chipped in: "T'army's bloody daft but not as daft as to tek thee; a'll 'ave a word in t'liberal club, sumbody theer'll know 'ow to stop it." But they did mean me, and Harry I's club contact didn't have the ear of the Commander-in-Chief. The Sergeant Major at the drill hall was most put out when I suggested that the order hadn't the likes of me in mind, after all I'd not attended even a single drill, never donned a uniform and I was only just 17. The Sergeant Major was terse: "4977691 'Ardy – yo're in t'army now sunny boy an' there's a flamin' war on!"

And so it came to pass that while on 31 August 1939, I was an alley lad who'd not have known the difference between the muzzle and the butt of a rifle, on 3 September, disguised in an ill-fitting uniform and toting an old Lee-Enfield .303, I stood on guard over our sacred realm – in reality a piddling little airstrip at Hucknell Torkard. An under-developed 17-year-old who'd hardly ever been away from Harriet's side, a proper 'mad arse' if ever there was one, I'd been pitched overnight into an empty aircraft hangar together with 40 or 50 brutish, foul-mouthed old sweats: my bed, not more than two feet away from the next on either side, was a straw-filled palliasse thrown on top of three planks of wood raised about 12 inches above the icy, concrete floor. All around me were stinking, rowdy, gross-witted, chain-smoking aliens.

The Sherwood Foresters

They were aliens to me anyway, those men, my comrades-in-arms, men portrayed by the nation's propagandists as 'noble, fearless crusaders against evil, idealists eager to fight the good fight for Christianity and democracy, every man jack of them a credit to his King and country' etc., etc. The reality of course was that they were coarse-minded louts who looked down on the 'Eyeties' and 'Dagos' as slobs who deserved to be pushed around by jokers like Mussolini and Franco but who thought the Germans were on the wrong side. As far as they were concerned a touch of Hitlerism wouldn't have gone amiss at home; they found a lot to their liking in the way the Fuehrer dealt with 'Jew Boys', gypsies and the infirm. I'd been given a World War I rifle and bayonet, an empty cotton bandolier, some thread-bare webbing 'equipment', a uniform that fitted only where it touched, a ridiculous tent-shaped cap that wouldn't stay on my head, a pair of second-hand, hob-nailed boots with puttees I never could fasten properly, a pair of well-used mess tins, a tinny knife, fork and spoon and a cap badge saying Sherwood Foresters. Robin Hood would have been disgusted.

Decked out thus, throughout the first winter of the war I stood guard over crappy little outposts that Hitler in his craziest, carpet-chewing moments couldn't possibly have wanted to seize. When I wasn't defending the Kingdom's barricades I was marching idiotically up and down responding to commands shouted out by spiteful hatchet-men: "Quick march! Halt! About Turn! Slope Arms" and many other inanities, part of a centuries-old routine that was supposed to rob men of their individuality, turning them into robots who'd kill and who'd get killed to order thus scaring the shit out of the enemy.

It was all too silly, too crass to be funny. I'd no books to turn to for escape because had I ever opened one my comrades-in-arms would've tormented the life out of me for being 'sissy'. No wonder then that I was desperately homesick.

I was only a few miles from Sutton but I daren't go home for fear that I'd never go back to the army again and land up in the 'glasshouse'. Instead, I blubbered into Muriel's ear over her telephone line and once or twice went to blub my heart out in front of Uncle Isaac who kept a pub in Hucknall. Isaac, who always presented a stony mien to the outside world, turned out to be softhearted and understanding. Eventually though I developed my own defence mechanism against melancholy and alienation (it was to serve me well most of my life), I switched off my consciousness and escaped into emotional isolation and fantasies.

Early in the new year of 1940 my rag-tag, ruffianly regiment was ordered to France, a deployment which if noted by his intelligence people would have done Hitler's morale a world of good. Not for me however the delights of the *filles de joie* or the culinary marvels of Gaul; not being 18, I couldn't be sent to the front-line. My dreadful companions marched away leering and practising their *parley vous*, while I was left behind in a suddenly deserted sort of depot near Hucknall to do more or less as I pleased. I joined the local library and taught myself how to type. I'd have been doing Hitler as much harm had I stayed with H. & C.H. Blinkhorn, Hosiery Manufacturers.

On the Border Line

The mob of Sherwood Foresters that straggled back to Hucknall from Dunkirk in June was in even worse shape that it had been before embarking for France. Its pathetic state had nothing to do with its having grappled with the enemy tooth-and-claw but all to do with its having fled in terror before a foe it now feared and with its having chucked its weapons away as it took to its heels. This ragbag was swiftly rearmed with whatever ancient weaponry was found to be lying around and, reinforced by 4977691 Private Stanley Hardy, it was despatched northwards, there to defend the southeast corner of Scotland (I'd made it to 'abroad' at last!).

We dug-in, World War I style, right opposite Bass Rock just below Edinburgh. It was all very well for Churchill to rave on about fighting in the hills and on the beaches and never surrendering but my trench companions were in no mood for a fight. They were still seething with shame over the manner in which they'd bolted out of France and they remained poorly shod, ill-armed and demoralised. The Scottish air was blue with curses aimed at the entire officer corps while profane oaths were sworn hourly against both Chamberlain and Churchill.

But as the days turned into weeks and the weeks into months without as much as an air-raid siren to disturb the peace, old habits were revived. Skiving resurfaced as a way of life; prodigious amounts of army supplies found their way on to the local black market, everybody was on the make and sloth became all-pervasive.

When the Germans didn't show up and the weather made it unlikely that they would, we moved out of our coastal holes to go inland into grim lodgings of one kind or another, mainly abandoned cotton mills in Scottish border towns where we once more began to play the same old, infantile military games. Our masters believed that by their positioning of highly polished mess-tins alongside the perfect edges of faultlessly folded blankets and by weekly infusions of the holy gospel, the common soldiery could be turned into efficient manslayers. Thus, on Sunday mornings, having first been inspected to make sure that our appearance wouldn't offend our ultimate Commander-in-Chief, the Christian God Almighty, we were marched to church. Drawn up outside its portals we were ordered to "Remove headdress!" and directed where, when and how ("Upstraight!") to sit. We were also cautioned to demonstrate silent, humble endorsement of the vicar's plea to our Good Lord that He dealt death, destruction and plague upon the German and Italian people. And there I'd sit ("Upstraight!") in my pew ruminating on the fact that German sermonizers were preaching the same gospel to German soldiers and that all German killing machines bore crosses!

My plans for escaping the Sabbath burlesques went horribly wrong. If only I'd had the sense to have registered myself as a Zoroastrian, Shaker, Anabaptist or Bahai I'd have been able to be on my bunk of a Sunday; instead, I told the truth: "I'm an atheist." The army wasn't having any of that; I was accused of "coming the old soldier" (me an old soldier!) written down as 'C of E' and told to get on church parade "or else". It was an experience that confirmed what I'd already learned – you'd never get the better of the system by protesting against it or by telling the truth, least of all by using common sense; no, to beat it you'd have to use guile.

The Smell of Grease Paint

For a while after Dunkirk the army brass lacked the guts to direct a return to the imbecilities of kit-inspection and church parades. For one thing there wasn't much kit left to inspect and for another, back in France, God had given the impression of being a Nazi, so they didn't dare risk mutiny by ordering the rank and file to indulge in such frolics. But, given time, soldiers who'd been bolshie returned to being their old, supine British selves again; their anger changed to resignation coupled with stupefaction. My future looked desperately dull; somehow or other I had to fiddle my way out of the Sherwood Foresters or go suicidal. In the end it didn't need knavery, just a stroke of luck. Perusing the notice board one day I came across a curious pronouncement inviting 'entertainers' to apply for auditions for work in the 46th Division's concert party – 'The Oaks'. The fact that I'd never once in my life set foot on the boards didn't deter me for a moment; in the need to try anything to escape I bunged my name in. Expecting only to get 'booked' for insolence or some other military crime, to my amazement not only was I auditioned without a question being asked about professional qualifications but also I was almost overnight signed up as a member of the troupe!

And so it came about that in less than a year after I'd joined the army straining to get at Hitler's throat, I was to be found prancing about acting the fool on town-hall stages covering the length and breadth of the Scottish borders. The Oaks must have been one of the oddest ensembles in the entire army. My 'Good Companions' were a middle-aged gay, Michael Ronnie, who'd seen better days with the Royal Ballet – or so he claimed; a pair of pianists, one tall and gay, the other whippet-like and neuter; a fine actor, Bunny Hare; a handsome Doyley Carte tenor, Tom Hancock, and a fat Yorkshire man, a slapstick, lavatorial comic, Tommy Kendall who'd spent years peddling smut in working-men's clubs in the North. It was a bizarre way of waging war but it was no more risible than the way in which I'd seen it being waged during the previous 12 months. No matter how it had come about, membership of The Oaks represented a gigantic turn for the better. My new friends were cosmopolitan, a human species from a different planet to that inhabited by colliers or Sherwood Foresters. And we all knew how lucky we were, and only too happy to load our mini-pianos, props and footlights aboard our coach and take the road to town halls, theatres and cinemas in places like Melrose, Galashiels, Haddington, Jedburgh, Selkirk, Hawick, Peebles, Dunbar and North Berwick.

What we performed was so picayune that I recall very little of it. I can see Michael Ronnie, oblivious to the catcalls from the rude soldiery, dancing quite charmingly without having to impersonate a ballerina because he already was one. Hancock's golden-voiced 'Take a Pair of Sparkling Eyes' silenced the ever rowdiest ruffian. Our pianists could be real hepcats when they tried; their 'Jamaican Rumba' always brought the house down. For my own part, what I enjoyed most was dressing up for, and playing, a stuttering 'wall' in a burlesque of 'A Midsummer Night's Dream'. "Th...th....th...thus have I ww..w... ww..wall my p..p..p..part d..d..discharged so". It was all preposterous, absurd but it really did happen!

Doreen Maud Fenner

Like the camp followers of yesteryear we entertainers followed our soldiers around. Which is how we came to be lodged in a warehouse above the Station Hotel in Ashford, Kent. Using this comfortable billet as a base we played Hastings, Canterbury, Bexhill-on-Sea, places in which the soldiery had so little need of our sort of rodeo that they had to be ordered to attend. Even so we faced a half-empty house in Ashford itself. Across the footlights however my gaze came to rest not upon the empty seats (we got the same pay whether we packed 'em in or not or whether or not we were hissed off the stage), no, my eyes locked as in a trance upon one particular incumbent of a front-row seat: a well-rounded, long-haired teenage female balancing an open note-pad on one of two entrancingly shapely knees.

To my joy this charming creature hung about after the show, not alas because she was star-struck but because she wanted one of us to help her with a report she was to file with her employers at the *Kentish Express*. My luck was in because for one reason or another I was the only 'Oak' in whom the delectable girl stirred romantic interest; hence it was left to me to deal with her. Doreen Maud Fenner had me in flames the moment she opened her mouth. Her voice was as seductive as her person.

She spoke with clear, clean cadenza, diction and articulation, the very tongue I'd fantasised about back in the ghetto, the voice of good manners, intelligence, education, taste and culture. The lovely sound issuing from its beautifully contoured outer-package was irresistible, like that of a nubile young female, DMF's mouth was made for kissing but added to this alluring detail, the delicious sounds it emitted produced a powerful aphrodisiac.

Elated as I was at first however I was brought down to earth with a bump when DMF informed me that her father was a retired empire builder, an ex-Engineer Commander in the Royal Indian Marine! What chance had I, a little, sway-backed, semi-literate, unrefined private soldier-cum-alley-lad-cum-amateur player who hadn't even made out with a butcher's daughter; what chance had I of romancing a daughter of the Raj? If the class divide between Joyce Beastall and Stanley Hardy had been wide as the Trent, then that between my exquisite wordsmith and the same me was as wide as the Bay of Bengal. But I progressed further with DMF than I had with Beastall; in the darkness of the cinema she allowed me to hold her hand! Our world was however too disorderly to permit orderly courtship and my hopes were short-lived. My sweet reported that she also wanted to take a swipe at Hitler; she joined the navy, upped-sticks and moved clear across the country to Milford Haven, thus adding physical separation to the social divide. So began courtship by letter, and always it seemed at ever lengthening distances.

Taking Wing

I thought of little else except how to improve my image before my Kentish enchantress, agonizing over the knowledge that the hands I'd held while watching *Citizen Kane* were now caressing torpedoes in the Welsh valleys. I tortured myself thinking of how she might hold me in contempt for acting the wall in 'A Midsummer Night's Dream' while she was arming torpedoes for firing at Hitler? Enough was enough! I volunteered for the Parachute Regiment, the army's newest task force and the one which according to barrack-room gossip was free from bullshit.

In the twinkling of an eyelid, I was in training at – of all places! – Hardwick Hall, Teversal: not more than three miles from Garden Lane! There, in authentic Lady Chatterley country, I got down at last to some really serious instruction in the 'brain-splitting, windpipe-slitting, art of war'. God knows it wasn't before time. Whatever lay behind the progenitor of the parachute regiment, it was so out of line at the time that it was spared the antediluvian stewardship by which the rest of the army was shackled. At Hardwick Hall for example, we weren't called upon to prance about like zombies to the orders of illiterates or to worship the Lord by numbers; all we had to do for 14 days was to push our bodies to their physical limits, the idea being to weed out those who, when it came to the pinch, might be found not brainless enough to throw themselves out of aeroplanes in flight.

Walking was out; once you stepped outside the barrack-room you had to jog. The regimen was so tough that men who outwardly resembled tanks dropped out within hours of arrival. But I was driven by high motivation. One, failure meant going back to the Sherwood Foresters;

two, I was fired with the notion that, by displaying a parachutist's wings on my sleeves, I'd show proof of my determination to do real battle with Hitler and so persuade DMF (who'd, incidentally, dubbed me 'Tim' and never again breathed the name 'Stanley') to permit the assuagement of my smouldering lust. Thus inspired I gritted my teeth and, somehow or other, I made it into through the backbreaking physical endurance tests.

Bent double under full battle order I pounded seven miles of rough track in just 60 minutes. Then, after scrambling through drainpipes; scaling high, slippery walls; and breeching barbed-wire fences, I'd managed to fire my rifle from my left shoulder (you'd to pretend your right arm had been busted) and hit the target. Next, once more weighted down with full battle-rig I'd puffed and pulled myself over loose netting as high as a house. I'd grabbed the end of a rope to swing across a noisome pond and so on. Finally, I was given boxing gloves and told for three minutes to trade punches with a person whose name was pulled out of a bag the same time as mine.

The Marquis of Queensbury's rules didn't apply to the ring at Hardwick Hall; a hulking heavy could be pitched against a puny flyweight. Neither did it matter who won the most points or got knocked out; all that counted was that both boxers kept slugging away at each other. My opponent was a massive young Austrian Jew who, stripped-off, looked like one of those huge, tormented Russian circus bears – all sinew and fur. He was a chap I'd taken a shine to, an intellectual whose rage against fascism had driven him to volunteer for the parachute regiment as the quickest route to Hitler's jugular. As the giant Semite towered over me in the ring, his long arms ending in outsize boxing gloves beside his knees, I swung my fists at him and waited for him to land me just the one clout that would have done for me. But the bell had the opposite effect upon the Austrian because he immediately buckled at the knees and slipped to the floor in a dead funk. Poor fellow, he was sent away to seek another way to cut Hitler's throat while I graduated from Hardwick Hall.

My next berth was at Ringway Airport, Manchester, where I was to learn the tricks of the new aerial way of killing people. Being a new art, its initiators hadn't had the time to work the old military frivolities into their routine (but before very long even seasoned paratroopers were square-bashing).

At its early stage Ringway had only one purpose: to teach soldiers how to jump from the skies and land on the ground undamaged. The regiment's attractions were thus well founded: a reputation for being free of ancient military humbug plus higher rates of pay. Dependent wholly on volunteers (ordinary mortals would've mutinied en-masse rather than obey orders to chuck themselves out of aeroplanes) the regiment drew non-conformists, hence few professional soldiers.

Our heads protected by sorbo-rubber helmets and our feet by high boots, we trainees were instructed not so much in diving out of an aeroplane but in the vital art of landing on the ground. Thrown off high towers we were told, much as public schoolgirls are instructed, to keep our ankles and our knees glued together. We studied film showing how Russian and German paratroopers did it. We were given fancy multi-pocketed zoot suits, machine guns straight from Chicago (yes, genuine Thompsons), gourmet food and the very latest in backpacks, etc. And, to gild the lily, not only were we paid two whole shillings a day extra but we were actually ordered NOT, repeat NOT, to clean any of our kit and never to polish its brass work!

The big day came at the end of a fortnight's hard slog. Six at a time we were locked into our parachutes as if in straight jackets and, in the charge of a 'despatcher', we were herded into a large basket suspended beneath a great big balloon that soared skywards until it reached 500 feet. One at a time, our despatcher told me, we were to swing our legs into the large, round hole that had been cut out of the basket's floor and when he shouted "Go!" we were to hurl ourselves through it, our bodies held stiffly to attention, into the open sky beneath us.

I'd been told off to be second man out – No. 2. No. 1 was the only other aspirant-parachutist who wasn't several inches taller and many pounds heavier than I was. Together, he and I formed a two-man minority of 'short arses'. On the command "One" my diminutive friend swung his legs into the hole alright but on the bark "Go!" he turned greenish in the gills, opened up his breakfast, crawled into a corner of the basket and whimpered that he'd rather not. Another who had to find a different way of waging his war.

It was up to me to preserve the honour of short people. I swung my own legs into the hold and, imagining myself to be a robot, I waited to be switched on. At "Go!" I straightened up, plunged myself through the hole like a man on the gallows and fell through the air like a stone. A hundred feet into the fall I heard a noise as if somebody above me was tearing a sheet of calico; it was the sound of my parachute bursting from its envelope and opening above my head. It filled out on the instant to spread above my sorbo-rubber helmet like a fantastic umbrella. Pulling first one cord and then another to regulate oscillation (a word I hadn't known until I took up parachuting) and to avoid plunging into the lake at Tatton Park, I dropped to earth a lot faster than I'd anticipated – in a matter of seconds. Knees together, bending into the fall, I subsided into the grass as gracefully as Nijinsky.

The real thing turned out to be a piece of cake; compared with jumping from the balloon, leaping from an aeroplane was a doddle. I was to be the consummate parachutist; seated in aircraft pitching around the sky like corks in a rough sea, I was always close to throwing up and always, therefore, more than ready to jump out. Indeed, I felt so awful at times that I'd happily have leaped without a parachute. After the seventh aeroplane jump I was given a red beret, a flashy cap-badge, cloth wings to sew on my uniform and two whole shillings a day extra pay. The question was would all the new frippery and affluence help me seduce DMF?

I was a paratrooper in the 6th Airborne Division. The 6th? There certainly weren't five others, the 6th I suppose was meant to fool the enemy into shaking in his boots thinking there might have been. In any case parachutists made up only a small part of the division. We were heavily outnumbered by glider-borne troops, wretched infantrymen who were stacked like sardines into flimsy, engineless flying machines that, once cast off from the engine-powered machines that towed them, floated slowly down to earth. Luckless fellows those, they wore neither parachutes on their backs nor facsimiles on their jackets and they were paid only half the danger money we got.

Second Fronts and Second-rate Generals

Hardwick Hall and Ringway were the high days, the heady days when it was possible to feel that at long last we really were getting close to sticking it to Hitler; from then on things drifted downhill again. The Germans were knee-deep in their own blood on the Russian steppes, the Americans had come into the war on our side bringing overwhelming amounts of power to our elbow; as Lenin would have said, Hitler, Mussolini and Tojo were 'dead men on furlough'. Strangely however there seemed little to shout huzzahs about, while Russians were still being slaughtered in titanic battles in the East we could run only to relatively little sideshows in Africa and Burma.

Both Oz and Harry II had been in North Africa where General Montgomery had insisted on massing advantages of nine-to-one in soldiers, five-to-one in tanks and artillery and 100-to-one in aircraft before he'd attack the Germans in Egypt. It seemed to us squaddies that it didn't take military genius to achieve 'a glorious victory' when the odds were so heavily weighted in our favour. Compared with Stalingrad and Kursk, Alamein had been but a petty skirmish; the bulk of the British army, including the 6th Airborne, lay around at home doing nothing.

The hero of Alamein, all the stops having been pulled out to hail him as the mightiest general since Alexander, came home to tunes of glory and one fine day he was brought, all conquering, into the wilds of Wiltshire there to try to rouse his paratroopers to his own level of blood-lust. We brave paratroopers, who hadn't yet fired a shot in anger, had been 'stood to' for hours in carefully pre-arranged 'spontaneous' welcoming formations overlooking a sort of platform waiting for the great military genius to arrive. When he did, he was in the middle of a flurry of flunkies who eventually hoisted him aloft on the podium. We couldn't believe our eyes; the unremarkable-looking little fellow who was pushed in front of the rest of the red-tabs couldn't possibly be anyone but a warm-up comedian but to our astonishment he was introduced as 'General Montgomery'. From this bank-clerkish figure there issued forth a bank-clerkish voice: a piping, snooty squeak in which we were informed that we were the world's finest (a statement I considered lacking in empirical evidence) that we were led by the world's finest (which had been vividly demonstrated to be untrue) that God was on our side (ditto as things stood) and, in peroration, that he, Montgomery, conqueror of Alamein, was "looking for an ocean he could push the 'Nazis' into". For a battle cry it was hardly Henry V but then Montgomery wasn't Olivier, more like Stan Laurel. We kept our hands in by leaping every now and then from aircraft and we tried to keep in good physical trim but, much as our bodies may have been tuned-up by 50 miles-in-24-hour marches (passing Stonehenge at four o'clock on a balls-freezing morning) didn't help poor Comrade Ivan over there in Voronezh.

To break the monotony we'd swap with American parachutists who, as we ought to have guessed, jumped with one parachute on their backs and, just in case it didn't open, another one on their chests. I recall the end of a long foot-slog to an American camp on the south coast; it fell to me to heft a horrendously heavy base-plate of a mortar over the last, bruising mile. It may have engendered a temporary blip in Anglo-American relations but, amicability was restored when we drank Budweiser, ate bacon and waffles smeared in molasses and scoffed lots of ice-cream (oh! the profligacy with which the Yanks waged war) and I marvelled at Yankee openness and friendliness. At the American camp there were hot showers and the 'hard' rations were food for the connoisseur; you could forget there was a war on except, of course, that the news from Russia soon brought you to your senses.

As I've said we jumped every now and then from aircraft, sometimes by day, sometimes at night. My favourite aeroplane was the Albermarle, a machine in which a dozen of us sat between each other's legs with our backs to the cockpit, perched on a slide running downwards from the nose of the Albermarle to the rim of a coffin-shaped hole cut out of the floor of the tail, the widest part of the coffin being nearest the tail. At the word "Go!" we slid like kids on a park slide, tumbling out of the hole with heads bent towards the wider part of the coffin. It was a lightning-quick exit from which we were parachuting within parts of a second of each other and which resulted in our landing nice and close together.

Then there was the Whitney, a slow, ungainly bomber from which we leapt through a tube projecting maybe a metre below the middle of its floor. Jumping through the tube was a bit tricky; you'd to make sure of flinging your head backwards. If you didn't the slipstream from the engines, catching your legs first, would pitch your torso and head forward in which case your face might collide with the opposite wall of the tube. Sorbo-rubber padding or not you'd come to earth sporting a bloody nose – it was called 'ringing the bell'.

Somewhere along the line we were introduced to the parachutists' Rolls Royce – the DC3 (Dakota). Instead of throwing yourself through a hole in the floor you just stood up straight and walked out of the back door. The Dakota took 20 of us, ten seated along either side, our umbilical cords (the straps by which our parachutes were connected to the air-frame) coupled to wires stretched taught above our heads. All we had to do when we got the word was step out of the door one at a time, turn to face the tail so that the slipstream hit our backs, and enter space – simple as that. As soon as your canopy had been pulled from its bag and was about to open, the cord holding you to the Dakota snapped and there you were drifting down to earth. Almost enjoyable!

This account might make it seem as if we were jumping, running and marching all the time but it wasn't so; most days we just loafed around, indeed we were more or less egged on to take as much leave as we liked or could afford. Ergo, I spent a lot of time laying siege to, but failing to breach the ramparts of, DMF with whom I engaged in overheated skirmishes in all manner of places: Cardiff, Bognor Regis, Portsmouth, Newbury, Littlehampton and, most memorably, Brighton where DMF chose a room in the YWCA as the battleground. What girl ever needed to wear a chastity belt in a YWCA?

It was the spring of 1944. Over four years had gone by since I'd burst into the Drill Hall on Alfreton Road straining to get my hands on a gun with which I'd shoot Hitler. Four years and I'd not yet seen a Nazi let alone fired a shot at one. Four years and I was still a lowly private soldier. Fours years and I was 22 and still a virgin.

Then at long last, something was about to happen. The 6th Airborne Division was herded into a camp on the outskirts of an airfield close to Burford. There was relief because it looked as if we really meant business and to crown it all we were actually let into the secret of what the generals had in mind for us. We were told that we were about to spearhead an assault against the German army in Normandy. What's more, we were given such precise information and with such cockiness that if we'd not been made cynical by past experience we might have been persuaded that, for a change, our generals might have known what they were talking about.

Take for instance the minute detail of my own platoon briefing: on the night before the seaborne armies were to land on the French beaches my platoon was to drop from the air close beside a little bridge that spanned the River Orne near the Normandy town of Troarn. Our job was to seize the bridge and hold it until glider-borne sappers, together with their explosives and a good number of infantrymen, landed close-by. We were then to give the bombardiers a hand to blow the bridge then settle down until 24 hours later when seaborne troops would relieve us as they dashed towards Paris. It was a simple plan: by denying the Wermacht use of the Troarn Bridge fewer of them would be able to get to the beaches to carve up our soldiers landing on them. It looked foolproof and, to make us feel even better about it, we were shown photographs of our bridge and we actually built a scale model of it. We grew so fond of it we didn't want to blow it up.

Our scepticism was however well founded; we asked ourselves whether or not this was going to be just a safe little curtain-raiser to the

main event or were we really going to put the Wermacht through the
mincer and end the war? Would our seaborne comrades relieve us within
24 hours as our colonels had promised and would they really capture the
city of Caen as a general had personally sworn to us they would do within
the first few days? And after Caen would the roads to Paris and Berlin
really be wide open?

Purple Fireworks and Red Faces

In the evening of 5 June 1944, together with 19 others (two-thirds) of
my platoon, I was rammed into a DC3 at an airport near Burford. I use
the word 'rammed' because, being encumbered by monstrously heavy
loads (besides the parachute and the usual battle-gear each of us toted
either a two-inch mortar tube or its base plate or one or two of its bombs,
bandoliers of extra ammo and extra rations) we had to be pushed up
the landing steps by loaders as if we'd been Japanese commuters being
sardined into bullet-trains.

Some of the relief and the excitement we'd felt about at last going to
war evaporated quickly and it didn't help to be told that our Canadian
pilot had never dropped parachutists before. To add to our misgivings,
once aloft we circled for what seemed hours while our prodigious air-
armada, history's largest, got into formation. Finally, buffeted by the
slipstreams of hundreds of aircraft all around ours, we flew bumpily
across to France. I wasn't the only one sick enough to hope we'd be shot
down and so be done with it and who greeted the order to jump with
glee. I stepped through the door, turned left and, like a ton of bricks,
dropped into the dark French sky. It was midnight. It was an unusual
mode of immigration I suppose but there I was overseas at last.

Knees locked together I rolled over nicely to settle comfortably into
French grass. I banged the 'box' on my chest to break the lock that closed
my parachute around me and I stood up to look for my mates and, I
hoped, for road signs reading 'Troan —> ½ km'. Above all I looked for a
flashing purple light, a signal we'd been told would be beamed by a scout
who had been dropped ahead of us. Our platoon was to converge upon

that light and, once formed up, we'd be led by a French resistance-fighter to our bridge. We'd also been told that there'd be no enemy soldiers about and that we'd be at our target within an hour of getting out of our parachute harnesses.

What met my eyes instead was a dazzle of brightly coloured lights; several of them purple, flashing from all directions. It was as if I'd landed on Blackpool promenade at illumination time. For another stomach-churning thing, the only other living creature I could see was a white horse I'd nearly fallen on; what's more, judging by the sound of gunfire blazing away on all sides, there were plenty of angry soldiers about, a good many of them, presumably, German.

Far from being on our bridge within an hour, by that time I'd not moved out of the field I'd landed in and I'd managed to rendezvous with only five other paratroopers, all of them, like myself, privates. We weren't to know until much later that the fireworks and the lines of tracer-bullets we'd seen and the din of small-arms fire we'd heard weren't being directed against us or our missing mates; no, they came from enemy guns alright, but far from the Germans having been alerted to our arrival by filthy spies, they were engaged in a night exercise, blasting away at each other with blank ammunition. Not understanding this we six forlorn creatures viewed our situation with alarm.

Looking on the bright side though we worked it out that if we weren't far away from our bridge then we were near to our platoon mates (another thing we didn't know was that the plane carrying the other half of our platoon, including its commander, had been shot down) who might be about to blow the bridge. Ergo, wait for the big bang and make tracks in its direction. The bang never came. All right then, we still needed to know the way to Troarn. Never doubting that we'd soon come across a place-name: 'Troarn – Bien Venue', we set out looking for a road – any road.

Sure enough we soon came to one and sure enough it had its name-sign. Mystifyingly however, instead of proclaiming the village ahead to be 'Troarn' it said that it was 'Herouvillette', a place we'd never heard of and a place moreover that on closer inspection appeared to be lifeless; not even a dog to bark. In no mood for heroism we six decided that the most sensible thing to do was to hide in the outskirts of Herouvillette and wait for daybreak. We chose to secrete ourselves about a quarter of a mile from town in a deep ditch beside the road. One of us, the platoon signaller, was humping a thundering great wireless set that he couldn't get a spark out of. He wouldn't dump it though because come the light he might be able to fix it and maybe find out what the hell was going on. Poor sod, he became the first man I saw die during the whole war. He perished, not by bullet or bomb or bug but, unbelievably, by sinking in a split second into the mire at the bottom of the ditch. He and his wireless disappeared with a sort of 'whoosh' – Roger and out. Abandoning him to his watery grave, the remaining five of us fled to higher, wooded ground where dawn found us hugging the earth while shells from our own ships out at sea screamed over our heads.

Our position an hour or so later was that while the shells told us which way was North we remained confused because we'd still no idea where we were in relation to Troarn. There were still no signs of soldiers either friend or foe and our spirits were lowering by the minute. Then all of a sudden, just as though he'd known we were there, into our hideout walked a 13-year-old local youth who introduced himself as Daniel. After telling us how he hated Germans he said that we were a long way from Troarn but he knew where there were lots of Britons who'd dropped from the sky during the night; he could lead us easily and safely to them. True to his word, on the night of 7 June Daniel guided us through woods and dales until on the morning of the 8th he brought us into a shambolic gathering of a couple of hundred stragglers from our own outfit.

God knows what Daniel thought of his first sight of the cream of the British army; we must have looked more like cutthroats on the run than liberators. When we'd all put our stories together it turned out that the Canadian airmen had cast us out of their aircraft while flying too high meaning that few of us had come to earth where we'd been supposed to and we'd been scattered so far apart that, for instance, those carrying the two-inch mortar tubes had dropped not metres but miles away from those carrying the base-plates and so on. Nobody knew exactly where we were, where the seaborne soldiers were or what was best for us to do. Everybody was in the mood to lynch Montgomery.

What it boiled down to was that the airborne operation, which we'd been conned into believing would be flawless (and heaven knows the brass had had long enough to make it so) had in practice been a right old snafu. (The next one – Arnhem – was to be an even bigger one). But maybe the church parades had paid off after all because there had been few casualties (even the rest of my platoon had walked away from their crash-landing into captivity) and the sea-landings had proved to be a lot easier than had been feared. We parachutists had done nothing but we still expected to leave straight away for England there to prepare, as we'd been told, to drop within weeks over the Rhine, opening up the swift dash to seize Berlin before the Russkies got there. But confusion was piled upon commotion; the dash for Paris ground into the Normandy soil and to our chagrin we were told to dig in like poor bloody infantrymen and help secure the beach-head against possible counter-attack. What happened to Daniel? Since we were unable to take him safely back home to Herouvillette he was sent to help in the field-kitchens; a stray shell (possibly one of ours) landed on the cookhouse and killed him. *C'est la guerre.*

Trench Warfare and Bald Women

Weeks later, just as I was 'borrowing' a duck-board from a nearby farm building to line my muddy slit-trench with, I collided head-on with a Colonel. On the following day I was wheeled up in front of him to be charged not with looting (no army ever took looting as a serious offence) but for 'failing while in the front-line on active service to carry his personal weapon' – an offence, according to the Adjutant, that was damned near a court-martial thing. My defence was that I'd been in the front-line for several weeks without having clapped eyes on an enemy soldier; I didn't therefore feel all that insecure without my gun and, anyway, I needed both hands to carry my duck-board. My plea must have hit the right note because although he pronounced me 'guilty', the Colonel excused me from punishment and in the next breath promoted me to Sergeant! His judgement was no doubt coloured by the fact that so many of our Sergeants had turned their ankles, caught pneumonia, been taken captive, gone bonkers or deserted that he was left severely short of them. The outcome was that he used his authority to confer a 'field promotion' on me.

4977691 Sergeant Hardy (Harry I would've had a pint or two on the strength of my meteoric rise) sat atop a hill overlooking the city of Caen, the city that the military genii had sworn to liberate within a couple of days of the initial landing. But there I sat, weeks later, watching as a thousand bombers belonging to my own side unloaded God knows how many bombs on Caen because that city was still held by the Germans! Berlin, it seemed, was still an awfully long way away.

While we sent a thousand bombers to liberate one city, we never saw a single German aeroplane in the skies; such a one-sided conflict could only end in one way and it did; all of a sudden the enemy turned tail and ran. We ran after them. Crossing the river Orne over – yes you've guessed it – Troarn Bridge we made for the fashionable watering holes of Deauville and Trouville; our ultimate objective, we were told, was Le Havre.

The country through which we chased the Germans, still never firing a shot, was calvados country. Everywhere you looked it seemed as if thousands of gallons of that corpse reviver was brewing away in enormous vats from which we liberators liberated buckets full. In every town happy, newly freed Normans paraded in front of us dozens of haunted-looking shaven-headed females, demented creatures with the eyes of caged animals. They'd been tried by kangaroo courts and convicted of having 'fraternised with the enemy'. Their summary punishment was to have their heads shorn by thugs wielding blunt, old-fashioned cutthroat razors; then, bloodied and horribly disfigured, they were put on display before a jeering populace and companies of their 'Tommy saviours'.

It was a sickening, uncivilised spectacle but one which nevertheless drew loud applause from a large majority of my fellow liberators to whom the loathsome practice was as much a spoil of war as looting. Just as they never paused to question the ethics of stealing from people who were supposed to be our allies, it mattered nothing to them to acclaim the torture of French, not 'enemy', women. They cheered on the ghastly Norman barbers and they ransacked every empty farmhouse they came across. Luckily, before we reached the fleshpot Deauville where I dreaded witnessing victory celebrations in even more depraved taste, we were ordered to turn about and fly back to Wiltshire. Hardly a man landed back home without carrying some booty he'd liberated from the 'Froggies'. It was an ignoble end to a fouled-up battle but almost every one of us had lived through it. As Marquez wrote, the greatest victory in a battle is to be alive at the end of it.

Quartermastering and Helicoptering

I'd flown out of England as one of the nation's military elite – the most macho of its machismo. Armed to the teeth and hyped up to a crazy pitch of blood lust, my company had spearheaded the greatest cross-water military action in history. But back in England three months later I walked away from a DC3 with my ammunition bandoliers unopened and my gun barrel as virginal as my body.

According to latrine rumour – and you didn't have to be a military genius to see that it might be true – our next job would be to drop on the east side of the Rhine. And I was going to drop on the Reich not as a mere Sergeant but wearing the crown of a Quartermaster Sergeant, a rank that was a much sought-after sinecure because a Quartermaster had first go at supplies, dishing out the rations, the pay and the clobber. Lord knows how they worked these things out but there it was; I'd helicoptered up four ranks in as many months; at that rate of promotion I'd have entered Berlin carrying a Field-Marshal's baton.

But I'd been promoted no more than a day or two when I was transferred to the 12th Battalion, 5th Independent Parachute Brigade, which the buzz had it, was to go to Asia. Meanwhile Montgomery gave the exalted task of crossing the Rhine to the 1st Airborne Division whose soldiers were told that the bridge at Arnhem, undefended, was theirs for the taking. We could've told 1st Airborne a thing or two about Montgomery's intelligence, especially where bridges were concerned, and we weren't surprised to learn that massive German forces had cut 1st Airborne to ribbons on the bridge and that its bloodied survivors had to swim for their lives back to the West Bank.

In any other walk of life, errors of judgement on the Arnhem scale would swiftly have led to the wholesale sacking of the principals responsible but, this being the walk of death, the generals weren't pressed even to say "Sorry". They went instead into an orgy of backslapping, of singing the praises of each other's heroic nations and armies and of awarding themselves fancier ranks, medallions, sashes, titles and higher pay. While they were thus fooling around – serves them right – the Russians reached Berlin first. Adolf Hitler escaped his people's wrath by blowing his brains out; the great cigar-smoker chose to go for an election which, to his astonishment, he lost by many a mile. But, of course, election defeat or not, Churchill's class held on to its domination of the British establishment. Atlee's so-called 'socialist' government made noises that provoked the bourgeoisie to anguished charges of 'bolshevism' and 'red dictatorship', but it lacked the guts fundamentally to try to alter the class structure. It remained easier for a 'working man' to be appointed Minister of War, for instance, than for him to get a royal commission in one of the armed services. True, the working-man Minister (one Fred something or other) set alarm bells ringing with talk of 'democratising' the services but he was easily neutered by being kept so busy inspecting parades that he lacked the clout even to promote lance corporals, let alone generals.

Wedding in Worthing, Bedding in Buxton

Our 'socialist' minister promised the rank-and-file that one day they'd wear collars and ties like the officers and gentlemen – but not yet; first he had to have the shirts and ties manufactured. That was about as democratic as Fred was able to go. In the meantime we hung around in

Wiltshire perfecting the art of skiving while pretending that we were men still at war, now with Japan.

In May 1945 the 5th Independent Parachute Brigade was ordered to go to help our American allies settle Hirohito's hash in the Far East. Maybe the news that I was to go to Asia reawakened DMF's reveries of her babyhood in India, thus releasing her broody instincts, or maybe she was turned on by imagining me in tropical shorts; whatever sparked her off it was DMF herself who put forward the idea that we might share a bed before I sailed for Bombay. The proviso, standard in those days, was that the bedding came only after the ritual of holy wedlock.

The deal was struck at St. George's Church, Worthing, on the morning of 8 June 1945 in the presence of Engineer Commander Sydney James Fenner, Royal Indian Marine retired, his wife Rose Fenner and Muriel Atkin. When you think that all that DMF and I could look forward to with any certainty was that I was just about to leap from aeroplanes over Asia while she was to return to servicing torpedoes in Wales, it was a brave, daft thing to have done. But we did it. We honeymooned in Buxton, yes Buxton, Derbyshire – old cycling country to me and a place not half as unromantic as it sounds.

Then we parted, neither for the first nor the last time, to go our separate ways, not just across county borders, not even to put only a country between us, but to be separated by continents. Always though to come back, happily, to each other.

The Gateway to India

Not counting DMF's infant years in Calcutta, our overseas life began in July 1945 when, aboard a troopship which had sailed along the old life-line of Empire – the Suez Canal and the Red Sea – I landed at Bombay, the Gateway to India; the city whose immense dockyards had once been in the charge of Sydney James Fenner among whose recollections was one of himself sitting behind a great desk while the wraith-like Gandhi sat cross-legged on the floor in front of him pleading for a better deal for the Bombay dock-workers and coolies.

The 5th Independent Parachute Brigade in which I was but a lowly Quartermaster Sergeant had been ordained as the advance guard of an almighty assault aimed at driving the Japanese out of what our ruling classes still called 'British Asia'. Much as such imperious terminology offended my anti-colonialist self, I nonetheless had to allow that before we could quit our Empire we'd first have to clear it of the Japanese who'd been far harsher imperialists than we'd ever been.

My first view of the Indian vastnesses about which Sydney James had eloquently waxed lyrical was from the open ends of a tent pegged to a hot, dusty plain a mile or so outside Kalyan, a railway halt-cum-bazaar-cum-cantonment just an hour by train from Bombay. At every opportunity I'd leap aboard the Calcutta-Bombay express that halted momentarily at Kalyan before making for Bombay.

The city at the end of the line was every bit as wondrous strange as Sydney James had described it. If there'd been nothing else in it but the railway station it would still have been worth a hundred train journeys. When you stepped from your coach it wasn't to enter an easily recognisable railway terminus but to be swallowed up within cathedral-like columns, domes, ornate stone-work, filigree, parquetry, cornices and fascias, a building designed to strike pride in the hearts of the imperial masters and awe in the hearts of their subjects. Part palace, part shrine, part temple and part railway yard, internally it was a mighty concourse whose first function, seemingly, was to serve as a vast doss-house. Everywhere one looked thousands of Indians, who lay as if they were bundles of rags, parted to allow passage to thoughtless railway men, who kept driving great big steam engines through their ranks and disgorged thousands more.

The air inside was steamy, smoky and full of effusions exuded by hordes or people not fully washed, from inefficient toilets, molten cooking oil, cheap perfumes, fruit and spices. Outside you inhaled incense arising from a hundred Hindu temples and wayside shrines and you choked on the stench from streams of rainbow-coloured sewage. The populace was staggeringly variable. Beggars exploited ghastly disablements while women, caged like animals, were offered for sale by pimps proffering testimonials that certified their nautch girls' services had been enjoyed by such luminaries as Count Ciano, Joe E. Brown, Edgar Hoover and the Duke of Bedford.

Groups of naked men of astonishing grace and beauty stood in the shadows of the mighty Taj Mahal Hotel while their fellows in dhoti, toting the instruments of their trades in little wooden boxes, plied their skills as ear-cleaners, nose-hair clippers, tongue scrapers, barbers, chiropodists, masseurs, manicurists and fortune-tellers. And, as if in a different world, down the stately steps of the Taj trooped stout, shiny-skinned, lordly sahibs, both brown and white, followed by female companions whose voluptuous crimson and gold saris blew seductively in the sea breeze. It was, by God, a long way from St. Michael's Street.

Alas, however, we weren't in India simply to marvel at marbled palaces, sublime temples, beautiful people and the grossest possible abominations but to mug up on ways of slaughtering Japanese. Long reconciled to expect little better than idiocy from our generals, we raised hardly an eyebrow when they told us that we were about to storm Japanese-held beaches from the sea. We, who'd been trained for years with one thing in mind: to drop on the enemy from the skies, we who'd never laid eyes on a landing craft let alone been aboard one, were nonetheless scheduled to sail into battle by sea. Sheep-like, fearing the worst but past complaining, one August morning only about two months since DMF and I had tied the knot, we set sail from Sydney James Fenner's Bombay docks aboard a troopship bound for Malaya.

'Operation Zipper'

To a cynical old soldier like me the plan for 'Operation Zipper' sounded familiarly hair-brained. It called for us to skim across the Straits of Malacca in shallow-bottomed boats from which we'd storm the beach at Morib, a settlement on the west coast of Malaya just south of Port Swettenham. The names meant nothing to us and all we were told was to trust the intelligence wallahs who knew what they were about. Given past experiences it was advice that made our hearts sink. Once we'd put the coastal defenders to flight, the plan went on, we were to race inland to seize a nearby air-strip whereupon aircraft from Ceylon (Sri Lanka) would land complete with parachutes, pick us up, take off, assemble in formation and finally drop us over our prize: the island of Singapore.

The one redeeming feature of the plan was that it involved parachuting but that didn't make it any the less loony for we dreaded to think of what the Japanese, forewarned by the landing at Morib, would have in store for us over Singapore. They'd have loaded every gun they had (including mighty howitzers captured from us in 1942) and they'd have pointed them skywards.

Bless our lucky stars however; we were spared having to enact that batty scenario because, as we cruised down past the Andaman Islands (where Sydney James Fenner's father had once gone ashore to escort Lord Mayo, the Viceroy of India, who was then assassinated in front of him) we got news of the atomic obliteration of Hiroshima and Nagasaki followed swiftly by word of the capitulation of the Japanese Emperor. We were at once as cheerful as men on death row hearing of their reprieve. Delighted to think that we weren't after all going to get our feet wet, we fell to conjuring up pictures of the orgiastic welcome we expected to get when we sailed, not parachuted, into Singapore. We danced on the decks.

But we danced too soon. As we might have guessed our generals had other ideas. Disappointed at being cheated out of a bloodletting, they still wanted to play their war games. Operation Zipper, they declared, would go ahead regardless. What followed, even without an enemy to fight on the beaches, turned out to be one of the greatest military cock-ups in history.

From the first step taken by the first paratrooper from the first landing craft on 9 September 1945, Operation Zipper went horribly wrong. We'd been instructed to "march off the ramps of your landing craft with your heads thrown backwards and make for the beach; you'll be in shallow water, not more than an inch above your knees at most". We did as we'd been told only to sink like stones into several feet of seawater, being dragged further under by the preposterously heavy loads we'd been saddled with.

I was one of the lucky ones because I could swim but many of my brawnier comrades couldn't even stay afloat. Spluttering, heaving and wagging my one free arm (the other hand held my carbine) I paddled my feet like a duck and managed to inch my way towards land without having to jettison anything more than a grenade or two but most of the others, panicking, chucked away guns, packs, boots, trousers, helmets, everything. Then, just as we were about to touch down on what we thought would be firm sand (we'd been assured that it would be 'just like concrete') we felt our feet being sucked into the gooey black paste of mangrove swamp across whose odious surface we flopped like beached whales.

It would have taken but two or three Japanese machine guns to have wiped out every man jack of us before we'd reached even the mangrove but, thanks to the Shinto Gods, having heard the order from the Chrysanthemum Throne, the machine gunners, together with the rest of the Japanese garrison, had bolted. Morib was ours! The rule of His Britannic Majesty was re-imposed upon Malaya.

Not a single Union Jack waving local came to greet us; the only witnesses to the return of King George VI's forces to that part of his vast empire called Malaya were primates, snakes, birds and fish. They couldn't have been favourably impressed by what they observed to be emerging from the ocean before their eyes, for it was not a smart, proud, triumphant army flying its sovereign's pennants but what must have looked like a mangy horde of half-naked, half-drowned, half-delirious, unarmed castaways.

Worse was to follow. Having slithered our way across the ooze on our bellies like mudfish, there fell upon us in late afternoon (our generals' 'ten-minute dash' having taken ten hours) a further, terrible misfortune. No sooner were we standing upright on terra firma trying to recover our wits than an electric storm crashed through the heavens to dump water over us, pitilessly, for hour after hour. Those few who hadn't thrown their rubber ground sheets into the sea now lost them to the gales so that in the end we all stood there in desolate union unprotected in the teeming, thundering jungle. There we stood, hundreds of us, stock still in the pitch-dark, deluged jungle, our bare feet sunk in mud, letting our blood to mosquitoes and leeches, cursing all officers and praying for daybreak. When at last the sun rose, its rays dappled through the forest canopy to pick out a ragged, famished, thirsty, demoralised riff-raff looking for all the world like the remnants of an army that by the skin of its teeth had just escaped from a Saturnalian battlefield upon which it had suffered a monumental defeat.

Looking through their binoculars from the distant troopships the colonels and brigadiers cannot have believed their eyes. They'd have experienced a night tossing, turning and plagued by nightmares about what would have happened to their brigade had the war not ended a day or two earlier? What would have happened was that the blood of their soldiers would have stained the sea crimson all the way back to the mother ships. Even as it was, when not so much as a single shot had been fired against them, their soldiers were in no condition to take the next step in the plan – to move a few miles inland to board aeroplanes. The generals had no option but to call the whole thing off. They didn't have to tell us what to do; as soon as we saw the landing craft coming towards the shore we took off from Morib, sliding, crawling, paddling and dragging ourselves back to the boats. To the Straits of Malacca we'd abandoned at least three quarters of the weapons and equipment we'd tried to land with. It was a ragged and demoralised mob that chug-a-lugged its way back to the troopships in which, eventually, we sailed away.

Man's recuperative powers are remarkable: after showers, food and a good night's sleep – and with the sight of Singapore on the horizon – our spirits recovered. And they soared higher and higher when we caught the mood of the welcoming populace and that of the prisoners-of-war whose loathsome camps we opened up and to whom we delivered food and medicines. The entire population, it seemed, was crazed with joy to see the backs of the hated Japanese. Ecstatic celebrations were in order. They handed over to us their fine city, lush in brilliant sunshine.

The Lion City

The war was truly over. Our job in Raffles' 'Lion City' was to haul down the Rising Sun (but to avoid the shame of doing that in front of their conquerors Hirohito's commanders had already done it) to run up the Union Jack (I wanted nothing to do with that) to release and care for our prisoners of war (easily done) and to disarm and then stand over the Japanese who were used as unpaid labourers to put right the railways, docks, drains and hospitals again. Even this last chore was dead easy. Before you could say "Kazuo", the Japanese had rounded themselves up, stacked their weapons in neat piles to make it easier for us to confiscate them, and then they'd assembled themselves in straight lines like robots ready – nay, eager – to obey our orders. One word and they'd march off to railway sidings, godowns or rubbish-tips there, pausing only for a ten-minute break at noon to swallow a handful of rice, to labour from dawn to disk. We were left with nothing to do but bask both in the tropical sun and in the peoples' adulation.

There can never have been a more agreeable place to roam around in than the Singapore of 1945. I lived in a little white room – once the amah's quarters – in a large, gracious colonial villa set in extensive, still beautifully tended gardens shaded with jacaranda, palm and frangipani. When I wasn't sun-bathing, romping in the warm sea, ordering up the pay and rations, cycling or playing either soccer or cricket, I'd canter round the city, drinking in a thousand new sights and scents an hour. One picture has stuck right in the forefront of my mind ever since. It is that of a cadaverous, ancient Chinese male dressed only in a pair of tattered shorts, laid flat out in the shade of casuarinas on the narrow ledge of the sea-wall, his head pillowed on a small, round cigarette tin. He was sound asleep, not twitching an eyelid. To him the change of armies had gone unnoticed.

Double-Dutch and Double-Cross

Just before Christmas (1945) we were put on board ships once again, this time to be transported to Batavia (now Jakarta), capital of what was then known as the Dutch East Indies. We were told that because the rightful colonial power, Holland, lacked the means to do the job for itself, its government had asked we British to go to its East Indies territories to round up the surrendered Japanese.

We disembarked into a great city, a hot chutney of bazaars, docks, palaces, villas, curio shops, mosques, churches and reeking slums, a city through which flowed a once-proud river now a wide, malodorous sewer, a city that appeared to have been overrun by millions of the loveliest, milk-chocolate-hued people I'd ever seen. And all of them were waving flags, not Hirohito's Rising Sun nor yet the red-white-and-blue stripes of Her Hellenic Majesty but red and white jobs which, from what we could gather from the cries of those that waved them, were those of a country we'd never heard of: 'Indonesia'. Neither had we ever heard a word about a man named 'Sukarno' yet plainly he was the idol of all of these gorgeous little brown people; indeed everything pointed to his being the boss of the place.

'Bung Karno' (the name by which the masses idolised Sukarno) was the man who, 20 years later, was once more to add considerable spice to our lives. But to go back to 1945; he was in his capital city which he called not Batavia but Jakarta. There he'd proclaimed himself 'President of the Republic of Indonesia', a claim that evoked for us a burning question: were we in Jakarta, capital of what everybody in sight said was the republic of Indonesia or were we, as our leaders insisted, in Batavia, capital of the Dutch East Indies? The 'President' said that we were welcome in Indonesia but only as long as we cleared out the Japanese and then cleared out ourselves; the Dutch, he warned, would be treated as pariahs.

Again, as in Singapore, it didn't take long to deal with the soldiers of the Mikado; they rounded themselves up and waited for our orders. Standing in front of us, in perfect order, their weapons stacked neatly at a distance, they waited only to be told to board whatever ship would transport them home. We were left, once again, with time on our hands; all we'd done was to swap one tropical playground for another. I lay around in the sun, played soccer and strolled around a worse-for-wear but still quite splendid oriental metropolis.

A week or two later my battalion, under a colonel who had the ghoulish name of Pine-Coffin and the nature to match it, was shipped a hundred miles down the Java coast to Semarang, a seaport in which partisan forces loyal to one Tan Malaka, said to be an Indonesian 'desperado', were harassing the Japanese, demanding they hand over their weapons to Tan Malaka, not to us.

Apart from the many gung-ho types among us (including all the regular soldiers) who were itching to spill somebody's – anybody's – blood, we were greatly relieved when landing at Semarang (another exquisite tropical seaside town) to learn that the guerrillas under Tan Malaka had slipped quietly away into Java's apparently endless, shimmering rice-fields. We were therefore free to resume our lotus eating in the magical climate I'd become very fond of. I swam in the sweet Java Sea and played football on surfaces the head groundsman at Lords would have been proud to have prepared.

Even the odd hour or two of work added sweetness to the time. Part of my duty as Quartermaster was to safeguard the soldiery against scurvy, dysentery and the like; hence, first thing every morning I'd make for the local market-place to purchase the fresh fruit and vegetables that would add nutrition to our rations. The traders, brown, sarong-clad females, turned me down theatrically refusing to touch the Dutch guilders which were the only currency I could offer in payment. They made it lewdly plain that the sight of the Hellenic Queen's head on the crisp new notes I held out to them made them feel sick. The trouble was that while Bung Karno had fashioned a flag for his new nation and for all I know a national anthem as well, he hadn't got round to printing a currency. But the market mammas were eager to do business and as a way round the problem they suggested payment in Japanese occupation scrip – the 'banana-money' the Indonesians were still using among themselves. In no time at all I was busy haggling with happy, betel-chewing matrons to whom I handed fistful after fistful of rupiah notes carrying a likeness of Hirohito so granite-like it made Wilhelmina on her guilders look positively lively. In exchange I took away sacks full of rambutan, pomelo, papaya, oranges, pineapples, bananas, mangoes, melons, tomatoes, pepper, limes, lentils and beans.

Our taste buds reactivated, our stomachs enjoying the treat and our metabolisms tuned-up, we sank deeper and deeper into our warm, humid, Eastern harbour, too languid to question the true purpose of our expedition into the Dutch East Indies/Indonesia. Lulled into believing that we were leaving the Indonesians to do their own thing, we marched light-heartedly out of Semarang bound for the docks where we were to board an old tub *The City of Canterbury* bound for Singapore. It was another golden morning but it was ruined by the sight half-way to the port of a large column of Dutch troops marching in.

I sailed from Indonesia with a nasty taste in my mouth. We'd sold those lovely people down the river; we'd made them feel safe and free and all the while we'd been giving the Dutch time to assemble an armed force with which to re-occupy their old colony. We'd merely been the bridge over which one Asian despot had marched out and a European despot had marched in. Bung Karno finally drove the Dutch out of his republic in 1949 but a lot of Indonesian blood had been spilled by then.

The Last Post
By the time my feet touched the dockside at Singapore my demobilisation number had come up (first in, first out) and I was no longer a soldier. Thankful to have left behind so preposterous a trade, I got straight aboard a troopship and headed for home. Prone on the deck I ran in my head a video recording of my brief Asian experience. What my mind reflected confirmed my schoolboy conviction that empires were run for the profit and glory of the rulers of the imperial powers. All attempts to justify colonisation on any other grounds – 'civilising missions', 'bearing the

white man's burden', and the colonialists 'moral and spiritual supremacy', were just cant. Especially unctuous was the line about how we Europeans were in our colonies only to help their backward peoples advance towards living standards enjoyed by our own 'civilised' masses. I'd seen no Southeast Asian communities as down-in-the-mouth, dirty, backward or as hopeless as the folk I'd lived among back home in Sutton.

As for His Majesty's armed services, I was glad to have done with their grim barracks, music-hall parade grounds, barking Sergeants, dithering chaplains, snooty colonels, chinless subalterns; indeed to have seen the last of their vulgar communality, their corruption, pretentiousness, pettiness, incompetence, bombast, bullying and baseness.

Footnote: Soon after I'd taken ship to Singapore the 5th Independent Parachute Brigade moved northwards into Malaya proper, indeed not far from Morib. Once there, the Brigadier unwisely decided that the time had come to turn his brigade into a spit-and-polish, peacetime outfit. It was the last straw. Having been misinformed and misguided for years (remembering Normandy, Morib and Indonesia) the rank-and-file – the irregulars at least and they were greatly in the majority – turned their backs on the officers. In plain words, they mutinied. Like other mutinies in the British forces, it was hushed up. The brigade was disbanded. It had a dishonourable history.

1946–1952
From Post-War England to Malaya

Escape

DMF and I had dreamed of sharing a simple, cultured life but the cold reality of post-war England drove us to opt for a less fanciful existence. The ugly truth was that I was lamentably short of the basic educational qualifications necessary for entry into even the lowest-grade education programmes on offer at the time. There was nothing for it then but to go to the very place I'd sworn to escape from: Sutton-in-Ashfield. It was the only place in which I was sure of getting both a job and a roof over our heads. Luckily, right out of the blue we came across, thanks in part to Sydney James Fenner, and straight away raised a mortgage on a brand new semi-detached in Chestnut Avenue, Kirkby-in-Ashfield, a town close to, and every bit as awful as, Sutton. Unbelievable as it may seem now, despite the fragility of our situation, DMF and I settled into Chestnut Avenue in exultant mood.

God knows we'd no right to exult – except in each other that is – for a mortgage of £1 a week out of a £5 wage saw us living from hand-to-mouth in two barely furnished rooms with the rest of the house closed off. My beautifully voiced, lubricious-bodied, bourgeois-conditioned DMF bent herself over a metal bucket in which she boiled clothes on a gas ring in the dark little scullery. Our only wheeled transport was my ancient bicycle and we'd hardly a carpet on any floor in the house. Sydney James Fenner came for a visit. Shaken by what he saw he bought a tin teapot, turned on his heel and never stayed with us again. And I don't blame him.

I still shiver at the memory of the raw, bone-chilling sleet that slammed into me on the night that Christopher was born in March 1947. But I also remember the fecund radiance of DMF enceinte, the super-impregnated milky DMF who stepped from the train on her return from a holiday with her parents at Worthing, all tanned and glowing.

Every morning at 0700 – come rain, shine or snow – I peddled the old bike three miles to, and every evening at 1730, three miles from, the factory still belonging to 'H. & C.H. BLINKHORN, HOSIERY MANUFACTURERS'. The old, sickly-green sign was still there, the dreadful driveway still pitted and sludgy, the surroundings still befouled with factory waste and chicken-shit (Harold kept a run of fowls) and Harold and Charles seemed still to be suffering from the same old distemper. But they recognised the change in the alley-lad who'd left them six years before.

"Same as that", they sang out in odious duet, "Same as that, yo've dun gud in t'war an' that. Seein' as 'ow yo've cum out as a Sergeant an' that, 'ow'd yo like to bi Assistant-Manager like?" Who knows what gave them the idea that they needed an 'Assistant-Manager'? I never fathomed what was behind it – probably something to do with company laws and evasion of paying taxes – and I can't say why I fell for it. There was after all never the slightest chance that I'd ever wear a business suit and sit behind a desk dictating to secretaries; there weren't any desks to sit behind anyway. Neither did money come into it for they offered me less than I could have earned working one of the great German machines that were still going strong. What swung me I suppose was the promise of regular hours and no shift work.

Hogarth himself never painted a tackier scene than the one presented by the Blinkhorn factory and no ruling family outside a Zola novel ever exploited its workers so calculatedly or so callously. It was entirely in keeping with the rest of the plant that its 'office' boasted not a single chair. The 'Assistant Manager' bashed out bills of lading on a cranky old typewriter screwed into the top of a high desk exactly like the one Dickens's Bob Crachit stood against to do his clerking. And all the while that unwholesome, barren, Blinkhorn tribe would keep up a barrage of sour abuse against 'wastrels' (their employees, every one), 'spongers' (the working-class, every man jack of it), 'traitors' (Tories who jibbed about using force to stay in India or Ghana or wherever), 'welshers' (all council house tenants), 'cheats' (all foreigners, especially those coloured sportsmen who did well against the English) and 'bolshies' (anybody who hadn't voted for Churchill in 1945).

Forty-five hours a week with the Blinkhorns was enough to derange anybody. And by 1950, same as that, I'd damned nearly reached that stage. Mercifully I had DMF and the babies, books, games of canasta and crib, the radio, evening and weekend classes with the Workers' Education Association (weekends I studied Marxism, weekdays I gained first-hand confirmation of what Marx had condemned about capitalism), gardening, cycling and working as Education Secretary for the local Labour party. Even so, the prospect of working for the next 50 years as the Blinkhorn's 'Assistant Manager' or of bringing up the family in Kirkby was appalling. The question was: how to escape and to where?

1950–1952: Malaya

The answer came, most improbably, from far, far away – from Malaya. In 1948 the Communist Party of Malaya had taken to the jungle 'to wage an armed struggle, against British colonial domination of Malaya-Singapore. Dreaming poetical, mystical fantasies of my days in Singapore and Indonesia, I read all I could about the 'Malayan Emergency', scratching my head the while because even though the Atlee government had pulled us out of India, it seemed determined to hang on to Malaya-Singapore. Could it be because Malaya was the Empire's biggest Yankee dollar-spinner? Perish the thought!

I ferreted out all the Malayan news, grilled my Workers' Education professor on the Atlee 'contradiction', sweated blood over arguments with local communists and I brooded and brooded, In the end I settled, uneasily, for Atlee's line: Malaya would be independent as soon as the insurgency had been put down; to pull out before then would be to hand over the indigenous (Malay) majority to the rule of an alien (Chinese communist) minority.

In the meantime the badly rattled colonial government in Kuala Lumpur went in for the urgent expansion of its security agencies; it advertised vacancies for police officers, preferring, men with recent military experience. Ordinarily, even under the so-called 'socialist' government I'd never have had a snowball chance in hell of getting into the class-ridden colonial services but in Malaya, 1950 who knew? Dowsing a troublesome conscience (in other words, kidding myself) with the idea that I wouldn't be a real colonist but a person of good leftist principles who wanted only to get in on the closing act of imperialism, with DMF's approval, I answered the advertisement.

To cut a long story short, one summer's day in 1950 found me in a baronial hall of the Colonial Office in London being grilled by half-a-dozen colonial stuffed shirts. I got the feeling that my inquisitors were unimpressed by a candidate whose sole qualification for a colonial office job was a six-monthly military stint in Asia – and even that, not as an officer and gentleman. I left London with my tail between my legs picturing the old boys straightening their Haileybury ties and either giving me their cigar-stained thumbs down or throwing six black balls into a hat. But, wonder of wonders, just when we'd given up hope there dropped through our letter-box an offer of an appointment (conditional) with the Malayan police.

DMF and I burned the midnight oil as we chewed it over; we'd not really expected it to come about. The sticking point was the condition: for the first three years the officer cadet would be unaccompanied – meaning that DMF would be left to take care of the children unaided. On the other side of the coin, acceptance meant rising from the poverty trap (our bank balance at the time stood at just £40), and escaping from the coalfields and the Blinkhorn's midden. Most importantly perhaps it meant getting my name in the establishment's lists; once on the colonial office list I'd surely be safe for life?

It was a good job we weren't given more time to think it over because we might then have found weighty reasons for turning it down. As it was we set our eyes on those first three years and I filled in the form. Family eyebrows were raised all round and it was a long time before the Hardys, Scotts and Fenners got over their suspicion that DMF and I were splitting up.

I still catch my breath when I think of how cold-blooded my abandonment of DMF and the babies must have appeared to our families for I left them to face the winter in a cheerless and, what was to DMF, an alien place with but £40 in the bank. The cold fact remains however that in the grey chill of dawn on 13 October 1950, I crept away from DMF and the children, leaving all three of them in the same bed, to catch a train south on the first leg of my journey to Malaya. From that day on though – and deep down that's what really counted – from that day on my name appeared on the colonial office list.

In those days long-distance aeroplanes carried only about 30 passengers. Apart from the occasional sandwich and a glance at the position chart drawn up by the navigator and passed back from passenger to passenger, they offered neither food, nor drink, nor entertainment. They bounced about a lot and, by today's standards flew in noisy, slow motion. On the other hand they flew much closer to the earth than modern jets do so that the passing scene was ever changing. And of course there was no such thing as jet lag; air-travel, if not serene, was at least not stressful. It took five whole days to fly from London to Singapore.

On day one for instance, at British Imperial Airway's expense I lunched in Rome, toured the city by coach while our 'plane was being re-fuelled, then dined and slept in splendour at the Heliopolis Palace in Cairo. I'd only been a colonialist for one day but I could already see why the colonizers didn't want to let go. On day two we juddered above the sands and oasis of Arabia to land in dusty Karachi where our overnight digs, while not up to Heliopolis, were to me still princely. The third night I lay under the majestic roofs of the Taj Mahal in Bombay, on the fourth at the Gall Face Hotel within the sound of the Indian Ocean in Colombo and on the fifth we touched down at Singapore.

The Setting

Malaya (known since 1963 as 'Peninsular' or 'West' Malaysia) is about the size of the United Kingdom. A blue-green mountain range runs along its spine all the way from Thailand southwards to Singapore, sloping down on either side to coastal plains: to the South China Sea in the east, to the Straits of Malacca in the west. The country's geography thus reflects its Indian and Sinic cultures. Demographers disagree where its *bumiputra* (native Malays) came from but it seems a safe bet that its *orang asli* (aborigines still living in their primitive state in deep forest) came down from Vietnam-Burma.

The British were drawn into Malaya in 1785 when the Sultan of Kedah, in return for the British East India Company's assistance in resisting Siamese incursions, gave the company the island of Penang as a gift. The company went on to develop the island of Singapore and from 1819 onwards it encouraged the immigration and settlement of Chinese and Indians into its newly acquired possessions. The Anglo-Dutch Treaty of 1824 defined the Malayan peninsula as the exclusive preserve of the British, leaving the Dutch with their East Indies (Indonesia).

The tin, rubber, palm-oil and timber industries sucked in immigrants at such a rate that by the 1930s they were close to outnumbering the Malays themselves. The Chinese, by far the largest immigrant community, operated their own schools, importing both textbooks and teachers from the motherland. Having no reason to owe allegiance to a monarch in London and because back in their own tumultuous country Kuomintang and Communist fought each other more fiercely than they opposed the invading Japanese armies, the Chinese in Malaya turned intensely and dangerously inwards.

Such was the situation when in December 1941 the Japanese invaded northern Malaya. The Malays stayed aloof from the conflict, the British fled in shameful haste. Many Indians, deeply influenced by Gandhi's campaign for Indian home rule, sided with Hirohito's army's slogan: 'Asia for the Asians'.

But the Japanese proved themselves to be the nastiest imperialists of all. They raged with terrible ferocity against the Chinese, tried to console the Malays and recruited an 'Indian National Army' to fight alongside them. For the masses of all races however, the Japanese years brought unequalled deprivation and harsh physical suffering, years so awful that when the British returned in 1945 they were greeted with genuine affection. Nonetheless, the Japanese had demolished the myth of British supremacy; thus the first question the relieving force was asked was "When will you be leaving?"

The one Malayan faction that had opposed the Japanese with force – even the British, albeit through clenched teeth, had to admit – was the Communist Party of Malaya (CPM). The British had smuggled weapons into Malaya for use by communist guerrillas but they'd been used only sparingly against the Japanese, the party preferring instead to cache the armaments away for future use against the British themselves. The rise of 'communists' to power in China, coupled with Soviet victories over Hitler, gave an enormous boost to the CPM.

Drugged by their own propaganda into believing that they were 'the wave of the future' and that the masses would rise as one to support an anti-colonialist insurrection, in June 1948 the CPM's old guerrilla force, restyled the Malayan People's Liberation Army (MPLA), returned to their jungle hide-outs swearing the while to wage 'armed struggle' against imperialism until the British colonialists withdrew from Malaya-Singapore. It was to prove, for them, a disastrous miscalculation:

By having already retreated from India, the British under Atlee had clearly demonstrated their intention to dismantle the Empire. Hence, over half the population of Malaya-Singapore – the Malays and the Indians – saw no need for an armed struggle to achieve independence when it would come peacefully. At the same time, influential Chinese opinion, voiced by the wealthy, powerful merchant class, was overwhelmingly opposed to the uprising. Most damaging of all though was the fact that 99.9% of the guerrilla force itself was Chinese while 90% of the government's security forces were Malays. No British propaganda was needed to win Malay support; the 'struggle' instantly became a war in which Chinese murdered Malays, a war of 'alien infidels' against indigenous 'believers'. From the very start the CPM had no chance of victory nor, having committed so colossal a political blunder, did it deserve to win.

Bahau, Bandits and Breakdowns

I breathed Malaya's soft, sedative air ('the sigh of the East'), mixed with coal-smoke, through the open windows of the night-mail from Singapore to Kuala Lumpur. And it was meet that it was so because I was destined during the next three years to ride so many Malayan and Thai trains (*kereta api* in Malay, *rot fai* in Thai – both meaning 'fire wagons') that in the end I might well have qualified to make a living as a railroader. On that first Malayan night I was on my way to the railway station at Bahau in the state of Negri Sembilan where I was to take charge of a police detachment going under the grandiose title of 'East Coast Railway Control'.

It says a lot about the condition in which a few thousand guerrillas had, in two short years, reduced one of the Empire's most esteemed colonial establishments that it was down to sending a raw youth straight from the shop floor of an English factory to take charge of a military-style operation aimed at keeping one of its two railway lines open.

I got down from the night mail at Seremban, a snoozy, immaculate little town in which the administrators of the state of Negri Sembilan were fortunate enough to live. There I stayed for a day or two in the near-perfect tropical setting of the town's Rest House (nearly every settlement in the country had its Rest House which for a ringgit or two a day would provide the traveller with a charpoy, a mosquito net, thunder-box, a *tong* full of water and plenty of good, plain grub) from which drowsy spot I was taken on rounds of introduction to different officials. This introductory process, always taken seriously, was known as 'familiarisation'. Collectively, the mandarins to whom I was presented knew everything there was to know about Negri Sembilan, everything that is except about the East Coast Railway. All I learned about my railway line was that 'bandits' were forever derailing the rolling stock (Government considered it clever at the time to call the communist insurgents 'bandits' – changed in later years to 'communist terrorists' or just 'CTs').

Thus 'put in the picture' I took the twisty, jungle highway from Seremban to Bahau, pausing midway to wonder at the Sultan's Istana at

Sri Menanti, a palace built entirely of red wood (menanti) every inch of it beautifully engraved, stippled and carved.

No destination in the world could have lived up to the expectations raised in the traveller by encountering Sri Menanti along his route; hence I wasn't too downcast to discover that Bahau fell a long way short of any such promise. Bahau was simply a long, one-street bazaar that gave the appearance of having been cobbled together in a hurry by unskilled labourers working only with saws, hammers, nails, corrugated iron and a little paint. Certainly none of the craftsmen who'd worked on the Istana at Sri Menanti had ever touched Bahau. Had it boasted boardwalks, bars and bordellos and had its streets been paved with gold, not rubber, it could have been a Klondike gold-rush town. As it was, the price of rubber was sky-high and since raw rubber stinks, Bahau, literally, smelled of money. And no wonder it did because it was the town nearest to the largest rubber estate in the world – Ladang Geddes.

Just at the bottom of Bahau's single street there ran a single-track railway line which, having started its life at Gemas, a town in southern Negri Sembilan, passed through Bahau on its way to Jerantut in Pahang state where it simply petered out. Known in the old days, and lately so re-named, as the 'Sumpitan Mas' (Golden Blowpipe), the line had at one time gone all the way to Kelantan on the northeast coast, but the Japanese had uprooted every single rail that ran north of Jerantut and they'd hauled the whole lot away to use on their infamous railway in Thailand.

My 'East Coast Railway Control' was charged (though not formally; it had no written charter) with securing what the Japanese had left of the line – a hundred miles of track stabbing like a sword through jungle and rubber. It exemplified the chaotic state to which the 'bandits' had reduced the colony (Malaya wasn't a colony but you know what I mean) that the police officer who was supposed to hand his command over to me had been whisked away to some more critical point leaving nobody in Bahau to help me find my feet.

The station master at Bahau was an even-tempered, courtly, silver-haired Tamil gentleman. Taking pity on me, he gave me one of his two waiting rooms to serve as my 'Headquarters'. On the platform waiting to greet me I found 20 young Malay 'Special Constables' (hastily recruited, inadequately trained, poorly paid, ill-motivated mercenaries) who, together with two armoured trains and their two drivers, made up all the resources with which I was supplied to fulfil my commission to keep the East Coast Railway running.

The line, as I've said, ran straight as an arrow through jungle and rubber, breaking cover every now and then at pocket-sized stations with names like Rompin, Ayer Hitam, Kemayan, Temerloh and Mentakab. Only four trains a day puffed their way through these wayside footings: two up, two down. Only one class of seat was on offer – wooden benches designed to accommodate three persons – each one overflowing with five or six, most of them hanging on to at least one child and several species of livestock while rubber sheeting was stashed higgledy-piggledy all over the place. The aroma arising from a mix of an excess of citizenry, non-house-trained animals and babies, over-taxed toilets and bundles of yellow rubber, took a newcomer like me by the throat.

The 'bandits' had train derailment down to a fine art. They'd leave their jungle cover, of which they needed no more than a square metre or two to be totally invisible, unscrew a couple of 'fish-bolts' that locked lengths of rail together, push the freed length of line just a teeny bit out of tune (more than a centimetre or two and the engine driver might spot the deviation and stop his train in time) and scarper back to the jungle. Nine times out of ten, over went some parts of the Sempitan Mas. Derailing a train was thus just a ten-minute spanner job (the 'bandits' stole the spanners from unarmed railway maintenance gangs) requiring neither explosives nor ambuscades.

On the other hand, experience had taught the railway people a thing or two as well. They governed engines to a maximum speed of 15 miles per hour for instance – a rate at which the severity of the consequences of a derailment was greatly reduced; and they ordered that four long, empty, flat-wagons be pushed ahead of each engine so that it was a wagon or two, not the engine, that went off the rails. Being lighter and moving slowly anyway, derailed wagons suffered little damage and were easily tossed aside to be picked up later and used again. Then again, our own Tamil gangers could screw fish-bolts home even faster than the 'bandits' had unscrewed them. By the time I arrived on the scene a sort of stalemate had developed – the 'bandits' put the train off the line once or twice a week and we put it on again. The only casualties were the timetables and government's face.

I had two armoured trains at my beck and call – one more than Trotsky had in 1918! Compared with Lev Davidovitch's mighty locomotives however, mine were but tin cans mounted on bogies. Their drivers were toddy-addicted Tamils, veterans brought out of retirement to man my trains. Like their engines they were fired-up all day long. Together with my fledgling special constables, my tiddly ancient train drivers made an amiable team but one which, thank God, the 'bandits' never put to the test of exchanging gunfire. My team could have had no more faith in me than I had in them for what the hell did I know about counter-insurgency; what did I know even about Malaya? All I could do was to go through what I thought might be the motions of my assignment, hope for the best, and escape into that state of mind I always found solace in: sense erasure, a practice made all the easier by the somnolent heat in which all of us were bottled. So, the wagons kept coming off the rails and the estimable Namarsavayan put them back on again.

Namarsavayan was a large, muscular, hairy, jet-black Singhalese (Tamils and Singhalese were to Malayan Railways much as Anglo-Indians were to Indian Railways) a Chief Engineer who rode his magnificent breakdown train in a style befitting his status as a railway sahib and master technician. He treasured his opulent private coach (something like an Orient Express suite complete with its own sumptuous kitchen) as much as he treasured the giant cranes and winching gears with which he performed his engineering magic. Upon news of a derailment he'd board his fiery chariot at Gemas, meet my little army at Bahau (the 'bandits' never attacked the line south of Bahau) and off we'd speed to the crash.

Once on the scene my army would deploy to defend the railwaymen from 'bandit' attack (which never once came about) while with much banging, whistling and grating of steel-on-steel Namarsavayan and his 'gangers' set to work. Tamil oaths bounced off the trees and the smell of curry wafted in the always-moist air above the breakdown train's kitchens. Namarsavayan bestrode the rails for all the world like a black demi-god, glistening with sweat, throwing a switch here, cranking a wheel there, staring down his theodolite (if that's what it was) and bellowing orders right and left. Great tubs of soft, hot, white, boiled rice would appear along with curries and spices and tangy local coffee. According to the civil list Namarsavayan's salary was four times greater than mine but it caused me no Blinkhorn-type blues: Namarsavayan was worth four of me any day.

Nobody ever came to inspect my 'headquarters' or to see how things worked: nobody, as far as I knew, ever checked on me; nobody asked me for reports. The result was that I had plenty of time for football, for studying the Malay language and the law (in which subjects you either passed exams or got the sack) and for learning about Malaya and its people – those who used and ran the Sumpitan Mas, for example.

The Malay passengers were small, brown, healthy-looking, neatly dressed, handsome, often penniless (which isn't the same as being 'poor') folk who'd turn up at a station at any old time – maybe minutes, maybe hours before their train was due. They'd squat, uncomplaining, in patches of shade waiting with inexhaustible patience for the next train going their way. Timetables had no meaning for them. The Chinese on the other hand, querulous and restive, knew their train times to the minute and would make a fuss over any delay.

The station masters at the small, one-cubicle wayside halts, dressed as carefully to greet and despatch the 9 o'clock to Jerantut as the station master at London Victoria might dress for the Royal Train. Spare, near-naked Tamil labourers spent their whole lives tapping wheels, testing sleepers, tightening fish plates, cutting back the jungle, re-setting telegraph poles, drinking toddy and making children, but it was the sweaty Chinese cooks in their dirty singlets and baggy shorts who held a special appeal for me. These greasy, nimble little kitchen wizards fried eggs, rice and noodles over small charcoal braziers set up in the guards' vans of the trains. For just a few cents a time they'd serve up their delicacies on palm fronds whose stock they'd replenish – snip, snip – from the side of the track wherever the train came to a stop. It was in these crude estaminets on the Sumpitan Mas that I became addicted to noodles.

One day, just when I'd got the idea that I'd been forgotten and that DMF and I together with the children would spend the rest of our lives in a room above a Chinese coffee shop in Bahau, there came from Seremban a large bundle of bilious-green file covers each stamped with an imposing crest above the words 'Federation of Malay Police Case File'. With the file covers came a note typed on official government stationery. "Dear Hardy," it said, "Now that you've settled in, the Chief Police Officer wishes to draw your attention to section x, sub-paragraph xx of Penal Code xxx under which it is a most serious criminal offence wilfully to damage a railway train or any part thereof. Consequently, you are required to complete a Case File (supply herewith) for each and every such criminal act that has taken place or that might in future occur upon the entire length of the East Coast Railway. You are further instructed to investigate each occurrence with the aim of bringing offenders to..." Or words to that effect.

I was thunderstruck. I hadn't the foggiest idea what to do. I'd never before in my life seen a file cover or been addressed on official paper as "Dear Hardy". Where for a start to put the letter and the file covers? My 'office' furniture consisted of a wooden bench that ran around three walls of a small waiting room, the fourth side was wide open to the station platform. My 'Headquarters' carried a Malayan Railway sign that said, simply, 'BAHAU'. As for investigating anything, most of what I knew about police modus operandi came from Dostoevsky's 'Crime and Punishment'. I couldn't see that anything I'd learned from the subtle ways by which Porfiry undid Raskolnikov might help me bring armed revolutionaries out of their tropical jungle fastnesses to the bar of justice. The very idea was so absurd that I chucked the lot, crests and all, into the firebox of one of my armoured trains. I expected the wrath of Seremban to crash upon me but all I heard from the state capital was a message encouraging me to carry on with my good work. I was learning more than the Malay language, more than the nuances of the Indian Penal Code, more than the art of using chopsticks, more than how to avoid prickly heat and crutch-rot; I was learning the ropes!

Tiffins, Tappers and Temerloh

Although I performed the minimum acceptable social interchanges I wasn't of course always on my railway line, burning files or mugging up on Malaya, Malay and the penal code. Almost by colonial office fiat, I was made a member of the Bahau Club; to have declined the invitation would have given gross offence to the large local rubber planting community and it would have been unwise to have begun my new career by provoking social ostracism.

The Bahau Club was housed in a long, squat building raised on stilts, its four sides protected from the elements only by chiks (blinds woven from atap). Its dominant feature was a long, horseshoe shaped bar to which golf, tennis and squash courses were but sideshows. The bar's proudest moments were the ritual Sunday tiffins. The booze began to flow at noon on every Sabbath, starting with trickles of gin that gradually, as the time for gorging approached, surged into cataracts of beer. Feast-time was about three o'clock when gargantuan helpings of rice and curries, along with trays of a dozen different *sambals* (condiments, nuts, dried fish, onion rings, chutneys, etc), *nasi goréng* (fried rice) and *gula Melaka* (an irresistible desert made of tapioca and brown sugar), were swilled down with Niagaras of Tiger and Anchor beers. At around five o'clock the brandy glasses were charged and the cheroots lit up; at sundown – about half-past six – it was time for a *stengah* or two before, legless and bloated, the *tuans* and their exhausted *mems* tottered to their cars to be driven off by syces to sleep it off in their princely homes. My very first Sunday tiffin was also my last, the gluttony and the bibacity was enough to put me off the practice for the next 32 years.

As I've said, the 'bandits' left my amateur policemen alone; they were not however so considerate to others who moved around the rubber estates. I'd not been long in Bahau for example when half-a-dozen specials were ambushed as they travelled in a GMC (a half-armoured truck, open at the top) along a laterite road not far out of town. As they'd passed through a defile with steep jungle slopes on either side the 'bandits' had dropped hand-grenades among them. The GMC's fuel tank exploded all about them and they were machine-gunned as well. The whole ghastly mess was towed back into the police cantonment, blood running from the floor through bullet holes. The corpses were half-barbequed; insects swarmed above them in black clouds. Scores of Malay females ululated endlessly while men folk peeled bark from palm-tree trunks which, then shining wet and starkly white, were cut into pillow-sized lengths upon which they laid the lifeless heads. Together with a few other non-Muslims I put in an appearance to demonstrate sympathy and support, but we were ignored as if it had nothing to do with us. There were no calls for revenge, no expressions of anger; only the ceaseless, dignified lamentation – 'Ululululu…'

Greenhorns like myself were encouraged to mug up not only on the Malay language, customs and law but on the rubber trade as well. To that end I took myself off for a couple of weeks with Roy Carter, a 35-year-old, rather vacant, morose loner who managed the Rompin rubber estate a few miles down my line from Bahau. I lived in his splendid house and for 14 days stalked his every footstep.

Because latex runs most freely in the cool hours before or just after dawn, Carter's routine began by being awakened at four in the morning. Without further ado – ado meaning breakfast – and dressed like a bee keeper (the mantilla was meant to keep mosquitoes, not bees, at bay) he tramped the plantation, escorted every inch of the way by cloudy hordes of mosquitoes whose appreciation of these ungodly hours was equalled only by that of the latex. Rompin mosquitoes were a particularly ferocious breed. They'd stab you through your khaki drill as if armed with laser beams, thrust steel needles through the lace holes of boots and throw darts at the backs of ears and necks. Thank the Lord for nepacrine: a tablet a day – albeit that it turned you yellow – kept the malaria doctor away. He'd pause every so often to check the work of his tappers, busy folk of both sexes who exercised a brain surgeon's skills slicing the bark of their trees with scalpels to make them bleed the white, gooey sap (latex) which, once running, dripped down a narrow tin runnel into cups suspended below.

After an hour or so of that Carter retraced his steps this time inspecting the emptying of the cups of liquid latex into tin buckets and, finally, he'd move to collecting points where the buckets were emptied into vats in which, mixed with chemicals, the latex coagulated before being put through old-fashioned mangles from which it emerged as the smelly, yellow sheets that stank up every little market place in the country. By the time we got back to the bungalow it was still only ten in the morning and Carter had already done six hours work!

Home again, he'd take a long, cold shower, dress only in a sarong and sit down to a greedy-guts 'brunch' of bacon, eggs, noodles, kedgeree, bread, marmalade and a wondrous selection of fruits. After a couple of hours paperwork at the office and a siesta he's playing sepak raga, a Malay game in which the trick is for a team of five or six to keep a closely woven rattan ball (sepak takraw – about the size of a grapefruit and light as a shuttle cock) from falling to the ground. All parts of the body apart from the lower arms and hands may be brought into play but no one player may touch the takraw twice running. To see young Malays heading, heeling, toeing, elbowing and kneeing the ball was to witness a ballet danced by youthful, brown Nijinskis. In such company Carter and I hoofed like a couple of elephants among a herd of gazelles.

Almost as invisible as 'bandits' but less evasive of government servants were the *orang asli*, tiny aborigines who did their own thing deep within the Malayan jungle and asked only to be left alone. The *orang asli* were spoken of as 'primitives' because they went about naked, recognised only three integers when counting (one, two and many) and because they believed that laughing at butterflies brought bad luck. Unfortunately for them they were out of favour with the military minds that held sway in Kuala Lumpur in 1950. Frustrated by their own failure militarily to make short shrift of the 'bandits', they sought to attach some of the blame on the *orang asli* by accusing them of 'aiding the enemy'. Remove the *orang asli* from the jungle the military wizards argued, and not only would the 'bandits' be starved out but the *orang asli* themselves would be better off: they'd be safer, healthier and, once they'd tasted 'civilisation' they'd never want to go back to the forest. The generals may have brought bad luck upon themselves by laughing at butterflies but, regrettably, their ill fortune was visited also upon the gentle *orang asli*.

I had personal experience of that calamity. It happened that a tribe of about 200 of those languid folk were known to roam the jungle across the borders between Negri Sembilan and Pahang close to Kemayan, a hamlet with a railway station on my line. I received instructions one day to provide the armoured escort for a special train which was to rendezvous with a company of British soldiers who were to round up those particular *orang asli* and march them to a given point on the railway line where they'd be loaded on to the special train to be taken to new 'civilised' homes already prepared for them on an oil-palm estate near Rompin, not far south of Bahau.

The aborigines and the soldiers emerged from the jungle right on time. The little people clutched blow-pipes, bamboo quivers full of arrows, flint stones, dogs, monkeys, sloths, tobacco leaves and supplies of reeds for use as cigarette tubes. Bunched tightly together in obvious fear of the soldiers, their terror was heightened further by the sight of yet more human giants waiting for them (to them even the Malays, a slightly-built race, were Goliaths). But that was nothing to the shock of seeing two great iron monsters puffing and blowing and belching fire. For our part we were confronted with 200 runny noses; 400 wide open, rheumy eyes; a couple of hundred naked, scaly skins over skeletal, small frames; and a thousand weeping sores. The special train had brought them food, medicines and clothing but what was sticky rice, solvents and sarongs to people who lived off insects, roots, berries, birds, monkeys, fruit and wild rice, people who'd never seen or heard of aspirin and who went about naked? What we did was wrong.

And sure enough, once they were in the Rompin camp they went downhill by the minute before our very eyes. They got colds, coughs, flu, ulcers, dysentery, and every damned thing. They wouldn't touch the food dished up to them; they fought against sleeping, refused to wear even loincloths and wouldn't talk to anybody. They shrank to the size of pygmies, silently wasting away on their feet. The soldiers had to give in; we put them back on the train and returned them to their own world.

Temerloh – My Idea of Shangri-La

Temerloh, a small town served by my railway line, reclined like a pair of satiated lovers resting separately but intimately side-by-side on two chaise longue – parted, in the town's case, by the mighty Pahang river. A coffee-coloured, moving highway, the river was forever busy with colourful sampans ferrying some of the most beautiful people on God's earth between two perfectly trimmed, ever-green lawns decorated with majestic royal palms, frangipani and pretty bungalows.

I was dreaming of how DMF and the children would adore Temerloh when, right out of the blue, came a call from Forbes-Wallace saying that I was immediately to go to Kuala Lumpur to be interviewed by the government's latest anti-communist guru, Sir William Jenkin. Sir William (who didn't last very long) was an old India hand summoned to Malaya to establish a professional intelligence service. Given carte blanche and a sack full of blank chequebooks, he declined to create a MI5-style boy's adventure outfit, preferring instead to build upon the existing police C.I.D-cum-special branch organisation.

I dashed to KL as ordered, had a hurried personal interview with Sir William who showed the keenest interest in my limited knowledge of Marxism, and then, acting on his instructions I hurried back to Bahau where I *namasteid* to the station master, to my do-lally train drivers and to the breakdown wizard, Namarsavayan; said farewell to my special constables, to Carter and the local planting community, packed my few belongings and made for Kuala Lumpur and into the embrace of Sir William Jenkin. I didn't know it then but my days as an orthodox police officer (unorthodox as they'd been in reality) were over and done with for good.

Muddy Creek

Kuala Lumpur (Malay for Muddy Creek) may have lacked Saigon's celebrated chic, New Delhi's Lutyen grandeur or Bangkok's brilliance, but with its multi-minaret Moorish-British Raj pseudo-oriental and its magnificent open playing field right at its centre, plus a botanical garden as elysian as they come, it was far less of a 'dump' than many of its citizens made it out to be.

Anyway, dump or not, it was in KL that a small group of Jenkin prodigies fetched up in the spring of 1951 to attend a two-week course on 'Thailand'. We were lodged in the 'Hotel de Luxe', a Chinese inn on Batu Road. The hotel whose food, thank God, more than made up for its otherwise total failure to live up to its name, lay quite close to the city's main shopping thoroughfare, a reading of whose shopfronts was as good as a history lesson in commercial imperialism: Thomas Cook, Cox and Kings, Whiteway Laidlaw, The North Borneo Company, Pacific and Orient, Robinsons, Bansteads, Harper-Gilfillan, Ben Line, Guthries, British Imperial Airways, Grindlays, Butterfields, The Chartered Bank of Australia, India, The Hong Kong and Shanghai Bank and more.

As for the seminar itself, it deserves mention only because our teacher was an elegantly minded old Malaya-hand, Guy Madoc, who was an authority on birds and butterflies as well as on Thailand. At the close three of us drew lots for one of three 'frontier intelligence' posts that Jenkin had ordered to be opened on the Malaya-Thailand border: Padang Besar in Perlis, Changloon in Kedah and Kroh in Perak. I drew Padang Besar. I took the night train to Prai (the station for Penang and Bangkok) and the following morning found me scoffing noodles in the guards' van of the slow local train from Prai through Alor Setar to Padang Besar.

Padang Besar (Big Field)

As I said before, Jenkin didn't last long. His carefully constructed, temperate approach towards defeating the insurgency was opposed by a combination of the military, hard-set policemen and the British intelligence community, a consortium that plunged shivs between his shoulder blades. His hopes for a more cerebral conduct of the conflict were in any case dealt a crippling blow when 'bandits' ambushed and killed no less a dignitary than the High Commissioner himself. It was an act akin to regicide. KL was in ferment. No sooner had Gurney's bullet-ridden corpse been pulled from the ditch alongside a roadway in Pahang than hawks like Robert Thompson (later a 'Sir' and, disastrously, later still, an adviser to Richard Nixon on Vietnam) resumed near-uncontested domination in Kuala Lumpur.

To cap the bellicosity, Churchill, now back as Prime Minister in London and still by nature a man of war, posted a dazzlingly bemedalled, hard-nosed army general, Gerald Templer, to KL as the new High Commissioner, an appointment that promised the mailed fist. In tandem with Thompson the general introduced a crude strategy that boiled down to taking it out on the Chinese masses. Templer knew from the start of his reign that the communist high command had already high-tailed it across the border to hide in the jungles of Thailand and that the Malayan forests were being emptied of 'bandits' as fast as the 'bandits' themselves could flee into southern Siam.

His strategy duly took account of the fact that, since most of the guerrillas had moved into the Thai border region, the conflict internally had become largely political, and he ordered the expansion of Jenkin's professional intelligence service – the special branch. Hence my transfer to Padang Besar as one teeny-weeny bit of that expansion went ahead.

Perlis is a mini-state, its internal communications system was shorter than that of Ladang Geddes rubber estate; there was only one road, a minor effort that ran from Alor Setar to Kangar, the state capital, Kaki Bukit and Kuala Perlis. The main artery was the single-track railway line between Alor Setar and Padang Besar at which point it connected with the Royal Thai Railways. Perlis boasted neither great estates nor tin mines. Apart from long stretches of green padi, several abrupt limestone outcrops and picture-postcard kampongs nestling sweetly in coconut groves and peopled with honey-brown Malays, the jungle smothered it all.

The state was nevertheless personified by a real-live Rajah and, albeit that its history was interwoven with that of Thailand, it rightly claimed its own distinctive identity. For simplicity's sake however, and to save administrative costs – the colonial administration bound the little Sultanate with its much larger neighbour, the state of Kedah. Its police chief, for example, sat not in Kangar but in the Kedah state capital, Alor Setar.

Kangar was a diminutive, soporific town, little more really than the setting for the Rajah's Istana and for its mosque both, in their miniature ways, buildings of harmony and balance. Pleasing to the senses and bewitchingly peaceful, Kangar was quintessentially Malay. The aroma drifting above its *kedai kopi* (coffee shops) arose neither from oil-frying Chinese woks nor from tandoori ovens but from curries based on coconut milk and fish and, in season, from durians. Its five-foot way (pavements that ran between shopfronts and storm drains; required by law to be five feet wide, sheltered and uncluttered) was wall-to-wall stained red with sireh-betel juice expectorated by Kangar's citizens.

Perlis's climate was no different from that of the rest of West Malaya: it was hot and damp. Day in, day out the temperature averaged 27°C, the humidity seldom fell below 90% and rainfall was well over a hundred inches a year. There were no seasonal changes and daylight varied over the year by no more than half-an-hour. The sun rose at 0500 and sank, with a rush, at 1700. There was never anything in the air to entice you into breathing-in deeply. Great and frequent storms blacked out the sky and hurled water everywhere. At these times you shut every opening but the wet got through anyway. There was no air-conditioning, louvres weren't sealed, everything then was liable to get sodden; shoes turned green, mats smelled badly, bedding was dank and mildew spread like paint from an upturned pot.

But, unfailingly, the sun always came out again and when it did sheets, mattresses, cushions, mats and clothes would be hung out to steam and to sweat and then to smell sweetly. And in the evening, provided you had some protection against mosquitoes, you'd sit in a sarong and vest and thank your lucky stars for living there.

It was best to wear the minimum of clothes. The 'emergency' had put paid to many of the more old-fogeyish colonial rituals – calling cards for instance – and much of the stuffiness regarding dress. Mind you, colonial strait-lacedness had never been a feature of life in Padang Besar and it had certainly never been a centre for *haute couture*. Apart from Nai Sathien, the senior resident Thai official, a dandy who always dressed like a courtier about to escort credential-bearing diplomats to audience with the Thai monarch, the only other citizen of Padang Besar who invariably turned out in full finery was Sathien's Malay opposite number who did it, I suppose, to keep his end up in the face of Thai competition. The rest of us were a scantily-clad, scruffy lot. *De rigueur* for men was vest (optional) above either a sarong, black pyjama trousers or shorts; for women, Malays and *nyonyas* – Malay-born Chinese – it was sarong, kebaya and head shawl, or for Chinese and Thai black cotton pyjama suits. Flip-flops were standard, unisex footwear. For the extremely rare occasions when I was summoned to the Istana in Kangar I had a tailor there run me up a 50-ringgit suit – the only such rig I was to purchase for the next six years.

The name Padang Besar ('Big Field') may not have been poetic but it was suitable because the little town stood on the edge of a feature almost unique in Malaya – an expanse of grassland upon which, for reasons best known to nature, the encircling jungle – which subdued every other inch of territory left clear for five minutes – was unable to encroach. But it wasn't grass; it was lalang, a coarse, grass-like growth akin to metre-high, green razor blades. Lalang was certainly not the stuff of poetry; cattle won't touch it, a person wouldn't dare lie down in it, you'd suffer the death of a thousand cuts if you ever played football in it, and you'd only walk through it if you were wearing armour. That was why that particular 'big field' lay undisturbed by man or beast. The town's most attractive environmental feature by far was a small lake fed by a brilliant, pure, cold stream that rushed down from the forested hills to the west.

The northernmost inhabited place in Malaya, Padang Besar owed its existence solely to the fact that it was where the tracks of the Royal Thai and the Malayan Railway systems crossed. Thus, my association with railway engines and railway people continued unbroken. The railway station, the centre of all activity, boasted platforms far too grand for the one-horse town it supposedly served, neither were they justified by the amount of traffic they handled. No, it was international rivalry that dictated the grandeur; Malayan and Thai officials vied with each other to show who was better; their separate ticket-offices and customs/immigration posts being kept apart, fittingly enough, by a Chinese-owned coffee shop shared by everybody.

Picture the railway station as Centreville. To the east ran the one and only street, a short, narrow, unpaved path lined on either side with an open storm drain above which stood a row of flimsy little wooden shophouses, more like market stalls than stores. Each emporium displayed identical merchandise, ostensibly for local sale: English cigarettes (mainly 555s, a brand to which the locals had evidently become addicted), Scotch whisky, French brandy, the ubiquitous 'DOM' and bales of brilliantly coloured cloth. At the end of the thoroughfare stood that classical standard outpost of Empire – the police station, a square, wooden structure raised above the ground on stilts, spick-and-span in every detail, rarely visited by citizens, even less so by outsiders and manned, even in those days of 'emergency' by just four Malay regulars: a Sergeant and three constables whose principal function was to display the Empire's orderliness by keeping themselves and their station in perfect trim and to raise and lower the Union Jack precisely at the regulated times. I don't suppose they dealt with more than one report a year.

Further on, still going east, up a bit of a slope, was the government dispensary (a smaller version of the police station but busier and without the flag) one or two biggish but by no means substantial houses and a school – all wooden structures and all, apart from the government buildings, looking as though they might collapse at any moment.

To the east of the railway track lay the trim lines of the Malayan Railway employees and government servants quarters plus a two-bedroom rest house and, the personal divertissement of the Railway Inspector, a tennis court.

To the north, just up the line, lay the Thai village of Pekan Siam (Siamese town) a dirt-poor, ramshackle strip of half-a-dozen shops with nothing more to sell than flyblown household basics and poor quality rubber sheets made from the product of trees grown nearby in mean little holdings. Across the street lay the shoddy, unsanitary lines of huts which housed the Thai railway men and civil servants and not far away at Klong Ngae was a tumble-down Thai police post which, no matter how slovenly in comparison with the Malayan post half-a-mile away, still flew its own flag with pride.

The grandee of Padang Besar on the Malayan side (apart from the rare days upon which we were honoured by a visit from the Railway Inspector), the real Pukka Sahib of Padang Besar, was the Immigration Officer, a Malay Tungku (Tungku means Prince, a common title in Malaya where each of the state rulers could enjoy four wives at any one time; the offspring of those ladies, combined with those of the many ex-wives, added up to a ten-a-penny proliferation of Tungkus). But we all bowed the knee to our Tungku not because of his royal title but because he was the boss and because he was a most agreeable fellow. The Thai supremo was their Customs Officer, Nai Sathien, an aristocratic-looking chap who allowed no glimpse of doubt as to where the Thai regnancy lay.

I was soon made aware that my sudden appearance as the first white official ever posted to that quiet, unchanging backwater had caused all-round alarm. It was an understandable reaction because, no matter that I didn't look or dress like one, the bush-telegraph system had soon informed the populace that I was a police officer. It was probable that they saw me as a law-enforcement officer appointed to a town in which, apart from the Malayan civil servants, the only inhabitants actually paid a living wage, and Seng Hin & Co, the only legitimate business in the place, everybody depended for their livelihood on smuggling. Even a half-hearted enforcement of the customs regulations would have bankrupted the town inside a couple of weeks. Even more certainly, without the bribes the smugglers paid, the grotesquely under-paid Thai civil servants wouldn't have survived, let alone been able to work.

It was therefore no wonder that to every citizen: station and school masters, tradesmen and tinsmiths, Malays, Chinese, Thais, Indians and Pathans, male and female, young and old, the sight of a white official stepping off the train one morning meant bad joss; that he looked as though he might be staying for good and not just passing through, spelled catastrophe. It must have crossed their minds that the white rulers in KL, despairing of Asians enforcing the rulers' laws, had sent one of their own kind to do the job. If it hadn't been for the heat, shivers would have run down every spine.

Fortunately, there was one merchant in the place who didn't depend on smuggling for a living – an English-speaking Hokkien Chinese, Khoo Hock Kee, better known as 'HK'. Besides running Seng Hin & Co, the only sizeable trading agency in Padang Besar, HK held the Rajah of Perlis' appointment as a state legislative councillor, a position that entitled him to the appellation 'Honourable' which made sure that the populace was suitably respectful towards him. He and I took an instant liking to each other and we became firm friends. He promised to spread the word around that the newly arrived 'foreign devil' would not interfere with normal business – meaning smuggling. It didn't take long for the town to return to normal; the populace, I think, believed me when I told them, through HK, that it was in government's interest to turn a blind eye to smuggling; after all, who'd benefit from the killing of the place stone dead?

So, smuggling resumed; into Thailand went contraband tobacco, liquor and cloth while into Malaya came small amounts of bootleg rubber. Thailand was the big loser particularly over tobacco because from the age of five upwards Thais of both sexes moved in a perpetual fog of nicotine smoke while, since tobacco growing and the manufacture of cigarettes were state-owned monopolies, the large-scale importation of foreign tobacco products hit the Thai government revenue hard. As for lawful trade, HK's company imported large quantities of the best, long-eared, polished Thai rice, always the favourite of Southeast Asians and a variety grown in enormous surplus in Thailand whereas, in those days anyway, Malaya's own rice harvests failed to meet demand.

For all the smuggling though there were no millionaires in Padang Besar, HK was worth a bit but he was no fat cat while Sathien probably stashed away a few thousand bhats a month to provide for his eventual retirement to Bangkok but for the rest of us, well, we lived down to our positions as petty traders and petty officials.

The contraband lifeblood of the town didn't go on all the time of course; oh no, for most of each day and for the whole of every hour of darkness, Padang Besar was asleep. It came alive only in two short bursts a day – when the trains arrived – at 0900 hours and again at 1500 hrs. At these times trains from Haadyai (Royal Thai) and Alor Setar (Malayan) met at Padang Besar before heading homewards at 1000 hrs and 1600 hrs. The purpose of this simple, untaxing timetable was of course to exchange passengers passing from one country to another but there were never very many of them; indeed, the Thai trains seldom carried more than the same 20 female smugglers who travelled backwards and forwards so regularly that, especially since they wore the identical uniform of black pyjamas, they might have been taken as members of the train crew.

Those ever-cheerful matrons, bearing large empty baskets slung on poles over one shoulder and a bag full of bhats over the other, would race swiftly to the bazaar (the word 'bazaar' covered all commercial centres in Malaya, from groupings of two or three stalls to thriving city high streets) where they'd exchange their bhats for the contraband, returning to the train with full baskets and empty bags. It was a black-market, black-costumed ballet performed twice daily with perfect syncopation. Its dancers, ever conscious of being under the eye of the choreographer, Sathien, traded never a cigarette more than they understood he would allow.

One Haadyai damsel ran a different scam, different because it was legit: this lady, who came only in the mornings, would get down from the train and immediately settle herself down on the platform – always at the very same spot – to sell her laksa, a rice gruel anointed with a rich, sweet curry sauce and topped with slivers of pork crackling. She ladled her nectar from one of two ladles into tin bowls which, in return for 20 cents, she handed over together with pairs of wooden chopsticks. Neither bowls nor chopsticks were washed between customers' use but then neither, I suspect, would the ladles have been washed overnight – an oversight that probably day-by-day improved the relish of their contents. That Haadyai breakfast was the best I've ever eaten anywhere. Every morning, often accompanied by HK and those not otherwise engaged in lawbreaking, I'd be pacing the platform, impatient for the Thai train to pull in.

Beyond the junior civil servants' lines to the west stood two more substantial – but still modest – wooden houses built in Malay kampong style on stilts. The larger of the two housed the Tungku and his family; the other, a two-room affair, the Tungku allocated to me. At least that's what he said. But, on my showing up clutching my *barang* (a marvellous Malay word covering wherewithals, shopping bags, odds-and-ends, everything), I found my claim to sole occupancy disputed by a white dog with a ridiculous curl to its tail. The ill-favoured creature, known in the bazaar as 'Boss', was already installed in a shady corner of the veranda. He gave all the signs (wagging of the twisted tail, a pulling back of the ears and a soppy 'I'm yours' expression in the eyes) of looking forward to sharing life with me. One other creature that, by the seeming custom of the land, had the right to share my abode was a snake, which lived in the rafters; I could hear my elongated non-paying tenant slithering around upstairs.

Two other people occupied the combined kitchen-cum-servants quarters separate from the house: a Malay police constable (appointed by Government as my 'orderly') and his wife. Let it be said here that it was not only white sahibs who employed servants; just about every Asian family above the low middle-class in the country, and indeed throughout Asia, had at least one. Mine was grossly under-employed.

By the standards of a country whose people ate and socialised while squatting on the floor and who had little use for curtains and knives and forks, my house could be said to have been furnished. In any event its one small, round table, two chairs, an almeira and an oil-lamp were enough for me. I pitched my camp bed smack in the middle of the bare second room and hung a ceiling-to-floor mosquito net around it so that Boss and I could walk round the bed and still not get bitten.

The bathroom was a square of concrete at ground level surrounded by wooden screens. I had to descend steps to get into it. In one corner stood a metre or more tall 'Shanghai Jar' or *tong* filled with wonderfully cool, soft water which, several times a day I ladled over myself with a *gayang* (scoop). The water ran away down a shallow trough in the floor and away into the lalang outside.

In another corner sat the 'thunder-box' whose receptacle (a large pan with a long handle) was cleaned out every morning by the same person who filled the *tong* – an Indian untouchable who trundled his 'perfume wagon' all round the bazaar before emptying its rich organic fertiliser straight on to the Chinese vegetable garden above the school. We, the residents, would eat the vegetables then defecate them into our thunder-boxes which would then be used to help grow more vegetables and so on in the perfect, environmentally-friendly cycle.

Up early I'd breakfast in the station shop on eggs and either *kopi o* (black coffee) or *kopi susu* (white, the cream being a huge dollop of condensed 'Carnation' milk), both made from local coffee and ground by pestle on the spot. Coffee was served in tumblers of such thickness that they were unbreakable. At 0900 hrs, I'd meet the trains from Haadyai and Alor Setar, eat a bowl of laksa and then do a round of the shops, taking tea here and there; lunch at a hawker stall (wherever two or three Chinese gathered together there'd be some entrepreneur boiling or frying food over a charcoal brazier) on *kueh teow* (rice noodles). Then, while the rest of the population had a siesta, Boss and I took a stroll round the lake (our love affair at those times was one-sided – an Asian creature, Boss didn't care for exercise in the afternoon heat), getting back to the station to meet the 1500 hrs train. Tea at 1600 was followed by tennis; supper (a big rice dish), I'd eat in the coffee shop at 2000 and by 2100, I'd be under the mosquito net with a book.

After I'd become an accepted part of the local scene I began to venture further afield. I'd jump on trains going in either direction, take a few, uncertain steps in the jungle; I cycled through shimmering rice-fields; and once with our Tungku I sailed aboard a slick customs yacht from Kuala Perlis to the peerlessly beautiful and in those days untouched island of Langkawi. Then, foolishly and arrogantly (was I underneath a colonialist?) I appropriated the railway jeep, a track inspection vehicle that, thanks to the 'emergency' lay idle in the yards. Apart from running on bogey wheels instead of rubber tyres and not having a steering wheel, the contraption was no different from an ordinary jeep. Anyway, Boss and I took to leaping aboard the thing as soon as the 10 o'clock had left the station and, side-by-side we'd be off to 'inspect' the line, Boss' spittle spraying like rain behind us. It was a mindless, madcap, self-indulgent thing to do.

Too well mannered to raise objections to my face the Padang Besar railway folk sent word to Prai. In response, from that headquarters came the Chief Railways Inspector, a jet-black, baby-bottom bald sahib of most imposing proportions, Tambiah. Tuan Besar Tambiah summoned me to appear before him in the Rest House, his Rest House. Dressed in spotless white dhoti and with a pristine white cotton shawl like a robe of authority over one massive shoulder, the Inspector looked for all the world like one of those fearsome yet benevolent deities you see in Bombay movies. He spoke in flawless English and with withering asperity: "I would ask, Sir, that you show me your credentials as a qualified rail-track inspector and for your authority to drive a motor vehicle on same rail-track. You have neither? I thought not. You, Sir, an officer of the law, should be ashamed of your law-breaking self. What's to be done with you – isn't it?" The interrogative 'isn't it?' was tacked on to almost every sentence uttered in English by the local citizenry. Thoroughly put-down I could but mumble apologies, promise never to ride his jeep again and beg for a non-custodial sentence. Whereupon the stern God was reincarnated as a kindly human being who invited me to join him in a game of tennis and afterwards to dine with him.

I'd always thought of tennis as a bourgeois pastime but Padang Besar changed my mind. With no class regard at all, local luminaries like Tambiah himself, Sathien and HK banged the ball about against, or in partnership with, sweepers, ticket collectors, clerks, porters and shop assistants. Tambiah, a tennis freak known in Penang for his booming serves, had brought the game to Padang Besar some years before, partly to pass the time away when he was visiting, partly to energise his inspection work, partly to built an appetite for dinner and partly because he was addicted to a nightly game. Anyhow, at Malayan Railways' expense he'd had his labourers lay out for him a fine, true court made out of brick-red laterite and they'd put up a little atap pavilion to go with it. He'd then looked round for tennis players. Sathien, no mug to this game, could keep the Thai flag flying high even against the Burrah Sahib himself; HK soon learned to become a handy player and I took to the game as though born to play it. The lower orders made the most of their chance to put it to their masters, the Thai underlings however making sure to lose against Sathien fairly regularly. I quickly became dotty about it. Every evening at 0500, I'd be the first on the court, putting up the nets and checking the balls, etc. The sweaty hours I spent chasing tennis balls all over that particular patch of sun-baked laterite were among the very best I've ever spent anywhere doing anything in my life.

Then one day there came from Kangar a startling royal pronouncement, the Rajah of Perlis (in his own right a tennis player of national repute) sent word that he was to captain a team from Kangar against a team from Padang Besar, the contest to be staged at Padang Besar! We rolled and rolled the court and then we rolled it again, marked the lines to perfection, repaired the holes in the net, recruited ball-boys from the Chinese school, ordered iced fresh-lime to be on hand by the gallon, laid on a *kenduri* (festive lunch) to be served in the Thai customs shed, instructed each other on royal etiquette (Sathien snootily denied the need

for such instruction for himself) called up Tambiah to captain us and
practised like mad. Somebody in town produced a black-wood Chinese
chair that looked a bit like a throne above which we mounted the status
symbol of all Asian monarchs – a large, yellow umbrella. We festooned
the pavilion and the bazaars with bunting in the green of Perlis and, on
the great day we gathered, all breathless, to meet the up-train.

His Royal Highness, dressed for an English public-school sports day
– striped blazer, white bags, checkered choker – and accompanied by a
dozen aides carrying tennis racquets, boxes of brand-new balls, thermos
flasks, umpteen changes of royal attire and a hundred 'Good Morning'
towels (small hand-towels made in China, thin as paper and stamped in
red in Chinese and English 'GOOD MORNING' – everybody in the
land seemed to carry at least one of them) H.R.H. stepped down from a
special bright yellow coach attached to the 0900. Waiting in ceremonial
attire to receive the Rajah stood our Tungku in a pearl-buttoned shirt
over black silk trousers and gold-piped sarong, shining songkok on his
head and kris at his waist, together with Tambiah in the plumage of a
Malayan Railway mogul.

Normally, nobody played games in the hottest part of the Malayan
day but on this memorable occasion, with H.R.H. being bound as tightly
as any ordinary mortal to the immutable train timetable, we had no
choice but to play our tournament during the very hours when the sun
turned the laterite into a scarlet inferno. And play we did, everybody kept
repeating – and meaning it too – "We are enjoying ourselves, isn't it?"
Only Sathien minded being beaten.

The 'emergency' and Gerald Templer's distemper not withstanding,
in the early 1950s most of Malaya slumbered as it had always done in
a bucolic heat-haze, nowhere more somnolently than Padang Besar, a
retreat beyond the reach of the motor vehicle and, therefore, Tambiah
excluded, prying senior bureaucrats. Apart from an electricity generator
that operated courtesy of Malayan Railways, for just two hours every
evening, the stillness was broken only by the puff and hoot of railway
engines, the ring of the two station masters bells, the clop of balls and

shuttlecocks on tennis and badminton racquets and the voices of people, animals, birds and insects. The silence that followed the shutting down of the generator at 9pm was so concrete that I'd lie on my canvas bed, Boss unconscious underneath the bed, and wonder if I hadn't died and gone to some sort of nirvana.

The head of the special branch covering Kedah/Perlis, 'Bottle' Hargreaves, was a sweet old boy of the pre-war school. He could read Jawi (the Arabic script), quote both the Koran and the Singapore stock-market prices and distinguish – or so he claimed – the difference between brands of claret by drinking them. I never once met him in his office but always on the veranda of his lovely house where, dressed in baggy shorts he'd recline in his chaise longue, assure me that I'd "get used to things in time", and promise that he'd take the train one day and call on me. Like every other police officer in the two states, he never did.

If I'd been 007 I'd have dashed around south Thailand dressed in the latest in tropical silk suits spending millions on bribing professors and seducing sultry, almond-eyed sirens to spy for me deep in the enemy's heartland. But I'd have looked silly to have worn so much as a neck-tie in south Thailand. I don't think Bottle Hargreaves would've given me millions to spend, while professors and scarlet women were in short supply in the vicinity of Padang Besar. So I went around doing things in my own sweet way – visiting Songkla for example.

Songkla was a comatose Thai town on the shores of an enchanting inland sea, the provincial capital of a very large part of southern Thailand. There I'd 'liaise' (a meaningful word in the bureaucrats' lexicon translated as eating and drinking at somebody else's expense) with the Thai local intelligence chief, Captain Chalong, a rather dull fellow who, despite our having little or nothing to say to each other about our common enemy, nevertheless always made a big fuss of me because he could claim expenses for 'liaising' with me, meaning entertaining me at an open-air restaurant beneath swaying palms on a superb beach. In my turn I too would claim expenses for liaising with Chalong, thus completing a cyclical rip-off of taxpayers whereby unrelated civil servants fed and watered each other at their taxpayers expense without the same ratepayers of three countries gaining as much as a baht's worth of value for their money.

Months passed and I hadn't collected even a smidgen of 'intelligence' to pass to Bottle Hargreaves. Then I got an idea. Thai officials were too proud to admit that any Malayan 'bandits' were living in their country (but it was no secret that they were). Indeed, they got very shirty if you as much as mentioned the possibility. But I guessed that they'd send truthful, secret reports to Songkla in which they might mention the subject. Could I bribe them to sell me copies of those reports? Sathien, who must have held an intelligence as well as a customs role, was too near home for me to risk losing his friendship and perhaps causing a diplomatic incident through making corrupt approaches to him. Instead, I made for Sadao, a rickety, flyblown little town about ten miles from Padang Besar where Police Major Choob, who had charge of the police in the district covering the Padang Besar area, had his headquarters.

Like every person in the pay of the Thai government, Choob was so grossly underpaid that he had no choice but to put the squeeze on his citizenry who for their part were quite ready to grease the palms of folks like Choob rather than pay taxes. In Sadao I ate with Choob in the greasiest, filthiest stinkball of a coffee shop I'd ever seen. Over a delicious meal (did dirt enhance the flavouring?) I put it to him straight: I'd pay him 500 ringgits a month (several times his salary) for a copy of his intelligence reports to Songkla or, as turned out to be the case, directly to Bangkok. Choob didn't need my 500 ringgits; underpaid or not he already possessed an imposing limousine that sat proudly by his front door and a kerosene-fuelled fridge that shuddered away in a corner of a living-room crammed with the latest in Scandinavian furniture. Madame Choob was costumed for St. Tropez rather than Sadao, her jewellery played a tune as she minced along and her excellent table (to which thereafter I was admitted rather than the coffee shop) proffered French wines and Havana cigars. Choob, fat as butter himself, smiled over my offered bribe, stuck out a podgy paw, pocketed the money and went to fetch a copy of his latest report. From then on, at the end of every month, we exchanged money for documents without saying a word about it.

Back in Alor Setar, Bottle Hargreaves had retired either to Tasmania, the Transvaal or Tunbridge Wells, to be replaced by another old-timer, Hughie Donaldson, who received me as Bottle had done, reclining in the same old long-sleeve chair, dressed though not in baggy shorts but trim linen slacks and, to hid his ageing Adam's apple, the cravat which was Hughie's hallmark (I ran across him in Hong Kong 30 years later; he still turned on the old courtly manners and still wore the cravat). Hughie's reaction to my announcement of the deal with Choob was one of rapture; anybody would have thought I'd brought him Chin Peng (our leading enemy) on the end of a rope. Translated, Choob's reports turned out to be barren, self-congratulatory accounts of the reporter's masterly stewardship of his district. Unruffled, Hughie called the deal 'a momentous coup' and he promised to write nice things in my personal file about it.

Choob continued to report the same fiction to Bangkok every month, repeating over and over again that his district was untroubled by the 'emergency' on the other side of the frontier, that his area was quiet, prosperous and worshipful of his Thai Majesty. I suppose it was intelligence of a negative sort in that it showed us how Bangkok was being badly misinformed. It also proved that the Malayan communists were taking great care not to disturb the Thai authorities. It could also have crossed Choob's mind of course that had he told Bangkok the truth – that alien, communist 'bandits' were living and organising almost beneath his kitchen window, he might have been ordered to do something about it.

Choob was transferred to Bangkok in mid-1952. His replacement, Sanggat, a leaner but no less venal officer, took over the Choob-Hardy compact as if it had been part of his official duties; the 500 ringgits part of his salary. Sanggat's reporting style was different, but his 'intelligence' remained the same: worthless. Nobody ever pressed me to ask for more, nobody suggested that we might be paying through the nose for nothing. Collecting the Sadao report, the only 'intelligence' work I ever did in Padang Besar, occupied half-a-day of my time once a month.

There was plenty of another kind of work to be done though. The Colonial Office ruled that failure for a cadet to pass law and language exams within the first three years of service would result possibly in dismissal and at any rate in the forfeiture of pay increments and promotion prospects. I found the Malay language to be both simple and extraordinarily complex. Nonetheless, in Alor Setar in December 1951, I passed the first of the two required Malay language tests (a standard one pass was expected within 12 months, standard two within three years).

The law exam was a tougher proposition. Although according to the civil list I was a 'cadet assistant superintendent of police' I'd had no police training or experience whatsoever, a factor that limited my acquaintance with the law. Moreover, unless you wanted to learn how to break the law and get away with it, Padang Besar was not the best place to study law. Mercifully, much experienced in the ways of colonial establishments, Hughie Donaldson wised me up on which sections of the law books to concentrate on and which to leave alone. Every evening for months I spent an hour or two beneath my pretty kerosene lamp mugging up on certain chapters of that holy writ of every British colony no matter how far removed from New Delhi: the Indian Penal Code. On opening the exam papers in Alor Setar in 1952 I found that most of the questions related to parts to which Hughie had directed me. I sailed through and within a week I'd forgotten all the law I ever learned. Never once in the next 30 years as a 'policeman' did I ever feel the need to recall a single word of the Indian Penal Code.

That left me with only one hurdle to jump before my name would be engraved in the Colonial Office's stud book of permanent officials: the second part of the Malay language exam. That stiff test, which included writing Jawi was made tougher for me because, although I was living in a predominantly Malay state, the local lingua franca was Thai. This fact, together with my having been given Thailand as my area of special interest, plus the sight of bundles of Thai newspapers being thrown off the train every morning, gave me food for thought. I'd had it drilled into me (though I didn't believe it) that people lucky enough to have been born anywhere beneath the Union Jack were advanced to levels of literacy unheard of in the rest of the 'uncivilised' world yet here, dumped on the platform before my eyes every morning, was evidence that Thailand, a country that had never experienced colonial rule, no, not for a single day in its history, was a more literate country than was 'British' Malaya and by a mile at that! Very few Malay language newspapers were ever delivered by the northbound trains; Thai newspapers by the hundreds.

I learned that nine out of ten Thai adults could read and write – a percentage that put many a 'first world' country to shame and a fact that accounted for the cornucopia of Thai newspapers, books, journals, comics, magazines and manuals, many of them in rich colours and flaunting illustrations vivid enough to excite the dullest imagination and preposterous enough to draw me like magnets. The front-page picture that finally turned my head around was one showing – or claiming to show – a woman (brown) giving birth to a snake (green). I ran straight to Sathien for a translation of the article and to beg him to teach me his language so that I could read such sensational stuff for myself.

Sathien, a well-educated man with plenty of time to spare (as all of us in Padang Besar had) was pleased as punch over my enthusiasm for his language; he promised me an hour's daily tuition but on two conditions: one that I'd begin at the beginning by learning the alphabet parrot-fashion as if I were a five-year-old and two, that I'd do homework as well. Knowing that I couldn't learn Thai and Malay up to standard two at the same time, I proposed to Kuala Lumpur (KL) that Thai, not Malay, be my required language. KL agreed with amazing alacrity, saying that a pass in Thai at a low level would see me through to confirmation in place of Malay standard two but that a higher Thai pass would be required later on.

I began five years of Thai language studies by sitting with five- to six-year-old Thais chanting in differing sounding tones: "kor, kor, kor, kor, kor: khai khai khai khai khai" and so on, graduating after a few weeks to Sathien's overflowing desk in the appallingly chaotic Royal Thai Customs Office. It was a right royal mess indeed, a battlefield of buckled chairs and rickety shelves breaking under the weight of mountains of dog-eared files, thousands of rodent/termite chewed ledgers, yellowing paper, balls of twine, lumps of red wax, spittoons, empty ink bottles, broken pencils, overflowing ashtrays, bales of stinking rubber and long discarded, busted pencil-sharpeners.

My guru, a living model of neatness and decorum but blissfully unaware of the clutter all around him, gave me a history lesson. A 13th century Thai king had lain long under shady trees inventing a written alphabet for his language. Dismissing the ideas of copying the Chinese calligraphy (the Thai language, like those of China, is tonal) he eventually came up with 44 consonants, 15 vowel signs and five tone indicators, a total of 64 ideographs altogether; unwieldy perhaps but much simpler than the Chinese. Being a language that is sung more than spoken, just as in order to sing well you'd first better learn the tonic *sol-fa*, so to sing Thai properly you must first learn the script. Sathien was right; sitting among children helped me understand the musical qualities. Now, assisted by the beauty of the tongue, my tutor's patience, my ample freedom and the lack of distraction together with necessity's sharp pinch, I too lay, metaphorically, under a tree slowly but surely beginning to grasp the meaning of the ancient monarch's doodling.

The Thais are a beautiful, good-natured race but who wouldn't be if they were lucky enough to live in a country where the padi grew strong and straight from well-watered loam, where fish leaped in between the rice seedlings and where the temperature never fell below 25°C? The very bountifulness of Thailand shone from its people's eyes.

One day I got a big surprise: a message ordering me formally to receive a personal representative from the Almighty Gerald Templer himself! I gave the news to Sathien, the Tungku, HK and Boss and together we informed the populace that on the day in question they should refrain from smuggling and open gambling. I laid on a fine lunch in the Rest House and, on the appointed morning I stood on the platform dressed as if the Rajah was making another call. My V.I.P. was a tall, snappy looking Colonel hung about with the red tabs and hatband of the general staff. He cut quite a figure in Padang Besar. He drew himself up to salute me (a gesture that won me a good deal of face among my smugglers) and told me that His Excellency Templer, mindful of the increasing importance of the border region, had instructed him to come to see this particular part of it for himself and then to report back to the General in person. I suggested an itinerary: coffee with the Tungku and Sathien, a stroll around the bazaar, a glance at a map, lunch and then more detailed discussions. The Colonel however had other ideas – he and the General had no time for pleasantries, they had a war to win. He intended to return on the very same train he'd come in on; ergo, he had about half-an-hour to see the frontier: "Now, Sir, kindly direct me to it."

Hardly believing my ears, I swept the Colonel down the platform and along the footpath leading to Pekan Siam until, in about three minutes flat, I brought him up against a very ordinary looking signpost that could have done with a lick of paint but which still read

After gazing upon with rapt attention for a few minutes he sighed, turned on his heels, hurried back to the train, saluted again, jumped aboard and headed for Kuala Lumpur, there, I suppose, to go straight to His Excellency and report that the frontier at its most northerly point was properly signposted, but could perhaps be smartened up a bit.

It was about this time – early 1952 – that a 'Police Jungle Squad', a platoon-sized formation of military-trained specials was posted to Padang Besar. I'd had no say in the matter and but for the fact that a section of the squad was deployed in an abandoned railway gang line about six miles south of Padang Besar, I'd have had nothing to do with them. But, after all, I was the senior police officer and I feared for ill-trained men stuck in a jungle outpost close by 'bandit' lairs in Thailand. I felt beholden to share the experiences with them, which is how Boss and I came to spend the odd night or two in the gang line.

A large area to the rear of the gang line – the railway track lay immediately in front – had once been cultivated by the Tamil labourers who'd lived there. But it had rapidly been reclaimed by belukar (secondary jungle) a tangled mess of vegetation by comparison with which the jungle beyond it would have seemed like a clean, windswept English meadow.

Life wasn't much easier within the shelter either, it being infested by millions of ticks, sand flies, cockroaches, ants and mosquitoes. To be outside the mosquito net after dark was unbearable. But even the nets couldn't keep all the blood-suckers at bay because, having been made small enough to stow in knapsacks, when erected the nets cleared the camp beds by only about 40 cm which meant that there was a good chance that some part of your anatomy – a knee, an elbow, a head or a big toe – would touch the netting while you slept and thus become the target for a thousand rapier-wielding mosquitoes. Trying to avoid such torture we went to bed fully dressed – boots and all – a practice that made the heat more suffocating than it ordinarily was. To add yet further torment you choked on the smoke from fires lit and kept smouldering in a vain attempt to keep the insects away. Squash a mosquito early in the morning and its blood – your blood – spurted many a mile.

The specials had been sent there to patrol the railway line to make sure it hadn't been tampered with. It was an invitation to an ambush. Time and again I lectured the patrolmen on the perils of repeating the same drill on two consecutive mornings and on the importance of keeping as close to the ground as possible. But I knew in my bones that they'd be ambushed and sure enough we got a radio message from the gang line one morning saying that the patrol was under fire and needed help.

I rounded up the rest of the jungle squad and away we went in one of the great freight-pulling locomotives, that by good luck had pulled in from Kelantan the night before and was steamed up ready to go to Alor Setar. But by the time we reached the stricken patrol its attackers had already high-tailed it back to Thailand leaving, to our enormous relief, only one of the specials wounded. That chap, no more than a boy really, had what looked that a badly mashed arm which was soon wrapped in bandages and strapped across his chest. We couldn't move him to Alor Setar however because our engine driver, a Tamil built like a great slab of marble, stood pointing his unshaven chin (Asians never point a finger) towards a hand-grenade that lay unexploded in the middle of the track in front of his locomotive. He wouldn't move until the grenade had been removed.

A police sergeant, a regular from the Padang Besar station and accustomed to command, took over. After telling us to get our heads down he moved well way from the grenade and then fired at it with his rifle. And he hit it; you could see the bullet holes, two of them. But it didn't explode. It lay there staring at us through the two eyes the sergeant had drilled into it. I tried to talk the driver into taking a chance, it was, after all, a dud wasn't it? But he wasn't having any of that. Wagging his great head and gesticulating, he said, "We are having bomb on line. I am thinking of the railway regulation, which is saying if we are having obstruction on track we are not risking engine. If we are clearing bomb away then we are driving train, if bomb is staying where it is we are not driving train and not helping young fellow getting doctor sahib and maybe bleeding to die. Which I am not liking, isn't it?"

Whereupon the sergeant, ordering us to get our heads down again, leaped across the line, swooped up the grenade like a kestrel pouncing on a mouse and in one motion hurled it high in the jungle opposite where we heard it land with a splash. Still without going off. Then the engine-driver sahib was picking up a Malay boy and carrying him, like an amah is carrying a baby, and taking to doctor sahib who is saving all of the boy except small parts of two fingers. Isn't it?

Then, all of a sudden, in mid-1952, Kuala Lumpur ordered me to pack up and move forthwith from one side of the country to the other; I was to resume my spying on Thailand from the state of Kelantan. The news roared around the bazaar a good 24 hours before it reached me officially. My Siamese smuggling sisters faked tears, the laksa lady gave me two bowls for the price of one, the fortune-teller read me a cut-price prediction (the more you paid him the brighter his forecast), the gamblers allowed me to throw their loaded dice, Sathien presented me with a handsome Thai-English dictionary, the Tungku laid on a *kenduri*, Boss went home to wait for his new provider and I, genuinely melancholic, promised to return. Which promise I kept.

Reflections
Scene I: The Miracle Performed Four Times a Day
Just to the east of the main railway line, behind the station. There was a large, open shunting area in the centre of which there sat a jumbo-sized gramophone record made of solid steel at least a foot thick. It revolved on massive wheels and bearings and carried a length of the railway line straight across it.

That wondrous strange contraption was employed to turn around huge railway engines so that they faced the direction from whence they came: Thai trains from the north faced north again, Malayan trains vice-versa. Once de-coupled from their rolling stock the locomotives were shunted on to the disc, which was then, rotated 180 degrees. Once facing the other way the trains were shunted off on to the main line again and coupled for their return journey.

The miracle was that the turntable's mechanism was so superbly balanced, tuned and maintained that it needed only the finger pressure of one puny little human being to spin it around – thumping great locomotive and all – as though it were but a roulette wheel.

Scene II: Background Music
The Chinese school was a big one-room shed with an atap roof, a beaten-earth floor and walls of unplaned planking reaching about a metre and a half from the ground to leave a space up to the roof open to the elements. Desks and benches were of rough-hewn timber, like the rest of the materials sourced from the encroaching jungle. Over the years they'd been polished glass-smooth by the bottoms, forearms, elbows and fists of hundreds of children.

The sole teacher, a gaunt, care-worn fellow imported years earlier straight from China, instructed his forty 6–12-year-olds, dressed uniformly in blue shorts/skirts, white shirts and close-cropped black hair, in the time-honoured way of teaching Chinese how to read and write their mazy language. This meant leading them parrot-fashion in articulating a sign by singing out in chorus over and over again until they reconciled forever the sound with the particular ideogram displayed on the blackboard.

Singing out the tone for 'Hai' (yes) for example they learned to identify the pictogram as being different from the one which went for the different toned 'Hai' (shoes). The result was that for four or five hours a day the bazaar rang with the sing-song of a choir of irrepressible youngsters – like an off-note glee club stuck with the same few bars of an anthem. The chant of Chinese schoolchildren at their language lessons was the background muzak in many a small Malayan bazaar. Maybe by now they've been silenced by air-conditioning?

Scene III: A Picture Postcard

The Malays of Perlis grew rice in fields fed by rivers and streams into which there poured over a hundred inches of rain a year. Their padi fields were swampy chessboards squared by raised earthworks and small enough to be taken in by the human eye in cinemascope. Depending on the time of year they presented landscapes ranging from newly turned loam to tall, waving rice. In the background were pretty kampongs with dinky little homes nestling under green umbrellas made of long-limbed coconut palms. The palms provided not only shelter from the sun but wood for the houses' supports and cross beams; atap for roofs, walls and floor coverings; rattan for lashing; coconut milk to scent the air and calm the stomach; shells to drink the milk from; coir to fill mattresses; oil to light lamps and to put a sheen on long, black, lustrous, seductive tresses; and, out of the mufti's sight, sap to foment into the throat-throbbing toddy that only fire-eaters could drink without suffering burnt insides.

Steep roofs protected against the rain; floors were raised more than a metre above ground to keep out both floods and snakes; steps were constructed unevenly so as to confuse evil spirits; jars of water were placed at the foot of the steps for the washing of feet before the upward climb; and, to provide sustenance perhaps for the resident snakes, special rat runs – *larian tikus* – were built into the apex of the houses along the whole length of their roofs.

Further away the backcloth was of dark-green, jungled hills while, to return to the proscenium, there in the padi fields were glossy, black water-buffalo, huge creatures who worked the land like shire-horses used to work in England, imposing beasts which fed the loam with their wastes and which acted as flight-decks and food traps for birds which'd take rides on their backs while feasting on ticks and leeches that fed upon the animals. And they also acted as magic-carpets for young Malay mahouts dreaming the while of Mecca. Every so often there'd be a best-kept buffalo competition; the mahouts would buff their charges until their hides shone like black velvet, their great horns glistened in a royal yellow and their hooves glowed with the lustre of a Sergeant Major's parade boots. But once the contest was finished these magnificent creatures would be allowed to do what they liked best of all – to sink slowly into a metre or two of treacly, tropical ooze until only their eyes, snout, crown and horns were to be seen.

Scene IV: Tickety Boo

The jungle came right up to the bazaar. It was known to be a dark damp place smelling of the tension between genesis and rot; the sun penetrated only to touch the widest of its streams and rivers or places cleared perhaps by the *orang asli*. Damp dripped ceaselessly from above and damp rose perpetually from below to create a paradisiacal environment for trees, orchids, pitcher-plants, creepers and thorn bushes known as *nanti sedikit* (wait-a-minutes) because they tugged at your clothing, tore your hands and snatched your hat off.

It was nirvana also for wild creatures that lived there in a profusion made all the more wondrous by their invisibility. So dense was the foliage that elephants, mammoths though they are, could move only a metre ahead of you without your ever clapping eyes on them; tigers, crocodiles, boar, apes and snakes were everywhere around you, yet almost never before your eyes. Insects, leeches and flies of every colour and size moved in enormous squadrons while centipedes and ants crawled and buzzed in trillions, all of them on the look out for a patch of bare human skin to land upon or apertures: nostrils, ears, mouths and eyes to screw themselves into.

It was a giant, natural incubator for skin-fungus, crutch-rot, athlete's foot, mange, cankers and dermatitis; a hatchery for a thousand species of parasitic vermin that threatened dysentery, yellow fever, black water fever, dengue, the flux, malaria, cholera, typhoid, rabies, hepatitis and tuberculosis. It was also an auditorium whose excellent acoustics made for the clarity with which you heard the almost non-stop noises of a myriad life-forms. Yet there were times also when, for no reason at all, the din would cease all at once, neither fading out nor losing individual voices one-by-one but all at the same time, just as if all those making the noises had received a signal, a radio wave that human ears couldn't pick up but which would instantly silence every bat, bird, insect and monkey simultaneously. Such was the silence at these times that you'd think that every single organism had stopped breathing. And then, just as suddenly and eerily, the heaving excitement of nature would start up again.

Scene V: Serpents

In order to reduce the 'bandits' 'cover' and provide a 'field of fire' for the jungle squad, Government ordered clearance of a strip of jungle immediately encroaching on the town behind the school. It was done in a big, collective, labour-intensive exercise carried out on three consecutive Sundays when there were no trains either way. Every able man, woman and child, and every saw, axe, changkul and parang was put to work.

The most remarkable aspect of the operation was that it uncovered countless snakes, scores of serpents who until those days had lived, minding their own business on Padang Besar's doorstep without hurting anybody. The exercise became known as 'the three days of the serpents'; the superstitious – and there were many – performed mumbo-jumbo to guard against snake bites and it paid off because although we were chopping down their dwelling places in a most unfriendly manner, not once did any one of them attack; our 'Doctor'; treated not a single snake-bite and, as for our part, we killed not a single snake. As we could have told government before we started however the area was swiftly covered in belukar to give the 'bandits' better 'cover' than they'd have had from the jungle.

Scene VI: The Sting

Talking of biting hands, I was unrolling the tennis net one afternoon when I felt a jab of pain as shocking as if a hypodermic needle had been stabbed into the tip of one my fingers. And then I saw the hypodermic needle disguised as a scorpion scurrying away across the tennis court like lightening, its purple poison sac raised to the skies.

Holding my wounded hand high in a Nazi salute I rushed through the bazaar shouting "Kala jenking, kala jenking!" ("Scorpion, Scorpion!") in the hope that our 'Doctor' would hear me wherever he might have been hanging out. Hearing me, everybody else ran behind me as if I were the Pied Piper. Luckily, the 'Doctor', a tall, lean, good-humoured Chinese trained in first-aid was in his dispensary. He laughed, gave my throbbing finger another injection, told me not to be such a baby, and sent me home. That night my hand grew to the size of a boxing glove; the next day I was playing tennis again.

Scene VII: The Princess and the Thunder-box

A glamorous Malay princess of the Kelantan royal family related to the Ranee of Perlis came into town one evening, missed the train connection, and was accommodated by our Tungku. The Tungku however, was ill so I was asked to entertain her. Luckily, a government film unit was staging a show on the station platform. The best two seats were reserved for my royal guest, sheathed head-to-toe in stunning gold silk, and myself, wearing my one and only suit. Halfway through a documentary on ways of preserving rice seedlings against weevils – a problem that my charming companion would never have to deal with – she turned to me and in a voice sweet as honey, whispered something in highfaluting Malay, ending with the one word I caught: *kenching* (urinate).

Not trusting my ears I hesitated to respond whereupon the princess, accepting that my Malay wasn't up to the royal standard, repeated her command in the language of the street: "Saya mesti-lah buang ayer dengan segara." ("I simply have to pee right away.") I leapt to my feet hurriedly to escort her to the thunder-box room of the Rest House and, afterwards, trying to kid myself that I'd heard the tinkling sound of running, regal waters, then back to the movie. The next morning, bending low to bid farewell to the royal dream from Kelantan, I couldn't help thinking to myself that princesses and thunder-boxes didn't go together.

Scene VIII: White Crocodiles and White Blood

A *perahu* sailed twice weekly between Kuala Perlis and Langkawi, a small sparsely populated island that came within my operational parish. There was never the remotest possibility of communist activity on the island. Nevertheless I made an excuse to visit. The Rest House was a two-room affair above one of Langkawi's few shops. It was owned by one of the island's few Chinese residents, a man who was also the comptroller of the island's transport system meaning that he had two broken-down bicycles for hire. That he also sold kerosene in jam-jars gives you an idea of Langkawi's economy. I was the only guest he'd housed for months, the only customer in his shop that day and, by the look of the machines, the only hirer of one of his cycles for a long time.

I pedalled through fields in which the Malays grew the rice they'd eat together with the fish they'd pull in effortlessly from the ever-warm seas and the fruit that fell at their feet in over-abundance and great variety. I climbed slowly until I stood on the lip of a milky-looking crater-lake in whose depths according to legend there lived a *buaya puteh* (white crocodile), in whose body dwelt the spirit of a young girl who, centuries earlier, drowned herself in the lake over a love affair and who has since shielded Langkawi from harm.

I didn't see the *buaya puteh* but the locals swore that she still worked her charms (they said that the only Japanese soldier to set foot on Langkawi was never seen again after he'd gone to the lake) and it must be said that the island gave every impression of being under divine care. The girl whose spirit was inside the crocodile wasn't Langkawi's only saintly female for there was also Mahsuri, a woman who, on being executed for allegedly committing adultery, is said to have spilled the white blood of the crocodile. I had the idea that somewhere along the line the two tales got mixed together.

Scene IX: Murdering Monks
The Thai pirates of Phuket raided Malay *perahus*, slaughtered the fishermen and made off with both boats and fish. They were feared and despised. Yet once back home those same murderers would likely have paid homage to the shrine of their Lord Buddha and even worn muzzles over their mouths so as not to hurt a fly by swallowing one and they'd sweep the path ahead of them to avoid treading on an ant. Who was the true Thai? The meditator or the murderer?

In my day Thailand was a country as close to perfection as you'd find anywhere; it was warm, fecund and populated by as lovely and apparently gentle a people as the most loving God might ever create. Hamlets flaunted brilliant green and gold temples while the humblest of homes had its own pretty little shrine. Most of its young males gave a year or more of their lives to wander the countryside as shaven-headed, barefooted, saffron-robed monks begging for their food. They were a race so submissive that, taught to keep their heads below those of their betters, they'd drop to their knees to crawl past the likes of Sathien.

How come then that every government employee from the man who stood on the station platform waving green and red flags up to His Excellency the Minister of Railways was uniformed and armed? A police constable packed a .38 handgun while His Eminence, Police General Pao wore both a personalised pearl-handled piece and a jewel-studded dagger. A splendid young King, Ananda, killed himself while playing with a revolver. How to reconcile one Thai with another?

Let me give you an example. Four or five young constables stood in the middle of Police Captain Choob's ramshackle police station beneath the proud national flag. Having completed their sacramental years as pious monks, instead of saffron robes they now wore military-style peaked caps with enormous badges and instead of begging bowls they now carried loaded rifles. They stood guard over a circular bamboo cage about three metres in diameter, a cage jam-packed with prisoners as downcast as you'd ever see on a cinema screen let alone in real life. Having committed offences hardly more grievous than failing to pay 'dash' to Choob and his men they were nonetheless shackled in handcuffs and leg-irons. In order to save Choob the cost of feeding them they'd be freed to go home for the night on condition they'd return at daybreak the following day to be manacled all over again.

There's another day burned into my head. It was noon in Songkla, the town heavy with heat and peace, its silence disturbed only by the wash of waves rolling over the beach and the call of Minah birds. Then, all of a sudden rifle fire burst out, it seemed, in every direction and men lay bleeding everywhere I looked. Then silence again. The news travelled quickly. The dead and dying were convicts who'd rushed out of the prison gates opened to allow a lorry to enter. They'd escaped into town, only to be picked off by policemen on beat duty, soldiers off-duty and other government employees using whatever weapons they happened to be carrying. No warning was given, no riot act was read, no quarter given; men were simply identified by their prison garb and gunned down. The murderers were the same men who'd lived in monasteries, the same people who, on the grounds that their religion forbade them to take the life of any living creature, would refuse to put a cat out of its misery after it'd been run over.

Scene X: The Butterflies of Haadyai
In the early 1950s rubber and tin were fetching undreamed-of prices. Haadyai, south Thailand's main rail-junction and market town, was

having a fine old time. A sprawling, untidy metropolis, right down to the swinging half-doors, it resembled a Hollywood gold-rush town. Every other half door on the high street opened on to a bar and every bar was a bordello and every bordello had its screen on to which blue films, many of them shot in the back rooms, were projected. Their customers weren't free-spending foreigners – they were blessings yet to come to Thailand – nor were they spielers from Bangkok; Haadyai's cat houses teemed with local blades tricked out in body-clinging, bell-bottomed pants whose pockets were hot with bank notes blown into Haadyai like confetti before the wind of the Korean war.

Haadyai was but an hour's train ride from Malaya yet, apart from the weather, the contrariety was total. Stepping down from the train in Haadyai you'd have thought that every female in town was for sale. Stop at any wayside stall for a tube of toothpaste or a lottery ticket and you'd be offered a 'butterfly' as well. Your trishaw driver, barber, concierge, boot-boy, hawker, fish-monger, newspaper-boy, dhobi lady and street-cleaner was a part-time pimp; they'd all press upon you a choice of doxies: take your pick, they'd promise – long-limbed or squat and bacon-fat, gauche or experienced, scholarly ("you like schoolteacher?") or 'primitive', school-girl or matron, black, brown, white or striped; Cambodian, Puerto-Rican, Mongolian, White Russian, Zoroastrian or *farang* (European), short-timer or all-nighter, exhibitionist or quiet housewife?

1952–1956
Malaya

The Kampong

I packed my few belongings (a camp-bed, mosquito net, clothes, knife, fork, spoon, tin plate, mug) and, courtesy of Sathien, boarded one of the mighty freight trains I've already told you about. It carried me slowly from Perlis in the west to Kelantan in the east, making an unscheduled stop to drop me at the town that was to be my new home: Pasir Mas. Second only in size to the state capital, Kota Bharu, had horses been able to live in its steam-heat, Pasir Mas would still have been a one-horse town.

Small as Pasir Mas was, however, it was still the administrative centre of a large area to the west of the Kelantan River. Hardly a single internal combustion engine disturbed the dust or churned up the mud; human movement was on foot or bicycle.

I was once again the lone white face in town and, blessedly, once again isolated from my colonial masters. They could reach me from Kota Bharu only by crossing the river and, if they had a *tuan besar* on board, the *sampan serangs* (boat men) were conditioned to flash warning signals to the Pasir Mas side to give us advance warning of his approach.

My immediate superiors in Pasir Mas itself, the District Officer (admin boss) and the Superintendent of Police were both charming, unhurried Malays who, without showing the slightest interest in what I was supposed to be doing, looked after me nicely. They gave me a simple Malay house set within a kampong which was itself set within the town boundaries – a sort of up-market ghetto. My warrant was a repetition of the vague authorisation I'd had in Perlis: 'Keep your eyes peeled on south Thailand'. But this time I was given a title – 'Officer-in-charge Special Branch, Pasir Mas', but officer-in-charge of whom? My 'staff' comprised but one Inspector, a local-born Thai, Siddhi Naparawongse, but he nevertheless constituted a 100% increase over Padang Besar. My designation (I was the first officer to hold it) probably caused many an official Malay eyebrow to rise because it implied that I was there to spy on everything that happened in the whole of the land area to the west of the Kelantan river.

They needn't have worried. Free of 'bandits', untroubled by the 'emergency', the state of Kelantan was blissfully peaceful. Kuala Lumpur (KL) was twitchy, not about Kelantan internally, but about the communists who'd fled Malaya to reorganise in south Thailand. Bangkok however saw the Kelantan border area from a different perspective. While losing little sleep over Malayan communists they were actively concerned about the large Malay population living within the Thai province of Pattani immediately to the north of Kelantan. The Thais feared that support for Muslim irredentism in Pattani was coming from Kelantan Malays. It was a standoff, with KL urging Bangkok to wage war against the 'common communist enemy' while Bangkok pressed KL to clamp-down on Kelantan Muslim assistance to irredentists in Pattani. The only gesture towards cooperation was the exchange of police liaison officers: a Malayan officer to Songkla, a Thai to Pasir Mas. Lieutenant San was a diminutive, dull fellow forever prodding me for information I never had but all the same helping me in my continuing Thai studies.

Sungei Golok

I dreaded every trip I made to the Thai border 10 miles away at a squalid, higgledy-piggledy bazaar called Sungei Golok. Its dirt lanes teemed with dogs ferreting about in liquid muck, cripples selling lottery tickets, women and boys selling themselves, barely-weaned youngsters flogging cigarettes, hashish and moonlight 'whisky' and policemen swaggering about in their slim-hipped, bell-bottomed trousers, grotesquely large hats and intimidating hand-guns. Golok smelled badly, it reeked of cheap perfume, wood-smoke, cooking-oil, sewers, incense, body wastes, unmade beds, mosquito repellents, hair grease, bad breath, tobacco, dope, rotting vegetables and uncleaned thunder-boxes. Since even the locals refused to drink water from the standpipes, there was a roaring trade in mineral water and empty bottles. Just as I'd seen in Padang Besar, the Thai government officials in Golok lived off the land; being paid next-to-nothing they took their food, cigarettes, coffee, water and peanuts from hawkers without handing over as much as a satang. Not one of them ever thought of paying for a railway ticket, a trishaw ride or a woman's favour.

The town boasted but one brick and cement building which the locals proudly claimed to be the most up-to-date hotel in south Thailand. Named 'The Southern Cross', for all its much flaunted modernity it offered neither, bar, elevator, veranda, nor anything to justify the description 'bathroom', to say nothing of running water. Conspicuous a place as it was, it was in effect a rowdy, dirty flop-house-cum-brothel, the focal point for gangsters, prostitutes and con men in the hundreds. Every time I returned home from Golok I'd empty a whole tank full of water over me and I'd wash my innards with gallons of water straight from the tap, thankful to live in a relatively clean, wholesome, orderly Malay society. Not that that society was without what Western eyes would regard as blemish. Its *kadis* (religious magistrates) for instance, enforced *khalwat* (a religious law) – which forbade 'close proximity' between unmarried males and females (young male and female pairs could be punished for holding hands in public) and they also enforced the *syariah* (Muslim law), whereby a Malay male had only to repeat the *cantrip talak* three times before a witness to divorce one of his permitted four wives.

As a result many female divorcees found their way into prostitution in the 'Biaritz Park', an open-air beer garden on the outskirts of Kota Bharu with little trysting places hidden among a maze of hedgerows. *Khalwat* was the stock-in-trade of 'Biaritz Park' but an official blind-eye was turned towards it partly because it was owned by prominent Malays (or so it was said), partly because it gave opportunity for the female divorcees to earn a living without displaying themselves on the streets, and partly because the *kadi-kadi* (Muslim judges) wanted to keep up the pretence that there was no such thing as a Malay prostitute. Compared with cant of this nature there was perhaps something to be said for straightforward, unashamed Thai debauchery. But when all was said and done, Kelantan's agreeable, safe and composed little towns were a million miles away from Sungei Golok.

The Tale of the Sultan's Sister

Work? I roamed all over the place talking and listening to anybody who'd listen and talk. Nobody knew anything about 'communists' but they were all sure that 'communists' were Chinese; indeed the Thais officially referred to them a 'Chon Chin' – Chinese criminals. In my 'office' for maybe four or five hours a week, I filled in expense claims and wrote letters home. Then out of the blue I got caught up in a criminal case having nothing to do with intelligence (except of course that you can find a political dimension in everything if you've a mind to). It was the only time in my career that I acted in the role of policeman; the whole whacky business absorbed me totally for a full seven days.

It all began with a hasty summons to lunch with the Chief of Police in Kelantan, Jack Slater, one of the by then dwindling number of old timers, a tall, trim, patrician who was in trouble with the Kelantan royal family, hence also with Kuala Lumpur: for the first time in history the Sultan's Istana had been burgled. The Sultan was outraged not only because millions of ringgits were involved but also because it was patently an inside job. One of his elder sisters had been robbed of several million ringgits worth of jewellery by a thief she herself had named, a Malay, a young stud who'd been servicing the ageing *puteri* (princess) for some time. He, we'll call him 'Mat', was believed to have fled, together with the loot, to the Pattani province of southern Thailand whence he came. Her Highness was never seen outside the Istana; all reports made her out to be an acerbic old bat suffering from an unpleasant urinary complaint. She said unless her precious gems were returned to her *dengan segara* (promptly), she'd blow the whistle on all kinds of scandalous things going on within the Istana. The Sultan had passed the threat on to Jack Slater.

Slater, acting on Kuala Lumpur's instructions, ordered me to drop everything else and go post-haste into south Thailand to induce the local police to catch the thief and recover the booty. Questions about the legality of the involvement proposed for me in a foreign country weren't even mentioned; it being assumed without enquiry that money could silence probes into possible infringement of sovereignty; I was given a few thousand ringgits 'for greasing palms' and told to get on with it.

I'd only to hint of the availability of backsheesh to inspire that usually somnolent police officer, Lieutenant San, to go charging off, with me at his heels, into the Thai town of Narathiwat, a blighted hole on the Pattani coast reputed to be the home of our prey. The feel of a ringgit or two in their hands quickly prompted the local gendarmerie to escort San and I to Mat's Kampong where we learned that we were only about 24 hours behind him.

We were told that he'd made an unhurried call on the kampong, picked up a favourite female and departed. To our astonishment, a slap-dash search of his girlfriend's house uncovered, beneath a pillow, a broach in which sat a diamond as big as a Narathiwat mosquito. From an illustrated list I'd been given back in Kota Bharu we quickly identified the fabulous bauble as one of our jilted *puteri's* most prized treasures. We'd only been on the trail a couple of days and we'd already recovered many a thousand ringgits worth of the swag. To add to our excitement and high hopes, we picked up a photo of Mat's 'amorosa', one Halimah, a lady whose beauty, shining through the grainy portrait, took our breath away. No wonder Mat had swapped his sour old *puteri* for Halimah.

It was now a case of *cherchez la femme* and a *femme* so exquisite that, even in a country as generously populated with comely femmes as Thailand was, she'd stand out. San and I set off in high spirits for that familiar, wicked town to which we'd been told Mat had made tracks – Haadyai. The news that I had ringgits in my pocket acted upon the Thai police in Haadyai like electric energisers. Within hours a hot tip sent San and I hurrying to catch the midnight train to Nakorn Sri Tamarath where we alighted into the first cool, minutes after dawn. Alongside Nakorn, a seedy dump with a reputation for violent criminality, Chicago was a Quaker settlement. We looked down upon a sprawling, filthy market-place already alive with peasants loaded down with their vendibles and within minutes thereafter with a flood of peddlers, hucksters, muggers, pimps and spivs each bent on swindling the other.

Because every market madam seemed to be about to sell pork, it wasn't the setting in which to expect the appearance of the Muslim Mat, still less his gorgeous Halimah. Yet there breezing through the squalor in high heels came that stunning, unforgettably shapely, beauty herself and, for an even greater wonder, on one of her fingers she flashed for all the world to see one of the old *puteri's* emerald-studded rings. Before you could say 'Mat' we'd seized several thousand ringgits worth of jewellery. Much more was found in their trysting place and Mat was clapped in irons within the hour.

The *puteri* repossessed about two-thirds of her jewellery, leaving perhaps a million ringgits worth at Mat's disposal. Some of it must have gone to his lawyer; there are no prizes for guessing where the rest of it went: suffice to say that Mat 'escaped' from jail.

Jack Slater was elated, the Sultan relieved, San in pocket, Kuala Lumpur soothed and the *puteri* – who knows? Neither do I know what became of the dazzling Halimah.

No sooner was I back in Pasir Mas than I was summoned once more to Songkla, this time to take my elementary Thai language exam at the British Consulate. For a couple of hours in one of the Consul's fine rooms, a Thai professor from the Bangkok embassy put questions to me in simple, correct Thai and chattered away with me in the lingo of the streets of Haadyai, had me write down the alphabet (a long list of consonants, vowel signs, tone indicators and typographical symbols) and tested me in the use of a Thai dictionary. Finally, he invited me to read a newspaper. The course of my family's life depended upon the outcome. I expected, gloomily, to be told that I'd have to wait while the results were passed to

KL but bless his lack of socks, cotton or otherwise, the professor there and then awarded me a pass. I'd made good in the very first Thai language exam held in the Consulate: the Consul, a charmer named Whittaker, laid on a celebratory libation. I went home feeling smug.

KL telegraphed Kota Bharu with good news in triplicate! (a) I was confirmed in my colonial commission, (b) I was given six months leave; and (c) on my return from the UK, DMF, Christopher, Jane and I would live in the choicest of all stations in Malaya – the island of Penang. My cup runneth over. I'd escaped from the ghetto for good, I'd broken through the class barrier. I was a somebody!

Wayangs and Layangs, Waengs and Washbasins

Drowsy and down-beat it may have been, but compared with Bahau and Padang Besar, Pasir Mas was a rampageous, sinful metropolis. There were few nights, for example when a *wayang kulit* troupe wasn't in town. *Wayang kulit* (which translates into 'skin theatre' but which emphatically doesn't mean what it does in the west) was a sort of movie that preceded Hollywood by several centuries, an entertainment that had a particular fascination for the Malays of south Thailand and Kelantan. All you the viewer had to do was sit on the earth in front of a grubby cotton sheet stretched between two trees with its lower edge on the floor. You'd watch the shadows of figures thrown by lanterns from behind the screen and manipulated out of sight by two or three puppeteers. For me however it was always more fun to watch from the wrong side of the screen where the ancient strollers (they always seemed to be old men) chanted time-worn fables, animating their stories by moving a cast of brilliantly coloured puppets against the back of the screen.

Wayang kulit was itinerant theatre; the mummers carried its props from place to place on their backs. Its repertoire was more limited even than that of D'Oyley Carte, the players' choice being restricted to a few sacred scripts, not a single word of which, nor a single puppet movement, was ever changed. The puppets themselves were made from animal hides (hence the name kulit – skin) and slivers of bamboo.

Performers, Every One

While *wayang kulit* didn't play every night, the wayang gambar (picture theatre) was open every day except Friday, the Muslim Sabbath. The Pasir Mas 'cinema' was no 1930s Odeon but, rather, a large, elongated, unpainted wooden hut with a bare-earth floor. At one end there hung a screen made up of once-white cotton sheets sewn together while at the other there stood a film projector old enough to have cranked out silent movies. Admission came in three grades: (i) for free you could take your chance on the weather and stand outside (the walls were but waist high) (ii) for 10 cents you sat under cover on rough-wood planks; and (iii) for 15 cents you sat on the same rough-wood planks but up on the 'balcony', a rickety gallery reached by way of a shaky ladder.

Sadly, certain species within Pasir Mas' vast range of different breeds of insect knew nothing about class differences. Indeed, I'd say that the worst of them preferred what was on offer upstairs. Because of that, one went to the cinema dressed for the jungle: trousers tucked into high boots, shirt sleeve down, collar up, hands in pockets and mosquito repellent at the ready. Even thus attired however the films were seldom good enough to take minds away from the squadrons of flying, crawling, marching, chewing pests which besieged the hapless patrons. To say nothing about the whirrings and clankings of the old magic lantern style projector; one could hardly follow the sound-track for the drumbeat of hands slapping exposed skin.

The films themselves weren't up to much either; they'd either have been turned out on low budgets in Indonesia or on the absurd extravaganza conveyer belt in Bollywood. Now and then though houses would be packed night after night for films starring Malaya's very own movie megastar: P. Ramlee who in the manner of most Asian leading men, was an overweight idol whose acting out-hammed any Western trouper ever to appear on screen.

Like the rest of his photogenic race however, Ramlee was a natural actor; indeed the whole Malay people, man, woman and child, can be seen as one single, gigantic repertory company; every one of them a tragedian, a beauty, a buffoon, villain, hero, heroine, jester, prima donna, hoofer, acrobat, ballerina or clown. The *wayang kulit* players, of whom I've already written, were perhaps the best exemplars; their job was to manipulate puppets and orate their lines while remaining hidden from view yet they threw themselves about as if they faced footlights and a packed auditorium. Watching Ramlee, you forgot the marauding fleas, flies and ticks – what greater tribute could be paid him?

Skin Houses

Thai cinemas (skin houses) were more memorable than the fleapit of Pasir Mas. Thai bugs weren't as baneful as their Kelantan cousins but you had to be alert to other distractions; the need, for instance, to be sharp on your feet as soon as the very first bar of the national anthem rasped out of the sound system at the start of every performance. Vigilante-cum-spies were present, their eyes peeled for the tardy. Anyone slow to rise to the hosanna – especially 'chinamen' – would be up before the local police chief in minutes accused of failing to show due homage to the monarch, a transgression that cost the offender a hefty fine.

When the lights dimmed to leave only proven Chakri (Thai royal family) worshippers in the cinema, what came over the loudspeakers, no matter whether the film had been made in Manila or Maharashtra, Liechtenstein or Lapland, what came over with a clarity that few sound-tracks could equal was a rich, melodic voice that sang or spoke in Thai. To make sure that no subversion was aired in a foreign tongue the Thai government made it obligatory that the sound-track of every foreign film be silenced in favour of the voice of a Thai actor who, live over a microphone in the projection room, dubbed every word of the script in the language of the motherland.

Flowers of the Sky

Nobody could fly *layang-layang* (kites) higher or more deftly than Kelantan Malays. Times were when the blue sky above Palekbang sparkled with brilliantly hued planets sailing the heavens.

They'd soar through space at the whim of small brown children or venerable sages down below; they'd glide, coast, skim, sweep, flow, swirl, skate, dive, soar and whoop. Or else they'd hover, poised in the glassy blue firmament like outsize, oddly shaped and coloured daylight stars. Their tails, sometimes 40–50 metres long, flashed in the sun's rays as if they were diamond necklaces worn by the Gods or they'd appear to burst into flames like the elongated fire-crackers you'd see hanging on high at Chinese New Year.

Voyeurism – Kelantan Style

Every January Kelantan was swept by extra-heavy storms, an unusual variation in a country that otherwise knew no seasons. Because of this Kota Bharu in January was Peeping-Tom time. Flood waters turned the town's five-foot ways into fast-flowing streams. Malay females, for 11 months of the year hidden from neck-to-toe behind voluminous-albeit subtly revealing – cotton cloth, were obliged as they tripped along the sidewalks to hike their sarongs up to their brown kneecaps. The shopfronts were then crowded with males hoping for cloudbursts and the consequential, rare, glimpse of a well-turned female ankle and calf.

Know Your Enemy!

That fearless, impatient, arch-enemy of 'communism', Gerald Templer, brought anti-red 'experts' into Malaya by the plane-load. 'Psyops' people, old-China hands, historians, spiritualists, philosophers, shrinks, Adam Smithites, PR men and, of course, spooks. One of the latter, billed by our Resident as 'an authority on international communism', came one day to Kota Bharu. His objective was to enlighten the 20 or 30 civil servants who, in one capacity or another, ran Kelantan, on the answer to Templer's incessant question: "What makes the enemy tick?" Sworn to secrecy before our visitor had opened his mouth, we sat in tremulous expectation of being let in on the dark secrets that lay behind our enemy's exploitable weaknesses. What we got however was a crude recitation about the vileness of all 'reds': they were gangsters ganging up in an international conspiracy to extinguish Western civilisation and belief in God. *Readers' Digest* stuff, it would have been beneath the average political awareness of boy scouts. And, afterwards, nobody challenged the cheap propaganda we'd been insulted by.

The Purple, Putrid Nutrient

Kelantan smelled wholesomely of the sea, blossoms, perfumes, steaming rice, kite varnish, palm oil, coconut-milk curries and babies. But, alas, in parts it also stank of the rotting corpses of little fish slowly putrefying in some sort of vinegar. Vapours to set the senses reeling wafted from open-topped barrels filled with a mixture called belachan, a seasoning concocted by dumping tiny marine animals into barrels of a kind of formaldehyde the origins of which essence it was best not to enquire into. After combusting in containers in the oven of the tropical outdoors for weeks, if not months on end, what eventually came out was an unhealthy-appearing, purple paste whose stink pained the sinuses but whose protein integrant, according to distinguished nutritionists, was sky-high. A dash of belachan over a bowl of rice, the dietitians said, and you needed no further nourishment for that day at least.

Waeng

Up until the day when Lieutenant San came to tell me that there'd been gunfire at Waeng, nobody on our side had ever heard of the place. According to San, having been harassed by 'Chinese bandits from Malaya', the citizens of Waeng had taken up their shotguns and driven them out. Pointing to a place on the map that indicated only dense jungle, to my surprise he offered to take me there.

We alighted from the train at a wayside halt about an hour west of Golok and there and then, as is the Thai custom at any time of day, we adjourned to a restaurant to eat. Restaurant? It was in fact a one-table coffee shop, easily the muckiest I'd ever been in. Following the maxim (the grubbier the estaminet the choicer the food) that particular *kedai* would have earned 'Cordon Bleu' status and indeed it served magnificent Chinese fare. Moreover, it entertained its customers to a, albeit grisly, cabaret staged smack in the middle of its only table: a flycatcher of diabolical design. The device provided a non-stop show (the trapping and demise of a hundred flies a minute)' which besides keeping the diners enthralled, took their minds of the squalor of their surroundings.

Fortified by our repast, San and I set off on bicycles along a well-worn track to a village the sight of which restored my faith in the Thais for unlike their hideous townships, all was tranquil, beautiful, unspoiled. We spent the night undisturbed in the village school, a rough and ready place with half-walls of untreated planking, a thatched roof, earth floor and furniture that had been hammered together on the spot. But for all its simplicity, it was a true centre of learning. At dawn the next day San and I mounted an elephant (elephants were used in the logging business) and, one on each side of the beast, we rode into Waeng like maharajahs.

No maharajah however, would have ever set foot in Waeng. Little more than a logging camp, it had grown into permanence without acquiring the frills that usually go with settlements; things like running water, pit-latrines, streets, shops and so on. It was a gloomy, scruffy, all-male enclave deep within the forest. A posse of Thai police sent from Yala with the purpose, San said, of slaying the 'communist trespassers', was billeted in a one-room shack into which San and I were invited for food and for a 'briefing'. There being no furniture of any sort, we sat cross-legged on a plank floor raised about half a metre above the slime below, there to listen to a baby-faced Thai police captain detail his plan of action. With all the drama of Olivier's Henry V oration before Agincourt, the captain told his braves that the honour of the nation rested upon their wiping out the alien intruders.

There we were, 20 of us huddled in a small, open hut. A hand-grenade through the door would have taken the lot of us out but, since I was there only as an observer, I didn't dare say so. At the end of the captain's peroration, the patrol, dressed for beat-duty in a town rather than for jungle bashing, lined up outside. They wore their everyday dun-coloured uniforms ablaze with polished metal buttons, belt buckles, whistles and with strips of red ribbon, topping it all with their monstrous peaked caps with their enormous badges glistening in the sunlight. Their feet were shod in black shoes that looked as if they were made of cardboard. They were armed with World War I rifles, cotton ammunition bandoliers circa Pancho Villa and they carried metal water bottles and mess tins. Spare ammo and first aid kits they lugged along in cheap suitcases, the sort that used to be used by people booking into Blackpool boarding houses. In short, they could hardly have been more badly prepared for an expedition into the jungle.

Away they went, marching parade-ground fashion in single file, buttons, buckles, water bottles and mess tins clanking loudly enough to be heard a mile away. The 'Chinese bandits' could hear them approaching long before they came in sight and they'd fade quietly into their jungle cover (to hide in the jungle meant moving only a pace or two). It was as if I were watching the filming of a Thai version of a Keystone Cops movie. Within 50–100 metres of entering the real jungle, half of the patrol would have lost its shoes, they'd be struggling to hold on to their hats, thorns would have torn their bandoliers spilling bullets into the mud and leeches would have made them bleed as if they'd been ambushed. I suspected that it was all for show, that after keeping to the logging track for half an hour hardly getting his shoes wet, the captain would sit down for a smoke and a chin-wag before returning to Waeng, then to Yala where he'd proclaim that he'd seen the bandits off. That's what I'd have done in his place.

Footlights, Fisticuffs and Fortune-tellers

Every sizeable Thai town had its nightly, all-year round, fairground. And every fairground had its boxing ring within whose ropes trim, slight young boys would dance around pretending to land punches on each other. They'd scowl menacingly, grunt with feigned anger, fling gloved fists at each other's faces, and kick with bare feet, seldom landing either glove or toe on one another. In between rounds they'd prostrate themselves in prayer – a piece of theatre as much as part of the show as the fake fighting. The onlookers, well-versed in the art, looked not for blood but for the ballet dancing complemented with more than a dash of sanctimony.

Every fair too had its brightly illuminated 'Ramvong' arena, a sort of boxing ring within whose ropes pairs of the opposite sex would glide around each other in much the same way as the boxers did. The air above the tilting ground was thick with sensuousness but, like the boxers, the dancers touched each other with not so much as a finger.

Then again there'd usually be a stage upon which a heavily Siamese version of the 'Ramayana' would be played out. At one point in that seemingly unending epic, a small figure – that of a child surely – covered from head to toe in a monkey costume with beatific face and long, curly tail, would race across and around the stage like a demented acrobat. From the left of the stage, a flamboyantly painted actor enters, sprouting a metre-long beak and magnificent wings, wings he'd flap so furiously they'd threaten to blow the footlights out. The monkey would leap on to the bird's back, and with an extra flash of the wings, they'd be away. Hanuman had flown to Sri Lanka to rescue Siva from Ravana.

For ten satangs you could have your future read by seers who, for an extra ten, would give you a cigarette and a light or a pinch of opium, hear your confession and offer a prayer for you. Five-satang-a-time lotteries offered the chance of a Portuguese passport, a weekend in Rome, a bottle of sure-fire cure for the pox, dinner with Elvis Presley, one of Marilyn Monroe's toe nail clippings or a trip to Mars at some unspecified time in the future.

Hooch was on sale by the gallon, grass by the bushel; pickpockets were as thick as mosquitoes. Oil flares and kerosene lamps were almost as plentiful as electric lights, all adding to the already suffocating heat as well as to the overriding tension caused by fear of the whole shebang going up in flames. But, said the Thais, the Lord Buddha made sure that it never did.

Mod Cons of the Day

Even when compared with the rest of southern Thailand's awful towns, Narathiwat was a cesspool. Its sole redeeming feature being that it didn't stretch very far: once clear of the short reach of slurry that was its main thoroughfare and you were back in the endless landscape of green, undefiled rusticity. I had the misfortune to have to stay overnight in its 'Hotel Narathiwat', a rickety, unpainted vermin trap that paid me the honour of housing me in its 'deluxe suite': "Our estimable police chief reserved our number one salon for you, Sire; all mod-cons for you, Excellency; nothing will be too much trouble to serve you with; our noble police chief will take care of every expense".

But my splendid chambers turned out to be a small wooden box whose walls and floor, in the particular manner of all hotel bedrooms in southern Thailand, were scarred by a zillion cigarette burns. Maybe the southern Thais couldn't bear to see a square inch of unblemished, albeit dead, timber? The room's furniture was a chair and a string charpoy with a sleeping mat rather than a mattress; the mat was a blessing because if offered less space for bugs than a mattress. Over the bed was hung the ubiquitous well-soiled, yellowish, well-holed mosquito net. But what did we have in one corner? Was it the deluxe element? It was nothing less than a genuine porcelain hand-basin made in Paisley, Scotland and sporting taps marked 'HOT' and 'COLD'. Regrettably however, nothing but cockroaches came out of either faucet which was just as well since the appliance lacked both plug and waste-pipe. Still, it was a nice touch and, after all, the management had promised that only "our VIP room is equipped with hot and cold taps", nothing about water.

The establishment boasted only one, unisex, 'comfort room', a sentry-box perched at the end of a wobbly, jetty running above a wide, swiftly flowing river carrying so much silt that it looked like a gush of cocoa. The end of the box facing the hotel had a door but on the riverside it was open to the gaze of passing boat people. The requisite aperture in the floor had been made by the simple act of removing the central plank and it was through that hole that one deposited one's waste matter into the chocolate stream swirling underneath. While running the depth of the sentry box, the orifice, above which one crouched was but 30 mm wide; your balance and your aim had to be good. Evidence a plenty showed that many of the hotel's customers hadn't been on target. For cleansing yourself you lowered a bucket on a rope to drag up water from the river below.

The End of Act One

What I remember about the end of my first three-year tour of Malaya is the exterior of a house I had lived in, doors and windows flung wide to admit beauty to those inside, enabling them to drink in the warmth, scent, and lazy, lovely languor of that sublime country. I recall a Malay *pantun* (quatrain): 'One can pay back a loan of gold but one dies forever in the debt of those who are kind to you'.

Reflections I
Chief Inspector Tambiah, Malayan Railways

The Chief Inspector, Malayan Railways, Prai (the station for Penang) was a big, boot-polish black, billiard-bald Singhalese who, difficult as it was to imagine him as anything other than a massively commanding presence, had been brought to Malaya as a baby. Without its railway station Padang Besar would have had no reason to exist; every soul in the village depended upon its trains. Ergo, when in residence, Tambiah was the Grand Mogul of Padang Besar. The bazaar was a different place when Tambiah was around; it was quieter, more orderly; all of us residents acted as if we too and not simply the railway terminus were being inspected. The coffee shop was cleaned up, platform casinos were suspended, the smugglers conducted their illicit deals out of sight, the Rest House keeper, Ah Seng (a railway employee) stayed off the samsu (alcohol) – though not the opium – the trains ran dead on time and, in order that the great sahib might bathe in light, the electric generator rumbled on for an extra half-hour.

But of course, there wasn't much for the Nawab of the Railway to inspect. After he'd paid his respects to Sathien, checked the station master's accounts, held court over the railway staff and spun the giant turntable like a Las Vegas croupier, he'd retire to the rest house to gather his strength for tennis. Ah Seng, who was normally too high on dope and booze to cook even a noodle without turning it into an inedible mush, would produce for Tambiah and Tambiah's chosen guest, a curry of a potency and delicacy as would have delighted the tastebuds of the most finicky Maharajah. Once having feasted, the huge man, who was covered head-to-toe in the whitest of white robes-de-chambre and looking for all the world like a great Oriental potentate, would settle back in his chaise-lounge and hold forth on the glories of Indian culture and the wonders of railways.

I last saw him on a September morn in 1953. Having been alerted over his railway signals network that I was travelling on the down train to Prai and then to Kuala Lumpur from where I was to fly to England on leave, there he was filling the station platform at Prai – the Emperor Jones, the Lord of Prai, huge hands clasped before him in namaste, first in greeting then in farewell and, in between these two gestures, to hand me a letter of introduction to some friends of his in Colombo: "Just in case you are having time to spare in my humble birthplace, isn't it?"

Thai Police Captain Choob Chinprayoora

At first sight you'd have sworn that Captain Choob was an actor playing the part of the obese, slant-eyed, oily, sadistic Oriental four-flusher in a 'B' movie about low-life in Chicago or New York. Upon better acquaintance you'd have known that Choob was not acting at all; he was 100% the real McCoy except that he was in Sadao, Thailand, not New York, America. He was so repulsive that I had to steel myself for my monthly visit to his headquarters. My stomach heaved every time I pressed a 500 ringgit bribe into his sweaty palm, into a hand so small that it seemed not to belong to so gross a person.

It happened that on one of these monthly pay days I entered the station just as he was personally engaged in the interrogation of a small, thin Chinese fellow who'd come all the way from Bangkok, he'd said, to visit an old friend. Unfortunately for him he'd failed first of all to pay his respects (meaning I suspect his bribe) to Choob. Consequently, the Captain was practising Thai boxing on him except that, instead of kicking with bare feet, Choob was lashing out with heavy boots. Not in the slightest embarrassed by my intrusion, Choob turned away from the bloodletting to welcome me, palm his 500 and signal to his underlings to carry on with the 'questioning'.

I loathed Choob. He was the personification not of the Oriental hoodlum but of the bullies of any race who are attracted to law-and-order outfits – 'security forces' – all over the world. Choob wore the menacing insignia of the 'Aswin'; a vulgarly whacking great ring by which he demonstrated that he belonged to a mafia whose Godfather was General Pao, the boss of the Thai police. As an 'Aswin' Choob was bonded to the villainous Pao, whose oft expressed oath of being 'sworn to the death of communism' made him beloved of Washington. Every corridor of power in the world had its General Pao, its would-be General Pao and its 'Aswins'. And there are always plenty of Choobs or would-be Choobs, gangsters cloaked in the varied uniforms of their establishments be they liveries, dhotis, pyjamas, regimentals, sarongs, burnooses or business suits; parasites more than ready to do the bidding of the world's Paos.

A Knighthood for the Porter

Sure of its masses' unshakeable faith in Buddhism, the Thai regnancy did not outlaw the evangelism of other religions and the celebration of foreign festivals, especially that of the Western New Year. The night of 31 December 1951 saw Haadyai en fête, sparkling with illuminations the most brilliant of which shone in the forecourt of the Railway Hotel, site of the grand, open-air festivity to which the town's notables and the guests flocked in all their finery. Drab as the work-a-day uniforms worn by Thai civil servants were, put them in full-dress and, sartorially at least, they were second to none anywhere in the world. Every public official was costumed, the higher the rank the more polychromatic the display of rainbow colours slashed across ivory whites. And, not to be outshone, those who paid rather than received government wages showed themselves off in magenta and cadmium orange dinner jackets while all the ladies flaunted the gaudiest, riches, most prismatic of Thai silks. The army wore cobalt green, the police midnight blue. Customs officers swaggered in quince yellow, sanitary inspectors in burgundy, but railwaymen, the bottom of the pile, in relatively anaemic beige.

'Mae Kong whisky' flowed by the gallon while an appealing little orchestra, impatient with waiting to blast out 'Auld Lang Syne', kept repeating 'Bye Bye Blackbird' and 'Home on the Range'. It was a dazzling scene. But shining through the incandescence like a glow-worm on a moonless night was the figure of a tall, pale, 'po-faced', round-eyed, middle-aged fellow in the dress uniform of a railway porter. It wasn't the beige tunic that made the porter stand out, nor yet the breathtaking brilliance of the wide marigold sash he wore across his chest. No, that radiant ribbon was but the backing for a flashing great orb that, on enquiry, turned out to be the illustrious Hellenic decoration: 'Star of Orange Nassau'.

Behind the star stood the 40-year-old offspring of an early 20th century liaison between a British Consul in Songkla and a Thai housemaid. The Consul had made off a couple of score years ago leaving our infant hero to be absorbed into Thai society, an assimilation the boy, then the man, had worked at all his life without quite ever achieving it. He had never married. During the Japanese occupation he'd been distressed by the sight of the soldiers' brutality towards a number of Dutch colonialists brought over from Java and imprisoned in a squalid camp hear Haadyai's railway station, where he worked as a porter. Looking on the white prisoners as kith and kin, for years he risked his life supplying them with little things like aspirin tablets, phials of quinine, a few eggs, needles and thread, pencils and dried fish. At the end of the war a grateful Hellenic Queen bestowed upon him a Knighthood in the order of Orange Nassau.

In Holland he'd have been a 'Sir' but here in Haadyai, as the year turned into 1952, he was just plain 'Nai' (Mr.), a mere railway porter. He took me into his pokey, grubby, one-room quarter in a slummy barrack behind the station and there he showed me yellowed Thai and Dutch newspaper cuttings telling of the ceremony at which he'd been knighted, on behalf of the Queen of Holland, by her Ambassador to the Thai court in Bangkok. Ever since that day, he said, he'd been saving every ticul he could in the hope that one day in, perhaps, 20 years time, he'd fly to the Hague to meet his Queen in her palace, a palace from which, as a Knight, he couldn't be excluded.

In the meantime that large, gentle, unlikely knight still clung to the hope that his father would come to Haadyai one day, gather him into his arms and take him 'home'. After all, he said, his mother had told him over and over again that his father was a good man who loved him dearly. Surely then, as soon as the old man retired from the diplomatic service (our hero accepted that as long as he was a diplomat his father could never acknowledge a child born out of wedlock to a Thai servant girl), as soon as he'd retired to his country seat in the home counties then, surely, this 'good man' would send for his 'beloved' child? I wished him a Happy New Year.

Smoothly and happily restored as a family unit (but oh what a risk we'd taken) DMF, Christopher, Jane and I spent the mainly wintry months between September 1953 and March 1954 in south England. We got to know each other all over again and prepared to go as a family into what promised to be an offbeat future.

And so, in the spring of 1954 we set off to make a home for ourselves in Penang, me by air, the others aboard one of those floating legends of empire – the P&O steamship *HMS Canton*.

Penang – Francis Light's Island

The night mail from Kuala Lumpur pulled into Prai just before dawn giving me time to catch the first ferry of the day to Penang Island. It was a moment to marvel at the way in which chance had smiled upon my family and me, moving us from grey, cold northern skies to blue heavens and perpetual warmth. It was a time too to reflect upon the generosity of the good folk of Malaya who were paying us to live among them and not the other way about. The self-acclaimed 'Jewel of the Orient', Penang is a small island lying in a warm, usually languid, brownish-coloured sea about three miles off the Malayan mainland. Small as it was exhibited within its shores was a surprisingly large pattern of imperial life: columned official buildings, an imposing Residency, a racecourse, clubs (of course), the ruins of a fort held together only by age and fungus, and a cemetery littered with the Empire's funerary statutory. It was a bustling, sweltering town beyond whose wide boulevards lined with flowering trees, lay miles and miles of clean, empty, sandy beaches. And crowning it all like an emerald tiara, stood Penang Hill whose peak could be reached in a mere half-hour by way of a funicular railway that glided smoothly upwards through layers of jungle to set you down at the top of a green upland 2,500 ft above the hot, teeming city.

From the summit you gazed across the green woodland over the city of Georgetown (there's a name with the ring of Empire for you!) and the sweep of the harbour on to Kedah Peak rising above the mainland background; a panorama that made it hard to suppress a sneaking feeling of pride in the old Empire and in its builders. Because you knew that beyond Kedah lay Hong Kong, Australia, Fiji, Canada, Jamaica, Nigeria, the Sudan and on to Burma and India. At that height, with that view and with those sort of, to me, subversive thoughts going through my mind it was harder still to stifle a yearning to throw myself into the Empire's panoply, authority, romance and adventure.

The harbour swarmed with gleaming passenger liners, dirty little coasters, fishing smacks, ferry-boats, sampans, brown-sailed junks, sleek yachts, barges, pilot boats and rusty tankers. Cheek-by-jowl with bicycle, coffee and jewellery shops were the quiet courtyards of mosques and temples. Whiteway-Laidlaw, a name redolent of the Raj, had a store there; so did De Silva, Wassiamull Assomull (textiles) Best Palaycat (sarongs), Jacobsen van der Berg, Joo Keng (grocers) and the Penang-Sumatra Mee Fong Co. Trishaws, hand-carts, buffalo-carts and bicycles bearing phenomenal loads, shared the streets with trolley-buses, taxis and private cars.

A mean temperature of 27°C, humidity of 80–90%, plus regular rainfall made for evergreen landscapes, fungi, waterfalls, immaculate lawns, orchids, palms, coconuts, cloves, cannas and snapdragons to be enjoyed by as cosmopolitan a population as could be found anywhere.

It was a watercolour of a place, a serene, tropical haven. We were all excited; the children's minds still awhirl with fresh memories of the gully-gully man at Port Said, the grandeur of de Lesseps' canal, Egyptian boys diving after coins at Suez, the Red Sea, the old woman's shoe-house in Bombay, dolphins dancing and flying fish flying. Waiting for us at the once-grand, now broken-down, entrance to our home lay the newest member of the family: a skinny, spider-legged, brown mongrel who, like Boss in Padang Besar, had been in occupation awaiting our arrival and who, again like Boss, had chosen to stay in residence. 'Rusty' was a highly impressionable creature. Smitten on first sight with the three new Hardys and with our equally spindle-legged 'housekeeper', Hui Boon Hua, and his studious daughter, she was bewitched above all with our little Morris Minor, one glance at the little green automobile and Rusty, a car freak if ever there was one, lived only to ride in it.

Imposing as it was from a distance, standing proudly with its back to the sea and its forecourt extending into gardens, our 'residence' had seen better days. Termites and brine-laden air had taken their toll; indeed the bottom half of the establishment had been closed off as being unsafe for habitation. The family may have travelled first-class in the manner of Empire builders of old but its first residence in the colonies fell a long way short of what the old-timers would have put up with. But, thrilled to bits with everything else around us, and having been promised a brand new house soon, the five of us settled in, in high old spirits.

Red Ants, Gods and Enche Kabin

The photos taken at the time tell of heat, pleasure, beauty and, surprisingly since Penang was the second city in a country in a 'state of emergency', of peace and security. Our windows were wide open day and night, our gardens were unfenced, we (later) rode around in an open-topped car, we tramped in forest and on beaches alike, we carried nothing as lethal as a Malacca-cane, and we were scared only by red ants, jelly-fish and falling coconuts. We'd already been, or regularly were still given shots and boosters against cholera, small-pox, dysentery, elephantiasis, jiggers, enteric fever, flukes, hepatitis, leprosy, typhoid, worms and yellow fever and we were warned to take precautions against prickly heat, rabies, dengue fever, rashes, sea-snakes and crutch rot. (The treatment for crutch rot was gentian violet, a remedy that, by painting the genitals a vivid violet, put a damper on romance).

Wide-eyed and bare-footed, we slid through the towering doors of the monumental Buddhist temple on Anson Road into a cavernous chamber in the centre of which, beneath sparkling chandeliers and flanked by disciples, sat a massive, gold Gautama. To either side of him were black-wood offering tables from whose holy vessels incense swirled, like the eternal flames at the burial grounds of unknown soldiers. Worshippers threw dried mango seeds to decide, according to which side finished uppermost on landing, which horoscope they'd need.

We gaped at the behemoth reclining Buddha – many times larger than life – in the Sri Lankan temple; then at the bodhi tree in the *wat* (temple) in Green Lane; at the coloured glass balls, beads, lanterns and winged deities in the Hindu shrines; at the hundreds of drugged serpents dozing in miasmic clouds of smoke at the 'Snake Temple' (a cruel fraud that); at little birds trained on payment of a cent or two to their Kapo to flip tarot cards over to tell fortunes; at medicine men on the five-foot way offering vials of a dark liquid ('tiger's blood') or wafer-thin slivers of pelt ('dried Korean bear's skin') either of which physic at 50 ("Well then, 40...30...20...15!") cents a time was guaranteed to cure rinderpest, warts, gripe, the common cold, 'women's troubles' and the bends; and at dark, stocky little folk who'd come all the way from Nepal to sit on the five-foot way selling coloured stones, miniscule gewgaws, and tiny carved figures. On the busy five-foot way we also drank lurid green syrup poured over the scrapings from large slabs of ice wrapped in dirty gunny sacks.

We stuffed ourselves with *enche kabin* (curried fried chicken), laksa, with the pungency of curried brimstone, satay (sizzling at almost every street corner at two cents a stick – the price including a dip in a bowl of spicy, sweet sauce) *kuey teow*, ikan kering, nasi goreng, nasi briani, birds' nests and a cornucopia of fruits including the local speciality – the small, succulent *pisang mas* (golden banana). And we drooled over *eu chow kueh*, a golden crisp fritter that looked like two croissants fused together, a fusion said to represent the coupling of a Chinese emperor and a favourite concubine. That morsel of edible pornography was delivered, appropriately hot, every morning by a man riding a bicycle and singing "*Eu chow kueh*! *Eu chow kueh*!" Seldom were we without Magnolia ice-cream, we drank 'Boh' tea and on the esplanade, we chewed salted peanuts sold in twists of newspaper by a large, jovial Sikh.

Senor Montana and Groceries

We bought a junior-sized violin for Christopher and to teach him to play it we engaged one Senor Montana who held his classes in a cubicle in a Chinese school. While Montana taught the violin, the school-teachers, intrigued to find a small 'round-eyed' boy in their company, gave Christopher extra-tutorial instruction in the appreciation of *dim-sum* (tit-bits) sold from stalls outside their common room. Montana was a Filipino – not much of a surprise since it seemed that his race had been chosen by the Almighty to be minstrels to all the rest of Southeast Asia; wherever you went in the region you'd find Filipino music-makers, conductors, tutors, cymbalists, hurdy-gurdyists, ballad-mongers and hep-cats. At Chinese funerals in Haadyai for instance you'd find Filipino ensembles playing 'Home Sweet Home' and 'She'll be Coming Round the Mountain'; Filipino dance-bands played in the leading hotels in Kuala Lumpur and Filipino baritones sang Handel's Messiah in Hong Kong. Anyway, there came the day when Christopher stood on the stage of the Chung Hua Middle School's concert hall to play a violin solo. Looking on from the wings his cherubic tutor, Maestro Montana, beamed as if he'd turned out a new Paganini. Then the Maestro himself, resplendent in white dinner jacket, a spot light bouncing off his baldpate, swept through a cello solo with all the panache of Rostaprovich. Another of his pupils, a Chinese youth, played on a solid silver flute so precious that he handled it wearing white silk gloves. The house being overwhelmingly Chinese, the smash hit of the evening, by a mile, was the flautist.

Penang embraced us with her damp heat and she breathed into us her oils, spices, saltpetre, charcoal, tin, garlands and incense. She could be relied on; at the same time every day of the year the sun leaped out of the sea like a stingray only to fall like a stone behind Penang Hill at about 1845 hrs. In her darkness we kicked phosphorescence from her seaside sands, the sparks flying as though we were fire-walking; we watched *bunga rajas* open and change colour like vegetable chameleons; listened to the chatter of geckos and cicadas and the unwelcome drone of mosquitoes; and we saw fire-flies flash like Catherine-wheels.

Not surprisingly then, for most of the time it seemed that we were on a never-ending vacation. But that wasn't so. Penang was as much our home as Kirkby and Worthing had been. We slept under our very own roof; we had our downs as well as our ups; mostly we ate not birds' nests and *kuey teow* but boiled eggs, cornflakes, baked beans and mashed potatoes; Christopher and Jane went to school; we had an account at the Chartered Bank; a local Chinese optician prescribed Christopher's first glasses; Jane went to a Chinese dentist; we played monopoly as well as mahjong; went to the pictures; borrowed library books; Rusty was vaccinated against rabies and wore a medal to prove it; and DMF was paid 50 cents per column inch for articles she wrote for the *Straits Echo*.

Work at the Border

And of course daily I went to an office (I was about to say that I went to work but that'd be stretching it a bit). I was allocated a share in a two-desk office at police headquarters, given a straight-backed chair behind a rickety, badly-stained table that was passed off as a desk and introduced to my 'Secretary', a pallid, raw-boned, chain-smoking, sourpuss who, after years of colonial experience knew every trick in the bureaucrats' book. Hyper-sensitive to the public's tendency to co-relate the status of the 'Secretary' to that of his/her official, my secretary –

the grave robber – transformed me in a flash from a second-rater to a
big-shot 'executive'. Before you could say 'red-tape' she came up with
much of the paraphernalia associated with the senior desk wallah: 'IN'
and 'OUT' trays, a desk calendar (to make sure that you didn't work on
Empire Day) a copy of colonial regulations (which told you when and
where to wear a sword) blotters, directories, pencils, bottles of ink, pen
nibs, writing paper, pencil sharpeners, erasers, a bell for summoning
peons to bring tea, ashtrays and blocks of wood, small stones, old fly-
wheels and bits of brick to use as paperweights, vital to retain order
when sitting under a ceiling fan and in front of open windows. The
trouble was that she couldn't find me any real work to do. From what
I'd learned from my first three years of colonial service I had to rely on
finding my own ways of passing time – far easier to do in the lanes of
Padang Besar and Pasir Mas than in an office within a large building.
But then, to my astonishment I was actually offered instructions and
guidance from without.

It all stemmed from the fact that KL had at long last allowed the
enemy's chief commissar, Chin Peng, and what was left of his 'army', to
retreat into the jungles of south Thailand. All the same, despite its having
swollen to mastodon proportions, the intelligence community spared only
a handful of its retainers to man a Special Branch unit set up in Penang
in 1954 and called, somewhat pompously, 'Frontier Intelligence Bureau',
changed by the time I arrived as one of its founding members to the more
sober 'Border Section'. Chartered to gather and collate intelligences on
south Thailand, the Border Section was placed in the hands of an MI6
import from London supported by myself, half-a-dozen indigenes, a pair
of secretaries and a host of local clerks and peons. The Section's problem
was where to begin. Chin Peng and maybe a thousand guerrillas were
holed up in jungle camps that we couldn't, and the Thais wouldn't, go
anywhere near. (The Thais laughed at the very idea of 'jungle-bashing',
armed forays into the forests to try to attack the enemy. "Give the bandits
time," they said, "and they'll rot away ideologically and then physically as
well". In the end, many years later – that's exactly what happened.)

The 'Wo Hup' Mystery

As I've said the question was where to start? We gazed stony-eyed at the maps we'd been given by the military. We scratched our heads and shuffled our paperweights as if they represented opposing armies but the only course of action we came up with was that we'd have to wait for something to turn up. And, sure enough, something did.

Checking on a pile of captured odds-and-ends that had been thrown into a cupboard in a Special Branch office in Ipoh and then forgotten, an officer came across a number of curious documents. To cut a long story short, when they'd been opened and decoded (work done by communists who'd come over to our side) those particular slips led the Penang Special Branch to a treasure trove of enemy secrets and to a cache of documents, some of which were handed over to us. The decoders told us that the papers related to what appeared to be Chin Peng's underground communications network in South Thailand; we licked our chops in anticipation of a real breakthrough. One link of the chain stretched from Betong in south Thailand to Bangkok: exactly the link we most urgently wanted to break into. Shadowy creatures in KL came up with the unimaginative title: 'The South Thailand Documents'. Excited over our prospects we quickly stamped them all 'Top Secret' (almost everything had to be classified, even extracts from the *Bangkok Post* were marked 'Secret') and, once they'd been translated into English, we placed them under our paperweights, and began to study them.

Alas, we couldn't make head or tail of them; they could just as well have been written about Swaziland as about Siam. It would have been bad enough had the place names been translated straight from Chinese characters into English but no, Chin Peng's encoders had written them in a code of sorts. One of our ex-communist friends had then decoded them leaving our Malayan Chinese staff to 'phoneticise' them into English. Every underground communist had a string of false names: back in the Malayan jungle each armed guerrilla had half-a-dozen; once you'd decoded one of those already fictitious names and then translated it into English your chances of attaching it to a flesh-and-blood individual were remote.

And we were forbidden to approach the Thais for help; our masters said they couldn't be trusted, that the Thais would sell the information back to Chin Peng who'd then change his communications system and leave us blind again – not that we could see far anyway.

The more we pored over the 'South Thailand Documents' the more baffled we became; we however, managed to piece together one potentially vital little piece of the jigsaw: somewhere in Betong there was a Chinese shop trading under the chop 'Wo Hup', which the communists used as a secret 'letter box'.

First of all, we tried what we thought would be the easiest step: locate 'Wo Hup'. Surely, we thought, we'd be able to find it. Betong, after all, wasn't all that big. The name 'Wo Hup' began to haunt us, I went to bed at night and awoke the next morning with 'Wo Hup' on my mind: we used 'Wo Hup' as a form of salutation to each other: "Wo Hup! Had a good night?"

We waded through directories, immigration records, business and hotel registers, indexes, customs' returns, bills of lading, newspapers, magazines, temple notes, trade journals, invoices, time-books, almanacs, circulars, sick-lists, notice-boards, time-tables and calendars. And we interviewed truck drivers, traders, motorists, tourists, salesmen, agents, bankers, hoteliers, clerks and harlots.

In the course of all the probing and with KL's guarantee of unlimited funds, we traversed northern Malaya and southern Thailand back and forth, over and over again. We went regularly to Ipoh, Alor Star, Kroh, Haadyai, Songkla, Changloon, Yala, Batang Star, KL and of course, Betong itself: up and down, up and down to Betong and back. We thought up ruses and disguises. Months went by, but for all we knew 'Wo Hup' could have been the name of a massage parlour in Tegucigalpa.

In the meantime 'Empire building' went on ceaselessly; as the security situation eased the law-and-order industry got bigger and bigger. For instance, although Border Section was reporting zilch to KL and was seriously under-employed, our controller despatched reinforcements to us. Bent on enlarging their part of the Empire along with everybody else, they insisted that as part of the machine we must take our share of the growth along with the others. Back in the capital city they spent millions on a 'Holding Centre' wherein suspects and surrendered communists were to be interrogated. A sprawling urban detention centre (though by no means a concentration camp), it was almost a city within the city and it was guarded like Fort Knox. In light of profligacy on that scale who were we to demur about KL's spending an extra few hundred thousand on us?

Not that we were in a mood to object. I was enjoying life; I may have experienced inklings of a seditious nature towards the intelligence game but I'd yet to see right through it. Indeed, I was tickled pink to be thought of as a cloak-and-dagger man, an underground crusader for the 'free world'. Far from trying to demystify my profession, I actually helped propagate the mystique generated for centuries to protect the intelligence community from being found out. I even exploited it myself just as all the others did. In our fruitless search for 'Wo Hup' for example, at a time when the roads were almost empty and motoring was fun, I took the tax-payer to the cleaners, charging him mileage allowance and expenses for driving thousands of colourful miles; for eating curry at a favourite stall run by a Tamil in the open market at Sungei Pattani; for taking the night sleeper to KL, flying to Kota Bharu, strolling round the perfect, green lakes of Taiping; swimming off deserted beaches at Songkla and playing tennis at Haadyai.

At the beginning, in 1954, we'd dash to our desks every morning eager to tear open our personal copies of the 'South Thailand Documents', confident that one fine day, something would click; surely at the very least we'd find 'Wo Hup'? Over a year later, we'd almost given up, leaving the papers to be closely examined only by the paper-eating silverfish who seemed particularly attracted to parchment salted with the sweat from hairy white forearms. As far as we were concerned the ants could chew their way through the dossiers until they resembled lace curtains stained by insect wastes, a fate that befell many old colonial records

Then, right out of the blue we stumbled over our prize. A hawker in Kroh mentioned the two magic words: 'Wo Hup'. Encouraged by a ringgit or two, he said that it was the name of one of scores of little wooden shophouses standing in rows behind the main street in Betong. Chinese locals knew it as 'Wo Hup' although the Thai nameplate said something else. To our mutual, total disconsolation however, by the time we reached Wo Hup's owner he'd had a cancerous foot in the grave for a long time. The man we'd imagined to be the hard-line revolutionary, indefatigable and indoctrinated to his toe-nails, turned out to be an emaciated, hairless, toothless, malodorous, sickly little fellow who could hardly put two words together. We gained nothing from what we'd hoped would be our coup.

All the same, over many months we were able to make sense of the 'South Thailand Documents' only to discover to our chagrin that they were a record of history long past; they were far too outdated to be of any use to us in 1955–56.

As an ultra-secret communication post 'Wo Hup' had closed down three or four years before. What's more, it had never been much more than a post-restante for communist other ranks with an occasionally important, high-level item thrown in. That's all there was to it. We were disappointed; all we could claim was that we'd cleared the mystery up. I was able to sit down and in my own good time write the unexpurgated English-language edition of the 'South Thailand Documents', filling the spaces with real, identifiable, locatable names. But we couldn't hide the fact from ourselves that we'd spent millions only to find a long defunct communist cell. Instead of being chastened however we acted in what I was to learn over the years was the typical way of all law-and-order elements: we proclaimed a great achievement, masking the emptiness of our minor accomplishment in an orgy of mutual back-slapping with our overseers in Kuala Lumpur and London. Official commendations were exchanged and we toasted each other over 14-course Chinese dinners paid for out of our (unchecked and unlimited) 'secret funds'.

Merdeka! (Independence)

Let's go back to the middle of 1955 by which time KL hardly needed its army of spooks to inform them that it had the remnants of Chin Peng's army on its last legs. The evidence was all around. Half starved, bedraggled, befuddled and demoralised, those comrades who couldn't make it to the relative safety and plenty of south Thailand were giving themselves up in droves. At no time during their seven years of 'armed struggle' had they come anywhere near to achieving the favourable revolutionary conditions for which they'd struggled: "to swim like fish in the sea of the masses". Long before mid-1955 their sea was positively toxic. Defeated, they threw their weapons down and, in exchange for a bowl of rice and a few kind words, talked their heads off. And they all said the same thing: their cause was lost.

That it had always been a heavily one-sided contest did not mean that the colonial regime could not, justifiably, claim its triumph; for all the people of Malaya, victory brought immense relief. For the imperial power itself, however, success was a mixed blessing for the defeat of armed insurrection robbed it of the only excuse it had for hanging on to power. The winds of change blew with gale force. It was time to lower the flag. The military strongman, Templer, was replaced by one McGilvray, a colonial time-server whose writ was to hand Malaya back to its traditional rulers. All of a sudden, a word hitherto untaught in Malaya's schools – *permilihan* (election) was on everybody's lips. Before you could say "Merdeka" (Independence) an avuncular Malay prince, Tungku Abdul Rahman, was our Chief Minister. He promised merdeka in no time at all.

The Show Must Go On

The people of Malaya behaved as if they had just got out of prison: they went on a binge, had a spring in their step and felt good. The collective intuition was that no matter that government advised caution and lifted hardly a single emergency regulation, the emergency was over. Rejoice! Only the Tungku's KL, prompted by the same colonial cabal who'd propagated the line all along, saw communists behind every rubber tree. Nevertheless, merdeka was on the horizon and there was no time to be lost in making cosmetic changes to the government machinery. By offering them generous 'golden bowlers', Abdul Rahman persuaded the bulk of colonial officials to go quietly. On the other hand, he was equally persuasive in getting many white stalwarts of the Special Branch as well as engineers, doctors, scientists and academics to stay on for years and years beyond independence.

Away from work, we acquired an open-top Hillman that looked sporty and classy but if you were just a minute or two late in getting the hood up in the rain (an inch an hour was not unusual) you'd soon get the feeling that you were at the wheel of a sinking boat. And, if you didn't get the thing started while you were stationary under the sun (like when waiting for the ferry), your brains would boil within your skull. Even in the best of times – at a good clip, hood down, in sunshine along an open, empty road – the slipstream would cool your brow but your genitals would fry in your lap while your clothes would stick to the red upholstery like band-aid.

But we adored the Hillman, it was dashing, different and it carried us through many rich and enjoyable experiences; in the cool of the evening the Hillman stood ready nearby. It took us through streets on which the sun shone: sheath-like cheongsams slashed high to show off lubricious female thighs, grimy shorts and singlets, demure kebayas, black-and-white check sarongs, gold-banded songkoks, glistening saris, dhotis, turbans and the latest in 'outings and shirtings'.

From Thai to Kiswahili

Safely as I already was within the colonialist establishment, it was made clear to me that a pass in the higher grade Thai language exam would improve my prospects of advancing up the establishment scale. As a further inducement I was offered a generous munshi allowance with which to engage a tutor.

For three evenings a week over two years my fat guru and I sat opposite each other across our kitchen table. Sweating under a slow-moving ceiling fan (if notched up another point it'd make the newspapers and text-books fly around like confetti) we plugged on until by the middle of 1956 I could refer to the McFarland Thai-English dictionary with about as much speed and accuracy as he could.

That was no mean feat because, while it's easy to get the hand of indexes that run only from A to Z, a Thai dictionary is a calligraphic maze, a complex, ingenious method by which is permutated no fewer than 15 vowel and 20 combined vowel signs, five tone indications and 44 consonants. This extraordinary script was the brainchild of King Rama Kamheng, a 13th century monarch who for years on end sat under a boh tree leisurely transcribing his people's language (a mixture of Pali, Sanskrit and Chinese) into a written scrip. The graphology he put together remains labyrinthine to this day – even to the Thais themselves (imagine interweaving the Roman alphabet with the musical staff notation and you'll get some idea of it) but it's also a work of art, beautiful, an intellectual wonder of the world and, most importantly, it works.

Anyway, in the middle of 1956 I was all ready to take an exam set by the British Embassy in Bangkok: 'The British Foreign Office Higher Standard Thai language examination'. I expected an all-expenses paid trip to the city I'd heard and read so much about but it wasn't to be; maybe the two examiners – one Briton, one Thai, had the same idea – they too wanted an all-expenses paid trip to Penang? No matter, in October 1956, I sat with my examiners – just the three of us in a large and otherwise empty college classroom. I was the first person ever to have sat the exam outside Thailand but it was hardly an event to hit the headlines. One month later I was being congratulated upon having achieved a pass mark of 73.5%.

Immediately upon becoming one of the first occidentals in colonial service to hold a Thai language diploma, I was informed that the colonial office wished to transfer me to Tanganyika!

It didn't take DMF and I long to make up our minds. We liked colonial life; we didn't want to go back to England; Malaya offered us, at best, a few more years but, possibly, only a few more months whereas, according to the colonial office brief on Tanganyika, Africa offered us 'a lifetime'. We chose Africa. Having passed exams in Malay and Thai I now went to the library in search of a textbook on Kiswahili.

Reflections II
City Lights

Only at intervals between dances did any lights, city or otherwise, pierce the stygian gloom of the Penang dance hall, 'City Lights'. And even then their voltage was so low that they resembled kampong oil-lamps rather than electric illumination. You'd be shown to your seat on terraced benches that ran in rows around the enclosed dance-floor; it was like being seated as a spectator at a Roman amphitheatre. The atmosphere was sultry; ceiling fans did no more than churn the sodden air round and round. Seated on chairs around the inside rim of the enclosed play area, a flock of 'butterflies', also known as 'taxi-dancers', faced inwards. They were Asian females – Chinese, Indians, Eurasians, Filipinos and permutations thereof. Aged anywhere between 15 (by law 18) and 50, they wore close-fitting cheongsams, saris, sarongs and skirts. Their common feature was jet-black hair which, as if to compensate for its standardisation of colour and sheen, they wore in individualistic styles: swept up, swished down, bobbed, frizzed, oiled, waxed, straightened and curled. They also shared another dubious blessing – they were all drenched in the same cheap, gummy perfume. Sitting within the fenced-off area, the women gossiped and chirped away like a flight of parrots rather than butterflies, appearing to be what they most certainly were not: beyond public reach.

The entrance fee into the clammy air of City Lights was one or more booklets of 25-cent tickets, each ticket entitling you to one dance with the butterfly of your choice. She'd first of all bank her token of esteem in her handbag, which she'd leave on her chair, and then submit herself to your clutches. The gramophone would start up and, timed to the split second, it would play a three-minute waltz, foxtrot or tango.

There was a touch of the slave-market about City Lights. On some nights business was so thin that the older and plainer of the butterflies went without partners, hence without a cent in income. On Saturday nights it might turn a bit bacchanalian and you'd see customers, butterflies and managers huddling together doing deals on extra-curricular assignations. But it was never a bordello; indeed for most of the time it was an uncannily innocent, unexciting, ritualistic, assembly-line sort of escort-service place. What the too-sweetly-smelling, too evenly smiling butterflies made of it you never knew because, except towards midnight when they'd yawn behind their frail little wrists, to customers at least, they seldom opened their mouths.

Oh Happy World!

They were called 'Great World', 'New World' and 'Happy World'. Singapore, KL, Ipoh and just about every big Southeast Asian town had one. They'd grown out of what in the beginning had been 'gambling farms', open-air casinos licensed by the early colonial authorities to operate on the outskirts of town for use by Chinese immigrants – many of them unattached males – who could roll their dice, suck on their opium pipes and use whores without disturbing the townsfolk. Taxed, they also helped the colonialists financially. In the course of time however, the towns had sprawled until the farms were smack in their midst. They were then fenced off, cleaned up, renamed and reopened for less obviously anti-social pastimes. Such was the history of Penang's Happy World. If in the 1950s you wanted to lay a substantial bet or if you were after a plug of chandu or a harlot then, rather than going to the Happy World, you'd best have gone to one of at least a hundred other places in town.

In our day the Happy World was a fairground surrounded by a high, freakishly decorated fence through whose gate you were admitted on payment of 25 cents. A glow with electric illuminations, it was a cabaret, bazaar, eating house, ballroom, theatre, cinema – a small-town Las Vegas.

Its centrepiece was the Chinese Opera House, a grandiose name for a huge, corrugated-iron roofed modern barn closed off along both of its long sides only by a metre high fence. There was a makeshift stage at one end and at the other a rough and ready foyer where you paid to enter the one-class auditorium. Well-worn, uncomfortable benches seated an audience of maybe 200–300 while there'd usually be about twice that number watching for free over the walls. The stage, made of rough-hewn planking, displayed the gaudiest imaginable backcloth but had neither curtains nor orchestra pit. The orchestra, a couple of gong-beaters plus a one-string fiddler, all three dressed like street-sweepers, sat cross-legged on the front edge of the stage.

On the face of it, the opera house was more the setting for a temperance lecture than for a spectacular display of subtle, not to say sublime, artistry. Yet no sooner did the players step on to the boards than you were in an enchanted world. Enchantment that in my case lasted only for the first half-hour; after which my concentration lapsed. Exotically painted, fantastically robed people strutted the stage; peacock's tail feathers glinted on long canes held high above sparkling tiaras and coronets; the cuffs of some of the performers brilliant mantles were a metre wide; spangled wands swept from 30 mm long finger nails; tinsel, baubles, paste, bangles, fobs and other knick-knacks jingle-jangled from the actors wrists, ears, ankles, elbows and knees; rich pantaloons faded into platform shoes 15 mm above the ground; and flamboyant plumes plus ornate chiffon banners swooned in the humid air above the scene. And all of that went on while the artists proclaimed in pulsating, ear-throbbing falsetto, the gongs clanged, the violin screeched and the whistles whistled.

Once the performers had begun you'd no longer notice the stagehands who, dressed like the orchestra as if for a day's labouring, flitted to and fro across the stage changing the props even as the drama was being played out. One of them might bring a stool to represent a holy altar, another would flick a silver ribbon to make do for the mighty Yangtse river, and another would hang a grubby little 'Good Morning' towel over the back of a trashy chair and behold! It became the emperor's gem-encrusted golden throne; everybody knew, or was supposed to know that much. Meanwhile, the audience shuffled, smoked (every Asian male above 16 smoked), hawked and spat, nattered, cracked sunflower seeds like muted machine-gun fire, fed babies, sauntered up and down the aisles, read newspapers, crossed legs to massage the toes (in a land where nearly everybody wore flip-flops day and night, there was a lot of toe stroking), dozed off and generally enjoyed the show.

Elsewhere in 'Happy World' there'd be men selling frogs tied together by their legs; a family of acrobats turning somersaults; stalls selling repellently coloured drinks in cloudy tumblers – not for the squeamish those beverages no matter how parched you might be. *Satay* morsels, skewered on bamboo spills basted and spat over charcoal braziers; banana fritters fizzed in rancid-smelling oil; and liquid pink squid and the gizzards of heaven knows what swirled around in glass bowls. You could buy lottery tickets, balloons, whistles and batek paintings, drink the sap of sugar-cane put through mangles on the spot; go to one of two cinemas or to a flyblown circus; crash dodgem cars, play tombola, fight with one-armed bandits, throw darts and have your fortune told by any of a dozen odd-balls who'd consult bones, seeds, cards, tea-leaves, scrolls, little caged birds and even crystal balls.

There was the dance floor that looked like a boxing ring. You paid your ten cents, climbed through the ropes and accompanied a dusky beauty with frangipani in her hair in a round or two of what amounted to shadow boxing. You were forbidden to touch – there was a referee to see there was no 'close proximity' as Muslim law put it – you'd be dancing, at arms length, the slow, shuffling, soporific *ronggeng*. Or you could do what most people did – spend your 25 cents just to wander around the wonderland, eyes open to the 'cosmorama', nostrils twitching to the smell of a mixture of wet sawdust, charcoal smoke, grease-paint, incense, chandu fumes, durians, beer, cosmetics, nicotine, varnish, animal-droppings, breath, cooking fats, perfumes, sweat and much-handled paper money; and ears pounding to the screech of Cantonese divas, the sweet dirge of ronggeng music, the jangle of cane-crushing mangles, the rasp of the dodgems, the cries of hawkers and the shrieks of lottery winners. It was worth every cent.

Kopi O!

Your average coffee shop was wide open along its entire front facing the five-foot way; above this pedestrian concourse its owner would have hung a couple of grubby sheets to keep the sun off his customers. The latter would sit at tables with round, solid stone tops and wrought-iron legs the combined weight of which must have made them difficult to drag within the shop on the approach of a diligent policeman (it was unlawful to block the five-foot way but the law was never enforced, a constable preferring a free cigarette instead). Being outside the shop proper offered advantages all round, being cooler it dispensed the need for electric fans, and the fact that the open storm drain ran down the street edge of the five-foot way made the disposal of leftovers, banana skins, orange peel and globs of betel and tobacco juice a simple matter of a flick of the wrist or a short-range expectoration.

Coffee shops (*kedai kopi*) substituted as bus-shelters, betting shops, telephone kiosks, post-office boxes, information centres, money-lending dives, venues for assignation and places for swapping messages on the sly. The customers had a choice of two beverages, both brewed from freshly roasted local coffee beans: Kopi O was black, thick and mind-numbing, *kopi susu* was a beige, gluey mixture one-third coffee, one-third condensed milk and one-third sugar. For those who preferred tea they'd pour it for you over crushed ice. Your drink, whatever it was, was served up in tumblers a millimetre thick and so heavy that it was said that you'd only to lift one glass a day to get all the exercise you needed.

Cigarettes could be purchased either by the hundred or singly with either a single match or a full box thrown in, or, according to taste you could buy stinky black cheroots from Sandakan or Moulmein, sold by the handful. The menu was a bit on the short side: nuts, sunflower seeds, sugar-cane sticks, fruit, toast (meaning slices of white bread scorched over a charcoal brazier) jam, tinned butter (invariably rancid and sickly yellow) sugar (for caking thickly over your toast) or, maybe, a lightly-cooked egg newly broken from its shell and, hardly heated at all, swimming in a saucer of dark brown soya sauce. And, of course, always *nasi goreng*.

Writing thus about coffee shops in Malaya doesn't make them sound memorable enough for me to have stored them away in a special place in my head but there they are all right. Their very special bouquet of roasting coffee, cheap tobacco, soya sauce and open drains is with me even as I write this down, 50 years later.

What a Mess!

My three years in remote outposts of Empire had spared me the ordeal of enduring attendance at officers' mess nights but once in the big city of Penang, I could neither escape paying mess dues and buying 'mess kit' nor from the social implications of involuntary membership of the gazetted police officers' mess. Copying the military in such errant practices as drilling, saluting, posturing, dolling-up and flashing medals and swords, colonial police formations had long ago got themselves into the bad habit of gathering together in 'messes'. Every gazetted police officer not lucky enough to be on duty (and few Special Branch officers could ever claim exemption on that count) was obliged to attend the mess on an average of one evening a month. Precisely at 2000 hrs to the beat of a gong we'd process in order of rank up the grand staircase to take our pre-determined places behind chairs around a U-shaped table quite exquisitely decorated with orchids and with stiff, beautifully folded table napkins and dressed, rather overpoweringly, with what was known as the 'mess silver': trophies, candle-sticks, sauce-boats, finger-bowls, pepper-grinders and goblets. Given permission to be seated we'd tuck into what, in order to fit into the ritualistic drinking routine, was invariably European food.

Afterwards, bloated, half-inebriated, untidy, nicotine-numbed and in a lather of sweat (this was before air-conditioning remember) we'd arrived at the moment when, whether we wanted to or not, we had to 'let ourselves go'. Egged on to drink more and more of the hard stuff (it's the manly thing to do) we were ordered to go on a wild bender of childish romps, a practice, again, borrowed from the military. Grown men of normally prim disposition went bonkers over a caper called 'High Cockalorum'. Spurs removed to preclude blood-letting, they jumped on each others' backs from all directions to form a human pyramid that eventually collapsed under its own weight accompanied by a great outpouring of curses, cries of pain, whoops of joy, belches, grunts and farts. Whereupon, following another go at the booze, they did it all over again and again. 'Leapfrogging' was another of our playground antics; in this we'd all collide gasping into each others' backsides while trying to leap over a progressively extending line, ending up, like our beer, spilled all over the highly polished floor.

Then, blindfolded and tied in pairs by our arms, we'd lie on the same by now scuffed and slimy floor and try to beat each other's brains out with rolled up newspapers thrust into our free hands all the while being cheered on in a way that'd make football hooligans sound like choir boys at practice. We'd go on all fours at full stretch, an empty gin bottle in each hand; the trick was, while keeping your knees off the floor, to place one of the bottles further away than the one that had been placed by the man before you. And we'd be invited to attempt to drink a pint of beer while at the same time – and invariably failing – to balance glasses filled with beer on our heads. And so, unbelievably, it went on and on into the small hours.

Chairs, tumblers, teeth, spectacles and sometimes even limbs got broken, curtains were ripped down, tunics were torn, patent leather was scuffed, lungs were choked, stomachs emptied, tempers frayed, kidneys abused and senses lost. Most of those dipsomaniac hours found me hiding away on the fringes of the arena bunkered down with a handful of Asian officers. It must be said though that most of our Asian brothers, in the belief that non-participation would be noted and then counted against them in the promotion stakes, joined in the high-jinks with – albeit feigned – alacrity. Others took the line that since all of us were charged pro-rata for the booze whether they sank a gallon of it or a glass of orangeade they might as well get the share they'd be billed for anyway.

Protocol, and attendant fear of demerit should it be transgressed, forbade anyone to leave the premises in advance of the Chief. This meant that the likes of me were compelled to wait miserably, headaches building, for release, which seldom came until one hour or two before dawn, by which time the place looked as if it had been ransacked by a disorderly mob, which was in fact the case. It looked indeed like a real mess.

A Binge at the E&O

One sweet-breathed Saturday sunrise when every plant dripped dew, when the sky was just turning pink and when the bulbuls were up and bobbling, the Chief Police Officer telephoned the news that a Thai Police-General from Songkla accompanied by a retinue of 30 officers, was to fly into Penang for lunch. The Chief instructed me to lay out the red carpet, KL he said, wanting the closest possible Thai cooperation in the fight against Chin Peng, had ordered that no expense be spared when entertaining Thai officials. I was to do my best to beat the Thais at their own lavish entertainment game. It was a formidable undertaking; the Thais had been perfecting the art of seducing influential foreigners for centuries; Thai officials weren't called upon to account for public money spent on backslapping visitors; hoteliers, restaurateurs and shopkeepers in Thailand knew better than to present bills to Thai officials. We had no such licence; our merchants had no fears about charging civil servants for their services.

Nonetheless, having been given a blank cheque I made straight for the best Penang had to offer: the Eastern and Oriental Hotel (E&O) where I ordered 33 places to be set for serving the hotel's finest curry tiffin: long grained Thai rice with a dozen different meats and fish, assorted sambals, satay and to finish with gula melaka. The repast was to be washed down with Italian and French wines, German beer and followed with Cuban cigars, English cigarettes, Swiss chocolates and whatever extra little delicacies the house steward might deem appropriate, regardless of cost. The hotel's magnificent banqueting room was to be decorated with orchids and with portraits of the Thai King and British Queen.

I ordered a fleet of taxis and arranged for outriders both to clear the traffic and add to the sense of occasion while the Chief persuaded the Governor of Penang to allow the use of his sleek, black Austin Princess together with its liveried chauffeur.

When the Thai Air Force Dakota, tricolour flying from its nose, drew to a standstill on the landing strip there stood the Chief decked out in full ceremonial while I, wearing a cheap suit, went to position myself at the foot of the steps. The Dakota's door opened and a coarse-looking young Thai male dressed in skin-tight blue jeans and sweatshirt skipped down the stairs and introduced himself as Police Sergeant Major something or other. Grabbing the astounded Chief by the hand he apologised, through me, for his General's failure to make the trip in person. The General, the Sergeant Major said, had been taken poorly all of a sudden, so swiftly indeed that he'd been unable to give advance notice of his disability. Anxious not to offend or disappoint his esteemed colleagues in Malaya and having no time to summon a senior officer to stand-in for him, the General had nominated the Sergeant Major to represent him on the goodwill visit.

The rest of the party – 30 other ranks – all dressed in what was then the Thai vogue: body-hugging, bell-bottomed jeans, wide belts with outsize buckles and polychromatic sports shirts, poured down the steps as if, like English tourists on a day drip to France, they had no time to lose in getting at the duty-frees. The Chief, speechless, managed only a sickly grin before, with a gesture that said 'It's all yours', raced to the Princess and took off, not to be seen again that day.

Being a duty-free port, Penang magnetised all Thais. I knew that what I had on my hands that Saturday morning was not a formal goodwill delegation but a raiding party acting on the General's orders. Its writ, I assumed, was to load the Dakota with as much contraband as it could carry: for the General, tobacco, liquor and shirts (those were the days when British-made clothing was still treasured in Asia) for the General's ladies – bolts of cloth, perfumes and jewellery; and for everybody else – transistor radios, cameras, electric shavers and vacuum cleaners. I wasn't therefore surprised to hear the Sergeant Major ask to be excused from the luncheon engagement.

But I couldn't excuse him. Just as he was thinking only about cartons of 555s, crates of Dimple Haig and gallons of attar of roses, my concern was for all those E&O curries simmering away in their golden juices; for all the fine wines and beer sitting on ice; for the maitre accoutred in his very best whites, drilling his superbly trained waiters; for attendants shining the brass work of the grandiose toilets, opening new bars of Pears soap, polishing already gleaming windows and heating towels; for the Manager fussing about, checking that the ceiling fans were swirling silently at full pace, that the orchids dressing the great table were fresh, that the silver and crystal sparkled; the same Manager who, I imagined, was even at that very moment nervously pacing the richly ornamented foyer awaiting the Chief Police Officer and his illustrious Thai guest, while his magnificently liveried Sikh chokidar practised the flourish with which he'd open the door of the limousine and the salute he'd give the two sahibs and their retinue. No, Sergeant Major, I said, I cannot excuse you; protocol doesn't permit it; I'll turn you and your entourage over to the bazaar only after you've dined at the E&O.

With its imposing foyer made all the more imperial by a domed ceiling, semi-circular reception desk, its regal potted palms, rooms that opened from floor to high ceiling to the ocean, and with its shaded courtyard gardens leading to a low sea wall, the E&O was one of the landmarks of Empire, ranking alongside the great Shepheard in Cairo, the Taj in Bombay, the Grand in Calcutta, the Raffles in Singapore, the Hong Kong Peninsula and Colombo's Galle Face. Sure, it had long since dropped its insistence upon gentlemen wearing ties at luncheons (though it invoked the rule in the evenings) and true, by the mid-1950s it turned a blind eye to the wearing of shorts so long, that was, so long as they were nicely cut, went down to the knees and were worn with long white stockings and were swapped for trousers at sundown. But it had never had to deal with the likes of the party I arrived with on that memorable Saturday noon.

I turned up with 31 roughnecks dressed more fittingly for a couple of hours carousing at a downtown shebang rather than for tiffin at the E&O. Their idea of a gourmet tiffin was a blow-out of a few bowls of Thai-Chinese scoff swilled down with Mekong whisky at a food-stall perched for ease of sanitation over an open storm drain. Instead, there was my Sergeant Major being shown by a fawning chief-steward to a throne-like seat of honour at the head of one of the most exclusive dining tables in Asia! Ignoring the silver-ware, the crystal finger-bowls, the starched, dressed linen napkins and the correct order of use of the cut-glass drinking vessels (for they were in a hurry to get to the markets) my Thai guests went at it with bare fingers, stuffing down the saffron rice, the chicken, beef and fish and the delicately scented sambals as if they'd not eaten for months. Following the dining etiquette of the eating-houses in Haadyai they spat the bones on to the floor – in their book bones were fodder for the scavenging dogs that lurked beneath every table. They gulped subtle wines as if drowning raging thirsts, swilled beer like Germans in a beer-drinking contest in Munich, puffed on foot-long cigars as if they were all Fidel Castros and, performing the only act in which their behaviour resembled that of the nobs who normally graced that table, they pocketed half-a-dozen Havana's apiece.

Their aplomb was unsurpassable; not one of them asked what it was all about, not one of them tried to make polite conversation let alone raise a toast of appreciation and not one of them – audibly anyway – put the question they must have been asking themselves, 'If the Malayan government does this for its lower orders just imagine how it must treat its officers?' No, they just dug in, concentrating on building their energies for the great purchasing expedition ahead. In less than an hour they were cleaning out the bazaars on Chulia Street. Their aircraft, dangerously overloaded, took off for Songkla just as the sun was going down.

The E&O manager was visibly shaken by the experience but his nerves steadied a good deal when I told him to add to an already exorbitant bill a further 10% for service.

The Thai general telegraphed his appreciation together with a message which, inadvertently, made clear the purpose of Saturday's buccaneering sweep through Penang's bazaars: he was off on immediate transfer to Chiang Mai. Thus the taxpayers of Malaya were a few thousand ringgits worse off with nothing to show for it. Nevertheless, KL sent the Chief its commendation.

Aswins

Aswins – 'horsemen; Vedic deities; twins of the sun; ever young; ever handsome; smart and swift as an arrow'

The District Officer of the Thai town of Betong was an 'Aswin'. He didn't proclaim it, there was no sign on his door or plaque on his desk to announce it, nobody ever breathed it out loud; no, the only way you knew he was an Aswin was by the insignia he wore: a heavy gold and emerald ring that bulged and blazed from a fat finger on a podgy hand. The District Officer would have been presented with that ring – the symbol of his local majesty in all things – only after he'd sworn, in the flesh, to do the bidding of the great supremo of the Aswin order: Police Chief and third hood in the chilling triumvirate that then ran Thailand – the infamous, overweight General Pao, Thailand's Herman Goering.

Aswins flashed their rings just as Anglican Bishops do to show they were in direct communication with the Supreme Being meaning, in the Aswin's case, General Pao. The Thais greet each other with the *wai*, a gesture that brings the palms together in front of the chest and below a bowed head while intoning the salutation Sawasdi. This winsome custom meant that when greeting an Aswin your eyes were straight away riveted upon, and your brain alerted to the purport of, that fearful orb on his finger.

Pao was Godfather, the Aswins his sworn henchmen, collectively forming a semi-covert mafia, an institutionalised secret society, a 'masonry' if you like, that controlled the major rackets: smuggling, drugs, prostitution, gambling, distilling and protection. Aswins were usually high functionaries such as District Officers or senior police, customs and immigration officers stationed in strategically important places like frontier towns such as Betong. Within their designated territories they ran the roost, handing down such punishments as they saw fit ranging from expulsion from the area to the imposition of fines, flogging and sometimes shooting. To defy an Aswin meant tilting not only against the mafia but against the state in the person of General Pao as well.

The official pay of the District Officer of Betong amounted to the wage of say, a Malayan police sergeant. That sergeant would have been able to afford a decent sarong and a bicycle yet the D.O., as Aswin on the same rate of official stipend, swaggered about in tailored uniforms, silk suits, sea-island cotton shirts, Italian shoes, Swiss time-pieces and American shades. He smoked Balkan Sobranie, kept a harem of exclusive harlots and was driven around in a Mercedes Benz from whose tinted windows he viewed his domain. Not that his domain was much to look at: streets a-jumble with poorish people: rubber tappers, tin-miners, peasants, shopkeepers, swindlers, bonzes, down-and-outs, plus great numbers of babies black with flies and naked except for good-luck amulets worn around their fleshy upper-arms and plump bellies. They were people who trusted in the stars and who pledged themselves to abide by the five commandments propounded by the Lord Buddha: 'Thou shalt neither steal, take life, tell lies, fornicate indiscriminately, nor imbibe intoxicants'.

They were also at the same time people who lived for the day, people who violated the Buddha's commandments in the same breath as they swore to obey them. And – and this is what brought the smile to the Aswin's face – to make amends for many of their violations of the commandments (when caught riding a bus without paying for example, eating dog meat, bedding a whore of the same sex, taking a drag on a chandu cigarette or swigging illicit booze) they'd fork out a fine to the Aswin's foot-soldiers and not without good cheer either; it's a fair cop they'd say. And of course, on the much bigger scale, the foot soldiers also squeezed shopkeepers, smugglers and, very probably, against a promise not to harass them, even Chin Peng's guerrillas. Everybody, up to General Pao, got a cut.

Sounds awful? Not necessarily so. Because what I saw in Betong, beyond its truly awful environment, was a populace full of energy, amiability, cheerfulness, even well-being. There was little sign of their being oppressed, no sign whatever of any *tonton macout*. Their disposition made untenable the analysis of despotism I'd formed in my mind when I'd first heard about the Aswin brotherhood. It was corrupt alright, yet, just as surely, it wasn't destructive; like everything else I'd experienced in Thailand, Aswinism left me feeling outraged one minute and lost in admiration the next.

Krungtheb (Bangkok)

The Chief of Police again summoned me to his presence to tell me the exciting news that I was to accompany him to Bangkok where the Thais were about to open a spanking new police college. Police Chiefs from all over Southeast Asia were to attend. I was to tag along as aide-de-camp-cum-interpreter. I was delighted: at long last I'd see the city the Chakris had built long ago, the city I'd read and heard so much about, and, as a bonus, I'd get a close-up of that walking headline, the notorious, terrible, Police General Pao.

We flew into Krungtheb (properly Krungthebmaharnkorn – City of the Angels or, to non-Thais, Bangkok) to be swept at once into a welcome on the scale of theatricality only Thai bureaucrats, freed from budgetary concerns, could have staged. Dozens of spectacularly turned-out flunkies bowed low on either side of a human corridor leading to a glittering Mercedes flying the union jack and flanked by glamorous motor-cycle outriders while the ladies in our party were smothered in orchids. The city's traffic came to a halt and parted to allow us to glide imperiously down the middle of the highway as though we were kings or presidents, not mere policemen. We went straight through every traffic light and over every pedestrian crossing until we pulled up at our villa (each police chief had his own villa) where we found waiting to attend upon our every wish an entire household: butler, chef, kitchen-staff, chamber-maids, waiters, porters, stewards, laundresses, valets, boot-boys, chauffeurs (we had a fleet of Mercedes at our beck-and-call) gardeners and secretaries.

Relatively speaking I wasn't much more than a menial myself; nevertheless I was ushered into a suite of rooms the like of which I'd only seen in movies. My bed, pitched in the centre of a large, high, airy room, was enclosed within a voluminous tent made of pearly-white mosquito netting, a rich vestment draped from ceiling to floor to which it was anchored by lead weights down into its hem. One entered that unique bedchamber by an opening to one side (an opening one had to remember instantly to close). Inside you could walk all around the bed, sit at a bedside table and do your morning exercises while remaining out of the reach of mosquitoes.

Bouquets of flowers and bowls of fruit stood at every turn. A fridge offered goodies from soya milk to champagne. Cigarettes and cigars lay everywhere I looked. The bathroom cabinets might have been display shelves in an up-market pharmacy; they contained soaps, towels, toilet rolls, shampoos, pomades, bath-salts, lotions, hair-dressings, talcs, toothpastes, tooth-brushes, razors and razor blades, manicure implements, lens cleaners, aspirin, Enos, deodorants, plasters, condoms and 'Optex'. The slightest press of a button brought instant attention from shoeshine boys, hairdressers and from waiters ready to serve caviar and brown bread, sausage and mash or a five-course meal.

Ready to add to our small splash of colour to General Pao's great event we Malayans were up and about at dawn on our first morning and were soon clothed in all our finery and raring to go. What a tremendous affair it turned out to be! The diplomatic corps, in all its plumaged panoply, was seated on plush chairs beneath an enormous, billowing, saffron-coloured canopy. The visiting police chiefs, creating their own vivid splashes, reclined on either side of Their Excellencies while we mere aides (among whom I was the only non-Asian) stood to one side beneath the probing sun. Just as I was about to liquefy into the ground, I became entranced by the theatre that unfolded before my eyes. The British might pride themselves on being the supreme exponents of the art of pomp and ceremony but the Thais can outdo them any day of the week.

Enter stage left, Police General Pao, a tall, jowly man with extravagantly coiffured white locks (his height and his hair led his enemies to spread the idea that he had Chinese blood because pure Thais were short, golden-skinned people with turbans of jet black hair) who made a dramatic appearance. Showing off a beautifully tailored richly-toned uniform from whose waist hung his famed bejewelled dagger, obviously enjoying the moment hugely, he saluted his guests with a *wai* that brought the sun to glint off his Aswin ring.

Next, dead on time (remarkable in itself since punctuality was a quality singularly lacking in the Thai race) the imminent arrival of the Prime Minister was announced. We ignorant outsiders looked for a sedately moving Rolls or Cadillac. Instead, a tiny, scarlet sports car, hood-down, came whooshing into view. It flashed around the arena in a red glow before screeching to a halt like a racing car at a pit stop, right in front of the pavilion. Out leapt the driver. Astonishingly, the driver was the great survivor himself: Prime Minister Pibul Songkram, a small, compact, good-looking man dressed becomingly in what I suppose was the cinematic livery of Thai prime ministers. As he took Pao's salute and as everyone else rose to him, his little red chariot was driven away: zip and it had gone.

Then, much more in character, there entered, royal ensign flying, a big, beautiful, golden (not just gold-painted either) limousine made especially for His Majesty the King of Thailand by a manufacturer in Bristol, England. It drew up before the marquee and everybody except the Thais who prostrated themselves rose to the sovereign. Under a huge, royal-yellow umbrella, out stepped the young Bhumipol in the uniform of Field Marshal, his eyes, as always concealed behind tinted lenses, and behind him his lovely Queen Sirikit robed marvellously in a military-style yet extremely feminine dress. A band struck up, flags unfurled, guns boomed, their Majesties sank into their brocaded thrones and across our front there charged hundreds of mounted police who, heads down, whipped their horses into a wild free-for-all, pell-mell canter; a most unusual march past that must have stirred even the coolest of diplomats.

Thousands of coloured balloons together with hundreds of kites swept aloft into the endless blue sky and that was that. Loudspeakers told us that the college would now begin to turn out police officers as good as those anywhere else in the world. On graduation, they announced, each cadet would be presented with a dagger just like General Pao's. (I had trouble translating the boast about the daggers because it implied that the school would turn out thugs in Pao's image.)

Trailing around the vast, ultra-modern, concrete and glass sprawl with its air-conditioned theatre-cum-briefing room complete with red-plush chairs, microphones, head-phones and velvet curtains and with its spectacularly hygienic kitchens and dining-rooms, one became aware of the fact that it wasn't authentically Thai. Paid for by the CIA, it was an American creation, a university programmed to turn out cloned anti-Marxists. Its Western-style crappers were furnished with toilet rolls, not tins of water and the cadets themselves were kitted out for showing-off in West Point display rather than for patrolling the dirty, humid back-alleys of Krungtheb or Haadyai. At the end if came as a welcome surprise – a slight concession to Asia – to find that the canteen offered chopsticks as well as knives and forks.

1957–61
Tanganyika (now Tanzania)

From Asia to Africa

The trans-territorial postings of colonial officials were decided upon by a handful of bureaucrats sitting in front of blazing fires in dark London offices. Without themselves ever visiting colonies they issued orders moving families clean across the globe. In our case they offered a transfer from a rich country in Asia to a dirt-poor protectorate in East Africa: Tanganyika.

It was November 1956. Eden's war on Egypt, one of the most ignoble of Britain's imperial spasms, had brought about the very thing it had been waged to prevent: it had closed the Suez Canal. As a result my ship, the P&O liner *Canton*, had to sail all the way round the Cape, calling at Colombo, Madagascar, Durban, Cape Town, Dakar and Tenerife on its way back to England. We rode the oceans for five whole weeks, entertained along the way with glassy ballets performed by dolphins, sharks and flying fish (those were the days before maritime pollution). We played deck games, swam in the pool, flirted, laid little bets on the ship's daily speed, dozed on chaise longue, snoozed in the library and ate prodigiously. The only things we had to put our hands in our pockets/purses for were booze and tips; the bill for all the rest – the passage itself, the fancy food, the tinsel, the deck quoits, cricket gear, outsize bathrobes, cinema seats and library books – the Malayan taxpayer paid for.

Such voyages were one of the most cherished perks of colonial life, a legacy of days gone by, days when it had been deemed vital for debilitated Europeans to recuperate their much-tried bodies and recharge their intellects by spending regular, long vacations on full pay in the homeland. The time taken in cruising the seas in stylish ships was added on to the holidays. Not until you berthed at the homeport or, in reverse, at a harbour in your colony, did your vacation begin and end. Each single, leisurely day throwing deck quoits and sun bathing brought a full day's pay. Never mind that life in the middle of the century in most colonies was at least as healthy as it was in Europe, the colonialists weren't going to give up any of the perks their predecessors had won for themselves – especially not the largess of the long vacation made longer by the voyages. Not likely. Indeed, their 'associations' – in other words though they'd admit to nothing so proletarian – their trade unions, screwed their masters in London into fattening that particular cumshaw until it became accepted practice for colonial officials to spend no fewer than six of every 36 months on paid holiday plus whatever time it took him/her to get home and back.

In May 1957, I flew from London to Dar es Salaam (Haven of Peace), the principal city of Tanganyika, in a Brabazon, the very latest four-engine aircraft. Until 1886 when European monarchs divided Africa amongst themselves, allocating Tanganyika (even the name was a western creation) to Germany, this enormous (364,000 square miles, twice the size of Spain), scantily populated (8 million in 1957) land had been the slave-hunting territory of Arabs operating, with some Portuguese assistance, from a sparkling cluster of small islands just off the mainland coast – Zanzibar. Even brutish German colonisation was an improvement on that.

Only 28 years after it had been taken over by the Kaiser, the country staged one of World War I's less bloody sideshows. In comic-opera fashion handfuls of British and German soldiers chased one another all over Tanganyika. What would the black masses have made of the sight of people who, having boasted that they were bringing 'civilisation', ran around trying to kill each other off? The outcome was that as part of the spoils of war the League of Nations mandated the territory to the care of the British.

Background
Fully nine-tenths of the country was dirt poor, much of its land infertile and much of its produce externally unmarketable. Poor communications made distances, already daunting, seem beyond hope of traverse. There

were pockets of well-being dotted about like oases in deserts: diamond mines at Shinyanga; sisal in Tanga, coffee, tea, pyrethrum, coal, wattle, gold and assorted minerals in the highlands to the north and south, but when their value was spread across the endless landscape, their contribution to the central treasury was miserly.

For all that however, destitution was rarely visible. And, despite the absence of a sense of nationhood and, bearing in mind that inter-tribal rivalries were argued over in scores of different tongues and that the law-and-order screen was gossamer-thin (5,000 policemen covered the whole territory as against, for example, the 25,000 that patrolled London alone – the Southern Highlands Province, almost the size of the United Kingdom albeit with a population of only one million, was policed with no more that 200 policemen with not a soldier in sight), for all that there was little fear that quarrels might be settled with fists, let alone firearms.

The native Tanganyikans left unseemly behaviour to their 'civilisers'. Different Christian missions competed with each other to recruit 'posho converts' and to poach from one another. They waged senseless religious warfare while all the time deservedly losing out to Islam. To their great credit however, it must be said that religious orders of all kinds were the principal providers of what few schools and clinics served the masses.

In short, the country we came to in 1957 – a mandated protectorate whose official title was 'Tanganyika Territory' – lived down to the description made by Western politicians: it was 'backward'. Its human population apart, the land was akin to one vast, open zoological garden canopied by wondrous bird life and traversed by herds of animals in fantastic numbers and variety. It was peaceful, pastoral country, unrefined, unspoiled and incomparably beautiful.

Dar es Salaam

The capital was a sultry, old-worldly, quixotic, comforting, down-at-heel, hot little city. Dearly would I have settled down there and then but I wasn't to be so fortunate. Instead, I was given time to do the statutory round of calls on officialdom, buy a car (a second-hand Peugeot 403 for which government advanced me an interest-free loan) and to kit myself up for my very first 'safari'. Within a few days of my arrival I began a 600-mile drive inland to the town of Mbeya, seat of local government in the Southern Highlands Province, where I was to take charge of the provincial Special Branch unit already established there.

Choking on the dust thrown up by his car ahead of me, I followed behind the officer I was to replace in far away Mbeya: a suede-booted, safari jacketed, upper class, public-school Englishman, Paul Coventry. En route, Coventry introduced me to a part of the so-called 'intelligence network' he was handing over to me: a kind of Masonic-fraternity of white settlers in the highlands. At the bar of the Sao Hill Club, a watering hole-cum-rest-house for white planters between the pleasant town of Iringa and Mbeya, I was pushed into the middle of a covey of 'agents': half-a-dozen beery, down-on-their-luck whites who planted tea, coffee and pyrethrum on extensive slopes of not very fecund hills. In return for having their glasses recharged again and again at Coventry's expense, they outdid each other with affirmations as to the loyalty of 'their' blacks both to themselves and to the crown. They made fun of 'that coon, Nyerere', swearing that for fear of being jeered at by the local blacks Nyerere wouldn't dare show his face in the Southern Highlands. I'd only been in the country for a few days but I knew racist claptrap when I heard it and I was dismayed later to hear Coventry describe it as 'political intelligence'. On our arrival in Mbeya he debited the drinks bill as 'expenses incurred on the 'collection of information' to his (soon to be my) 'Secret Fund' – money allocated secretly by the government to its Special Branch. As soon as the hand-over had been completed I determined that the Sao Hill mob had seen their last easy shilling.

The next morning, some 50 miles further on, we stopped to take coffee with another of Coventry's 'agents', one David Ricardo, an off-beat English 'aristo' shacked up with Barbara, a titled daughter of the Duke of Newcastle. I was charmed by the Ricardos; I couldn't get over the piquancy of their situation: a pair of English blue-bloods living on their uppers (off a small herd of cattle from which they supplied meat and milk to the white planters) in the middle of Africa in a rude, albeit spacious, mud-and-wattle homestead called 'Matanama' many a parched mile from their nearest white neighbour. An abiding memory is of two of the Ricardo's Masai friends who'd trekked hundreds of miles just to pay a call. I can see them now, a couple of long-limbed, slender Morans, naked, ochred from the hair on their heads to their toes, each carrying a spear while standing heron-like on one leg on either side of an oil portrait of the Duke of Newcastle that hung wonkily on one of the whitewashed adobe walls.

I kept the Ricardos on the 'agents' payroll, not because they ever gave me any 'information' but because it was always a pleasure to call on them and also because they always snatched at the shillings in desperation. Scraping a poor subsistence from the dust of central Africa, they yet lived a life that many a prince and princess might envy. The Ricardos regaled me endlessly with 'intelligence' about the trout streams in the Mporoto mountains, the movement of elephant herds across the plains of Chimala, the sightings of prides of lions 'nearby' (like 50–100 miles from Matanama) and they'd keep me abreast of all the latest scandals pervading the small, widely-scattered white community. But they knew nothing about any local political developments; their ignorance meaning perhaps that there was nothing going on: a sort of 'intelligence' in itself.

Coventry didn't leave me with much of an organisation. He was in a hurry to leave; the old boy net having found a diplomatic niche for him, he was keen to take the earliest possible flight to New Delhi. It took only a couple of days for him to hand over a house, an office, a Land Rover and a hundred files and to introduce me to the handful of colonial bureaucrats who ran the Southern Highlands Province. Almost at once I took off for Dar es Salaam to meet DMF and the children at the dock.

The New Africa and the Real Africa

The family's first two nights in Tanganyika were spent under yellowing mosquito nets at the 'New Africa Hotel' in Dar. The smartest hostelry in the country, back in Asia it would have ranked as a flophouse. Nonetheless, it had its charms; it was cavernous, unkempt, leaky, served the sort of fare you'd expect in a low-rated boarding house in Blackpool and it had a thoroughly deserved reputation of being the nerve-centre for invasions of mosquitoes in swarms akin to sand storms or locust raids. Its plumbing being out-of-whack meant that guests regularly succumbed to vigorous bouts of the Tanganyika two-step, known in Mexico as 'Montezuma's Revenge'. Anyway, following a couple of nights in the New Africa we faced the adventure, me for the third time in as many weeks, of two long, bone-shaking, dust choking days in old Africa: on the Dar-Iringa-Mbeya road. The prospect was however made enticing by the promise that every turn in the road could reveal a wild animal, an exotic bird or an extraordinary human being.

The first 100 miles, on a passable, tarred surface, brought us painlessly to Morogorro, a leafy little town set against noble blue mountains and blessed with a small, chummy hotel that was run, as were a surprising number of Tanganyika's small-town inns, by Greeks.

The next 500 miles was traversed on plain dirt roads pounded for long stretches into an iron-hard, washboard surface that shook every nut and bolt in the car and every bone in our bodies and which sent stones crashing against the (specially reinforced) undercarriage of the Peugeot at such a rate that it sounded as if we were under machine-gun fire. We were however, able to forget the discomfort and the noise because immediately beyond the town we ran through a long spinney of baobabs: huge, grotesque trees looking as if they were growing upside-down. Their wood was said to be useless to man because it had the consistency of cheese but they gave shade to elephants, herds of which we saw that very morning.

There followed 300 miles of corrugated red, yellow, white and purple dust, or, during the wet season, glutinous, porridge-like mud. Apart from the crossing of the Great Ruaha River, water was nowhere to be seen. Hour after hour, we hugged mountain slopes, gazed down from precipices, sweltered through valleys, passed hardly a single place of human habitation, saw scarcely another motor vehicle and never a petrol pump, but, in overwhelming recompense, we came into eye contact with hundreds of wild creatures.

Worn out and caked with a thick layer of grit as if we'd just emerged from a sandstorm, we came to Iringa, a good, clean, German-founded town offering a choice of lodging: (i) a comfortable 'Railway Hotel' (even though there wasn't a rail track for a couple of hundred miles) that served good, plain, home-cooked food; and (ii) the Greek-owned 'White House' which made up for its blousiness by providing a challenging, spicy table. What tipped the scales in favour of the Railway Hotel was its promise of deep baths filled with piping hot, reddish-brown water.

Between Iringa and Mbeya lay 200 miles of even more gruelling track. Every single metre jolted every last screw holding the Peugeot together and strained every nerve and sinew in our bodies. We juddered past the sad centre of white settlement, the Sao Hill Club; the snobbish Southern Highlands School, a private prep-school to which those few Tanganyika whites who could afford it sent their spoilt children; the monstrous Roman Catholic Cathedral-cum-cantonment that rose like an ugly great oil-tanker on an empty, calm sea from the barren landscape of Malangali; and the shanty hamlet of Igawa on one of whose run-down shacks made out of old oil drums and cardboard there hung the sign:

$$\boxed{\text{HOTEL}}$$

Hours later, hoping to build up our strength before tackling the last, crippling drive over the Mporoto hills, we pulled up at Chimala, a strange, mystical place not worth showing on the maps of the time. It boasted of only one building – a hotel of sorts, or so it claimed though I never met anyone who'd ever stayed overnight in it. In keeping with the whacky nature of many of the whites who had settled in remotest Tanganyika, the innkeeper was a portrait painter! It was said that he painted only warthogs:

Jaspar Warthog, Mathilda Warthog and so on but even if he'd been Rembrandt he'd still have had a struggle making a living in Chimala for within a radius of many hundreds of miles he'd hardly have found a single soul able to afford as much as a shilling for immortalisation in oils. His hotel was famous to travellers for three things: (a) its donkey, an outlandish beast in such a spot; had it not been fenced in day and night it would swiftly have been devoured either by wild animals or the local populace; (b) a monkey on the bars of whose cage the painter had slung one of his better works, a notice saying 'I BITE', a statement incomprehensible to the illiterate local Wasafwa who, if they'd had it translated phonetically into Kiswahili would have heard 'Eee bee tay', the name, they'd assume, of a species of primate; and (c) a guitar-playing teenage daughter who, poor child, having been virtually struck dumb by years of isolation, spoke only through her pensive eyes and the strings of her guitar.

Every pulverising inch of the last 40 miles up and over the Mporotos was corrugated and pot-holed, its dust like pink talcum powder. A few miles only and we were reduced to such a mood that we gave only a passing nod to the brilliantly plumed guinea-fowl which took up their abode in the Mporotos foothills, spared to proliferate because, radiant as they were in appearance, their flesh, we were told, was unappetising to man.

The summit of the Mporotos was swept ceaselessly by a perishingly cold blizzard. Yet there on either side of the road, crouching low to escape the worst of swirling, icy dust, you'd always find half-a-dozen ladies silently holding out cabbages and eggs for sale. Unclothed above the waist, those African Amazons remain in my mind as the only Tanganyikans from whom there arose the whiff of melancholy.

Mbeya

Mbeya, a small township nestling at 7,000 ft within a bowl of gentle hills, was home to 2,000 people: 500 Asians (merchants, artisans and, mainly Goan, civil servants), 100 whites (50 colonial officials, a couple of dozen traders and clergymen, a handful of landowners, one or two pensioners) and the rest blacks, of whom the local tribe, the Wasafwa, was outnumbered by black civil servants coming from outside the Mbeya district and often from outside Tanganyika itself.

The town's high street was lined on either side with one-storied *dukas* (shops) leading at the bottom of the hill to a big open-air market selling excellent local vegetables and fruit and, two or three times a week, fresh meat. There was a 'railway station' which served only East African Railways' buses, not trains; Catholic and Anglican 'cathedrals'; a Baptist church; a quaint, weather-beaten little hospital; and two hotels: the 'Railway' which offered bed and breakfast at seven shillings and sixpence but which reflected the district's water supply problems by charging five shillings extra for a bath, and the Greek-owned 'Mayflower'. The two hotels stayed in business only through bar and restaurant sales, their rooms being only spasmodically occupied by outstation colonial officers in town to report to their provincial headquarters, parents visiting offsprings attending the government boarding school on the outskirts of town and the occasional tourist who came to fish the trout in the Mprotos streams or who passed through travelling to and from the territories to the south, what were then known as Nyasaland (now Malawi) and Northern Rhodesia (Zambia). For relaxation the town offered three separate outlets: small clubs for the whites and Asians and *pombe* stalls – dirty, lice-ridden shebeens – for the blacks. Racial segregation came not from any legally based colour-bar for there was no such thing in Tanganyika, but just as effectively as if there had been one, from economics, privilege and prejudice on all three sides.

Mbeya was an orderly, well-swept, neat town, which, small and unrenowned as it was, yet housed a headquarters from which was administered a province almost the size of England.

No. 5 McMahon Road

We moved into house No.5 in a road named after one McMahon, a late notable whose personal history I never enquired into but who I presumed had been a colonial official who'd made a contribution towards the development of Mbeya. The Wasafwa would have had as much trouble pronouncing 'McMahon' in Kiswahili as they'd have had in figuring out what he'd done to deserve commemoration but, looking down the short stretch of red earth that bore his name, McMahon's road wasn't all that much of a memorial. No.5 was identical in every outward detail to almost every government-built house in the entire country, the only exceptions being larger, more stylish editions provided for colonial pashas like Provincial and District Commissioners, Superintendents of Police and judges. Sensibly, government's Public Works Department (PWD) had designed the simplest of dwellings, the intention being that they could be built using mainly unskilled labour out of locally available materials.

Besides the house and its furniture, we inherited from the Coventrys a 'houseboy' named Jumah, an impish teenager who promptly introduced us to, and gave us no choice but also to 'employ' as 'assistant', Joni. That playful pair of illiterate adolescents (Joni was hardly more than a child) were 'employed' at a rate of pay that, had we asked anything very much in return for it, would have been akin to slavery. As it was, in return for free lodging, some posho and a few shillings a month for sweeping up, chopping logs and building the fires, Jumah and Joni were free as birds; they lay in the sun a lot and strutted around the town as if they were bankers. They were endlessly cheerful and, seemingly at least, more than content.

Never a cross word passed between us, that is until, in our third year, Jumah came home with a battered, hand-wound, gramophone. It wouldn't have been so bad had he been able to afford, or acquire by other means, more than the one already badly scratched disc; but there it was – all the residents of 5 McMahon Road were subjected to the ceaseless repetition of a Swahili ballad which, sweet as it may have been first time round, began at the hundredth to wear on nerves, set teeth on edge and led to a confrontation.

Restrained as our objections were, they were ill received. In our ignorance of some obscure tribal ethic, we'd offended Jumah's deepest sensibilities and, bearing his precious gramophone, he took off in a great huff, bound, he declared, for his native *kijiji* (village) hundreds of miles distant (the distance lengthened with each declaration) and, he said, for good. But his tribe never got to hear his music because within a week he was back at No.5, tail between legs, apologetic, wistful, sans gramophone and exhausted. After hiding away in unaccustomed silence for a day or two he emerged to chop some wood and tell of his safari.

He said he'd never even set foot in his *kijiji*. Determined on harming him, a hostile sorcerer had placed a voodoo snare across Jumah's path: a spent matchstick. If his ever-vigilant guardian spirit had not riveted his eyes upon the diabolist's trap in good time, Jumah would have passed over it or even, heaven forbid, trodden on it. Had that happened, he said with a dramatic shudder, he'd have been cursed to spend the rest of his days as lifeless as the spar of wood from which the dreadful matchstick had been cut. That was his story and we never tried to reason him out of it. Bewitchery was common in Tanganyika and Jumah would have to pay a *mundungu* to exorcise the voodoo clear away, there was nothing else for it. In the meantime he was uncommonly morose. Joni, fearful, ran away.

Norina

To add to the six human beings and countless thousands of myriopoda, ants, hoppers, lice, skeeters, lizards and worms resident in No.5, there in trooped a veritable menagerie starting with the Empress herself: H.R.H. Norina I, better known as 'Nina'. A sleek black-and-rust female puppy-hound, Nina was presented to us as a welcoming gift by an Italian PWD road-supervisor, Pirelli, who lived just round the corner. That's how Nina came into her Italian persona: her jet-black eyes; deep warmth, grace; a tendency to be placid one minute and tempestuous the next; a love of pleasure; and, immediately post-adolescence, an inclination towards stoutness. She was adorable and no La Scala diva was ever idolised more fervently. From her liaison with a noble-headed, full-blooded Alsatian, 'Kim', who lived down the road, she produced a litter of astonishingly glamorous puppies of whom one, 'Pepe', grew into the most handsome mutt you ever saw; he stood with his mock-heroic head above what appeared to be padded shoulders, higher than his worshipping minder, our daughter Jane.

Malaria, the Rift and Wankie

The climate was bracing: for eight months of the year, predictable almost to the hour, brilliant sunshine out of clear blue skies; rain for the rest. Local diviners could tell to the very day of the year when to pack or unpack your wet-weather gear.

Days were cool and sharp, nights just short of freezing. It fell short of perfection however by reason of aridity; after a couple of months of the long dry season the air was bone dry, the earth baked. The roads turned into talcum, the skies a pitiless, metallic blue, the dust so penetrative that daily it coated every flat surface in the house.

To escape the dryness and its accompanying dehydration we'd drop down into tropical humidity either at Lake Nyasa (Malawi) at Mwaya or beside the Great Ruaha River near Chimala. Either trip meant 80 miles of grinding torture over one of Pirelli's so-called roads but the craving for the feel of moisture in your skin and the promise of the rapture that came from sitting alongside running water drove us on Sundays to endure it.

It was on one such Sunday, while skipping in the shallow, rushing waters of the Great Ruaha that one particular mosquito stung Jane. It was no momentous event at the time; after all, back in Mbeya mosquitoes were forever bayoneting us. What made that particular sting different was that it came from a malaria-carrying anopheles, a member of a species of mosquito absent at 7,000 ft in Mbeya but which thrived very nicely in the hot dampness that attracted them – and us as well – to Chimala. We'd happily thrown away the paludrine tablets that in Asia had turned us yellow but had also protected us from malaria. Unwittingly, by abandoning paludrine we'd left Jane without defences against a malaria-carrier down at the Great Ruaha.

Precisely eight days (the incubation period, we learned later) following our trip to Chimala, Jane's brain suddenly switched off. One minute she was her usual breezy self, the next a zombie. By a stroke of the sheerest good fortune however, she'd succumbed on the best possible day for it because when we carried her into Mbeya's Albert Schweitzer-type (no trimmings) hospital, we discovered half-a-dozen physicians gathered for a conflab. Diagnosing cerebral malaria – by far the most dangerous type of malaria – on the spot, they abandoned their conclave and set to work as a team to pull Jane through.

Now, much as the coincidence of the doctors being gathered together played the major part in it, Jane's recovery also came from her being a Mzungu (white). That's not to say that the doctors would have acted differently had she been black but that had she been black she'd probably have been out of their reach in a *kijiji* where maladies were treated only by voodooists (there were only a dozen qualified physicians in the whole province) and where invasion of the brain cells by tertiary fever (cerebral malaria) daily took the lives of blacks, young and old.

We clocked up thousands of safari miles without going outside my province. We'd drove to Lake Nyasa (Malawi) to the south; to Iringa 200 miles northeast; Njombe 100 miles east; to Lake Rukwa to the north-west; and to the border with Nyasaland (Malawi) and Rhodesia (Zambia) to the southwest. And, as if my territory wasn't far too wide already, because it was quicker to approach from Mbeya than from its provincial headquarters in Tabora, I was told to 'keep an eye' on the Sumbawanga district of Western Province. The trek to Sumbawanga may have been easier from Mbeya but it still took a bone-crushing day-and-a-half's drive to reach that town, a drive that incidentally passed through many miles of designated tetse-ridden wilderness where no creature could live for very long but which was miraculously relieved by huge swarms of brilliant butterflies.

Kiswahili

First things first; given that I'd already toiled for six years over the Malay and Thai languages; the colonial office excused me the higher grades of Kiswahili examinations. Nonetheless I was told that annual increments of salary and promotion prospects depended on my passing the lower, colloquial Kiswahili exam. A mix of Bantu, Persian, Hindi, European and, largely, Arabic tongues, Kiswahili is a much more complete, sophisticated language than Malay and is today ranked as one of the world's most important languages; the one that will, it is said, help you get from Berber to Beira, Zanzibar to Zaire. Pounding Pirelli's 'roads' in the company of black assistants helped me quickly to pick up enough of the lingo to pass the required exam and I did it within six months of arriving in Dar. But I never spoke it half as well as it deserves to be spoken, for when spoken fluently Kiswahili is a joy to the ear.

On Safari

Having such a vast area to cover I spent much of my time 'on safari' – travelling to the distant corners of the Southern Highlands Province and beyond. Attempting to give you the flavour of colonialised Tanganyika I've chosen to take you first to Njombe, a district whose administrative pattern mirrored that of all five districts in the province – and, apart from differences in topography, climate and local customs – the rest of the country as well. A description of Njombe will therefore serve all of them.

Njombe

The Njombe district, the size of Wales, was a parish of rivers, plains, mountains, swamps, valleys and lakes; of cold bare hills and steaming jungle; of wattle forests and mangrove, but not of roads. Even a four-wheel drive wouldn't get you far in Njombe; no, you needed stout boots, a sun hat, a walking stick, good lungs and plenty of patience. The native population was sparse, scattered, unlearned and unrefined. A tiny Wazungu community (Wazungu, the plural of Mzungu – a white person) had settled roughly but contentedly in wild, hallucinatorily beautiful – albeit less than verdant – highlands where they farmed coffee and pyrethrum, grumbled about prices, the vices of their black labourers, the baseness of the 'bolshies' back home, the shortcomings of the colonial government and the clumsiness and venality of their ill-paid domestic servants – and where they boozed mightily on South African hooch.

All that Njombe had going for it economically was the relatively thin, hardly profitable, cash produce of those same settlers and nobody was ever going to grow fat on the crumbs that fell from their tables. Some ill-placed but understandable optimism was placed in a sprawling plantation of wattle grown in the hopes that one fine day a market would be found for the tannin it produced. But, at least, when we were in Africa, no such market had been found. For all its material privation, however, Njombe was blessed; none of its children ever went to bed on an empty stomach.

It was said that the district was run not by government but by the 'White Fathers' (Benedictines) from their Mission at Uwemba just down the road from Njombe Township. Certainly the Fathers' mission complex was more imposing than anything the Tanganyika administration ever built but the Africans knew best who was the boss. True, the Fathers, who'd created an impressive collective around a church, school, clinic, workshop, farm and priory, plied a great deal of influence but it was the District Commissioner (DC) who imposed – or tried to impose – taxes, who coerced – or tried to coerce – people to dig ditches and who sent people to prison. The Fathers, known throughout the entire expatriate community for their lavish hospitality, kept a splendid table but precious few Africans ever sipped Rieslings and hocks from it; neither did many Africans sup with the DC but on Empire Day a few of them would get a cup of tea and a bun with him. The Fathers had built a replica of a Bavarian Priory, completing it by importing a great bell that had been cast in the fatherland and which had even been cracked by experts along the very same fissure as that which had cracked its German original, so that when hung in Uwemba the imported bell gave off the same discordant peal as its parent. I never learned what the locals made of that particular piece of the Wazungu's obeahism but the DC's *boma* (town hall, meeting place) couldn't hope to compete with it.

The *boma* was the formal, central point of colonial authority. Designed by unimaginative Public Works Department (PWD) engineers and built by unskilled labourers out of the material available on the spot, the Njombe *boma*, externally at least, lacked the slightest sign of authoritarianism. (By contrast, the Sumbawanga *boma*, built to the same PWD design, was given a regal appearance because it was dressed in the rich, red stone of the locality). Indecorous as it was however, and stiffly formal as it was intended to appear, nobody whoever went near the Njombe *boma* would have got the feeling that they were close to a bastion of heavy-handed, imperialistic bureaucracy. Its approaches were always alive with crowds of light-hearted, 'aweless' folk: litigants, complainants, defenders, supplicants and, predominantly, nosey-parkers who came just for the fun of it. They carried the paraphernalia needed for a long stay: fly-switches, coconut shells (for eating and drinking from), tobacco leaf, witch doctors' bones, blankets, palm-fronds, gourds of water and nose flutes. Inside, you'd find a confusion of dusty books, discarded files, out-of-kilter portraits of 'Mama Queenie' and Bwana Gubonor, empty ink-wells, over-spilled ash-trays, ramshackle cupboards and the smell of folk who hadn't bathed for a long time.

It might have been the size of Wales yet the district was run from a building no larger and perhaps even less pretentious than the average village hall in the Welsh valleys. Moreover, it was run by far fewer civil servants than would be on the payroll of the smallest Welsh town-hall: a white colonial contingent of just six – District Commissioner (DC), District Officer, a PWD official, an agriculturalist, a forester and a vet, backed up by maybe a dozen Asians and a score of Africans. And it was run on a budget so small that it would have had the lowest town clerk in Wales jumping down the nearest mineshaft. When activated the machinery conveyed not the impression of an all-powerful, all-seeing autocracy but of an easy-going community centre whose purpose was to inscribe details of individual and collective problems upon reams of cheap foolscap which, two or three times daily, were tied up in bundles and stacked higgledy-piggledy all over the place – and then forgotten.

A good deal of the stewardships – some said too much – depended on the DC; in Njombe's case he was, fittingly since I've used Wales allegorically, a Welshman, Peter E. I. Lee. Peter Lee embodied the genus of the public school, men whose boarding-house disciplines made it easier for them to turn the confidence trick of portraying themselves as supermen while also adhering to the code of administrative good manners that was applied everywhere from Njombe to Nauru, from Blantyre to Belize.

Peter Lee was at one and the same time mayor, town clerk, magistrate, police chief, supervisor of communications, surveyor of public works, town planner, chief accountant, registrar of births and deaths, inspector of health and sanitation, chief scout, collector of taxes, paymaster, fire-chief, bailiff, commissioner of oaths, notary public, overseer of schools, principal advisor to the local tribal chieftains and chairman of the chiefs' *baraza* (meeting). And here it must be said, to comment on Tanganyika's situation, that he was not overworked. Wearing full regalia, plumed hat, sword and all, on empire and armistice days he'd read the lesson in the Anglican church; dressed in a business suit he'd host garden parties; and, decked out in calico-denim with mosquito-proof boots, floppy hat and fly whisk, he'd preside over *barazas* deep in the bush. He'd spend half his days tramping his domain on foot, knapsack on his back.

He imposed law-and-order on his untracked vastness through the medium of no more than 17 policemen who were under the day-by-day charge of a Goan police inspector (the colonial service in Tanganyika employed a good many Goans, some of whom came from Portuguese – hence the Goan connection – Mozambique) and he did it with ease too because, there being next-to-nothing in the district worth stealing, his only law-and-order headache was caused by a high incidence of murder. And even then no fancy detective work was needed to bring the killers to book because, almost without exception, they gave themselves up. All the Goan inspector had to do was handle the paperwork, leaving Peter Lee with the grim business of sending the cases to the High Court for, much as he was King-of-the Castle, he couldn't pass sentence of death.

Lee's most telling demonstration of his lordship over the White Fathers was his house, by many a mile the best house in the district, the only habitat indeed that merited the approbation: 'residence'. Coming into Njombe Township, which was nothing more than half-a-dozen miserable *dukas* selling the usual beggarly provender that paupers could afford to purchase from the west, from Makambako or Igawa, you came upon a bridge that crossed the Mbarali River. Just beyond the bridge a sparkling curtain of water was thrown up from the trough of a shallow weir, a moving, wet screen that attracted the eye and also drew upon it clouds of dazzling butterflies. It was best not to stop to admire the scenery because the same spectacle also drew swarms of nasty insects whose stings were savage enough to keep most other living creatures – butterflies apart – at a distance. Beyond the weir and, mercifully, at a safe distance from the dreaded flies, there stood a gem of a low-slung, stone-bungalow – the DC's residence.

Built by the Germans, its metre-thick, solid-rock walls and its no-nonsense corrugated iron roof were, as you'd expect, appropriate to the climate and to its purpose as a sort of mini-Vice regal lodge. The overall impression of its being the focal point of authority was emphasised by a forbidding entrance deeply recessed into which was a massive door. Its windows were heavily shuttered and its great brick chimney stacks looked as if they'd been meant to serve as obelisks. Inside it shouted out its Teutonic origins: concrete floors, whitewashed walls, tremendous fireplace, heavy, sombre furniture and lots of space. One expected to see hunting trophies all over the place. But, for some reason or other, rather than communicating the intimidatory over lordship of a vizier of a strong, iron-fisted Kaiser, the DC's house in Njombe breathed an environment of serenity, lightness and simple comforts. Here was the confidence trick I've already alluded to made plain: whereas armed German soldiers may have goose-steeped around the bungalow warning off any native who dared approach, never a single watchman stood guard over Peter Lee and his like elsewhere in Tanganyika. In their days, at least when the weather conditions favoured it, the great door was always open to everyone.

Peter Lee personified the best of the 'heaven-born' DCs – whether in Africa, Asia or the Caribbean; he ruled light-handedly, his laxness being occasioned by a mixture of financial stringency, tropical torpor, the hushed voices of opposition and a leaning towards genuine altruism.

Iringa

Mbeya may have been the provincial capital but Iringa, 200 miles northeast, was the larger, more economically active town. The pugnacity of the Wahehe, the local tribe, had endeared them to the Germans who'd made Iringa their provincial headquarters. A glance at the tombstones in the white men's section of the cemetery (yes, even in death, there was apartheid) showed that the Kaiser's choice of the Wahehe to make up the bulk of his native army was a two-edged sword because, as the tablets bore witness, during the *maji-maji* rebellion in 1905–06 his askaris turned their weapons on their German officers.

Under the British, the Wahehe settled to peaceful pursuits and by 1958, led by a progressive, educated and ambitious 'Mtwa', Chief Adam Sapi, the town had grown into a centre for marketing the produce of the immediate surroundings: tea, coffee, pyrethrum and a little tobacco. The few Wazungu settlers grew almost all of that produce. To express their thanks for the blessings of the Wazungu's Almighty, the Consulate Fathers built a thundering great, hideous cathedral not far from Iringa at Tosomaganga – a nice name anyhow.

Iringa's relatively lively businesses didn't mean that it was a bustling metropolis whose air was filled with the jingle of cash registers or which boasted smart boulevards lined with chic emporia. No, what it meant was a dozen dust-coated Asian-owned *dukas* peddling single cigarettes, pots and pans, salt, tinned fish, kerosene by the pint, cheap, cardboard-like 'Bata' shoes and fabrics rejected by Western factories. Also, notwithstanding the fact that their shelves carried bottles of the cloying, sweet rotgut South African 'sherry' so beloved of Tanganyikans, they all publicised appeals for boycotting South African produce. Perhaps the saddest thing about the *dukas* was that they did a relatively brisk trade in tubes of 'skin-lightening' and 'hair straightening' creams which Africans purchased in the despairing hope that if they could only whiten their skins and iron out the kinks in their hair they'd soon be driving around in cars like the Wazungu and drinking all the 'sherry' they wanted.

Iringa boasted neither museums, libraries, cinemas, public auditoria, sports stadia nor public parks; the only institutions relating to its being a town in the 20th century were a bank and a garage but, everything being relative, Iringa was different; as you enter it, you felt that quickening of the pulse that comes with setting foot in a lively city.

Tukuyu

Your pulse, however, didn't race as you entered Tukuyu, a mere 25 miles south of Mbeya. By the time you'd traversed those few miles on the most back-breaking of highways, you felt as if you'd splintered every bone in your body. Small as it was compared with the other five districts, Tukuyu encompassed cold, dry uplands and, beside Lake Nyasa (Malawi) at Manda, a country so hot and humid that it grew rice. Mangoes were so abundant that you crushed them beneath the wheels of your Land Rover; it was as if some crazy Italian engineer had tried to surface the road with fruit; and green oranges grew in such volume that you could fill the back of your Land Rover to its roof for just two shillings.

Tukuyu was relatively prosperous. Its tribe, the Wanyakusa, were coloured a deeper shade of black and were smaller, more wiry, than their neighbours. By growing and selling coffee through a Co-operative they'd acquired a composite head for commerce. By Tanganyika standards they thrived. They had, however, a less admirable capacity for selling their younger males to the Wittwaterstrand Mining Company of (apartheid) South Africa. Every year, through an agency in Tukuyu Township, thousands of Wanyakusa young men were transported over the border to Fort Hill in Nyasaland (Malawi) from which dreary hole they were flown like so much merchandise to work in gulag conditions in the gold mines. At Wittwaterstrand, they were paid only one-third of an already meagre contract rate of pay, the remainder being held back for payment on their return home. The idea was well-meaning enough: it was intended that most of their pay would find its way to their families in Tanganyika but it didn't work out like that. Instead, homeward bound, the miners were fleeced of their money almost as soon as they collected it from the paymasters in Fort Hill where crooked white and Asian traders lay in wait to sell them all kinds of trash. Hence they'd return to Tukuyu wearing sham Stetsons, goofy sunglasses and cheap, loony clothes while carrying useless, fake-designer luggage. They sported fat cigars and much hooch but they'd hardly a Rand left in their pockets. Exposure to Western business methods when selling coffee and young men led a number of Wanyakusa to try to ape the Westerners in dress and deportment. The sad result was that, despite their relative affluence, the Wanyakusa who roamed Tukuyu's only street looked shabbier than the tribes next door.

On the outskirts of the town there was a leper settlement supervised by a humourless but high-minded Salvation Army couple. Their institute was run like a barrack: it was scrubbed, everything was in its place, commands were obeyed on the blast of a whistle; and all of it was totally contrary to what the lepers would have been used to back in their villages. Supervisors and patients alike however, shone with confidence in the belief that leprosy was a thing of the past, as indeed it was. The admirable pair of Yorkshire self-abnegators allowed themselves just one amusement: they played ancient gramophone records, thick and heavy as dinner plates, on an antique, hand-wound machine whose whacking great tin horn was a good metre across. The sound propelled by the pressure of fat wooden needles on wax cylinder was rich indeed but pity the lepers who, maybe shorn of fingers, toes and ear lobes, could still hear well enough and who had no option but to listen to the alien sounds of the owners' martial-spiritual-brass band repertoire. Onward Christian Soldiers!

Mbeya District

The district of Mbeya which to the south bordered on Nyasaland (Malawi) and Northern Rhodesia (Zambia) had but two marketable commodities: titanium and mica, both of which were mined in infinitesimal quantities; and a eucalyptus forest too far removed from possible markets for profitable exploitation. A handful of retired colonial officials grew coffee at Mbozi but, luckily for them, they didn't rely on its sale for their living: had they done so, they'd have starved to death. They were neither greedy nor arrogant, just well content to live out their lives in rough wooden bungalows without running water, push-and-pull sanitation, television or a reliable electricity supply; all they wanted – and rejoiced in – was empty space beneath an immense African sky. The main local tribe, the Wasafwa, was noted far and wide and even among its own brethren for its lassitude, which probably came from the subsistence level of their lives. It was a characteristic that sorely tried the DC Colonel Wilson, a very pukka, bean-pole of a man and a brilliant Kiswahili scholar who had enough energy for all the Wasafwa put together but, unfortunately for everyone in the district, he spent most of it on hunting, shooting and traducing the Wasafwa at every opportunity. Ergo, not in any sense was the Mbeya district well-endowed.

Chunya

A hundred miles west of Mbeya, next door, by Tanganyikan standards, lay the poorest district of all – Chunya. Yet it had once been, by many a mile, the richest. Way back in 1922 alluvial gold had been discovered on its windswept hills. Known as 'The Lupa', the area was instantly invaded from all over Africa by white diggers, dealers, chiselers, loan-sharks, bankers, romancers, four-flushers, quacks, clerics and whores. Dwellings sprang up overnight followed by a bank, a hotel, shops and even an airstrip. Chunya in the 1920s was the Klondyke of East Africa; 30 years later, like the Klondyke settlements, it was a ghost town, the shutters on the windows of the now-abandoned bank, hotel and shops swung open day and night.

But a few one-man 'mines' still cranked over, every week extracting from several tons of rock and shale as much gold dust as would fit what by then had become the accepted measure for the mineral: a small matchbox. The living was tough but then so were the ageing men and women who, banking on striking a nugget next week or the week after that, stayed on year after year buoyed on by their mania and by their memories. Sitting in their tin-pot houses with their matchboxes on the mantelpiece they'd tell stories over and over again. They'd tell of there having been so much gold on the old Lupa that clumps of it were used as doorstops, about champagne running like a river, about ball-gowns and tuxedos and about glamorous women stepping from aeroplanes wearing the high-heels and slinky outfits they'd flaunted on the boulevards of Paris and Rome only a day or two earlier.

The Mbeya-Chunya road went up to 8,000 ft. From that pinnacle you could look down on the Rift Valley, a view that, if your dust-reddened eyes were up to it, would take your dust-parched breath away. Not far from the eyrie, at what a road-sign said was 'THE HIGHEST ROAD IN TANGANYIKA', a dozen traditional, mud-walled, grass-roofed, earth-floored rondavels stood in a circle around a wooden shed that served as kitchen, dining room and social hall for the inhabitants of the encircling rondavels. The residents comprised a score or so of ancient, white, ex-gold prospectors. Whatever fortunes any of those geriatric diggers had ever struck (and they too talked of the fabulous 1920s when they'd drunk champagne at breakfast and when the ladies had been draped in mink) they'd long ago squandered them. In the 1950s, still unable to tear themselves away from 'The Lupa' in case somebody struck lucky again, they were trapped in their minute one-roomers on a high, chalky, alien plateau, their sole means of sustenance a pittance doled out by the colonial government to the manager of their camp, an honourable old stick who, against their never-ending chorus of complaints and abuse, spent it on their Spartan upkeep, every now and then meeting out a shilling here and there for pocket money.

I was welcomed into one of the rondavels by a neat senior citizen who'd arrived on 'The Lupa' 25 years earlier as a priest. Sent by his church to save the souls of the gold-crazed prospectors, he immediately lost his own to his brethrens' madness for gold. Defrocking himself there and then, he'd spent the next 20 years scouring 'The Lupa', digging for, but never striking, the fortune he expected to come across 'tomorrow'. And there he was in 1959 toothless, penniless, unrepentant, and full of grace. Through the gloom (the rondavels were short on windows) perched on an empty orange-crate as though reclining on a Chippendale sofa, I spotted his wife, dressed as if she were at tea in the drawing room of some grand Victorian vicarage. With gracious decorum she offered me her hand. Every other inch of space was filled with journals – thousands of them – on oceanography. Having first thrown away his cassock and then his digging tools, my host, at a distance of 600 miles from the sea he'd not seen in many a year and would never see again, was engaged in the study of the oceans!

I write as if there were no Africans in Chunya. There were, of course; the country was theirs after all. They were indeed in a majority of tens of thousands to one, scattered thinly and grubbing subsistence livings from poor land. If there was anything to be said for colonialism it was that it didn't inflate the natives' expectations. It didn't for example teach them dental hygiene – which was just as well for neither did it provide a single, solitary dentist for the whole of the Southern Highlands Province.

Ergo, ignorance was bliss; not having a clue about dentistry the Africans never complained about the lack of an orthodontist; neither did they express disappointment over the absence of toothbrushes on the shelves of the few *dukas* in town, they couldn't have afforded them had there been. Their staple diet of *posho* or *ugali*, a mash made from maize boiled into a thick white paste that tasted like bread dough and which was eaten with fingers from a communal pot – would have kept them from dentists anyway. Much as the twice daily intake of their unappetising porridge may have kept the dentist away, it failed to give them the energy they'd have needed to copy the white intruders hunt for gold, an enterprise they regarded with contempt. Away in their *vijijis*, out of the colonialists' sight they did their own thing. Few were to be seen in Chunya Township, a district centre reduced to hardly anything more than a flyblown *boma* with nothing to offer the masses.

Nevertheless, there were still more Africans than others in town; clerks employed at the *boma*, domestics working for the handful of whites who ran the district, half-a-dozen police *askaris*, labourers who toiled on the 'highway', a tribal chieftain and his entourage and, by far the most numerous, the crowds of camp followers that came with anybody lucky enough to draw a regular wage in cash; the humblest peon on a government pittance would share it with a dozen hangers-on. One drawback of urban life for the masses was a feeling of being under the surveillance of the white bwanas, their memsahibs and their attendants.

Unlike their rural cousins for instance they couldn't flout the white man's paternalistic law forbidding Africans to booze in their own homes. Out in the *vijijis* such an iniquitous ordinance was simply ignored but in town the mucilage known as *pombe*, a hooch fermented from maize, could only be brewed and consumed – and even then only consumed by adult males – in the government supervised *pombe* stall.

The stall was a quadrangle, something like a small, square bullring floored with well-pounded earth surrounded by a high, whitewashed stonewall. You could enter and leave only by way of a single fortified portal, a cumbersome great door like those on the outside walls of prisons. Except when admitting or releasing customers it was kept bolted shut. If not perhaps a bullring then the quadrangle was like a prison yard except that at its centre there sat a huge cast-iron pot presided over by three elderly, fat females, the only women permitted through the gate. One of those shapeless mamas drew the brew from the cauldron and ladled it into heavy, scum-encrusted, litre-sized tin mugs held out in Oliver Twist fashion by the customers. A second refilled the urn from slime-coated four-gallon cans while the third took the money. A good bite of the takings went into the Chunya treasury that had precious few other sources of revenue.

Clutching his badly dented jug of good cheer, the reveller would climb aboard a raised concrete emplacement that stretched around three of the inner walls. Lying back on the platform as if it were a catafalque he'd guzzle his heady potage down to the last dregs. The cheesy mash left at the bottom of his mug, he'd chuck into an open sump running beneath his perch. He'd rouse himself now and then to urinate and at times to vomit into the said drain. A Dantesque place, the *pombe* stall was cheerless, inhuman, without a shred of dignity and apocalyptically unsanitary. It served only as a cold and smelly venue to get plastered in, a piggy bank for collecting money for the purpose – or so the drinkers believed – of lining the pockets of the 'Bibi Queenie' in a distant, foreign *kijiji*.

Kazi (Work): Mbeya

I'd only been in the colonial service for a few years but I was already wise enough to its ways to know that I could expect no clear-cut work directives from my new supervisors. And I didn't get any either. A doltish police superintendent in Dar had given me the standard pep-talk recited to intelligence agents throughout Western colonialist territories: there was an urgent need to combat an international communist-inspired plot to defeat imperialism. My instructions were to identify such agents of the plot lurking in the Southern Highlands Province and to mark them down – together with the names of their toadies – so that 'when the time came they could be cleared away'. With that I was sent on my way. From Paul Coventry I'd inherited a neat, three-room, brick-built office staffed by two white female assistants. I'd also taken charge of an even smaller bureau in Iringa staffed by a junior white officer and his white female secretary. My Mbeya team was reinforced, without my having been consulted about it, by a military intelligence Captain who was required only to get to know the local scene in case it ever became necessary to station soldiers in the province, in which eventuality he'd help logistically in their deployment. In addition he was to 'follow instructions' – mine – but since I'd scarcely enough work for myself let alone for anybody else, I gave him none. He didn't make a fuss about it.

Then there were the Africans – a half-dozen, barely literate, male so-called 'detectives' who knew nothing about communism nor about any other ism including anti-imperialism but upon whom the rest of us, and ultimately the state itself, depended for any political intelligence worthy of the name. The most senior African was one Peter Obale, a handsome, Nubian-featured Ugandan whose predilection for *pombe* and prostitutes was to cause me more trouble than he was worth as a 'detective'. The other Africans, whose names I've forgotten, roamed the province attending *barazas*, listening to soothsayers, mingling with churchgoers, dancing at *ngomas*, eavesdropping at meetings of Co-operatives' shareholders, wallowing in *pombe* stalls and picking up rumour and gossip from them all. They'd come home to Mbeya every now and then if only to collect their pay and expenses and they'd report – as they did invariably, at least in the early days, 1957–58, that everywhere was quiet. That fact was in itself, of course, political intelligence.

My Mbeya team, including even the army Captain, John Tate, who turned out to be an unmilitaristic and witty companion, shared an iconoclastic rejection of the gospel according to Special Branch headquarters and behind it MI5 and MI6: that communists lurked in *tembes* and *pombe* stalls all over the place. Influenced perhaps by my own protestations on the subject – I was, after all, the boss – none of us ever took seriously the 'security threat' as proposed by headquarters. The youthful pair in Iringa however, David Hale and Sheila Bailey, swallowed it whole. David, a serious-minded, ambitious young policeman, and Sheila, born in Tanganyika to old Africa hands, were so solemnly and earnestly conformist that both were later welcomed into MI6.

The thrust of it was that we all wasted most of our time on idle pursuits and that all of us, except for Hale and Bailey, laughed about it. For myself, I safaried my vast territory listening to yarns told by district commissioners, assorted officials, policemen, coarse rustics, clerics, *imams*, hoteliers, crocodile breeders, coffee growers, poorly-paid menials, make-shift so-called trade unionists, Italian road foremen, wandering minstrels (of whom there were a great many) and black hitch-hikers whose unwashed bodies gave off a sharp but inoffensive odour that penetrated every nook and cranny in the Land Rover and lingered forever.

On top of all the 'intelligence' gathered by my 'professionals', every man jack on the government's payroll was charged with passing on to me every scrap of political information that came his or her way.

Every scrap of 'intelligence', be it the factual truth or tittle-tattle, from whose mouth or pen: chief, commoner, Carmelite clergyman or crackpot, came into my red brick box in Mbeya to be pawed over, sifted and (what little of it was not thrown into the incinerator) 'collated'. The collation then formed the basis of my draft of a monthly issue of the 'Southern Highlands Province Security Intelligence Report' – 'Sitrep' for short or, according to my irreverent team, Comic Cuts or Beano. Towards the end of each month that draft ended up in front of the 'Provincial Security Committee', a foursome made up of the Provincial Commissioner, his deputy, the Provincial Police Commander and myself as 'Secretary'. The four of us would drink tea while plodding word-by-word through my draft, altering the placement of a comma here and, to show off, adding a Swahili proverb there before clearing the Sitrep for despatch to Dar es Salaam where our masters would consider what bits, if any, to insert into the territory's Sitrep to London.

I trod very carefully in the beginning. A new boy in Africa, I was afraid of advancing views that might not find support with people like the Provincial Commissioner (a kind soul named Jock Griffiths) who'd spent a working lifetime in Tanganyika. I stuck to the Coventry line, drafting Sitreps reflecting the bromidic views of the district commissioners. I put the budding anti-colonial movement in its true perspective, which was more of a distant rumble than a thunderclap. I wrote of continuing African support for, or rather lack of antagonism against, the status quo. From late 1957 however, our Sitreps began to tell Dar es Salaam what it surely knew without being told by Mbeya: that it would very soon need to put the question: was Julius Nyerere to be given a great deal of political clout or was government preparing to use force against him, force by a government almost devoid of soldiers? Whether the question was ever asked by Dar of London, I don't know, but from the way things turned out, if it ever was asked London's answer was – give Nyerere his head.

The Tanganyikan African National Union

It had taken Julius Kambarage Nyerere but three short years to transform his political party, the Tanganyikan African National Union (TANU) from a laughing stock into a movement that clearly challenged the continuation of colonial rule. But, mirroring the penury of the country itself, TANU was so impoverished that it took it until late 1957 to get enough cash together to send its leader to one of the country's largest and most important provinces – the Southern Highlands. Anyway, together with a few thousand Wasafwa, I clapped eyes on Nyerere for the first time when he entered Mbeya standing in the back of a lorry he'd borrowed from an Indian trader when his own Land Rover – DSK50 – the only motor vehicle his party possessed (and second-hand at that) had broken down on the dreadful Mporotos. And there he was in the flesh, hanging on to the overhead framework of the back of a clapped-out truck as it chug-chugged up the hill into town past Rothbletz's garage.

Transport wasn't Nyerere's only problem that day. His loudhailer was gummed up and the dust had left him with a sore throat. Eloquent and witty as he was as a conversationalist, he was no great platform orator; he always needed the amplification of his loudhailer to make himself heard in front of crowds. There were two other loudhailers in town: one belonged to the Catholic mission, the other – never used – to the police. Fearful perhaps of invoking the wrath of the colonial establishment the holy fathers turned down Julius' entreaty flat. But, without even being asked, that lovely fellow, the Provincial Police Commander, Harry Dufill, offered his. And to top it off, when handing it over to a surprised Nyerere, Harry gave him a salute.

Dufill's salute to Nyerere up there by Barclays Bank in Mbeya in the autumn of 1957 probably made history as the first ever made by a uniformed white colonial officer to a black commoner in Tanganyika. And who knows what its significance may have been for the future political development of the country? Nyerere, I believe, was alive to its importance because time and again during his speeches over the next few years he warned his listeners to follow him in opposing colonialism and not the white people who ran it, many of whom, he said, were their friends and helpers. During that first visit his progress among his own kind, who were totally unaccustomed to what was happening anyway, was a good deal less than triumphant but he touched to the quick those who counted – white officialdom.

Small and spare built as he was, Nyerere nevertheless cast a long political shadow. And he did it in spite of, rather than because of, his party. That was what I tried to convey in my draft Sitreps and, by and

large, it was the approved account despatched every month to Dar.
TANU was made up of thousands of penniless, illiterate peasants. At
local levels it was run by politically innocent, semi-literates typified
by its 'Provincial Secretary' in Mbeya, one Wilferemu Mwakitwange.
A young, mission-educated Mnyakusa, Wilferemu dashed around
the Southern Highlands with tremendous energy preaching, in
denial of Nyerere's policy line, insurrection. He was a colourful rascal
and a genuine opponent of colonialism but was intellectually and
temperamentally quite incapable of leading a mass movement with the
restraint and dignity that Nyerere asked of it. What's more, and in this
way too, he typified most other local TANU figureheads, his fingers
were seldom out of the goat-skin bag in which he stashed his members'
pitifully meagre subscriptions. Very little of the money made its way to
TANU headquarters. Very few people – even of his own tribe – took
him seriously.

Mwakitwange's organisation had no committees, no records, no
accounts, no offices, no membership registers. But where after 70 years
of colonial rule could Nyerere have found Africans versed in committee
procedures or in political or any other organisation? Where were his
clerks and accountants to be found? Nowhere. Mwakitwange wasn't the
thug the white settlers made him out to be; neither was he a criminal
and neither did his satirising of Western missionaries make him an
atheist and therefore, according to Hale and Bailey, a Marxist. He was
smart, a good orator and, off the platform, a good companion. I knew
that much because he and I played football for the same Mbeya team:
'Lebuka'. Sure, it would have been better for TANU, for Nyerere and,
ultimately, for the country had the party been able to find local leaders
of a higher calibre than Wilferemu, men who could at least have earned
the respect of tribal chiefs to say nothing of *wasettlers* and colonial
officials. But they just weren't there. Nyerere had no hope of exercising
day-by-day control over his Mwakitwanges whose gross escapades, even
where performed among people not overly censorious of bad manners,
did much to harm TANU.

Nonetheless, Nyerere's machine was unstoppable. By the time of his second visit to Mbeya in 1958 the bush telegraph had long heralded his coming as a new, all-powerful, black Messiah. No colonial governor had ever been welcomed by such crowds or with such reverence, excitement and near-adoration. There was no need for our Sitreps to tell officialdom the way things were going. Even so there were still those blimpish enough to disbelieve their eyes and ears, District Commissioner George Baker in Tukuyu for one. In spite of the evidence before his very eyes, George, on the day before Nyerere was to address a meeting on the outskirts of Tukuyu town, swore that he, George Baker, was dearer to the hearts of the Wanyakusa then "that so-called 'Mwalimu' (teacher)" would ever be. And he let it be known far and wide that he'd be displeased to see a mass turnout of Wanyakusa to hear Nyerere speak. Moreover, by publicly declining Nyerere's invitation to attend the rally, he set an example he wanted all the chiefs – and consequently the masses – to follow. But when the roars of the huge crowd penetrated the thick walls of George's German-built *boma*, he conceded, and with good grace too, that it was time to get behind the 'Mwalimu'.

When, during the same 1958 visit, Nyerere arrived at the provincial capital, the witless Mwakitwange bounced him into attending a 'cocktail party' thrown by the local TANU branch in his honour. That few whites accepted their invitations was a blessing in disguise, for those that did found plenty to sneer about. The venue was untidy, the reception chaotic, the service sloppy, the glasses filthy, the food inedible and the drinks home-made liquid fire.

There was much to be learned from the evening though. Like the political escapologist he was to become, Nyerere appeared to be above the squalid confusion and he was all cool charm. He welcomed the few Wazungu not as creatures of a regime he was out to overthrow but as passers-by in need of tuition in local customs. He personified a good person, perhaps physically too frail to stand up to the struggle he'd embarked upon but sharp, on the level and unrevengeful. He stood at arms length from the corruption and incompetence of Mwakitwange and appealed, wordlessly but effectively, not to be judged along with Wilferemu and company. To me he was akin to the heroic. I had a feeling that night that we wouldn't be long in Tanganyika.

Kwehiri (Goodbye) Mbeya

Three years flew by as if they'd been three weeks. Life was good in Mbeya; we were never to be more comfortable with each other than we'd been there. Apart from Jane's brush with the mosquito-borne angel of death and DMF's having to hitch-hike a 1,200-mile round trip to Dar to get a tooth fixed (there wasn't a single dentist in the whole of the Southern Highlands Province) we were as fit as cockroaches in the Governor's kitchen.

To put the icing on the cake I was promoted. I'd still not spent a single hour in a police station but I was made a Police Superintendent! What's more, I was told that on our return from home leave, I was to take the plum intelligence job in the country – I was to take charge of the Special Branch unit covering Dar es Salaam city. There were clouds in our sky though: the end of colonial rule was nigh, meaning job hunting in prospect and, blackest of all, the time dreaded by all colonialists was upon us – the family was to be split: Christopher would have to stay at school in England when we came back to Dar. Mercifully, by that time in colonial history London's undertaking to fly the children of its officials to their overseas territories twice a year free of charge had eased the pain of family separation. It was an excellent, generous concession.

After five months leave on the south coast of England, DMF, Jane and I flew to Dar in the very first Comet (an ill-fated aircraft) to fly to East Africa. We saw Kilimanjaro just a few feet, it seemed, beneath us, then followed the sun-baked coast from Mombassa, past Tanga, and then came in over a turquoise sea to land at Dar es Salaam, a place so different from Mbeya that it might have been in another hemisphere. Where Mbeya had been cool and arid Dar was torrid, its air damp, its vegetation lush and its environs just a touch metropolitan. Small as it was, it was still the capital city and seat of government of an immense country; in less than two years time it would house a hundred foreign embassies. It was a clean, sweet-smelling town sitting quietly on the edge of the Indian Ocean minding its own business.

The very first thing we did, right there and then at the airport, was to post letters written aboard the same Comet that'd carry them back to Christopher, the first of hundreds, probably thousands, that were to pass between the four of us over the next 20 years.

Dar was populated, but not overcrowded, by a confusion of people: exuberant black indigenes (not noticeably in the greatest number), ever-cool Arabs (the descendants of those who, under the sultan of Muscat, had ruled the roost in Tanganyika from a headquarters in Zanzibar until only a hundred years before), handsome, slim and, by reputation, arrogant Somalis (favoured as servants by the better-off), blacks from neighbouring lands some of whom stood out a mile – the stick-insect like King of Burundi for example, a 6-ft 7-in tall political refugee hemmed in day and night by bodyguards of Watusi, a tribe famous throughout Africa for its height, slenderness and ferocity – aloof Asians of as many different shades of brown as there are religions and castes on the Indian sub-continent; head-turning mixed-raced beauties, a handful of busy-busy Chinese; and a scramble of the Wazungu hierarchy: true-blue Colonel Blimps; pale uppity, learned barristers, swaggering 'white hunters', theatrically costumed clergy; neat upright bankers, nondescript businessmen, a few boozy beach-combers; and a goodly number of red-faced lumpish engine drivers and work-a-day engineers who finished every day swilling ale in the New Africa Hotel.

For the first time in our colonial life – and by the time we reached Dar in 1960 we were almost veterans – we were to live smack-bang under the eyes of our ultimate overlords: Governors, Chief Secretaries, Attorneys and Accountants-General, Commissioners of this and that and the other, and later, Chief and Prime Minister, Cabinet Ministers, Parliamentary Secretaries and so on. In many other colonies and dependencies our arrival at the seat of government would have meant going through starchy formalities such as the leaving of calling cards but Tanganyika's economic misfortunes were such that we were spared much of the ridiculous protocol beloved of colonialists elsewhere.

By the same economic token however, the treasury couldn't run to furnishing our homes and offices with cooling systems; hence for nine months of the year (May–July were the least humid), we lived like creatures in the middle of a compost heap. Dar was so hot and clammy that day and night we felt in danger of melting. Even so, it was an agreeable place, a relaxed town in which only the highest and mightiest wore collars and ties, few buildings were higher than four stories; there wasn't an elevator anywhere; and the fanciest emporia were like the corner shops seen in the back streets of European towns.

Our allotted house, about two miles out of town in 'Oyster Bay', was a copy of No.5, McMahon Road, Mbeya except that it stood in more verdant pasture, lacked fireplace and chimney, was blessed with an electric cooker and fridge and simmered in 24-hour heat and moisture. With sundown bringing hardly a dip in temperature or humidity, we'd lie in our mosquito-netted beds uncovered by even as much as a cotton sheet, stifled and smouldering. Daytime we wore as little as we could get away with, exposing large areas of skin to the attention of a zillion *dudus* (bugs) and ignoring the advice that come nightfall, DMF and Jane should have worn high 'mosquito boots' beneath long skirts.

Exhausting and uncomfortable it may have been but Oyster Bay had much to offer in compensation for heat in extremis and for pests in unstoppable hordes. Only rarely did we wish we were somewhere else. Only a minute's stroll from our front door, for example (a door incidentally never locked and, for that matter, seldom even shut) and we were at the edge of the Indian Ocean whose waters were warm, clear and salty, bliss to submerge into and which, when they ebbed, left an exposed coral wonderland that was almost an extension of our front garden; a reef alive with curious, colourful, sometimes outlandish and occasionally grotesque creatures. In the trees in our garden flew bulbuls and flycatchers, shrikes, kingfishers and sun birds, while overhead sailed vultures, eagles and brown kites.

Nina, who'd lodged in Dar with a fellow officer, was beside herself with joy when we picked her up, immediately resuming her place as head of the household (which now included a guinea pig) and taking to the Indian Ocean as though it had been poured out purely for her pleasure.

The city of Dar was an ornamental garden lying beside a salty lake. In full bloom its main street, Acacia Avenue, was a long arcade of yellow fragrance the sight and scent of which made you want to look up the name of the colonialist who'd first planted the trees so that you could write to his grandchildren saying how much was owed to their grandfather. Our little house itself permanently displayed dazzling bouquets of cannas and frangipani; every bush was a resting place for an exotic bird while the inner walls crawled with a profusion of geckos gorging themselves on *dudus*. We suffered the old financial headaches but our social entanglements were minimal and we made do.

There being in those days not a single plastic bag in the entire country, we swam from golden, unpolluted, deserted beaches almost on our doorstep. When Christopher came on holiday we put on a show for him: we swam, goggled and explored the reef; we spent a night 10,000 ft up in the blue Ulugurus overlooking Morrogoro. We motored along the appalling track that went under the name of 'Coast Road' to Bagomoyo, once the transhipment port for slaves and the take-off point for Victorian explorations. At Bagomoyo we picnicked on the steps of the old *boma* built by the first German Governor of Tanganyika. These German *bomas* with their firing-apertures, watchtowers and enfilading positions were fortresses built to withstand sieges; that was the German way, they came not with medicine chests, seedlings and exercise books but with weapons of war – it showed clearly in Bagomoyo.

While we ate our picnic in front of the crumbling *boma*, we watched dhows sailing in and out as they'd done for more than a century, the incomers furling their great sails like swans coming down to water; they came from India and Arabia bearing dates and Persian carpets, loaded with ivory, coconuts and ebony for their return. In the afternoon we trod warily in dark cemeteries, tiptoeing past tombs decorated with shiny bits of pottery. We walked in silence in respect for the hundreds of thousands of slaves who'd been driven down those same narrow alleyways, pausing, as the slaves would never have been allowed to, to wander at the massive, ornately carved, brass-studded doors that once opened upon the homes of Arab slavers.

Kazi (Work): Dar es Salaam

My Special Branch team in Dar es Salaam was made up of a cultured, Tanganyika-born, orthodox Sikh, Harindah Singh Gill; a handsome, tall, very black, very talkative Ugandan, Livingstone Lubega; a fat, middle-aged, alcoholic Englishman, Stewart Langley; a dozen locals; two white secretaries and myself. I wonder if any other capital city in the world was watched over by fewer security intelligence spooks?

By now I don't need to tell you that I had no specific direction. I worked on the assumption that I was to watch Julius Nyerere's movements, not with the objective of providing government with cause to obstruct him but of helping government the better to understand him. It wasn't a difficult task because everything he did politically he did right out in the open for everybody to see and hear. Because he had only two or three clapped-out Land Rovers at his party's disposal and because he couldn't afford the 66 cents a mile at which Campling Brothers and Vanderwall offered an aeroplane, he hardly ever set foot outside Dar. This of course meant that all the political information worth gathering lay in the capital city.

When, in May 1960, elections were called for the Legislative Council, TANU won 70 out of the 71 seats and from then onwards Julius Nyerere was the country's paramount chief, then Chief Minister, then at breakneck speed, Prime Minister.

Nyerere first heavily influenced and then controlled the choice of intelligence targets for what was now his special branch. However, apart from removing the concentration on the 'red menace' that had obsessed his colonial predecessors, he changed our role surprisingly little. What my own charter boiled down to was that Nyerere's person was to be protected against physical assault (he feared cranks) and I was to keep close tabs on what few political opponents he had. It wasn't much of a task, even for so few of us. He never had more than one bodyguard in attendance; sometimes none at all, and they were never armed. Indeed, never at any time in Tanganyika did any of my offices house a single firearm and I can think of no time in my five years there when anybody at all – except for game hunters – anywhere in the country, fired a shot. That left just three of us – Harindah Singh, Livingstone Lubega and myself – to do all the spooking in the capital city. Our job was made easier by the impoverishment all around the land; just about everybody was willing to sell 'secrets' for a shilling or two.

The three of us each 'handled' two or three 'agents' who were well placed both within TANU and its opponents but, since everything was done in the open, they had no 'secrets' to reveal. The best they could do, and it was a useful if negative best, was to affirm and reaffirm that no politician in Dar es Salaam had an idea of winning his or her political goal through anything but peaceful, lawful ways. One of my own, personal, 'secret agents' – the jewel in the special branch's crown – was the Secretary General of the National Union of Tanganyika Workers, Michael Kamaliza. A tall, good looking, educated, English-speaking, polite young man, Michael was the country's leading trade unionist, a top TANU official and a pre-ordained Cabinet Minister in Nyerere's first post-independence government. In most other countries, his status and prospects would have won him a good living but this was Tanganyika where, no matter how low the dues were fixed, few members of political or labour organisations ever paid them, a state of affairs that meant that it was never possible to figure out the size of the membership of any such organisation. In consequence, party and union officials seldom had anything in their pockets. Inevitably then, more than a few of them (but always excluding Nyerere himself) were on Special Branch payroll. At bottom, we spied first on anti-colonialists and then on anti-TANUists simply for the sake of spying. Spying was, after all, what Government paid us to do.

It made for an absurd situation but one that was never subjected to public accountability, both truths being by no means peculiar to Tanganyika.

The Special Branch's clowning in that country wasn't exceptionally bizarre; it being in the very nature of all 'intelligences' to be ill-directed, unaccountable and wasteful, why should we have been any different? Just consider, for a prime example, how I personally 'handled' (the word comes from the universal lexicon of all secret services) our prize spy, Kamaliza. For all the 'secrets' he passed to me we might as well have met in the full glare of the lamps that hung in the courtyard of the New Africa Hotel but that wouldn't have done at all; 'secret' agents and their 'handlers' are supposed to come to their rendezvous by separate, circuitous routes, meeting on the sly in 'safe houses' where they'd speak in undertones.

Michael and I kept strictly to those rules, our meetings were right out of the spy novel. We met twice a month at dead of night (which in Dar meant anytime after 1900 hours) in a railwayman's hut just off Gerazani Street, hardly 007-style but still. Seated on old railway sleepers beneath a flickering, weak little lamp, breathing in the stink of engine-oil, creosote, rats' droppings, pombe sediment, oily rags and wheel grease and doing our best to ward off swarms of bugs, while Kamaliza smoked a cheroot and sipped brandy and I drank Tusker beer (cigars, brandy and beer courtesy of the Tanganyika treasury) we'd gossip about what was going on in our respective constituencies. I'd dish the dirt on the establishment while Michael went on about his lot.

Kamaliza was an intelligent, erudite idealist speaking about the most exciting and promising time in his country's history; hence, despite the awfulness of our 'safe house' our trysts were most agreeable. Besides cheroots and cognac, I paid him 200 shillings a month meaning that I gave him government money for information that that same government already knew. Had Michael ever got wind of a plot to harm Nyerere he'd have told the Chief/Prime Minister – and for nothing, before he'd have told me. Every now and again we'd laugh over our mutually ridiculous situation but we kept it going, he because he badly needed the money, me also because I was paid to do it; I'd have been in terrible trouble had I dropped our star turn. On the very eve of independence however, when Michael knew he'd be going on to the payroll as a Cabinet minister, we met in the grimy railway shed for the last time. We clicked mugs to each other and went our separate ways.

For the next eight years I'd get a kick out of news reports telling of Tanganyika's Minister of Labour addressing gatherings in Geneva, Kuala Lumpur or wherever. But in 1969 I got a kick in the stomach when I read that Michael Kamaliza had been placed under 'preventative detention' in Dar and, later, that he'd been sentenced to 10 years imprisonment for 'plotting to overthrow the government of Tanganyika'.

Uhuru na kazi ('Freedom and Work')

As the great day approached, the talk amongst the planners of the Independence Day civilities and celebrations (most of whom, ironically, were white colonial officials who, to give them their due, bent their backs to the tasks) was of impending pandemonium. With only a month to go, everything was in shambles. There weren't for instance, anything like enough hotel beds to accommodate the host of foreign big-wigs who'd been invited; hence the colonialists were asked to host them in their own homes; the best motor cars in town, irrespective of ownership and together with their drivers, were appropriated to shuttle to and from the airport to welcome incoming ambassadors, royals, commissars, guerrilla leaders and hot-shot journalists, all of whom were given escorts. For the rest, tongue in cheek, we simply assured Governor and Prime Minister that everything was under control and hoped for the best.

As always in Tanganyika, the planners had to have an eye on the budget; there was to be no costly razzmatazz. The Uhuru monument for example, the very shrine of the independence movement and centrepiece for the festivities was but a rude block of cement poured by the PWD overnight on a spot at Mnazi Mmoja. The supply of knick knacks was left to an enterprising British company, which, led by a retired Colonel, was cashing in on the rush of colonies to independence. It specialised, believe it or not, in the art of staging Independence Day festivities, offering to lay on high jinks in accordance with whatever the country in question was prepared to spend.

Tanganyika of course, went for the cheapest package: knock-down price flags, bunting, invitation cards, car-stickers, leaflets, menus for banquets, seating cards, portraits, slogans, fireworks, bill-boards, posters and so on. Besides getting the song sheets and the sheet music of the new national anthem printed locally, all the planning committee had to do was dish out the flags, hang the bunting and fill the word TANGANYIKA plus the date and the catch-phrase UHURU NA KAZI in to the spaces left blank for that purpose. The posters, leaflets, cards etc. were otherwise exactly the same as they were for the many other emergent colonies that also employed the Colonel. Bang on schedule, without a hitch, and to great rejoicing in the streets, at midnight on the 8 December 1961, it was done. *Uhuru na Kazi*!

Kwaheri Tanzania

We were beset with problems long before Uhuru: to add to the fact that our parents were ageing and ailing we were anxious about the prospects of future employment in a fast shrinking empire. It looked as if our short colonial life might be ending. DMF worked it out that it was best for Jane to go to school in England and for DMF to set up house there. That we were able to buy a house came about through the independence agreements between London and Nyerere that provided for the British taxpayer to advance 'lump-sum' (golden handshake) payments to compensate colonial officials for 'loss of office and opportunity'. The money was paid whether you asked for it or not, whether you were staying in Tanganyika or not. Ours came to a respectable (in those days handsome) £8,000 most of which we spent on buying a house near Worthing, Sussex.

As it happened, our colonial lives were far from over. Right out of the blue London offered me a Special Branch post in Sarawak, a colony on the northern edge of Borneo. It only took a bat of an eyelid to accept and once again our meagre effects were packed up and once more they were sent off by ship across the Indian Ocean, this time from west to east. After saying goodbye to many good folk including Julius Nyerere who,

I confess, gave not the slightest indication of regretting my departure, while DMF went to England, I took off by East African Airways for Nairobi and Bombay from where, after a blissful couple of days in the Taj Mahal Hotel, Air India carried me back to the Far East.

It was only because we were headed for a part of the world we remembered with great joy that we shed few tears about leaving Africa. Even before we set off for Sarawak that colony had already been designated for incorporation into a new 'Malaysian' Federation; hence we were, in a way, going back to Malaya, a prospect that boosted the corporate family morale no end. We weren't to know it then but we were to spend another 20 years overseas.

Reflections

Tanganyika had been very kind to us; indeed, in retrospect, our time in Mbeya had been the very best of our family years, starting with the space of it: I see enormous expanses of sky; the limitless, often awesome, extent of the earth; the grandeur of green and blue mountain ranges; and the boundlessness of lakes. I hear the first rains drumming down on the taut, dry hide of Africa to be heard miles away and see them turning everything to sludge overnight. Yet in the long, parched months everything was burned to hard-caked stone, the rust of the laterite coming through the surface like blood swelling up beneath scraped skin.

Then I see its people, first of all the native Tanganyikans. They were much maligned by most whites and by many Asians because, went the most common scoff, "they'd never invented the wheel or a system of writing, they couldn't lay a straight path, plough a straight furrow, screw on bottle-caps or tighten a nut without shearing it". And so on. But the fault for their backwardness lay to a large extent upon their white overlords: as long as they treated the blacks as children the blacks would behave like children. White opinion was in any case based on their contacts with the relatively few blacks who'd gone into the townships, not with the masses strewn over huge landscapes in small *vijijis*. And many of those in the townships wore clothes specially imported from Western second-hand markets, pawnshops, jumble sales, cheap theatrical agencies or army surplus stores.

Thus on the streets of Mbeya, Iringa, Arusha or Sumbawanga you'd see blacks dressed as London bus drivers, down-and-out French gendarmes, tacky Canadian lumberjacks, destitute American legionnaires and out-at-the-elbow Italian railwaymen. In their cast-off clothes they were caricatures of white artisans being judged by values not their own, patronised and derided. But they could make you catch your breath in delight whenever they gathered with their women to sing hymns in Kiswahili (*Munguibariki Africa* – God Bless Africa) or to *ululu* in joy, grief and anger. Then they became strong, proud, lively, individualistic people.

Within their vast, open spaces the very same people – but without the Western garb – moved with grace, beauty and purpose. Travelling through the emptiness you'd suddenly come upon *watoto* (children) standing by the roadsides offering tiny, soft-shelled eggs at ten cents a dozen; less than an old penny apiece. And you'd encounter travellers-cum-hitch hikers, men with neither fixed destination nor even any specific direction in mind but who wanted only to go along the line in which your vehicle happened to be headed. You'd come across folk who believed that snakes bore the souls of once great men; that some men could outdo Jekyll and Hyde by turning themselves, temporarily, into lions or that benediction was greatly assisted by spitting. And there were those who, because death in the house meant burning the place down, took their dying people outside, there to sit with them during the final hours. How was it then that so many whites saw, and to this day still see, such folk as being dull-witted, unimaginative and inferior?

Outwardly the Asian community seemed to be as lively, picturesque and interesting as it was in Asia but on more searching observation, perhaps because Asians were immigrants overwhelmingly outnumbered by the host community and because they were uneasy in their relationships with the whites, and most certainly because they were apprehensive about their future, they were relatively inexpressive. On only one day a week could they be seen to let their hair down a little; that was on Sunday afternoons when, *en famille*, they'd pile into their motor cars and drive around and around on any few miles of metalled road that happened to be accessible.

Among the most remarkable people in Tanganyika were the Somalis who were usually to be seen in small groups trading cattle or as individuals employed by the better off as domestic servants. A Somali 'houseboy' was a status symbol. Instantly recognizable by their tall, slim, noble figures, Nilotic features and immaculate dress (no cast-off clothing for a Somali) and because their women, with an Oriental cast to their faces, were among the world's most beautiful, Somalis nevertheless irritated their fellow Africans with their proud demeanour and with the way they had of objecting, and loudly at that, to their being classified by the colonialists as 'natives'.

The most numerous tribe of all was that of the animals in the wild. I'll mention here just one individual of that tribe: the Colobus monkey who sat, solitary, high on a tree within the compound of the rough-and-ready two-room 'Hotel' at Tunduma on the border with what is now Zambia to the south of Mbeya. He (or maybe she?) perched on his/her tree like some magnificent, dark eagle, his/her black cape pulled around him/her, stony-eyed until he/she blinked in disbelief whenever the rare guest showed up, a disbelief shared by that establishment's strange, ancient, proprietress.

Dar es Salaam had never been either a focus for the arts or a staging port for the world's leading artists. It was therefore a truly historic day when 'Satchmo' – the great black American jazz artist, Louis Armstrong – stopped off in town to give a show – backsheesh – in celebration of Uhuru. There he was in the open air, his big, black face streaming with sweat, blasting on his horn while a fat, black mamma belted out songs. For a couple of hours, tens of thousands of bedazzled Tanganyikans whooped it up. Nyerere had never told them that Uhuru would give them the likes of 'Satchmo' free of charge. If that was Uhuru, hooray!

There was an annual miracle: all that one could see on one day in November was that the landscape all the way to the distant horizons was burnished sand; the air was heavy with dust. Yet if on that same November night there fell the first shower of rain for seven months, you'd awake in the morning to find a soft, yellowish-green carpet covering the earth; the air would smell fresh, clean and sweetly scented. It was marvellous.

Sumbawanga – a fine name eh? – was right out of Graham Greene, a distant fastness he'd have revelled in describing, a far-flung (few were further flung) outpost of empire that was almost inaccessible by road. Approaching it from what is now Zambia to the south and just before entering a tetse belt that stretched between the frontier and Sumbawanga, there stood by the wayside a tiny, grass lean-to similar to those built by cattle minders as shelters. With not another living soul for miles, it was home to a wizened, wobbly, messy Mzungu. What he was doing there and from whence he'd come, he couldn't say for he was beyond speech and there wasn't in sight a scrap of paper that might have been helpful. Heaven knows how he existed. He haughtily refused offers of money, food or clothing and angrily rejected mimed suggestions that he might be better off elsewhere.

Beyond the moth-eaten hermit in his smelly hideout there ran mile after mile of tetse fly-infested scrub (stopping was prohibited and all vehicle windows had to be shut tight) uninhabited by any living creature except those that flew. Then all of a sudden you came upon the tetse free oasis surrounding Sumbawanga. You went round a corner on the exposed, back-breaking track and there you were driving up a half-mile avenue between beautiful trees whose branches closed overhead to give dappled shade: you might have been driving through one of the most fertile and prosperous of French provinces.

Even by Tanganyikan standards the township of Sumbawanga was pokey – a couple of *dukas* was about all there was, but its *boma* was something special. It wasn't big, nor did it deviate architecturally from the standard *boma* pattern but it was faced with the local, burnt sienna coloured stone. Standing at one end of a square shaded by flowering trees and with its front broken by a profusion of thick, blue-blossomed liana, when the sun shone upon it, and especially after you'd endured the horrors of many hours battling your way through scrub towards it, it made a most pleasing sight. There was a hush about Sumbawanga, a serenity that caused a man to pick his steps carefully lest he bring on the 20th century.

At Mwaya, the township that lay just inland from Tungi Port, a rickety wharf on the northern shores of Lake Nyasa (Malawi) there dwelled a bald, chubby, half-pint Afro-Italian who ran a bar that, if it didn't qualify as the world's smallest establishment, would surely have made it as the world's dirtiest. He resembled, and indeed glorified in the name of, 'Mussolini'. It was said (the windowless interior was so dark that one couldn't see to confirm it one way or another) that 'Mussolini' kept a bevy of whores on tap. I believed that tale because I couldn't see how he could make a living solely out of his meagre bar sales. Taken altogether his entire stock couldn't have been worth more than 50 shillings; a dozen bottles of 'Castle' beer smuggled in from Nyasaland, a half-empty bottle of water-diluted whisky, a bottle of raw, bargain basement 'Beehive Brandy' brewed in South Africa and a couple of bottles of the ubiquitous South African 'sherry'. But 'Mussolini's' scored with its floor covering. Sited beneath kapok trees whose fluffy, white blossoms blew into the bar, its floor was covered wall-to-wall with a softer, deeper, whiter pile than any Hilton foyer in the world.

December 1961–March 1968
Sarawak

Dum Spiro Spero: Motto of the Brooke Rajahs

The colony of Sarawak to which we were transferred in 1961 was as big as England with a population of only 1 million. It was 80% covered by rain forest, the rest mainly with magnificent, wild rivers. She lay on the northern shores of the great island of Borneo. Tropical, she was as peaceful as a soft-blowing breeze.

For just over 100 years (1841–1945) the country was in the keep of a buccaneering English family – the Brookes – who, in fairyland mode, called themselves 'Rajahs'; inevitably they became internationally famous as the 'White Rajahs'.

They failed to create the 'modern state' they aspired to but, if only by default, they produced something perhaps better: a harmonious collectivity. For all its dottiness, primordialism and absolutism, the rule of the 'White Rajahs', freelance imperialists as they were, was still decent and dignified.

Following the Japanese occupation (1942–45) the third Brooke, Rajah Vyner, recognised that Sarawak could no longer exist as a viable state under an outmoded, bankrupt, monarchical system of government. In face of serious opposition from the populace, Vyner ceded his country to Britain to be run as a colony. With the Attlee government in London mandated to withdraw from Empire, 1945 was not a good year to form new colonies. No sooner had London colonised Sarawak than successive governments cast about for ways to get rid of her.

London and Kuala Lumpur came up with a solution: an independent federation combining the territories of Malaya, Singapore, North Borneo, Brunei and Sarawak centred upon Kuala Lumpur and to be named 'Malaysia'.

President Sukarno ('Bung Karno') to whom I introduced you way back and who in the meantime had charged into megalomania, was outraged and swore that he'd do all he could to abort the Malaysia project. From the early 1960s he spoke darkly about 'confrontation'; hence the word Konfrontasi entered into the local lexicon.

That's where the Hardys came in; while I was marking time in Dar es Salaam and seeking employment elsewhere in the shrinking empire, the embattled Sarawak government was engaged upon beefing up its intelligence arm – the Special Branch. And by shocking coincidence the deputy head of the branch fell dead, so London offered me the job. Overjoyed at the thought of going back to Asia it took DMF and I about five seconds to accept the offer. Flying from Singapore, on reaching the coastline of Borneo we ducked under heavy, low cloud to emerge above lines of casuarinas standing behind the black mangrove shore. We then followed the grey, nipah-lined Sarawak river until we touched down to a welcome that sang out the country's name in a long, gentle sigh: "*Selaamat datang ke Sarawaaaak*".

The Brookes' motto for Sarawak, '*Dum Spiro Spero*', irreverently translated by some as 'While I sweat, I hope', proved to be apposite when I was shown my first, albeit temporary, quarters in the Kuching Rest House, a weather-beaten wooden structure that epitomised in spades the old Brookes' ideals about spartan living. The Rest House proper was perched high on a hill overlooking the town but my own billet lay in the 'Annexe', a row of what looked like stables sunk in swamp beneath the main building. My room, which had been commandeered by ants, mosquitoes and geckoes, was large enough only to hold a termite-infested wardrobe, a washstand, a shower stall (superfluous since all you needed to do when you wanted a shower was stand outside the door for a minute or two) and a cast-iron, metal-sprung charpoy. A solitary, unshaded electric lamp drew to it a cloud of suicidal bugs, among them the Borneo banded hornet, an insect that looked like a brilliantly painted mini V Bomber – triangular and flashy as a fisherman's spinner with a sting to match. The banded hornet's home thrust, delivered without warning from behind, left you numb with pain and incredulous at the thought that so small a creature could bear such a grudge against the human race.

The carcasses of millions of aerodynamic suicides against the lamp littered the top of the mosquito net, coagulating into a cheesy mess that was continuously being devoured by armies of ants. The busy feet of those self-same termites then raised a carrion dust that filtered through the netting to coat me in a sort of greyish face powder. Geckoes, known locally as *chichaks*, swarmed over every inch of wall and ceiling, hunting and copulating in such numbers that after a while they were seen as part of the décor. I lay nights on my soggy mattress under my smelly net, dozing in a slick sweat while gagging for air that was 90% moisture and I wondered what I'd let us in for?

My fellow Rest House guests included a veteran of the Brooke monarchy, a doddery, laugh-a-minute circuit judge, Justice Smith, who indoors and out wore a solar topee, not because he feared sunstroke (he'd as much chance of suffering sunburn during the rainy season as he'd have done in Moscow in January) but because the populace might lose some of its reverential regard if, without his magisterial wig, it caught sight of his pink, bald skull.

Called to the dining room by the striking of a Chinese gong, whose boom echoed round the town like a gun salute, we'd sit, Justice Smith under his topee, at a sturdy, rough-cast table covered by a grubby bedsheet stained, I suspected, not only from the colourful seepage from a score of bottles containing a variety of flux-inducing condiments but also by the night emissions of people who'd slept on it weeks before. As for the aforementioned seasoners, you had a round-the-clock choice of Tabasco, Ajinomoto, raw chillies, salt that you spooned out like wet sand, black pepper, soya, chilli and Worcester sauces, ketchup, vinegar, several antipastos like dried minnows, a tin of shoe polish, and a decanter of gin mixed with arrack and topped with raw chillies – an appetiser that brewed away ever more lethally as the decanter was emptied a spoonful at a time. Breakfast was rice gruel, eggs, bacon and, for Asians, big wedges of bread and jam. But the item on the menu that nobody passed over was the yellow mepacrine tablet that shielded you against malaria. Lunch was curry and rice, *nasi goreng*, fried fish and *sambal*; the evening meal was usually warmed-up leftovers for which you did battle against battalions of voracious creepy crawlies. And of course, there was always a cornucopia of fruit.

Settling in at Special Branch

Washed, nay drowned, by the *landas* (monsoon), Kuching at that time of the year offered little cheer; the great waterway on whose banks it stood rushed threateningly, overwhelming its open storm-drains to flood its streets under a red tide. Never a break appeared in the clouds that hung black and low enough, it seemed, for you to reach up and touch them.

But my spirits soared to hear once more the sing-song of the Malay, Chinese and Indian tongues; my nostrils twitched to the familiar scents of the East – of blossoms, aromatic wood, incense, hair-oil, swamp gas, sweat, ripening and decaying fruit and open drains; and I felt again the enveloping warmth that, no matter how dark the skies, promised sunshine one day.

In any case I'd little time for introspection. I'd come to Sarawak as deputy head of the Special Branch only to find that my only meeting with my boss was on board a boat that was taking him to Singapore on the first leg of six months home leave. The handover period was limited to a beery handshake and "Good to meet you, cheerio."

I was acting head of the Special Branch only a week or two after my arrival. I was offered a top flat in a six-apartment block known as 'Rock Court', a modern place that nevertheless blended nicely into the parkland it shared with the Rest House. Its living room offered a spectacular, panoramic view; along the entire length of its frontage – about half the length of a cricket pitch – there ran French windows whose plate-glass sections slid open to give full, unimpeded access to a veranda almost as big as the room itself. When these great windows were open, which was for most of the daylight hours – we were as good as living in the open air.

Better still; right in front of our eyes there stretched immaculate lawns dotted with palms, frangipani and clusters of crimson and yellow cannas.

The lawns swept down to a relatively quiet main road immediately on the other side of which there sloped, gently upwards, the gorgeous municipal gardens. Landscaped for the Brookes and treasured by them, they were crowned with the Sarawak Museum built for Rajah Charles in 1886 and said to be one of Asia's loveliest buildings. Thus, sitting in our Rock Court living room, we were given a glimpse into what it would have been like to live in a house with an uninterrupted view of the Taj Mahal – well, nearly. Cooled by soft, scented breezes, shielded from the elements (the landas having cleared away) we'd sit of a Sunday afternoon, gazing upon an entrancing scene; upon the police band playing from an ornate, circular, old-fashioned band stand (another nice Brooke touch) around which Kuching paraded in a pageant of sarongs, saris, parasols, cheongsams, skirts, trousers, *songkoks*, turbans, topees, fezzes and headscarves.

The bamboo telegraph worked well because, within hours of my being told I'd got a Rock Court flat, there appeared at the Rest House an applicant for the job as housekeeper. She was a fat, untidy, middle-aged Indian lady who, announcing herself to be 'Pakiong binti Jeffrey' (Pakiong, wife of Jeffrey) thrust into my hand a sheaf of 'references' with a smile so engaging that I didn't need to read any before setting her on. Pakiong was to stay with us for every day we were in Sarawak. She became part of the family, greatly cherished.

My office desk was cluttered with an abundance of weights ranging from defunct Japanese hand-grenades to horseshoes said to be from the Rajah's stables. They held down paper that turned to sponge by the humidity even as I wrote upon it. My initial jottings were recordings of the wisdom I'd accumulated as I went around the country on my 'familiarisation' excursions; knowledge imparted by those I'd listened to: the Chief Secretary, 'Residents', longhouse headmen, *penghulus*, merchants, peasants, Kapitans China and river-boat pilots. In effect, I'd been told that Sarawak had weathered – with aplomb – its transition from being under the thumb of an alien but resident potentate to being at the feet of another alien, but this time absentee, monarch. More than that, she looked likely to ride out the insurrectionist fevers racking many of her neighbours with serenity. While 'French' Indo-China, 'British' Malaya, the 'Dutch' East Indies and the 'Yankee' Philippines had all been peppered with shrapnel blown from Mao Tse Tung's explosive revolution in China, Sarawak was so tranquil that few of my tutors doubted that an unarmed constabulary, just 1,000 strong, was more than enough to keep the peace. And fewer lost a moment's sleep over the fact that there wasn't a single soldier in the land.

But beneath the surface the Malay fundamentalists who'd shoved a kris through one of the first colonial governors and a growing number of young Chinese who believed that everybody in the world would be better off under Mao Tse Tung were near to joining forces to oppose the plan by which Sarawak would be absorbed within a grand 'Malaysian' federation. Under the banner Barisan Pemuda Sarawak (Sarawak Youth Party) Muslim loyalists spread fears at prayer meetings warning that if Kuala Lumpur and London had their way Sarawak would simply swap alien monarchs: a white colonial Queen for a brown colonial Agong. Meanwhile young Chinese 'communists' organising clandestinely, preached essentially the same message, adding for extra zip that 'the motherland' (China) was also dead against the 'neo-colonialist' idea of 'Malaysia'.

But what set ulcers flaring in London, Kuala Lumpur, Jesselton (now Kota Kinabalu), Washington and Kuching was the reaction of that old acid-sprayer, Bung Karno, in Jakarta. The Indonesian dictator began to rant and rave against the 'American Godfather masterminding the imperialist mafia to swindle Asians'. Using street language as only he and Mao among Asian politicians could, Sukarno swore to 'strangle at birth the half-breed, born-through-rape infant, 'Malaysia''. Indonesia, which had one of the world's largest standing armies, shared several hundreds of miles of open border with Sarawak whose government had hardly a weapon to hand.

Early 1962 wasn't, therefore, the best of times to walk into the office of Sarawak's security intelligence chief. My main interest was in the young Chinese 'communists'. I could see how 'communism' might inflame young Chinese burning to free Sarawak from colonialism. It was easy to understand that when they were told to be proud of 'the motherland' where 'communism' was already working miracles, young Chinese might breathe rarefied air.

With every page I turned, I tuned in a little closer to the wavelength the youngsters were on; those children huddled together in two's and three's under flickering oil lamps on the floor of sheds in pepper gardens or in clearings in the *belukar* (secondary jungle far more dense than virgin jungle) on the outskirts of towns and villages listening to broadcasts from 'the motherland' or turning the pages of handwritten copies of treatise such as Lenin's 'Imperialism, the Last Stage of Capitalism', a most favoured work. They were teaching themselves 'revolution' in preparation for the day they'd be called upon to kill 'running dogs', not out of blood lust and not for loot but because the 'foreign devils' left them no other way of reaching their glorious goal. Ridding the earth of alien oppressors was not villainous; it was heroic. They were inspired to dream of creating a high-minded 'government of the proletariat' that would distribute Sarawak's wealth equally and without regard to race or class. Utopian? Yes indeed, but evil? No.

'O' – the Communists in Sarawak

Much as my heart sympathised with the lofty ideals of our would-be revolutionaries, my head told me that they were mistaken, and that somehow or other they'd have to be persuaded to desist. Put simply, the 'communists' or as they styled themselves in secret 'O', would never be able to recruit more than a handful of non-Chinese. For religious as well as racial reasons the Malays would have turned them over to the police as soon as they were approached while with only one or two exceptions, the Ibans, light years away from political consciousness, still saw Chinese as itinerant merchants passing through, bartering goods as they'd done for centuries past. What's more, they could count on the support of no more than a few of their very own race. Agrarian Sarawak just wasn't the right territory on which to wage a proletarian revolution. Where for a start was the proletariat?

What swung the argument further, finally and unarguably against 'O' however was that it presented a red rag to the Indonesian bull. One of Bung Karno's pet ideas was of a pan-Malayan empire centred on Jakarta and embracing the Indonesian archipelago, Malaya and the Philippines. A chauvinist up to his eyeballs, even as he was swearing eternal brotherhood with Mao Tse Tung he was ordering Chinese in his own country to remove the outward signs of their racial identity by adopting Indonesian names and by decreeing that all shop signs and account books be written in Indonesian. He approved of Sarawakian opposition to both colonialism and the Malaysian concept but he'd have seen an independent 'communist'-dominated government in Kuching in its racial, not political, clothes and he'd have moved like lightning to have it crushed.

It was in large measure to keep Sukarno out of Sarawak and North Borneo (now Sabah) that the Malaysian concept had been advanced in the first place. Compared with the grim conditions under which Borneans lived in Indonesian Borneo (Kalimantan) the lives of the people in 'British' Sarawak were paradisiacal. Hence Albion at its most perfidious could never have abandoned Sarawak to the mercy of Bung Karno; the Brookes who were British to their toenails would have turned over in their English graveyards. So, independence was out of the question; Sarawak on its own wouldn't have lasted five weeks. The proposition that the Union Jack be lowered leaving Sarawak and North Borneo to federate with countries which shared a common imperialist background might not have been the ideal solution to the problem of de-colonisation (many colonial officials were as opposed to it as the local 'communists') but it was a damn sight better than opening the gates to Sukarno's storm troopers.

Almost all of our information about 'O' was to come from documents either recovered from imperfect hiding places, purchased for cash from informers, confiscated during police raids or intercepted on their way through the 'O' network. In short, the comrades used their pens far too much for their own good. The papers came in a rich, voluminous variety: clandestine news sheets, samizdats (Mao's essays on guerrilla warfare for instance were mailed from China a page or two at a time, the whole at the end to be cyclostyled, bound together and distributed for study in secret cells) 'rolled slips' (messages on gossamer rice-paper whose every centimetre was covered with miniature Chinese ideograms that often needed a magnifying glass to read, then rolled into tight spools which were sealed with wax to ease their transportation within one of the courier's body orifices), study notes carelessly dropped, journals, diaries, self-criticism statements, 'work plans', letters, periodicals and even love letters. The astonishing abundance of the material – all of it handwritten – demonstrated the depth of learning, the ingenuity and the industriousness of 'O' and of those who aspired to join it.

Take 'O's 'newspapers' for example. Sitting in hiding, stylus in hand, a single youngster scratches page 1 in minute calligraphy straight onto a wax stencil. At the same time another youngster in another hiding place scratches page 2, yet a third deals with page 3 and so on. When each has finished his stencil he delivers it to a dropping off point where another youth, unknown to the scribblers, collects it for rolling off copies either on a hand-made roller or, more usually, by using a rubber roller, printers' ink and a piece of flat board. In yet another stage of the operation the finished pages are stapled together and bound in waxed brown paper. When 'published', 20 or 30 copies of a ten-page 'newspaper' will leave the 'printer'. Using the same secret procedures the readers themselves will reproduce handwritten copies which will be reproduced time and time again until in the end each issue will reach 400–500 readers who'd pass them on to 500 more and so on. How could one not admire such ingenuity and zeal?

What support there was for 'O' came not from its advocacy of Maoism which few people either understood or desired but from its uncompromising opposition to plans to federate the country within Malaysia, a prospect that left the majority of Chinese fearful of Malay domination.

Danger Within

Popular or not, Malaysia was coming up fast. The affected governments wanted information. Malayan and Australian Cabinet ministers together with Singapore-based brass hats and big-shot spooks came to Kuching searching for on-the-spot news. They were keenly interested in what the colonial government called the 'Clandestine Communist Organisation'. In order to pacify the visitors the Governor ordered the production of a definitive paper on that organisation. It fell to me to write it. I spent most of three months on the draft that was ready by November 1962. Thereafter, under a 'SECRET' chop, the paper went the rounds of those who mattered in Kuching, Singapore, Kuala Lumpur, Jesselton, London, Canberra, Wellington and Washington. Sometime later, the Information Service published an abridged version called, over my objections, melodramatically, 'Danger Within'.

Travelling in Sarawak

For all the time I spent on 'Danger Within' I was still busy as a bee elsewhere. I did the customary 'new boy' rounds of the colony, calling on heads of departments; generally wise, compassionate, skilled folk from whom I learned about local and tribal politics, husbandry, crime rates (practically zero everywhere) customs, traditions, taboos, migrations, resources, industry (ditto for crime – non-existent), communications, religions, class differences, gossip, tittle-tattle, and rumour.

Only 13 people lived in each square mile and lines of communication were such as nature had made them. True, each significant population centre had an airstrip of sorts but there were few aeroplanes, no railways and very few miles of paved road. People lived alongside watercourses: majestic, turbulent, red-brown rivers, narrow silver streams, cataracts, maelstroms, bores, trickles and rapids. There was water, water everywhere; meandering one minute, coursing frenziedly the next, racing from the hills in the interior down through fruit, vegetable, rice, rubber and pepper gardens on its way to the coast, all the while accumulating masses of sediment to create fertile deltas and tremendous mangrove swamps.

Thus was I borne by long-boat or marine department launch along Sarawak's liquid highways; down the Lupar for a start, the Lupar vividly described in Maughan's tale 'Yellow Streak', down the Lupar to Simanggang, the Rajah's favourite place for blooding new officers and the only settlement in the immense 2nd Division to merit the title Township and then only just. All that Simanggang had going for it were two rows of single-storey, wooden shophouses facing each other over a strip of tarmac stretching perhaps for 200 paces; a market place (large square of beaten earth covered by a vast expanse of corrugated iron resting on uprights but leaving the market open on all four sides), a nasty little modern, red-brick Rest House infested with creeping, crawling, slithering, flying parasites including mosquitoes said to be big enough to require permission to land on the airstrip; a few government offices; a grass airfield with a one-room, unmanned 'airport terminal'; and a rattan shed that proclaimed itself to be the 'Roxy' cinema, displaying crude copies of portraits of Hollywood, Hong Kong and Bombay film stars with no relevance to what was being shown within. Raised high above the unhurried town on a knoll cleared of *belukar* stood the old Brooke Residency, a humble guildhall guarded by a formidable wooden fort in front of which a cannon pointed its nose menacingly down the main street and the river. The same gun protected a clean, orderly, sensible clinic and the post office where Rajah Vyner Brooke was once said to have licked stamps.

I boarded the *Rajah Brooke*, a stately old, sea-going tub belonging to the Straits Steamship Company, a vessel that had seen at least 50 years of service plying between Kuching and Sarawak's second largest town, Sibu. She steamed high above the Sarawak river at Kuching, once at sea turning right to follow the coast eastwards before turning inland again to enter that rajah of all rivers: the Batang Rejang. Twenty hours after raising anchor at Kuching the *Rajah Brooke* pulled into the bustling dockside of the seat of government of the 3rd Division, Sibu.

Sibu boasted hotels, bars, banks, cinemas, tennis courts, an all-weather airport, post office, hospital, jail, clubs, docks, two-storey shophouses, restaurants and maybe five miles of paved streets. Every other store in town was an eating-place; every 'hotel' had its room-service prostitutes, its short-term rates, and its champagne and VSOP brandy that flowed like the Rejang.

Being Sarawak's commercial centre, Sibu had the most 'communists'. Accordingly, we had a large Special Branch unit there, calling for more frequent visits than my physical constitution approved of.

Miri

Colonial officials lucky enough to run the 4th Division had control over immense stretches of undisturbed rain forest. The region's main artery was another of Sarawak's regal rivers: the Baram. To get to the division you could travel by sea but the vagaries of the tides off Lutong, the port for the main town, Miri, meant that you had a good chance of lying off for days before landing by lighter. That was all very well in the Brookes' days when time stood still but colonialism was less patient. Hence an airstrip was laid into which, at least by the airways' timetables, there was a daily flight. The problem was whether or not the plane would fly out on the same day, the next day or even next week. Being simply a strip of mown grass and its navigation aids being limited to a windsock, one heavy shower and it was a quagmire, unusable for hours, maybe days.

Miri was my favourite town. Its very birth owed everything to the discovery of oil in the 1920s. The wells soon ran dry – although in 1962 one or two 'nodding donkeys' were still cranking out a trickle or two – but by the time they'd run out, Shell was refining much of Brunei's super-abundant supply in Miri, assuring the town of spin-off prosperity. Small as it was, Miri had style; its roads were broad and it was blessed with the finest *laksa* restaurant in Sarawak.

The sight of the Sarawak flag flying over Limbang, the flyblown capital of Sarawak's vast 5th Division only a couple of hours sail down the river from his gleaming 1700-room palace, must even today set the Sultan of Brunei's teeth on edge for his ancestors once ruled over it all. Like all Sarawakian officials, before passing through the Brunei Sultanate to reach Limbang, I had to get the royal assent. Once aboard the *perahu* bound for Limbang however, everything was perfect. The first stage took us through the wooden city built on stilts above sea on the outskirts of Brunei's capital, Bandar Seri Begawan; an Oriental Venice swarming with handsome, lithe, golden-skinned, healthy people (medical services of the very highest quality were available to all free of charge) who were at home in water as tadpoles. Thereafter for a couple of hours the boat raced down a great waterway whose banks on either side were draped in mangrove so green and shiny they looked as if they'd been brushed over with gloss paint and so dense that it was hard to believe that any creature larger than an ant could move through it. Whenever the *perahu* touched the black ooze from which the mangrove sprouted, a smog of decay would arise to attract a million butterflies, moths and birds. Beyond the swamp there stretched the endless *ulu* (wilderness). Apart from the burr of our outboard motor there was total, all-encompassing peace.

There was no sign proclaiming 'Limbang' nor was there anything to suggest you were approaching a human settlement, let alone a seat of government housing anything so pompous as a 'Residency'. Instead, without warning, the boat turned as if out of control to lead straight for the mangrove. But, instead of burying its nose into the slime, it drew up alongside a rickety *pengkalan* (landing stage) that was the port of entry into the capital city of the almost boundless 5th Division. Limbang slumbered in its tropical heat, its sleep disturbed only by the 'whoo-whoo-ha-ha' of hornbills. Yet, unbelievably it was in that dreamy, boggy place that Sarawak's peace was bloodily to be shattered.

Kuching

Viewed from abroad, Sarawak's towns could have been seen – in the 1960s anyway – as mere outposts. But to the vast majority of Sarawakians who seldom ventured beyond their kampongs and longhouses, the divisional capitals – even Limbang – were metropolis. Kuching, which some claim was named after the Malay word for cat (*kuching*), was a truly capital city. No matter how small it was the fact remained that, thanks to the

Brookes, for many years it had had international recognition as such. A slow-moving town, its only outwardly visible claim to front-rank status was the sight of the Brookes' Istana, an edifice that dominated the town but if truth be told wasn't much of a palace; the Sultan of Brunei wouldn't have had it as a cloakroom.

The Brookes influence remained visible and pleasing. Close by the *pengkalan*, opposite the Istana, stood the Supreme Court-cum-Legislative Council building, a quietly imposing structure redolent of the Brookes' predilection towards simplicity; fittingly a bust of Rajah Charles stood in its forecourt. Behind the courthouse was a charming, whitewashed, circular tower that before colonialism had housed the country's offices of state in their entirety but which was now barely big enough for the education department alone. Opposite was the nicest building in Sarawak – a massively pillared, classically 'Empire' Post Office which incidentally, with a typically Sarawakian touch dating back to the Brookes, opened on Sundays so that those who couldn't wait for the next day's delivery could collect their mail themselves.

The prison was a grand old whitewashed building in Tabuan Road built on top of a hill so small at its plateau as to deny any prospect of extension. I doubt if any other state capital in the world could have claimed a smaller house of correction. Lastly, Rajah Charles had laid out a horse-racing track whose every stable, betting booth, restaurant, viewing platform and royal box was made of rough, unpainted timber – a commodity which Sarawak possessed in great abundance.

Kuching didn't aspire to greatness but was content to sit in its shade, avoiding sunstroke. Its acres of *belian* roof tiles sheltered white walls, mildewed by decades of rainstorms and blistering heat. Shops bursting with merchandise opened straight onto the 'five-foot ways', while the five-foot ways themselves opened directly into deep, open storm drains. Angsana trees blossomed in riotous yellow and everywhere you looked there was jacaranda, frangipani, royal palms and cannas of unbelievable size and variety of colour. A heavy aroma of coconuts, bananas, pineapples, durians, green oranges, rambutans, mangoes, mangosteens, pomelos, locally grown coffee, pepper, cucumbers, tomatoes, lettuces, pickled cabbage and cassava filled the streets which were trapped by the dark rain clouds hovering over Kuching. The town was nature's greenhouse; it was said that if you dropped a seed from the prison roof it'd germinate before it hit the ground.

Right in Kuching's heart there stretched an extensive area of concrete turned green and slippery by years of coatings of vegetable and animal fats. That great piazza was roofed over by an enormous, leaky umbrella patched together from sheets of corrugated iron, strips of canvas, rolls of waxed paper, fronds of atap, beaten-out kerosene tins, old doors and windows and animal skins. Dotted about underneath that weepy membrane scores of charcoal braziers stood near to grimy, glass-fronted cupboards inside which hung rows of hooks from whose ends dangled strings of sausages, slabs of fat, pork, feathered chickens, innards, whole ducks that looked as if they'd been steamrollered, and strings of noodle dough. Round tables, their tops thick with grease were scattered like draughts on a chessboard and each one had the company of half a dozen unsteady stools. That was the 'Open Market', a 24-hour open-air eating place whose bewildering choice of specialities ranging from the common Cantonese fried rice to Mongolian hot-pot was probably unsurpassed in Asia. Chinese, Thai, Indian, Indonesian, Filipino and Malay cooks vied with each other to attract customers.

Curries, kebabs, sambal, sweet corn, purées, chilli-con-carne, *inche kabin*, dhal, *gula Malacca*, fish bladders, egg rolls, frogs' cheeks, *satay*, *bobo*, tofu, marrow soup, soya milk, chitterlings, black pudding, *nasi goreng*, *kueh teow*, noodles, *kai lan*, *eu cha kueh*, *choi sam*, *kangkong*, *ikan merah*, Szechuan dumplings, 'steam boat', hard boiled eggs, *chow mein*, birds' nests (Sarawak was the world's leading exporter of this dubious delicacy), sharks' fins, white rice, Tahi rice, brown rice (local unhusked), *biriani*, pillao, scented rice, sweet and sours, curds, peanuts, brinjal (aubergine), salads, century eggs, turtles' eggs, crabs, oysters, shrimps, vindaloo, chutneys, toast, jam, HP sauce, milk, Ajinomoto, bread, eggs and bacon, Irish stew, fish and chips, *laksa* and a whole lot more....

The open market was for everybody; for 50 cents you'd get a bowl of *chok* (porridge) at three in the morning; for five ringgits, steamed garoupa; knives and forks would be produced but only after a lot of grumbling about some folks' filthy eating habits. The restaurateurs, most of whom were fat, sweaty Chinese males of whom propriety seemed to require a standard dress comprising a grimy singlet; oily, baggy shorts; and well-worn flip-flops, were indifferent towards hygiene. The leavings of a departing party (whose leftovers, given the locals' appetites for shell-fish, could be mountainous) were swept to the ground with a couple of sweeps of a smelly rag there to be fought over by packs of dogs, flocks of minahs and sleek, big-bellied, curly-tailed cats. A quick wipe of the stools with the same scummy dish cloth and the mores of sanitation had been complied with; the incoming customers were invited to be seated as if they were in the dining room of the Ritz. There might have been Malays who, doubting the halal purity of the fare dished up, preferred not to eat there but otherwise, day and night the open market was a conflagration of the hungry of all races in the country.

Perched on a hill to the south of the town there was Kuching's very own centre for colonial social intercourse: the Club. Once a small Brooke period piece, a good few trees had been cut down to roof its post-Brooke expansion. It was now graced with tennis courts, swimming pool and even a golf course. Even so it remained a far cry from the swaggering opulence of the sahibs' clubs in India, Malaya and Singapore.

It was never an exclusively white domain; but it was the venue for the games the British played in their colonies: over-dressed, over-boozey celebrations of nationalism such as piping the haggis (when just down the road there was *rending sapi*!) and for rowdy expressions of chauvinism.

The Military Build-up

Back at Badruddin Road the heat was on. The Americans were prodding London – what are you doing about the lefties in Borneo? – London prodded Kuala Lumpur and Singapore, and at the end of the chain it was Kuching that took the jabs. The Chief Secretary was one Snelus, a man nearly as unpleasant as his name somehow implied. If hawkishness was graded 1–10 Snelus would have been a 12. Mercifully, he didn't last long but before he took off for Cheltenham or wherever, 'Snarly' as he was known, ran the red bogey for all it was worth. One or two of us tried to calm him down with the argument that while 'O' might talk about 'preparing for the armed struggle' it also depended on getting the necessary weapons from, as Mao advised them, 'the enemy'. But, we pointed out, 'enemy' weapons were pretty well non-existent because the only force of law and order in Sarawak was the constabulary that, to all intents and purposes, was unarmed. Ergo, without arms, where comes the 'armed struggle'? Snelus was more than equal to such logic. Bung Karno, he'd taunt us, had arsenals bursting with armaments not more than 50 miles from where we were sitting. We weren't the only ones who'd read Marx, Lenin and Mao, he'd say, and, from what he remembered, one constant theme was 'the enemy of my enemy is my friend'. Well then, Snelus said with undeniable justification, Mao was against Malaysia, Sukarno was against Malaysia and 'O' was against Malaysia; ergo, 'O', already Mao's friend, would befriend Bung Karno who'd give it all the guns it could handle.

Oh, Henry!

In June 1962, bursting with renewed vigour, Roy Henry, the substantive head of Special Branch, returned to the fray. A six-footer and heavy with it, he was blessed with an iron constitution that withstood anything that kampongs, longhouses, istanas, fancy homes, wayside stalls, coffee shops and posh restaurants could put in front of him: snake, dog, entrails, insects, worms, quails' eggs, snails smorgasbord, ambrosia, black forest gateau and caviar (his favourite was steak and kidney pudding) without ever feeling even a mite queasy. You could pour enough beer, brandy, samsu and *tuak* down Henry's throat to sink a battleship and he'd not even blink.

He was intellectually endowed though he wasn't perhaps always wise with it, but then, who is? He'd take any amount of information and repeat it days or weeks later as if he'd been programmed. He was not for slogging through Marx in the original; he'd only to listen to Radio Beijing's English-language service and he was ready to debate *Kapital* or Mao's *On Contradiction* with any political scientist. What's more important he was very likeable withal.

But he was a real policeman (he'd never been in Special Branch until he'd been made its director), hence he was restless, almost as touchy as Snelus. Roy saw 'O' not as a mentally stimulating political phenomenon that threatened only lightly but as something he had to deal with as a policeman. 'O' was breaking the law and couldn't be allowed to get away with it. Simple as that. He couldn't see the sense in collecting information and then doing nothing with it. It so happened that by the time he was back in the chair we knew who 'O's three leading figures – its politburo – were: a certain Wen Min Chyuan, his wife, and one Wong Kee Chok – and we knew where to find them. Ergo, on 22 June 1962 the three were arrested and deported to China. And that, we thought, was that. But we were to hear of them again. Coincidentally in mid-1962, the Sarawak Festival took place in the botanical gardens right in front of our veranda. We had front row seats. However, we didn't know then that we were witnessing the last manifestation of unrestrained public gaiety to be staged in Sarawak for a good few years and the last expression of joy being not Brookeian or Malaysian but simply Sarawakian. In an unplanned way the festival brought the final curtain down on the White Rajahs and, for good measure, although a year before it became official, also upon colonialism.

Coming Together
In July 1962 a British-Malayan commission named after its Chairman, the Briton, Lord Cobbold, toured the country with a brief 'to measure public opinion' on the Malaysian question: For or Against? It reported, some thought with undue haste, that the majority of Sarawakians supported the concept.

Jakarta, Beijing and Moscow sneered at Cobbold. The airwaves echoed

with pronunciamentos redolent of the 1930s–40s in Europe; there was to
be a 'Maphilindo' (a federation of Malaya, the Philippines and Indonesia),
a 'Beijing-Jakarta Axis', and then Pakistan joined in by voicing Islamic
misgivings over Malaysia while Moscow condemned 'neo-colonialism'
– altogether an alliance of forces that on paper committed a billion
people against 11 million. For all that, the Sarawakian masses showed
no signs of fear; it was as if they knew something we didn't, something
that made them smile at Bung Karno's ravings. Consequently, Roy Henry
continued to pit 90% of Special Branch against 'O' leaving only half a
dozen Malay 'detectives' to look out for signs of unease among the non-
Chinese population. But whatever the outward calm, things were coming
to a boil; sooner or later, it seemed, there'd have to be a reckoning with
Sukarno. In the corridors of power there were whispers about a worst-case
scenario: an invasion from Indonesian Kalimantan coinciding with an
'O' uprising internally. We weren't playing games any more.

Azahari

The climax was reached in Brunei, a neighbouring state reduced by 1962
into a Gilbert and Sullivan polity floating on an ocean of oil. It was said
in Brunei that oil was a divine gift to Muslims in order that they need not
toil in the hot sun. The streets of Bandar Seri Begawan were filled with
air-conditioned limousines owned by royals. There was also a profligacy of
Datuks (Knights) and Pehins (honorary members of parliament) brought
about by the Sultan's generosity in awarding titles (together with gratuities)
to just about anybody who stayed in his service for a few years.

To secure his throne, the Sultan employed grossly over-fleshed military
and police services backed up by an outsize Special Branch. Like every
other department of the Brunei government the Special Branch had money
to play with. Trapped inside plush offices by air-conditioning, expensive
electronic toys and wall-to-wall Afghan carpeting, the branch's white
officers, decked out in brand-name safari suits with silk cravats, and with
the support of British females secretaries, were hopelessly out of touch.

While the Sultan's bodyguards postured in a cool, dry 20°C, out there in the oxyacetylene environment of the nearby Temburong jungle, hundreds of small, sweaty Muslims were preparing something that would send the Hang Seng index into shock.

For a good few years a mercurial Brunei Malay/Arab, one A. M. Azahari, had nursed a romantic dream of a resurgent Brunei, a Sultanate restored to its old glory, the centre of an Islamic empire stretching, as it had once done, clean across the northern region of Borneo. While the Anglophilic Sultan was quietly musing over whether or not Brunei might further diminish itself by joining the proposed Malaysian federation, Azahari was receiving assurances of Indonesian assistance to restore Malay Muslim – not Malaysian – domination over what was called 'British' Borneo.

In November our man in Limbang began reporting tales of armed, strangely uniformed men gathering in the Temburong jungle just on the Brunei side of our border. I despatched an officer to inform the Brunei Special Branch about the reports.

The director of Brunei Special Branch, an aloof, old-school-tie Englishman, showed our man the door, saying that he wanted no help from Sarawak, thank you very much. The 'information' he said was mendacious; the only armed and uniformed men in Brunei were the Sultan's own and none were deployed in Temburong.

On 8 December 1962, two or three hundred 'soldiers' of the self-styled 'Tentera Nasional Kalimantan Utara' (National Army of North Borneo) overran police posts and oil installations throughout Brunei and were virtually on the point of seizing Bandar Seri Begawan itself when they stopped to await further instructions from their commander-in-chief, A. M. Azahari. The commander however had taken off for Manila to await the call to return in triumph as Brunei's viceroy. The cock-up theory applied. The rebels, who could easily have gone on to raise their flag above the capital's clock tower, instead sat down to wait for orders that never came.

A battalion of British soldiers shipped hastily from Singapore found the Tentera sitting in wayside coffee shops, sleeping in the grounds of the grand mosque and bathing in the river. Azahari hadn't warned them to be on guard against counter-attack. They were sitting ducks. Hardly a shot was fired. The rebellion was at an end almost as soon as it had begun.

Not much blood and not a drop of oil had been spilled. The political shock waves however, spread far and wide. Bung Karno sneered at a Sultan who'd had to be rescued from the wrath of his own people by red-faced, foreign infidels. Smarting from such insults the Sultan withdrew from the Malaysia negotiations. It was a bizarre little overture to Sukarno's Konfrontasi of Malaysia.

Konfrontasi!

Complacency suddenly gave way to uproar. Coded telegrams flashed between London, Singapore, Kuala Lumpur, Bandar Seri Begawan, Jesselton and Kuching. Military aircraft brought red-tabbed army officers to Kuching, their nostrils twitching happily at the whiff of cordite in the air. A destroyer anchored off Fort Marguerite and, for the first time since the end of the Japanese occupation, armed soldiers were seen on the streets of Kuching, Sibu and Miri. The legislature was hustled into passing into law those life preservers of many a colonial regime: 'Emergency Regulations'. The question arose: Who were they to be used against? The Tentera Nasional? In the whole country we'd identified only one true Sarawakian who might have been connected to it and he, being one of the most senior local officers employed by government, was considered politically to be out of reach. No, the target had to be 'O' but until then they'd not fired a shot nor, as far as we knew, had they any guns from which to fire one; Sarawak wasn't Chicago.

Nonetheless 'O' was up to no good and there was a chance that it would be armed by Sukarno. Ergo, we had to do something about it. But what? Mass arrests? No, because the constabulary couldn't handle them and our only little prison couldn't cope. Nothing could have been further from a gulag than the 'Across River' camp we built. That old veteran champion of human rights, an idol of my youth, Fenner Brockway, flew out from England to look at it. 'Heaven forbid,' he said, 'that I should ever be a detainee anywhere in the world, but if it were so then I'd choose to be detained here in Kuching.' It could of course only have been done in the tropics where the raw materials lay plentifully to hand: timber, bamboo, atap and twine and where just about everybody was a dab hand at building with them. Neither was there any need to worry about water or even to think about heating; no inmate required more than a sarong, a rattan mat, half a coconut shell and a pair of chopsticks.

The detention camp being ready we went ahead to pick up precisely the number of detainees it could hold: 75. The immediate result was what we feared – the Special Branch was buried under a mountain of paper: arrest and search warrants, seized documents by the hundreds, orders for detention. It was an alp from underneath which for the next five years we were unable to dig ourselves.

To its great credit the colonial government resisted calls for the imposition of martial law. And its successor, the Malaysian government similarly dismissed all appeals for it. Sarawak was to remain under civilian/political control, a factor that was to prove decisive.

Outwardly, Sarawak and Brunei returned to their normal somnolence but Bung Karno repeatedly raised the ante by ever-increasing the decibels, rattling in his Hitler-like guttural voice that he'd 'strike' any state that chose Malaysia. In no time at all, there was movement afoot everywhere you looked. British soldiers moved into positions on our border with Kalimantan, Indonesian soldiers moved into position on their border with us and hundreds of Chinese youngsters took to the jungle. The once niggardly treasury came up with staggering amounts of ringgits to pay for thousands of new constables, prison warders, propagandists and for the raising of an Iban vigilante corps to be known as 'Border Scouts'. Every public servant was hassled; few paused to ask themselves what they were doing.

The rhetoric on both sides became so offensive that Konfrontasi became unavoidable. Jakarta and Manila offered Kuala Lumpur a way out of its 'slave relationships with imperialism': join them in the anti-imperialist federation – Maphilindo. The Malayan PM exchanged the contumely by sneering at the way Indonesians were forced to eat rats. Given the atmosphere the question wasn't if there'd be an armed clash but when.

The answer came on 12 April 1963 when a posse of armed marauders from Kalimantan sacked the police post at Tebedu, an isolated kampong just inside Sarawak and only 40 miles due south of Kuching, murdering several constables and looting the place. From that moment on anyone still harbouring dovish views was well advised to keep them to himself.

Tebedu spelled Konfrontasi – undeclared war. Things moved fast. A British army general was appointed Director of Borneo Operations with his headquarters on the island of Labuan, off Brunei. State Emergency Executive Committees were convened in Sarawak and North Borneo. Following their regrettable custom the military moved in with displays of machismo and bullshit. Come May 1963 and the verandas in front of Kuching's government offices, passages that had been hushed for many a year, throbbed to the sound of heavy boots and raised voices. There could hardly have been a less fitting time for me to go on home leave but I was overdue for it and nothing was more sacred to colonialists than home leave. For an officer to suggest that he might defer it or for a superior to suggest that a junior's leave might be held back was unthinkable.

And so, in mid-1963, I flew to Sussex for three months holiday.

The Winds of Change

The Sarawak to which I returned in October 1963 was already a Malaysian state. And, thanks to Bung Karno, much more than its constitution had changed. For a start Kuching airport was now alive with ugly military aircraft and there were soldiers and airmen everywhere you looked. But Rock Court was the same; Pakiong and family welcomed me with salaams and grins as if I'd come back from the dead. The botanical gardens still stretched lazily in the sunshine beyond the veranda. They gave no hint of being no longer jewels in a Brooke or a Windsor crown but in that of the King of Malaysia. Similarly, the eyes of Stanley Hardy, eyes that still delighted in the garden's glory, were no longer employed to watch over the interests of a white sovereign in London but over those of a brown one in Kuala Lumpur.

The most dramatic change awaited me in Badruddin Road where I found my old, small team already outnumbered by newcomers brought in on what was hoped would be short-term contracts to help cope with Konfrontasi, most of them Brits with Southeast Asia connections. Into the bargain London sent us no fewer than five 'Military Intelligence Officers' (MIOs), army officers trained for 'intelligence' work and posted, in mufti, to help Special Branch units in places where the British army might one day be involved in shooting wars.

There was more. Drawn to Kuching like ants to sugar came the intelligence community, which, as always, accompanied the diplomats (Britain appointed a Deputy High Commissioner, America a Consul). Overnight we had MI5, MI6 and CIA people to handle. By prior agreement they had to declare themselves to Special Branch and they were forbidden to do anything without our blessing.

The most effective and most welcome of our reinforcements came from our new bosses in Kuala Lumpur. Having more or less settled the hash of the Malayan Communist Party they were able to part not only with seasoned Special Branch officers but also with ex-Malayan Communist Party cadres as well. A good deal less welcome, more a millstone round our neck than a helping hand, was the military's intelligence corps, not to be confused with our MIOs. These army officers frequently turned their attention towards the 'enemy within' – 'O'. They claimed legitimate interest. After all, their argument went, if 'O' was going to shoot anybody in Sarawak it might well be soldiers. Soldiers therefore needed to know their enemy. Like their American counterparts in Vietnam, they were obsessed by the numbers game. How many communists are there? How many guns do they have? There was logic to their enquiries. The army was trying to figure out how many soldiers it would take to win the war; ergo, "don't know" answers to questions about the size of its possible enemy were unhelpful. All the same, I pointed out to one Colonel after another (they changed over with startling rapidity) that since 'O' itself didn't know its own strength (I mean an underground organisation wasn't going to keep membership records, was it?), how on earth would we know?

In the end, I was cornered in Kuching by the Director of Borneo Operations' top intelligence chief, Farrar-Hockley (then a Brigadier, later G.O.C Northern Ireland) a needle-witted soldier-intellectual who put it to me that the army simply had to have a figure – one, two, five, ten thousand – they had to have a figure to work on. Repeating our case but conceding that he too had a case, I proposed that we settle for an inspired guess – say 2,000. The next Joint Intelligence Committee report issued in London had it that "the local Special Branch assess active communist strength in Sarawak to be 2,000". Such was the way such weighty matters were resolved in wartime I suppose; we had a figure and we lived with it. We never found out how near to, or how far from, the truth it was.

Vive le Roy!

Roy Henry, a man with a sense of drama in his blood, was on a high. To him Konfrontasi meant excitement, flag-waving, danger, bagpipes, travel, camaraderie, generous public funds, derring-do, beatings of retreat, the chance of glory and an ever-expanding command. He took to the army's helicopters as if they'd been supplied with him in mind, he exulted in being greeted by guards-of-honour at military outposts now scattered throughout the land, delighted in drawing himself up confidently to address the State Emergency Executive Committee against a background of maps and he relished the carousing that was as much a product of Konfrontasi as the guns were. Not that he was just a showman or that he failed to appreciate the dangerous subtleties within the situation, far from it. Behind the exhibitionist there dwelt the serious political analyst, a man with the common touch the like of which I never saw equalled by another, and a tactful, respected leader. It says much of him that he was everybody's favourite from the lowly Border Scout clutching his shotgun against a bare, tattooed chest in the longhouse to the medal-bedecked Director of Operations in his air-conditioned lair on Labuan Island. Roy was away from Kuching frequently and for long periods, leaving me to manage what had grown into a large command made up of people of as wide a disparity of natures as you'd find anywhere in Sarawak – and that's saying something.

'Armed Struggle'

Early in 1963 we'd began to confirm the disappearance from their homes of maybe hundreds (there's that numbers game again) of young Chinese. The exodus alarmed us because it was assumed they'd taken to the jungle en route to Indonesian Borneo where they'd be trained and armed by Sukarno for participation in Konfrontasi. It was the worst-case scenario: the Indonesian army raiding from without, communist guerrillas making trouble within. But at Badruddin Road we thought that 'O' would regret its decision to take up the 'armed struggle' because it would mean an ultimately decisive drop in its already weak mass support. And that view was strengthened from a surprising source.

Miri wasn't the place we expected to get much intelligence from, but purely by fluke our people there stumbled across what they thought at first were just some more 'O' news sheets but for one very interesting document. It was a copy of a report in which the 4th Divisional Committee of 'O' advised the politburo to consider the racial consequences of going into 'armed struggle'. Given the ethnic composition of the opposing sides, it said, 'armed struggle' would pit Chinese ('O's people) against non-Chinese from whom the imperialists drew their armed forces. Ergo, what was meant to be a 'people's war' would turn out to be a civil war. The non-Chinese masses would blame the bloodshed on the only people who supported 'O' – the Chinese; the 'armed struggle' would then become a racial struggle with the Chinese being the losers. The 4th Divisional Committee's farsighted analysis corresponded exactly with ours at Badruddin Road where we'd already concluded that if 'O' persisted in 'armed struggle' it would never achieve the mass support necessary to achieve its political ends. The Malaysian government went as far as to give shotguns to Ibans in remote longhouses – hardly a sign that it feared mass insurrection.

The 'O' leadership however saw things differently and there were those on our side too who shared 'O' appreciation of the situation. It was easy to imagine them sitting in their secret places listing the things they had going for them: Azahari's nearly successful coup in Brunei had raised some local revolutionary fervour; Sukarno was threatening to pitch 100 million Indonesians into Konfrontasi; Manila was conducting an insulting jeremiad against Kuala Lumpur, laying claim to a bounteous slice of Malaysia; Pakistan had joined in reviling the Malaysian concept; Moscow, Beijing, Havana and the rest of the socialist brotherhood made concerted diplomatic onslaught against Malaysia; and in Sarawak itself there remained a solid core of anti-Malaysian sentiment. If to all these powerful manifestations of support for their 'struggle' added the anti-colonialism still being generated by Afro-Asian-Latin American countries, then 'O' had good reason to believe that Lenin's 'revolutionary situation' already existed in Sarawak and that the time, therefore, was ripe for 'armed struggle'.

What neither they nor we could appreciate at that stage was that things weren't at all what they seemed. Hindsight shows that, for a start, Azahari was already a fallen star; moreover, Sukarno would turn out to be a paper tiger; the Americans would buy off the Philippines (a transaction anybody should have foreseen), China would be torn apart by its cultural revolution and lose her influence in Jakarta, and the Soviets, sensing dangers close to home from an unstable China, would back off.

But all that was unknown, as things were in 1963 and considering their ideological objections to crystal gazing and slavish adherence to the gospel according to Mao Tse Tung, it was inevitable that 'O' should reach for the gun. Ignoring the fact that it had no guns to hand and that its influence extended hardly a metre beyond the urban boundaries, the politburo ordered its non-existent troops to 'besiege the cities from the countryside' – straight out of Mao's teachings on 'people's war'; lacking a single square mile of 'liberated territory' from which to direct its sieges and without reliable weapons, most of 'O's 'soldiers' sought refuge and support in Indonesian Borneo. They were to besiege Sarawak's 'cities' from the Indonesian countryside. Inevitably, however, once in Kalimantan they were forced into servitude to the Indonesian military.

Those who stayed behind, mainly in the 3rd Division, fared little better. Taken in by their own propaganda they honestly believed that the 'hirelings of imperialism' (mainly British soldiers) then entering Sarawak in numbers would be unwelcome by the local populace. They took it for granted that, just as Mao had told them, the peasant masses would turn to 'O' for protection against the 'invading barbarians'. It didn't work out that way at all. Far from recoiling from the 'foreign dogs of war', the longhouses greeted the white strangers with open arms, welcoming the gifts – bribes if you like – they brought with them: radios, cigarettes and aspirin tablets. On the other hand, when the 'liberator' approached the longhouses all they could offer were long, incomprehensible words; indeed, rather than having any aspirin to give away they were likely to beg some for themselves.

Unable to go near a longhouse for fear of being informed against and lacking the weapons to take on either the army or the police (they carried one or two home-made shotguns which however ingeniously crafted out of bits of metal piping, wood, wire and nails, were more likely to damage their owners than their intended targets), the 'underground army' had to grub down in appalling conditions on the edges of urban areas from which they could cadge food.

To illustrate, let me take you to a 'revolutionary outpost' I once visited on the outskirts of Sarikei, a small town in the 3rd Division. It was a camp typical of several uncovered during Konfrontasi. You reached it by burrowing like a mole through a few hundred metres of tangled *belukar*, creeping along on your belly through a green tunnel that left thick foliage overhead making you invisible to helicopters.

After half-an-hour's crawl, your front from chest to toe fouled by smelly sludge, you arrived at the 'camp', an outpost providing five sleeping berths circling a clearing the size of a ping-pong table. Laid out like the spokes of a wheel, the five sleeping places had been hollowed out of the bottom of the *belukar*, just as birds would build nests within the thorniest of thickets, to leave a natural canopy of green foliage which, however, afforded little shelter from the heavy rain that fell almost daily. The tiny open space that served as a recreational-area-cum-parade-ground was the only part of the camp in which you could stand up or in which you could be touched with sunshine. A separate length of slime-floored burrow led to the latrine, a stinking, water-logged hole swimming with faeces and alive with insect movement.

There was also a 'larder', a cache made out of split bamboo to hold half-a-dozen, wax-sealed, four-gallon tins, four large, wax-sealed glass jars and several plastic boxes. The tins and jars held biscuits, nuts, dried fruit, cooked rice, shrimp wafers, squid, coffee, tea and sugar. The 'kitchen', another burrow, contained a tiny, one-ring oil burner, bottles of kerosene, one small saucepan, one or two enamel mugs and a dozen chopsticks.

There was a medicine chest – a sealed jar containing aspirin, iodine, mepacrine tablets and bandages. There were tatty oilcloth sheets used to protect the revolutionaries from the worst of the rain. Escape burrows ran in all directions with the intention of reducing the possibility of all five guerrillas being caught using the same route. And of course there was a tin full of documents aimed at willing their readers to be prepared to sacrifice their all for the glorious armed struggle.

I stood on the parade ground experiencing camp life at its rosiest but overwhelmed by the awfulness of the place. Conscious of the fact that there were few days that didn't bring cloudbursts I tried to imagine what it would be like in the rain. The burrows would become instant sluices, the parade ground a swamp, the latrine an overflowing cesspit, every leaf would be a water spout, there'd be no hope of a cup of tea or a cigarette (the male revolutionaries were chain-smokers to a man) and how on earth would you keep your gun dry – provided of course that you had one?

And what about mosquitoes, ants, scorpions, spiders, snakes, leeches, crutch-rot, athlete's foot, canker sores, ulcers, fever, fungi and menstruation? Four or five 'proletarian revolutionaries' had occupied the camp for months before we found it; they had indeed escaped by scurrying on their bellies along these dreadful grass tubes. I wanted to call them back for a hot meal in town, talk to them, listen to them, and take them back to their mother. I said nothing of this out loud. My companions, policemen who'd stumbled across the camp earlier in the day, would have scorned ill-placed sentimentality. And what happened soon afterwards made me glad I'd kept my feelings to myself. I was 'helicoptered' to Sarikei town to view the hideously mutilated corpses of three Chinese merchants who'd almost certainly been murdered by the young guerrillas from the camp I'd seen.

Badruddin Road under Siege

Badruddin Road came under siege, invested not from the jungles but by British military men on our doorstep. Their appetite for action, stirred by Indonesian reluctance to take them on, turned the restless military to look to Sarawak's 'communists' as mouth-watering objectives. Lacking political education beyond sloganeering ('the only good commie is a dead commie') and yearning for a chance to teach the Americans in Vietnam a lesson or two on 'commie bashing', army officers, from generals in Labuan to colonels in Kuching and captains in the hinterland, began to pester us for information and for leave to take swipes at 'communists'.

Army officers beat a path to our door; pleading for permission to go on 'search and destroy' operations based on 'information' they'd either purchased from brigandish locals or picked up from gossip. It got to the point where Roy Henry and I found ourselves wasting time talking the military out of madcap ideas and reminding them of their own rule of engagement: to focus on the external enemy and leave the rest to the police. The turnover of military officers was so rapid that we'd no sooner cooled one batch down than another was clamouring for our attention. I was burning myself out trying to help the new Malaysian administration keep control of events that threatened to tear Sarawak to shreds. The only set routines in my life – only when in Kuching – were the daily conferences known as 'morning prayers', the weekly State Emergency Executive Committee meetings and tennis.

From Guerrilla to Governor!

In trying to figure out who in Sarawak might be soulmates of Azahari (he of the Tentera Nasional Kalimantan Utara, friend of Bung Karno) the only prominent name we came up with was that of the Education Officer to the 2nd Division, Ahmad Zaidi bin Muhamed Noor, M.A. (Edinburgh). Zaidi had been stranded in Indonesia when the Japanese seized that country from the Dutch in 1942. He'd joined the liberation movement (not as much anti-Japanese as anti-Dutch) and he'd been made a Captain in Sukarno's Tentera Nasional Indonesia. According to our intelligence, Zaidi would have preferred Indonesian domination of Sarawak because he considered the 1960s Malaya to be neo-colonialist whereas Sukarno's Indonesia, unruly as it was, was at least a truly independent, proud Asian state.

Zaidi's personal opinions wouldn't have mattered had he not carried considerable influence within the Malay community. He was President of the Barisan Pemuda Sarawak (Sarawak Youth Party) one of the largest open political organisations in the state. What were we to do with this politically turbulent fellow? Our political masters would have been happy to see him flee to join Azahari in Indonesia but, alas, he showed no signs of doing that. In the end it was given to my Malay friend Hamdan and I to go down to Simanggang to sound him out and to persuade him, at worst, to keep his thoughts to himself, at best to get on a soap box and shout for Malaysia.

We found no raving nationalist firebrand, no fundamentalist Muslim cursing all infidels but a dignified, courteous intellectual living modestly in a house packed floor-to-ceiling with books on philosophy, religion and politics including a section on Marx for the possession of which, we could have arrested him on the spot. We were spared the embarrassment of explaining our mission because he'd obviously been waiting for us. He served us tea, exchanged pleasantries, guided us round his library and hinted strongly that he'd stay politically silent and would welcome a move to Kuching where his impeccable behaviour could be more closely observed. We took our leave.

Passing Zaidi's battered little car on our way out, Hamdan, in a goodwill gesture, bent to close a door that had been left open. He noticed in the glove compartment a document in Indonesian printed on the cheap parchment favoured by underground organisations. It's hard to believe but it was Zaidi's commission as a 'General' in Azahari's Tentera Nasional Kalimantan Utara. Even less believably Zaidi immediately acknowledged its authenticity. We could hardly ignore it. Hamdan and I were empowered to take even the lowest foot soldier in Azahari's army into custody. Here we were face-to-face with a self-confessed 'General' but we were forbidden to arrest him.

After some decorous parleying, it was mutually agreed that Zaidi return with us to Kuching for further negotiations. One good thing about it: he'd no need to worry about his family because, as was usual in Sarawak, Zaidi's house was home to so many in-laws that his absence would hardly be noted. I got the feeling that Zaidi was pleased to have been found out; he wouldn't have to take the field as a 'General' in an army that hardly existed any more. In Kuching he lived under a kind of house arrest with Hamdan. He reached a secret agreement by which in return for government financial aid to his family he would be allowed to 'escape' across the border into Indonesia where he'd lie low until the end of Konfrontasi. Both sides honoured the agreement. Zaidi, a convert to the Malaysian concept, returned to Sarawak in 1968; by 1974, he was State Minister for Housing and Development; and in 1985 he moved into the Brookes' old Istana as Governor of Sarawak.

Sigint (Signals Intelligence)

Early in 1964 it was calculated that 12 Indonesian army battalions were deployed close to the borders of East Malaysia to *mengkonfrontasikan* British, Australian, New Zealand and Malaysian troops who, if not equal in numbers were vastly superior to them in firepower, air and sea support, equipment, supplies, medical services, food quality, leadership and, crucially, morale. The wretched Indonesians lived off the land, the same land that barely sustained its own sparse local people, let alone hundreds of hungry scavenging Javanese. Their communications were pitiable; there were no roads, they had nowhere near enough river craft to permit easy movement and only one of the six Russian helicopters in Indonesian Borneo was ever able to fly, and even then only when fuel was available. Once in the 'war zone', the unfortunate Indonesian askar would be there 'for the duration', undernourished, cut off from family, scared, ill-housed, badly protected and poorly motivated.

When it came to intelligence, the contest was even more one-sided. The British brought in the latest signals intelligence system: 'Sigint' through which, helped by gross Indonesian mismanagement, they plugged into what the Indonesians called their radio communications system but which consisted in fact of World War II wireless packs whose signals depended upon old-fashioned crystals, crystals which, in defiance of all military rules, they never altered. I was told that wireless operators who changed their crystals weekly reduced their chances of being intercepted to almost zero. The Indonesians either didn't know about the simple safety measure or, more likely, couldn't come up with replacement crystals. Through the years of Konfrontasi, the British, on behalf of all the rest, were tuned in to Indonesian army communications.

Internally, what we'd feared most – Indonesian soldiers and irregulars providing the backing for an 'O'-led insurrection – didn't materialise. Most of the Sarawakians who had internal insurrection in mind, the 'O' youngsters, fled the homeland to subjugate themselves to Indonesians who had no love for Chinese from anywhere.

The Indonesian foot soldier simply wasn't hyped up enough against Malaysia to be prepared to risk his neck trying to destroy it. As a result we had an Indonesian army hanging about dispiritedly on its own soil, passing messages between formations claiming victorious incursions into enemy territory that had never happened. Worst still for them, by passing messages of any sort, true or false, they disclosed their locations and invited pre-emptive attacks upon them.

There were so few Indonesian incursions that they can be dealt with in one paragraph. Following the opening attack on Tebedu there came the most daring and successful penetration, an incursion of about 100 miles into the 3rd Division by a crack Komando unit that, with no loss to itself, murdered a good many unsuspecting Ghurkas. Then there was an attack by Indonesian soldiers guided by 'O' guerrillas upon the police post at the 17th mile bazaar on the Kuching–Serian road killing among others, the brother of the Chief Minister. Then Indonesian irregulars made a real cock-up of a bizarre attempt to infiltrate the Sarikei area of the 3rd Division by sea; they got no further than the mangrove on the beach. Finally, a Komando unit attempted an audacious penetration aimed perhaps at Kuching airport only to be easily and bloodily driven off. By far the most common Indonesian offensive activity – and it says all about the depth of their demoralisation – was for its warriors to move close to the border, lob a few mortar bombs in the general direction of local habitation and then scarper fast. Apart from causing damage to vegetation and no doubt to wild creatures, those ambuscades did little or no harm to the state of its people.

Regardless of the sound and fury in the background, Sukarno's troops stayed put in their miserable positions inside their own borders. Indeed, Konfrontasi was turned on its head because it was the soldiers on our side, ostensibly employed in a defensive role, and not the Indonesians, supposedly sworn to assault Malaysia, who did most of the border crossing. Bored with sitting in their dug-outs waiting for attacks that never came, longing for the chance to go hunting on the other side and with Sigint locking on targets with pin-point accuracy, our military ached to have a go.

Operation 'Claret'

There was, however, one major snag. What was straightforward military logic held the worst possible implications for the politicians. War had after all not been declared. Sukarno still pretended that it was indigenous insurgents, not Indonesian soldiers, who threatened Sarawak, and diplomats on all sides were still trying to find a peace formula. Above everything else the politicians feared that the death of a single Indonesian soldier at the hands of foreign invaders on Indonesian soil might trigger a real war involving major powers. Blindingly obvious as those dangers were to the politicians, they cut no ice with the military that, as always, saw things in straight 'us' and 'them' terms.

"Either we kill them," they'd argue, "or they'll kill us. Our own chaps could die in an Indonesian raid tomorrow but we have the means of pre-empting that raid by going over there and taking them out today. Using Sigint information we could raid one Indonesian unit today, another in another place tomorrow and one or two somewhere else next week. They wouldn't know where to turn; they'd be totally demoralised. On the other hand, if we don't do anything it'll be our boys who'll be demoralised. We've got the intelligence, why collect it and then not use it? You brought us here to fight a war; right then, let's get on with it." Relentlessly, tirelessly, they'd go at it like that.

The military had all the time in the world to argue its single-issue case. For the politicians and administrators however, Konfrontasi was just one more, albeit major, issue to deal with; they still had a country to run – and a brand new country at that. At the end, no matter how reluctantly and fearfully, London and Kuala Lumpur authorised a super-secret military operation code-named Claret. With the important proviso that the incursions be 'unattributable', Claret sanctioned shallow incursions into Indonesia.

'Unattributable' became the buzzword among the military planners in East Malaysia. Claret teams were to cross into Indonesia on the strictest possible understanding that they leave behind not the slightest shred of evidence with which Sukarno could prove violation of his country's territorial integrity. That was in the beginning. The first raids were conducted with all the restraint the politicians had insisted upon. Small bands of lightly armed, well-briefed soldiers would dart across the border, shoot a few Indonesian soldiers whose location had been fixed by Sigint, then hurry out again leaving behind not so much as a fag end.

But over the months it became apparent that for reasons of its own (maybe Sukarno couldn't bring himself to admit that 'colonialist' soldiers were entering and leaving his country at will?), Jakarta didn't make a row about the violations. Nor did the Indonesian military on the ground swear to avenge the slaughter of its young men (Sigint reported a sickly lack of concern). Hence, the more gung-ho military officers began to press for more frequent, deeper and bloodier raids.

No Commonwealth soldier in Borneo was more gung-ho than the very top one: General Sir Walter Walker, a ramrod-straight chauvinist to whom even President Johnson of the USA was 'a pinko' because he'd drawn back from using nuclear weapons in Vietnam. To give an idea of what Walker stood for, after his retirement in the 1970s he declared his support for apartheid in South Africa and indeed for the extension of its practice elsewhere; he advocated the formation in the UK of an 'armed vigilante corps of Royalists' to root out 'communists and fellow travellers'; he associated himself with a born-again American religious movement that presented the violent obliteration of 'international communists' and he became a leading figure in the CIA-funded, Taiwan-based 'World Against Communism' movement.

Walker's secret weapon was the SAS operation. Claret was tailor-made for the SAS. It offered jungle training with an edge of danger, physical toughening and shooting practice with new weapons aimed at live targets; and all this out of the sight of pinkos, liberals, do-gooders and commie lovers. While other units taking part in Claret (Malaysian forces never did) stuck more or less to the rules, the SAS did much as it pleased.

Not all the soldiers enjoyed it. Expressions such as "It's like shooting rabbits!" were heard. But not from Britain's toughies, the SAS. Secretly supplied by MI6 with Iban 'guides', the SAS went for Claret with relish. They first built a secret longhouse known as 'The Island' off a remote beach west of Kuching not far from our picnic spot at Karangan. From 'The Island' mixed SAS-Iban gangs took off for Indonesia where guided, or so they claimed, by Sigint intelligence, they slew Indonesians. They'd return to 'The Island' bearing gory trophy heads which hadn't, I suspected, belonged every time to the Indonesian military.

None of which criticism gainsays the fact that without the military shield the Indonesians would have been in Kuching within days of the Malaysia declaration and that, imperfect as the Malaysian solution may have been, Sukarno's would have been a thousand times worse. The soldiers provided the fortification behind which the politicians and administrators were able to build.

Get the 'Reds'

Hour after wearisome hour Roy Henry and I rejected military and police officers' pleas to round-up 'communists'. The fixed idea of the military was that every Chinese was a 'red', and this implied the mass chastisement of Sarawak's Chinese population.

A typical discourse between myself and, say, a couple of General Walker's aides, a Brigadier and a Colonel briefed no doubt to echo their master's voice, would have gone something like this. The Brigadier would have opened with what had become a tiresomely familiar lecture. "The Indonesians aren't the underlying threat here; they were beaten before they even started. No, the real 'insidious threat' (how the military loved those two words!) lay with 'international communism' against which Malaysia's Internal Security Regulations gave the security forces a free hand. Why then were we sitting on our hands denying the military the means of dealing with a threat that was growing every day?"

During such times, I thanked God that we hadn't gone down the American road in Vietnam where the military were the masters. My reply to the Brigadier would have been to question the proposition that the 'communist threat' was increasing. The real communists, I'd have said, as opposed to those conjured up in military minds, were either already in custody or over the border in Indonesia. Apart from a few score who'd taken to the jungle locally and who were being easily contained by the constabulary field force, there remained abroad in the land only weak-willed, poorly-led novices who'd be more of a threat in detention than they were outside because once inside a camp they'd be 'steeled' by the hard-core 'professional revolutionaries' already in there. Better to leave them alone, inoperative. And I'd have pointed out for the umpteenth time that, contrary to common misconception, the Internal Security Regulations did not give the security forces a free hand. It wasn't true that evidence wasn't required or that the word of an army officer was good enough; it certainly was and it certainly wasn't. If a Brigadier's soldiers delivered suspects into the hands of the constabulary together with evidence that added up to a strong case, then these persons would be detained. But if he were to set his men loose on 'commie bashing' exercises, then we'd release people as fast as his soldiers picked them up. And that would be bad for the morale of the army, the constabulary and the population alike.

I'd then talk to them as if they were children. Without spending millions more on new detention camps, I'd say there was a limit to the number of detainees we could house. Moreover, the Special Branch was already over-extended; mass arrests would swamp us, dragging us away from more important, albeit less publicly dramatic, operations. I'd invite them to stop and think. For every suspect 'commie' they'd pick up, they'd alienate at least a score of people: parents, grandparents, wives, husbands, children, friends, neighbours, aunts and uncles, school mates, work mates, play mates, brother, sisters, cousins, sweethearts and so on. By throwing just one Chinese into the back of a Land Rover a score of people would be made dissidents. Was that the way to win the day? And finally I'd remind them of the basic strategy: the military would defend the borders against incursion while the civil authority dealt with internal matters.

The Brigadiers and Colonels (and on one occasion General Walker himself) would take their leave muttering about 'making representations elsewhere', an implication that troubled us not one whit because 'elsewhere' could only mean Kuala Lumpur where the Federal Cabinet was less than enthusiastic about suggestions that foreign – albeit friendly – soldiers might run around in one of its states rounding up locals. Safe in that knowledge we could always call the army's bluff.

Spending on Soldiers

The military squandered men, materials and, consequently, money on a scale such as to make it seem that the Director of Operations had declared profligacy to be the order of the day. They weren't as spendthrift as their American cousins in Vietnam (the British drooled over the Americans' excesses), but to those of us who'd spent our working lives 'making do', they were like spoiled kids.

Take helicopters for example, machines costing thousands of ringgits an hour to fly. The army had an insatiable demand for them. Undeniably the best means of supplying jungle outposts, helicopters were much fancied by staff officers wishing to cut a dash. Colonels weren't satisfied with air-conditioned staff cars to take them to and from Kuching airport, a pleasant journey taking maybe 20 minutes and costing maybe as many ringgits, nor were they happy to take their cars to Bau or Serian, journeys of an hour or so that'd set the taxpayer back about 30 ringgits. No, they had to have 'choppers' by which they made bravura entrances and exits, dropping from and rising into the skies like deities but at several thousand ringgits a time. Domestic flights between Kuching and Sibu at 50 ringgits a seat were sniffed at in favour of spending a couple of thousands on going there by 'chopper'.

Enough of the military. Trying as its presence was, it's worth repeating that by comparison with the Indonesians who pulled the final curtain down on Konfrontasi by slaughtering half a million home-grown 'communists', Walter Walker and his men behaved like saints.

Constables and Cabinets

The Constabulary too had taken advantage of Konfrontasi to raid the then open public purse. Following decades of holding the peace with but a few hundred unarmed constables, almost overnight the Commissioner had under command around 10,000 variously armed men and women (this amounted to a four-fold increase in his regular force plus para-military units and a few thousand 'Border Scouts' – a sort of vigilante corps with a presence in every longhouse in the border region). Where he'd once been concerned only with trying to catch a few petty criminals and the rare murderer, and performing at state ceremonials, Konfrontasi made him concentrate his extended force against what the state called 'communist terrorists' and what 'O' called 'freedom fighters'.

The snag was that most of the 'terrorists' had fled the country and were beyond the Commissioner's reach; few of them stayed behind in Sarawak and ever came to light. The result, with the exception of the Special Branch, was a grossly underemployed constabulary, a state of affairs that led to boredom which, as with the military, led police officers to plead to be allowed to have a go at the 'communists', to allow harsher interrogation of suspects and to recommend sterner conditions of detention for those 'communists' already behind bars. But, because Roy Henry and I were senior enough to instruct the rest of them to keep quiet, the dissident constabulary officers were easier to deal with than the soldiers.

Some of the local politicians also favoured witch-hunts. Having had no previous experience in the art of governance they weren't too understanding of its niceties. The Sarawak United People's Party (SUPP) had been the first political organisation of any significance and in the pre-Malaysia days was far and away the foremost party in the state. It suffered one howling weakness: while boasting multi-racialism its membership was almost exclusively Chinese. Its aims were simple enough: independence and liberalism. Its leaders, Ong Kee Hui and Stephen Yong, were able, highly respected Sarawak-born Chinese fiercely jealous of Sarawak's individual identity and, consequently, firmly opposed to the Malaysian proposition. They were however, busy professional people with little time to oversee the day-to-day business of their party, the guidance of which fell into the hands of young Chinese ideologically close to 'O'. Unsurprisingly, Kuala Lumpur viewed with alarm a situation in which the only serious political organisation in the largest state in the federation was opposed to the concept of the federation and which was Chinese to boot. To counter the SUPP the Malayan government (pre-Malaysia days) more or less openly promised to bankroll any political party that would do its bidding in Sarawak. It got more than it bargained for.

Five brand new parties registered in quick succession, each claiming to represent group interests but each in truth doing no more than provide the screens behind which opportunists hoped to lay hands on Kuala Lumpur's money and influence. KL knocked them all together into a pro-Malaysian 'Alliance' which by 'winning' the 1963 general election cleared the way for KL and London to claim that absorption within a Malaysian federation was confirmed as the choice of the majority of Sarawakians.

The result was that the only genuine political consciousness resided in the minority opposition party while the state government was in the hands of novices. The Chief Minister was a semi-literate Iban, Stephen Kalong Ningkan and the Federal Minister for Sarawak affairs with a Cabinet seat in KL was a totally illiterate Iban Chief, Temenggong Jugah. Ningkan, Jugah and the rest had yet to grow the politicians' thick skins. Ningkan had moved almost directly from longhouse to the residence of the former Colonial Secretary, the second most prestigious dwelling in the country, while Jugah overnight swapped his loincloth for the spectacular, fussy robes of a Cabinet minister. In assuming the appurtenances of high office they supposed that they'd acquired the powers that went with them. Ergo, they resented criticism from any quarter; feeling for example that if they felt slighted by an opponent they could turn to the Commissioner of Constabulary for redress. Like the soldiers, they saw the Internal Security Act as giving the Commissioner the power to arrest and detain anybody they didn't like the look of. Happily however the authors of the federal constitution had posited authority over state police forces with the PM, not with state governments. Roy Henry was promoted to be Commissioner of Constabulary and I was promoted to Assistant Commissioner of Constabulary, head Special Branch, Sarawak. I became the third-ranking police officer in Sarawak, a bizarre elevation when you consider my background and the fact that I'd not had an hour's police training in my life.

'Lada'

Once exalted, I'd no option but to move into the more exalted dwelling that went with the job of head Special Branch. Any reluctance we felt on

parting with our splendid Rock Road apartment was soon swept away as
we settled into 'Lada'. By no means a mansion, indeed one of the more
modest of the houses built for the Rajah's top officials, Lada (the Malay
word for pepper) gave all the appearance of having been the idea of some
Brooke hand who, having been allocated a couple of acres of pepper
garden within which to build himself a house had, in full understanding
of the climate and the terrain, come up with its design.

Perched above, but screened by high foliage from, Bampfylde Road (a
lane named after one of the Rajah's faithful administrators and possibly
the projector of Lada) the house wasn't all that grand to look at from the
outside. But what the squat, square bungalow with its belian roof lacked
in architectural merit, it more than made up for in the taste with which
it had been fashioned internally. Sarawak was short of many things, but
space wasn't one of them; Lada's grounds ran to a couple of acres much less
formally cultivated than the gardens of most other colonial homesteads
in Kuching. Its lawns weren't merely carefully mown backgrounds for
floral displays, rather they were lush, green slopes dotted with flowering
shrubs, ferns and trees all strewn around in unaffected, colourful, pleasing
disorder. Sitting in Lada was like sitting in a summer house gazing as
the sun filtered through the foliage to pick out flying lizards as they
glided from one casuarina landing strip to another. Casuarinas, perfectly
harmonious to Lada, grew close enough to the house for you to touch
their gossamer tendrils without stepping a foot outside.

Early morning was the time for kingfishers to flash brilliantly through
the clearing; midday was the turn of the flamboyant yellow and red
woodpeckers to put on their show, red-whiskered bulbuls buzzed about
all day long and at night the tock-tock bird beat its irregular drum.
Frangipani and jacaranda scents hung in the warm, damp air, palms
swayed (yes they really did) and tiger orchids, cannas and poinsettias
grew as tall as Pakiong. The seemingly haphazard nature of Lada's gardens
was, of course, a fake. Left unattended they'd have been secondary
jungle within a fortnight. To keep them in order in came yet another of
Pakiong's family, this one a tall, barrel-chested, middle-aged brother who

for a few dollars a month and as much rice as he could eat (I bought rice for Pakiong and company by the sackful) appeared two or three times a week to scythe the grass and the undergrowth; we eschewed motor-mowers, Lada was as peaceful as the jungle.

Riding the Pigeon

Suddenly, disaster struck – I got tennis elbow. Like a drug addict, without my daily tennis fix I couldn't sleep or function properly. Heat treatment, wax baths, pills, a Malay bomoh's fomentations, massage at the hands of Pakiong's mother (like being trampled on by a day-old kitten) left my elbow still as sore as a boil. Whereupon my good friend Wong Kie Keong recommended a certain acupuncturist: "He's a miracle worker, he'll have you back on court in no time." I couldn't get to the famous healer fast enough. From what I'd learnt about acupuncture, I'd be pierced somewhere removed from my ailing elbow – in my left big toe, perhaps. Or in one of my ear lobes? Not a bit of it. Once he'd located the exact location of the inflammation, the great 'doctor' stabbed his needle into that very point and twisted it round and round between his fingers like he'd have used a swizzle stick. The pain had me leaping higher than a tennis net. Three days, three stabs and three swizzles later and my elbow still throbbed at the very sight of my tennis racquet.

Unfazed, Kie Keong introduced me to another Chinese 'doctor', this time one of the scores of necromancers who set up stalls in every town in Southeast Asia. The high sense of drama and dedication to the noble cause of healing with which those diabolists advertised their skills would put any old Western medicine-monger to shame. Take the 'dentists' for example. Outside the surgery (which might have been anything from a rented space of a square metre of the five-foot way to a gleaming modern clinic), there would invariably hang a vividly coloured blow-up of a human head split down the middle to display its inside in profile. The passer-by was thus informed at a glance of the dangers posed by streams of yellow, green and purple toxins making their way from rotting molars to destroy noses, eyes and brains. The calligraphy underneath rubbed the message in: to avoid such miasmic destruction taking place within your head, all you had to do was call on the 'dentist' there and then. Crude as they were however, the orthodontists' signboards had nothing on the haemorrhoid 'specialists' who, faced with a huge potential market (maybe because of their habit of squatting, their lack of exercise or their addiction to hot spices, Asians were particularly susceptible to piles) were easily the most imaginative exhibitors. Their advertising hoardings, sometimes illuminated as if they were advertising a desirable product, presented spine-chilling, graphic, technicolour close-ups of festering anuses from which erupted serpent-like fiends, balls of flaming tar and unspeakable leeches.

But to get back to my elbow. Being a 'world-renowned dermatologist' my new 'doctor' proclaimed his skills with relative restraint. His exotic signboard showed a unisex bare back and shoulders from whose every square millimetre there spurted a pustule, each pustule emitting mucus of varying colours. Even if the passer-by had trouble as bad as that depicted, the sign said he or she would be cured by the miracle worker within. I suggested to Kie Keong that since my elbow looked nothing like that poor creature's back he might have brought me to the wrong place but he insisted that the skin specialist was also an osteopath who'd have me serving aces within a day or two. Why, I nearly asked, if he was so exalted a physician did he practice his profession in his living room, a sleazy bed-sit overrun with chubby, snotty-nosed, naked children and underfed dogs and why didn't he wear a white or green coat instead of a pair of baggy, tatty shorts beneath a bare torso?

My new physician, who'd have taken an oath to a triad society rather than to Hippocrates, swept one or two smelly babies from a canvas chair and invited me to be seated. Without further ado, calling an attendant, a vacuous-looking youth dressed in the same skimpy style as his master, the 'doctor' proceeded to build a small pyramid of a green powder right there above the elbow. He then set a match to a fuse that stuck out of the apex of the pyramid like a candlewick. The fire burned slowly downwards until, at the moment when I was about to jump up and run for it, the 'doctor' blew it out. Next he spread a malodorous white paste over a large, green leaf, making a stinking poultice, which he strapped around my elbow with twine. Then, delivering himself of incantations, he waved his joss-sticks over my arm before putting it in a mucky sling. Warning me not to remove the dressing for 24 hours, he charged me five ringgits and made an appointment for the next day.

The stench of the dressing would have stunned a five-ton bear; thankfully, it was Saturday afternoon, meaning that I didn't offend anyone at home except poor old Pakiong who, however, contrariwise as always, was mightily impressed by the 'noisesomeness' of the appliance; anything that ponged as evilly as that, she said, was bound to do good. On the Sunday I went through one more ordeal by fire but then gave it up. Despairing of ever reaching Wimbledon I bought myself a Chinese-made 'Pigeon' bicycle, which was to substitute for tennis. Pedalling around Kuching I learned how little I knew about the town, riding down its side streets, back lanes, alleyways, footpaths and embankments (like the one that had once carried the track of the Royal Sarawak Railways). I fell in love with the place more than ever. It got to the point where I was recognised, albeit as a crackpot, as a sort of daily event, children waited on corners to laugh with me, old women came out to wave, and my old tennis chums stopped playing to jeer.

Practising medicine in Kuching and preaching the Bahai faith to a few non-Muslims at the same time was one John Fozdar, son of a famous female proselytiser of the Bahai religion. It says much for Fozdar that, forbidden to attempt the conversion of Muslims and a believer in a religion banned by its parent Islamic state, he yet had many Muslim friends. What has this to do with anything? Well, it was the excellent Fozdar, eloquent in many tongues, who finally cured my tennis elbow. Profoundly respectful of traditional Asian nostrums and naturopathic medicines as he was, Fozdar nevertheless very swiftly shot an expensive Western concoction into my elbow by hypodermic syringe and hey presto, I was back at the tennis court. But I never gave up my circling of Kuching on my 'Pigeon'.

Lubok Antu

Come with me to Lubok Antu, a two-shophouse settlement smack on the Indonesian border some 20 miles south of Simanggang. Lubok Antu existed only to give an address to which government could send tax demands to a pair of Chinese merchants who made a living by buying rubber smuggled in by Ibans from the Indonesian side of the border and then selling it in Simanggang. The Ibans didn't know they were smugglers; total innocents, they recognised no border; there was no signpost (not that they could have read one anyway) to tell them that at such-and-such a point the path crossed from one people's jungle to another people's jungle and the river, which was the boundary line, was just the same on one bank as it was on the other. There was a flag waving but they'd have thought it signalled a birth or a death, not different nationhood. They understood nothing of any communal groupings beyond those of longhouses in their stretch of the jungle.

As far as those Borneans were concerned the trading post at Lubok Antu was the nearest one to their longhouse, the only place they could barter their rough rubber for things they couldn't get back home. I stood beside the jungle trail at Lubok Antu one day watching a line of diminutive, honey-coloured, near naked men, women and children, most of them tattooed from finger-tips to toe-nails, walking towards the shophouses. They bore incredibly heavy loads of sheet rubber packed tightly into rattan back-packs of which, when emptied, I bought two of the smallest from among those being carried by children. Those happy-go-lucky little folk had walked for several days, eating what they found in the jungle, sleeping by the side of the track and there they were at long last throwing their loads to the ground, their foreheads showing wheals where the headbands of their haversacks had bitten into them. When their smelly strips of the poorest quality rubber I'd ever seen had been weighed, haggled over and finally priced, they took in exchange bars of coarse soap, scoops of sugar and tins of corned-beef and sardines; then, their mouths blood-red from chewing betel, they began their long trek home.

Tropical Heat

I am unable to eloquently describe the heat in which we were enveloped in those days before air-conditioning. Just seated at my desk in Badruddin Road without picking up a pencil the sweat ran down my arms to leave little pools of water beneath my elbows. Getting into the Dauphine after it had been parked in the sun for ten minutes or so was to climb into a kiln. In Lada at four in the afternoon, whether the sun outside buzzed like a fluorescent lamp or the skies were dark with rain, was to be imprisoned within a personalised sauna. You baked into a stupor, the heat a leaden weight on your shoulders.

For that reason when the family was at home together we'd escape, often to spend those numbing hours before dusk sauntering through secondary growth that was rapidly reclaiming an old, disused airstrip. There, just off the road seven miles out of town, we'd, as the Malays put it, *makan angin* (eat the breeze). It was a place where the bush fused into a combustion of burning and flowering, of myriad orchids and a rank profusion of algae that looked like deep green excrement; of giant pitcher plants carrying a pint of poison in each; of lianas thick as the ropes round a boxing ring; of *lalang* (grass) sharp as razor blades; of gorgeous cannas, moulds, yeasts and a riot of other flowers so wild, grotesque, lovely and exotic that it diverted our minds from the pressure cooker in which we were boiling.

'Hardy' – a Secret Enterprise

To return to Badruddin Road, where an exclusive Special Branch team, backed by a large range of ingenious gadgets, pushed through an extraordinary, secret enterprise which, deep down, few of us ever thought would come to much. We clandestinely rented a large house off Pending Road; it was so well concealed that I personally never set eyes on it. Into this place, known only to a few of us, and despite fears that it couldn't be done in a place like Kuching, boffins from KL installed machinery for tapping telephones, intercepting mail and bugging premises.

With the help of the Malaysian air force (who doubted they'd pull it off without being 'blown'), we flew aeroplanes into Kuching in the dead of night. They brought strangers carrying false Sarawak citizenship papers, specially equipped automobiles bearing bogus registration plates, tons of technological gadgetry, even household furniture and appliances – all for the Pending house. There was never the slightest leak.

In the open we rented a sprawling, ramshackle old place lying behind thick bush on the top of a hill off McMahon Road. The house, whose innards were torn out and rebuilt, became our 'holding centre', a designated place of detention in which we could hold and interrogate half-a-dozen 'communists' at a time. Within it we installed the latest in electronic gadgets and we also installed some remarkable people, the most special of all being an aged Chinese couple who went under the unlikely pseudonyms of 'Mr. and Mrs. Hardy', 'Hardy' having been the code name given years earlier to the distinguished-looking, silver-haired gentleman who then became a key member of our team.

A former member of the Central Committee of the Communist Party of Malaya, for ten years 'Hardy' had waged 'armed struggle' against the Japanese, British and Malayans until he awoke one morning in his jungle hideout to admit to himself that the 'armed struggle' was doing the masses more harm than good. He fled from the jungle and volunteered to work for the Malayan government trying to persuade his old comrades to give up; he had much success. In Sarawak, we wanted him first of all to diagnose the strain of Maoism that ran through 'O', then to come up with an antidote to it. And then we hoped that he could ideologically reclaim the 'O' members we'd already detained so that they could be sent out into the countryside to induce their comrades to abandon the 'armed struggle'.

'Hardy' was assisted by a frequently changing team of four or five ex-CPM members, above all by his *tai-tai* (wife) a plump grandmotherly figure who kept excellent house for everybody in the holding centre. Detainees, interrogators and visitors alike all enjoyed her superb food. While there's no such thing as a good prison and while 'Hardy's' cerebral approach to interrogation didn't always pay off, the McMahon Road house was a civilised place from which scores of young Chinese went free still clinging to their dreams of building a better, more equable society, but convinced that in Sarawak's circumstances their dreams could never be realised through the barrel of a gun.

Once coupled with our major operation, 'Hardy's' programme bore fruit. By mid-1965 it told us, straight from the horse's mouth that 'O' in Indonesia was in desperate straits; its Indonesian masters left its 'soldiers' ragged-arsed, half-starved, ill-armed and bottled up in camps like prisoners. Unable to make contact with Beijing through Indonesia, the 'O' politburo-in-exile decided to try via Sarawak and Hong Kong. Always holding our breath we marvelled when our operation intercepted their communications to and fro. To cut the story short, we got hold of a secret instruction telling 'O' that, while 'O' had Beijing's spiritual support, China wouldn't lift a finger to help it materially. Only by going through the furnace of armed struggle unaided from outside, said Mao, could a revolutionary movement be steeled to win, and made strong enough to govern once it had seized power. For it to triumph with the assistance of outsiders would be no victory at all. In short, Beijing wished 'O' the best of luck but left it on its own.

This account might seem to be no big deal but way back in the 1960s, it was a priceless piece of intelligence. However, the few top people who were told about it received it with mixed feelings. All were happy to hear of 'O's plight and of China's refusal to help but some of the heavies in KL, London, Labuan, Washington and Kuching were none too pleased to be shown proof that one of their articles of faith – that Mao handed guns to every third-world troublemaker who asked for them – was, simply, untrue. They'd exploited the line that Mao was behind every gun pointed at Western interests in Asia to support their continuous – and successful – clamour for more weaponry for themselves. They didn't change their tune. Nonetheless, several years later, Farrar-Hockley (by then a General and a very big wheel indeed) told me that my letting him into the 'O'-Beijing secret had been, for him, the most dramatic event of the Borneo 'war'.

Exploring Inland

I was insanely busy. Indeed, those years in Sarawak were the only ones in my entire colonial career that made me feel that I truly earned my keep. All the same there was more to life than a desk. I travelled regularly to KL and was constantly on the move in Sarawak. I went for instance to Oya/Mukah which could then be reached only by a long, lovely, serene journey by long-boat up the Batang Igan from Sibu to Kut and then by the Batang Oya to the Kampong of Oya. As we neared Kut our boat was escorted on both sides by iguanas just as we'd been flanked by dolphins while sailing on the *S.S. Canton* in the Indian Ocean. From Oya we travelled by jeep along the beach to Mukah, a one-street town from where it was possible once a week to take a single-engine aeroplane to Sibu.

Tapioca was Oya's only cash crop and a poor one it was. It may be good to eat or, in its finished pearl-like state, to look at, but the way in which it was processed from woody pulp (the Malay name for it is *ubi kayu* – wooden yam) into edible grains was a foul enterprise. Tapioca is the pulverised soft wood of a certain type of palm. An immense amount of the wood is cut, stripped of bark, soaked, beaten by hand into a pulp that is then fed through ringers to produce a tiny amount of the pap to be turned into tapioca kernels. There remains a prodigious amount of waste to be thrown upon huge heaps of the stuff to burn very slowly and to give off a putrid smell. Tapioca cultivation brought a subsistence living at its lowest possible human level; the Melanaus who lived on it appeared to be worse off than any Ibans I ever saw, not because they were equally impoverished but that they lived in a badly polluted environment as well.

Mukah, with better soil, presented a more cheerful aspect. No more than a speck on the map it was yet noted through the land for its *umai*, a raw-fish delicacy washed down by those who could afford it by 'four-star' brandy. Since to refuse it would have given offence I steeled myself to eat an *umai* breakfast in one of the town's coffee shops. The whole of the shopfront opened out on to the five-foot way; a counter ran along one side in front of open shelves displaying canned food from Amoy, China, or Lee of Singapore whose cans pictured cows, chickens and fish. There were cigarettes (every male over the age of ten and many of the older women smoked; on every shop counter there'd be a candle flame from which the cigarette purchasers of anything between a single 'stick' and a tin of 50 could light up), tins of cooking oil, jars of boiled sweets (a great favourite were the English-made cough lozenges, 'Hacks'), tins of Jacob's biscuits (a great colonial snack enjoyed by the natives as well; wherever you couldn't get bread there'd always be Jacob's – a Jacob's biscuit on either side of a spoonful of Lee curry chicken was to me the food of the gods), bags of rice, beans and nuts, and jars of Chinese pickles which, on being opened, gave off a smell noxious enough to choke on.

At the back of the store below a patch on the ceiling black with soot, stood charcoal braziers, pots and pans, knives and cleavers, a bloody butcher's block and kerosene-burning refrigerators full of bottles of beer, cheap carbonated-water drinks and, of course, *umai*. In the dining area, standing on a beaten-earth floor, were half-a-dozen round tables topped in imitation marble and sporting the usual amount of lethal condiments, each table surrounded by several not always reliable stools. The whole caboosh: shelves, kitchen, eating area and five-foot way gave off a powerful and, to old hands, agreeable miasma smelling of oils, greases, vinegars, excretions, charcoal smoke, kerosene fumes, joss-stick reek, roasting coffee beans, cheap scent, sweat, pickled cabbage and scrubbing soap.

My host was a laugh-a-minute, brush-moustached, gap-toothed Malay district officer who waved me to a stool at the 'VIP' table (so designated because it was positioned directly beneath the establishment's only ceiling fan – not operating at the time because the electricity supply ran only for a few evening hours a day) and summoned the *towkay*, a Chinese clad only in a pair of pyjama trousers (not that he'd only just got out of bed but because such attire was *a la mode* for coffee-shop owners) to serve "*umai dengan brandy ampat bintang punyah lah!*" *Umai*, a dish I'd been warned could eat through the stomach walls in minutes, was served up on saucers with chopsticks. Rubbery to the mandibles, it was undeniably fishy. One bite and I knew why the habit of eating *umai* for breakfast or at any other time for that matter – hadn't spread beyond the boundaries of Mukah. I raved about it, of course, praising *umai* as the finest refreshment to be found outside of France but I was thankful not to be pressed into consuming a second helping. I was permitted to drink excellent local coffee instead of brandy and I eventually took off by air for Sibu none the worse for wear.

I went up the mighty Rejang all the way to Kapit in a small boat whose beam was just wide enough to admit mine (boats were made for lean-hipped locals). Kapit had once been an important stronghold of the Brookes who'd built there one of their imposing, indestructible, wooden forts from whose ramparts they'd 'kept the peace' in the upper reaches of the greatest of their rivers. I spent a couple of nights in a Malay house high above the town; steamy, heavy nights, nights made tumultuous by the clamour of a billion bugs. Disturb the mosquito net or touch a garment handing on a nail in the wall and the flapping of the wings of many thousands of disturbed insects set up a loud, harmonium-like drone.

I next went to Kapit in a broad-beamed luxury launch taking the Deputy Prime Minister of Malaysia, Abdul Razak, to pay a call of potentially great significance upon Temenggong Jugah, the Federal Minister for Sarawak affairs and uncrowned 'King of Kapit'; he of the dramatic hairdo and shoulder-length ear lobes. Jugah was just beginning to voice public concern over the poor status of the Ibans in their own land, in effect but not in so many words muttering disquiet over KL's good faith. Razak was going to Kapit to excise the cancer before it spread; KL had enough on its hands without having to deal with a rebellious Jugah. Razak's mission was openly to pay respects to the great chief on his native territory, hand out gifts, make promises and speak soothing words.

Jugah had laid on a fabulous blow-out, a smorgasbord of Asian delicacies (minus of course, in deference to Razak's religious rules, that most favoured of all Iban dishes: roast pig) spread in the Brookes great fort across a huge iron-wood table standing on heavy legs carved in the Iban characterization of dogs, each corner of the immense table being held as it were within the jaws of an animal whose upper head rose about a foot above the table's surface. It was a medieval scene – two high chiefs together with their entourages being led into a citadel by a procession of maidens to gorge upon a gargantuan array of meats, spices, legumes, rice, fruit and nuts piled in mountainous heaps upon a massive block of black wood running almost the length of the hall.

I remember the day when I flew in a slow, single-engine, two-seater aeroplane skimming the lordly Rejang like a kingfisher all the way from Sibu to the northeast of Kapit to Belaga, almost in the centre of the country and the only trading post for miles and miles in all directions. Not that it was much of a market because it had but one Chinese-owned store which also did duty as coffee-shop, post-office, doss-house, airport lounge, motor-launch jetty and first-aid post. It stocked a cornucopia of the usual, much pawed, sometimes decomposing merchandise: coarse soap whose smell made one's nostrils twitch, solidifying sugar, rock salt, honeycomb, brown rice, cigarettes, loose tobacco, cheroots, tinned Irish stew, canned curried goat, sardines, bottled beer, 'Fanta' soft drinks, broad-leafed tea, 'Carnation' condensed milk, dried sausages streaked with unhealthy-looking lines of white fat, Jacob's biscuits, Ajinomoto, Hacks, corned beef, sarongs, betel and stamps. Above this display, which to an outsider may have looked primitive but which to the locals was what Harrods' windows must be to Londoners living in cardboard boxes, there hung the obligatory picture of the Malaysian king. And the king who looked down on me from the top shelf of the Belaga supermarket was none other than my old friend from early Malaya days – the cherubic, cheerful Raja of Perlis who'd been elected to be the first King of Malaysia (the crown rotated every five years among the Sultans).

That was all there was to Belaga – a silence whose depth the Western world had long forgotten and which by now may also have gone beyond the recollection even of the native folk around Belaga.

I once took a lift in a small aircraft belonging to an Australian Bible-thumping outfit based on Limbang, flying from Lawas into Ba Kelalan with an Aussie preacher-pilot and a boyish Malay police officer as my fellow passenger. At Ba Kelalan, close to the Indonesian frontier, we landed on the remotest and strangest of Sarawak's airstrips: nothing more than a windsock flew in the middle of a piece of countryside unique in Sarawak: a plateau bare of trees and scrub. It was breathtakingly beautiful. It was at Ba Kelalan I tried to comfort an Indonesian soldier who, together with a companion, had wandered across the uncharted border by error and had fallen into a trap laid by local Ibans to catch wild pigs. Besides twisting an ankle and breaking a finger he'd suffered wounds from the tips of bamboo *punjis* (spears) that pointed up from the bottom of the hole. His mate had been impaled, mortally, on the *punjis* leaving the wounded askari to lie helplessly for the night while pigs devoured his dead comrade only a metre away. It was his good fortune to be found at daybreak by hunters checking their traps. Physically he was easily retrievable but I feared that day for his mental state. All was well however; he was 'helicoptered' to Miri, where he made a rapid recovery.

I wish I'd collected some of the posters the Australian God-pushers stuck up in longhouses, on trees along jungle tracks, on long-boats and everywhere outside Muslim areas where their evangelising was against the law. For me, communist propaganda, which was banned, would have done less harm to the Iban way of life than what was, to me anyway, religious pornography. Produced down under and totally pictorial (in those days few Ibans could read) each poster's central motif was a hideous, multi-coloured serpent whose deadly poisons (illustrated by depictions of the dire fate of those who partook of the snake's toxins) were alcohol (shown by coconut shells full of *tuak*) nicotine (rolled leaves with strings of tobacco poking from each end), pagan worship (men and women prostrating themselves before animist symbols), superstition (a picture of a wooden head like those placed by Ibans to mark their dead), and nakedness.

People who indulged in any of those 'sinful' practices were shown to be hurtling straight down into a pit filled with writhing, loathsome serpents, the offspring of the central, satanic snake. What angered me was that apart from their home-grown *tuak* and tobacco, dancing to imitate the wild creatures who lived in their forests, and their uninhibited joy in nakedness and sexual congress, the Ibans had little to be cheerful about, yet wealthy folk from a foreign land were warning them that enjoyment of a few fun things would be paid for in terrible suffering later on. And how could those innocent, unworldly creatures not obey the rules imposed upon them by strangers powerful enough to fly in the sky like giant hornbills? I'm pleased to tell you that they didn't.

I took passage to Sibu aboard that romantic old tub *The Rajah Brooke* which sailed as it had done for donkeys' years always of a late afternoon from Kuching down the Sarawak River to reach the South China Sea at sunset. The ship's *nakhoda* (captain) was an ancient, corpulent Malay, a sailor who, after decades of repeating the Rejang run, knew every frond, mangrove root and monkey on the river. Unusually for a Muslim he was a renowned tippler. He'd sit on the foredeck in his weather-worn wicker chair, bald as a football, his belly hanging over his black-and-white chessboard sarong, pipe between stained, broken teeth, a glass of oily looking brown samsu in his hand, every occidental's idea of the slothful native. But once his ship began its approach towards the jetty at Sankei he'd be on his bridge, decked out in the white rig bearing the insignia of the Straits Steamship Company, every bit as smart, commanding and alert as any P&O captain. Once safely alongside, he'd perform a solemn ritual: saluting his friend and fellow toper for many a year, the official pilot for the Rejang ports (whose services weren't required for the *Rajah Brooke*) a man who lived at Sarikei and who was, incomprehensibly, an old, weather-battered, heavyweight German right out of Joseph Conrad.

One fine day I hired a bicycle in Bau bazaar and rode out of town along narrow paths that had been pounded by bare or sandal-shod feet for so long that they were as smooth as the best laid Olympic cycle tracks. They took me through padi fields, rubber and pepper smallholdings rented by Chinese peasants whose hand-to-mouth existence belied the myth that all Malaysian Chinese were well off. The fact was that eight out of ten Sarawak Chinese lived at subsistence-level. Characteristically determined not to dilute their Chinese identity (from which trait springs most of their troubles), the Chinese masses wouldn't even admit to the wisdom which had it that houses in the Bornean hinterland not built on stilts would frequently be invaded by water, snakes and a trillion creepy-crawlies. No, just as if they were in Guangdong or Amoy, they pitched their square wooden shacks on the ground and then dug drainage systems all around them. Again, more concerned to keep thieves out (even though burglars were almost as rare as snow in Sarawak) than admit cooling breezes and shafts of sunlight, the only openings through which light and air could enter were one heavily barred door and a couple of wooden, shuttered, iron-barred windows. Their outside walls were invariably plastered with strips of 'lucky-red' paper and pictures of gods pasted up at festival times: they were never taken down but regularly covered over with new ones until every Chinese peasant dwelling looked like the exterior of a Parisian pissoir.

It was dark inside these homesteads, often smoky and invariably they stank of low-quality, raw rubber sheets. Every family, be they padi, pepper or vegetable farmers, had a few rubber trees to tap. And every Chinese peasant whether male or female, young or old, smoked tobacco, a vice that was encouraged because smoke helped keep mosquitoes at bay. No portraits of either a white or brown monarch looked down ceremoniously from on high; instead there'd be a picture of that Chinese destroyer of emperors: Sun Yat Sen, a man whose countenance was hardly censorious or even mildly authoritative but whose portrait was safe because it was esteemed by the Kuomintang and communists alike. Extended over the door of almost every house was a corrugated-zinc roof supported by two poles two to three metres from the house. Thus was created a forecourt in which, whenever it wasn't raining too hard or they weren't in bed, the family would spend a good deal of its life: cooking, sewing, eating, doing school homework or just plain sitting. Life was hard and life was earnest. The houses themselves were always spotless yet you'd only to step a pace or two beyond the drainage ditches and you were up to your knees in trash. To be fair though, another few paces further on and you'd see vegetables galore, orchids, roses, fruit trees, all lovingly tended and fed every morning with the family's night soil.

I took a cup of dark green tea with a dark elderly pepper gardener. His black pepper grains, he explained in crude Malay (few Chinese peasants bothered to learn the language of their host country), fetched a lower price than white – just as un-husked rice, for all its enhanced nutritional value, fetched less than polished – so he packed his beans into gunny sacks which were then anchored with stones to the bed of a fast-running stream. The water coursing through the sack for a week or two would wash away the husks leaving the little white beans to be sold in Bau as 'white pepper' while the husks at the bottom of the sack would be fed to chickens and pigs.

The Soldier Prince

The Malaysian army chief was a prince of the Pahang royal family, General Tungku Nazaruddin. He was a flamboyant, gentle Anglophile, also known as 'Bruno'. Unlike the large, noisy, smelly helicopters used by others, Nazaruddin's 'Alluette' was a chic little French three-seater, for all the world like a flying soap-bubble in the centre of which one sat in comfort to enjoy an uninterrupted, all-round view. Bruno happened to be with me when the news came in of some particularly bestial terrorist murders in Sarikei. He at once offered to fly me to the scene in his Alluette and within minutes we were airborne, skimming across treetops, coastal swamps, the South China Sea and then up the Rejang to land in Sarikei just an hour after I'd heard the news.

On another day we flew together to Bario, one of the largest longhouses in the country, the seat of an important Iban chief and located only just inside Sarawak's 4th Division but a few miles from the Indonesian border. Using boats and Shanks' pony it would have taken us a week to reach Bario from Miri but Bruno and I were in and out in the same day, dropping in through an opening in the vast jungle canopy that stretched for as far as the eye could see from the Alluette. The chief, a tiny, wizened ancient (he was probably no older than 50) wearing nothing at all but a lap cloth, heavy ropes of coloured beads and tattoos, his ears hanging down to his shoulders, his hair basin-style fashion and carrying a blow-pipe as if it were his badge of office, ran to meet us. What on earth could he have made of Bruno dressed as he was like a royal envoy sent to pay a state visit to some 19th century European monarch?

In the spirit of Konfrontasi, Bario had cut an airstrip out of the jungle and hoped to make use of it commercially by transporting meat for sale in Miri. The weather conditions however, were always so unpredictable that it was never known from one hour to the next whether a plane could land or take off; the last thing the Barios wanted on their hands in that climate was a dead water buffalo. Hence the beast whose time had come was tethered near to the airstrip to be slaughtered only at the last minute when the plane had landed and confirmed that it could carry the carcass out of Bario within the hour. Our headman, therefore, was not overjoyed to witness, on a perfect day for flying, the arrival of an aircraft that couldn't have carried a dead chicken let alone a buffalo. He was further put off when Bruno, a strict Muslim, declined the offer of a stiff slug of *tuak*. There was nothing for it, after that, but to fly away.

Operation 'Hammer'

The Sarikei murders had been bad enough but what happened at the 17th mile bazaar, halfway between Kuching and Serian, in June 1965, was worse. Within just two hours of darkness a bridge across the road at the 18th mile was damaged by a rocket fired into one of its supports: logs with upturned nails were strewn across the road at the 16th mile; two young men mistakenly identified by the attackers as police informers were murdered, one of them most bestially in front of his family who were either injured or driven crazy by the horror of it; and, worst of all perhaps, the Constabulary station was overrun, its Sergeant shot dead, several constables wounded and all their weapons stolen. The attackers then hijacked a lorry and fled in it far out towards Pedawan, en route, presumably, to the Indonesian border.

All hell broke loose in Kuching. The military, still mostly British at the time, were most hurt by suggestions that their frontier shield had been penetrated by marauders from Indonesia. They counter-charged that the terrorists were more likely to have been local 'communists' and that therefore the Constabulary was to be held to account for it. At first sight, before we knew about the lorry hijack for instance, we were inclined to see it that way too. One man who certainly agreed with the military and whose rage against the Constabulary was unconfined was the then Chief Minister, Stephen Kalong Ningkan. Ningkan had good cause to be outraged because the Sergeant who'd been riddled with bullets was his younger brother. To add to our woes we were without the one person who might have been able to calm the waters: Roy Henry. Roy was on leave in the UK and in his place we had David Goodsir from Johore. A man with a persona everyone would have wished to see in a police chief, David, with no experience of Borneo, was no match for the likes of the colonels who came at us like a bull at a red flag.

Having weathered worse days during the Malayan emergency without being savaged in unison by the media, the public, politicians and the military, Goodsir was nonplussed by what he saw as the extreme reaction to the 17th mile atrocities and stunned by Ningkan's furious response to them. Summoned to the Chief Minister's residence he and I couldn't have turned up at a worse time; we entered the hallway not a moment after the Sergeant's corpse had been delivered, literally on ice. Ningkan, his wife, the widow and numerous relatives of all ages were prostrate round the body chanting their grief, totally uninhibited in display of mourning. Sobbing and gesticulating in chorus with his family and then later on in his private rooms upstairs, the Chief Minister let Goodsir and I have it with both barrels.

The Chief Minister, 'in the name of the people', charged David and I with the responsibility for what had happened at 17th mile. The 'communists', he said, must have been in the vicinity planning the operation for months. Scores of locals must have seen them and even fed them and yet we'd got not so much as a sniff of information about it. What had the Special Branch been up to? What did it do with all the money secretly given to it? (Ningkan wasn't the sort of person who could be let into the 'Hardy' secret.) The Constabulary, he said hysterically, had failed him. There was no comforting him and since we could offer no excuses at that time, Goodsir and I hung our heads. Eventually we tendered our condolences, David promised a fitting Constabulary funeral for his brother and, ears burning, we crept away. It wasn't long though before we were getting apologies.

Ningkan was right on one thing: KL was indeed hopping mad. Having heard only the military's side of the story it was convinced that the Constabulary was to blame and who should appear in Kuching in person, breathing fire but the Great Panjandrum himself: the Inspector-General of Police, Claude Fenner. Fortunately, he was a man with a very short fuse; by the time of his arrival we'd a different tale to tell him and things cooled down. Even Ningkan was begging our pardon. Within minutes of news of the murders coming in, I'd sent our brightest officer, Koo Chong Kong, hot foot to 17th mile. Gathering together all the unscarred constables and their families, Koo re-enacted the raid over and over again, insisting upon their repeating every word uttered by the attackers. It turned out that what few words had been spoken had been in Malay without the slightest Chinese inflection. But, since the two languages were basically identical, could it have been Indonesian? Koo latched on to one word, the Indonesian for 'time-piece', one of the words in general usage that differed totally from the Malay. The raiders had repeated it over and over again as they went round looting wristwatches from the helpless policemen. Use of that particular word (which, though etched on my brain for years, I've forgotten) as opposed to the Malay *jam tangan*, led Koo to the likelihood that the attackers had not been Sarawakian Chinese but Indonesian. For one thing the Indonesian word for watch was never heard in Sarawak; indeed Ningkan's brother may have been killed because, failing to understand the word he hadn't swiftly handed over his own wristwatch. And for another, our home-grown 'communists' wouldn't have stolen watches or anything else because they'd had it drilled into them that they must wage 'armed struggle' in the strictest accordance with Mao Tse Tung's 'three rules and eight points': 'Do not take a single needle or piece of thread'.

Confident that he was on to something, Koo ordered up a large police field unit to search the *belukar* surrounding the station inch by inch and time and time again. Sure enough they came up with things like empty cigarette packets – packets that were distributed in Indonesian army rations. Then he spoke to a terrified local Chinese teenage female, gradually drawing from her the admission that she'd helped a young Indonesian soldier who'd broken his shoulder (we learned later that he'd been the one who'd fired the rocket at the bridge support, doing more damage to his shoulder than to the bridge). Finally, by discovering the lorry in which the raiders had fled towards Indonesia, we were able to virtually prove that Ningkan's brother had been killed by Sukarno's soldiers and not by local 'communists'. We were off the hook.

Our detective work was nothing to crow about but neither had the army any reason to hang its head. The soldiers after all had sealed the border so well that in nearly three years the Indonesians, for all their ranting and raving, had broken through only once or twice. Even Ningkan came to see it that way. No, the worst and most lasting effect of the '17th mile incident' was the way in which the hawks exploited it. They cried for revenge and since they couldn't overtly march into Indonesia to get it they went instead for the Chinese living in and around the 17th mile bazaar. Innocent or not, they had to suffer, vengeance had to be exacted. A special Emergency Executive meeting was summoned; this time even Ningkan himself overlooked the customary charade that he, the Chief Minister, was in charge. He had personal scores to settle and Claude Fenner, who dominated the meeting, looked the man to help him settle them.

Fenner took the stage; Kuching hadn't seen his like before. A burly figure, a pre-war colonial police officer, in the post-17th mile atmosphere he was a dictator. Speaking for the Cabinet in KL (until the day he died he carried enormous influence and respect in KL), he demanded that the 'communists' in the 17th mile area be 'hammered' (*di longkan*); smashing his huge fist repeatedly on the table he shouted "Hammer! Hammer! Hammer!" The effect was dramatic; it was resolved there and then to mount a punitive operation code-named 'Hammer'. Recalling the Brooke tradition of traducing any place that greatly offended authority, it was even resolved that the 17th mile bazaar be renamed 'Hammer', a name it possibly bears to this day. My lone, feeble voice appealing for a short delay while we confirmed the fact that the residents of the 17th mile had not been involved in the incident might have given the committee pause but it was silenced with expressions of contempt. Fenner had wound them up, the mood was too ugly for reason to intervene; evidence was not an issue, right or wrong were no considerations; all that was needed to be done was to determine the form and degree of punishment to be meted out.

To cut a long story short (how unimportant it seems today yet when it happened, it engulfed me totally) in a throw-back to the darkest days of the Malayan emergency the 17th mile bazaar was ringed around with a high barbed-wire fence and designated as a 'new village'. Curfews, searches without warrants, harassment and even rationing of foodstuffs were the order of the day. All Chinese within a given radius were ordered to live within the perimeter fence and permitted to attend livestock and cultivation outside the wire only during specified daylight hours. It was a cruel and unnecessary chastisement of people I knew to be innocent of the crimes for which they were to be harshly punished; in retrospect it was harsher still because the punitive apparatus was still intact and functioning when I left Sarawak three years later. 'Hammer' was vindictive, unjust, small-minded, politically daft and materially wasteful but, since I was a foreigner in the service of a sovereign Asian nation whose Cabinet decided policy for me to carry out and, having failed, massively, to argue against the action, I had to keep my opinions to myself.

The End of Konfrontasi

'Hammer' left a bad taste in my mouth but 'Hardy' sweetened it somewhat, giving me plenty of full-bodied intelligence to pass on to the Emergency Executive Committee which loved being sworn to secrecy (you could see them puff out their chests and sense their increased alertness) and which was overjoyed to hear my description of 'O's sorry plight. I remember Jugah, he of the elongated ear lobes, coming up to me at the end of one meeting, bubbling over with glee at having heard me going on about the comrades' misery. To Jugah, who liked nothing more than hearing bad news about Chinese and Malays and who'd been brain-washed for years by British officials preaching to him about the evils of 'communism', word of Chinese communists suffering was bliss indeed.

The Indonesian army turned its back on Malaysia and aimed its weapons at its own people. Declaring that it was putting down an internal 'communist' insurrection, it slaughtered hundreds of thousands of Indonesians. The whole country was turned into an abattoir. In Kalimantan, for example, the Iban population was encouraged to return to its old practice of headhunting, the only condition being that the beheaded should be 'communists'. Konfrontasi was over and done with but for those who lived close by Indonesia, there wasn't much to rejoice about for the news from just across the border was horrifying. The Indonesians behaved even more appallingly than our own overcharged propaganda had alleged at the height of Konfrontasi.

All Good Things Come to an End

In December 1967 I was summoned to KL by Abdul Rahman Hashim, my boss in KL, on the face of it not an unusual summons but one which immediately felt different because I was met at the airport by the director's aide and taken to one of the capital's leading hotels to be told that 'all expenses will be met by the director'. And I was welcomed into his opulent office with excessive cordiality. There the reason for the special treatment was revealed. Abdul Rahman told me that his Minister had ruled it to be politically unacceptable for a non-Malaysian any longer to be head of the Special Branch in Sarawak. Both he and the minister hoped however that I'd stay on; I'd hold the rank of Assistant Commissioner and the title 'Adviser' to the new Head, Koo Chong Kong. I flew home feeling down in the mouth but what should be waiting for me back in 'Lada' but a telegram from London offering me the job of head Special Branch, Fiji.

An exchange of telegrams with DMF who said 'OK' and it was all over. Just like that.

I went on a round of farewells: a formal 'dining out' at the police mess at Fort Marguerite, a stuffy dinner with the Governor at the Istana, lunch at the old Aurora with Chief Minister Tawi Sli, one last great Foochow blow-out in Sibu, a *laksa* breakfast in Miri, a *kenduri* in Limbang, a sweaty lunch in the market place in Simanggang and, touchingly, a splendid set-piece dinner laid on by 'Bruno' Nazaruddin decked out in his most colourful attire and attended by all his officers in gleaming full dress uniform plus the Malaysian ambassador to Singapore who just happened to be in Kuching at the time and who, attired in his brilliant diplomatic uniform, added yet more lustre to the occasion. How drab the guest of honour must have looked in his simple black tie.

The largest gathering and the one that took the highest emotional toll, was a grand dinner attended by just about every Special Branch employee in the state. Dining elsewhere in the same restaurant was Temenggong Jugah. He popped in to see what was going on in the ballroom and, being Jugah, to get at some free booze. Wonder of wonders the Minister for Sarawak Affairs hadn't been told that I'd been replaced. Rushing across the room, over-dramatic as always, he threw his arms round me and tearfully swore that he'd get the order changed; he'd fly to KL first thing in the morning and demand that the Minister change his mind and... and... he stood in disbelief when I calmed him down, told him that I wanted to leave because it was time for a change and that anyway he'd discover that Koo was better at the job than I'd been. So, long ears flopping as he tipped his head back to down a few *yam sengs* he bade me goodbye.

Dear old Pakiong's lamentations were endless. After days of resistance to her pleading I at last gave way to her dogged insistence that she perform a ceremony over me, an act she said that she simply had to perform in order to escape punishment in her next incarnation for failing to honour her departing benefactor in traditional fashion. With her mother holding a bowl of water, she knelt to wash my feet and then to dry them with her hair.

To Pakiong's tribe I gave my Pigeon bicycle, an old refrigerator and

the Renault car from the proceeds of whose sale they were able to move
into a decent little house on Green Road.

Most fittingly I spent my last three nights in Sarawak where I'd spent
the first three – in the Kuching Rest House, mercifully though, not in
the dreaded 'Annexe'. And, equally, appositely, I left Kuching airport on
an early March morning in 1968 when it was pouring with rain from a
dark, heavy, hot sky.

There's a saying that you may leave Sarawak but Sarawak will never
leave you; there's truth in it. Nowhere else in the wide world have I felt as
much at home as I did in Kuching.

Postscript

Indonesian abandonment of Konfrontasi, followed by the bloodbath of
'communists' drove 'O' (by that time blooded enough to call itself the
North Kalimantan Communist Party) to flee Indonesia and settle into
jungle bases in Sarawak. To add to the inescapable fact that 'armed struggle'
had failed and couldn't be regenerated, it became clear that there was no
political way forward either. In short, from 1972 onwards 'O' was on its
own in opposing Malaysia, a far cry from what had been the position nine
years before and furthermore it was disowned by China, the Soviet Union
and Indonesia. Friendless, 'O' was finally reduced to a corps of 300–400
Chinese adrift in the pitiless jungle, hopeless. On 21 October 1973 nearly
500 'communists' laid down their arms. It was all over.

May 1968 – May 1971
Fiji

A Dangerous Diversion Avoided

Just before the colonial government in Fiji showed an interest in my post-Sarawak employment, in January 1968 the CIA in Washington, through its Kuala Lumpur mission, offered me a job in Saigon (now Ho Chi Minh City) as 'intelligence adviser' to the secret side of the so-called 'Republic of Vietnam's' police force, General Loan. Like everyone else in the Republic's service, from its President down, Loan was but a hireling of the Americans whose conduct of the war in Vietnam was so repugnant to me that I'd sooner have gone on the dole in Sutton than lift a finger to help them. Nevertheless, the idea was enticing; I'd always itched to see for myself the city known in the past as the Paris of Asia but which in 1968 had become the nerve-centre of what surely was the dirtiest war of all time.

Rather than refuse point blank, I therefore suggested to the CIA that to help me make up my mind I might do a seven-day, on-the-spot study. This was agreed and I was handed a Vietnam visa; a return plane ticket; a pre-paid Saigon hotel reservation; a message of welcome from the police chief; and US$500 in cash (equal in those days to my monthly salary) for 'pocket money'. Having received the nod of approval from my own masters in Kihi, I prepared to take off for Saigon.

But it wasn't to be because on the very February morning that I was about to leave 'Lada' en route for Vietnam, I heard over the radio the startling news that Vietcong irregulars were rampaging through Saigon, into the American embassy itself, and that 'communist' shells had put the city's airport out of action. Clearly, my trip was off. I unpacked and sat glued to the radio. It was the beginning of the Vietcong's 'Tet' offensive, the battle they were to lose but which, by destroying all that was left of American self-confidence, was to win them the war. The next day's papers carried the first of hundreds of horrifying pictures of the carnage in Vietnam; one of the most appalling being the one that became, perhaps, the most infamous of all: it showed General Loan – the very creature I'd been lined up to 'advise' – standing in the middle of a Saigon street, gun in outstretched hand, shooting a 'communist' through the head!

Shuddering at the thought that I might have shaken the hand that held the gun, I handed the air ticket and the US$500 back to the CIA and turned to a telegram offering me the job of head of Special Branch, Fiji, to start in May. I asked to be released from the rest of my contract with the Malaysian government, got DMF's telegraphic OK and started to read up on Fiji.

Bula (Greetings)

Arising from a fusion of Polynesians moving west and Melanesians moving east, Fijians, I read, came in all sizes and shades of brown from the large, almost black and fuzzy-haired to the small, lightly tanned and straight-backed. Against all the scientific evidence debunking it, many of them still cling to the legend of their descent from Degei (pronounced Ndengeyi), a legend that could have been ignored were it not for the fact that it still bore within it many of the features of 20th century Fijian culture: chieftainships, the communal ownership of land, the worship of *daku waqa* (sharks which piloted Degei's canoe by the phosphorescence of their wake) and of snakes (from whom Degei was said to have sprung), the cultivation of *yaqona* (kava), and the system of *keri-keri* which imposes on the host the obligation to present to his guest anything the visitor may covet – a custom which in the days of electronic entertainment systems and refrigerators, had created a social minefield.

Fiji, the books went on, was made up of hundreds of islands, some of them no more than outcrops of coral sticking up above the surface of the Pacific ocean, others covered in thick forest; many without fresh water, others running mighty rivers. Until the 1860s the Fijians had been polygamous, warlike cannibals who buried people alive. Even so, in spite of the islands' reputation for savage inhospitality to outsiders, they drew towards them a riff-raff of Westerners: liberated convicts from the penal settlements of Australia, adventurers, missionaries, beachcombers and involuntarily, shipwrecks. They made up a ragtag of remittance men, soldiers-of-fortune, shysters, thugs, cutthroats, clerics and slave-traders, the latter supplying plantation labour by 'black-birding' people from other Pacific islands. Possessing, and ready to use firearms, of which the native Fijians had none, that motley, white mob pillaged, swindled, shot and prayed its way into setting up a 'seat of government' at its settlement at Levuka on the small island of Ovalau.

There at Levuka, in 1867, they proclaimed as 'King' one Cakobau (pronounced Thakombau) the chief of the tiny island of Bau. For Cakobau, a man renowned for a gargantuan appetite for human flesh, the whites, using tin, gold-coloured paper and fake jewels, fudged together a crown. They also ran up a flag, currency notes and postage stamps. King Cakobau's capital, Levuka, was no more than a single street of pawnshops, bars and brothels running alongside a shore-line that was said to glisten with empty gin bottles. It was no place for a King and Cakobau, despairing of ever being able to make anything of his drunken, corrupt, incompetent and disputatious 'ruling council' cast around for a saviour. Eventually, after countless attempts had failed, he managed at last to persuade Queen Victoria to annex his realm. On 10 October 1874 Fiji involuntarily entered the imperial bond. British warships fired salvoes across the flotsam that lapped Levuka's harbour, Cakobau's standard was lowered (he went back to being paramount chief of Bau) and the Union Jack was hoisted above the scruffy little capital. The first thing the new colonial governor did was to erect a new capital at Suva on the main island of Viti Levu.

First Impression: What Threat?

It was to that busy little metropolis that, nearly 100 years after Cakobau's abdication, I flew for 36 hours across the Atlantic, over America and Honolulu to touch down on Saturday night in May 1968 at Nadi, a town close by the spot where, as folklore had it, Degei's sharks had guided him to land – how many centuries earlier? It was pitch dark, silent, and, it being the first of Fiji's so-called 'winter' months, quite cool. I awoke on the Sabbath to an exquisite morning. The sun was huge and had a sheen to it; the sky was enormous and all of it was blue; the rest, everywhere I looked – the grass, the palms, the sugar-cane, even the sea – was a rich, emerald green. The people I woke up to were black, brown, slow, well-fed and handsome. I was put aboard an old DC3 (thus taking me back to parachuting days), which leapt eastwards over the mountainous spine of the island of Viti Levu to deliver me a mere half-an-hour later at Nausori airport, from where I was gathered up and taken to check in at the Grand Pacific Hotel, Suva.

It not yet being the age of universal air-conditioning, the stately Grand Pacific was a sort of mini-Singapore Raffles: wide open to the elements, neck-laced outside with royal palms and gigantic cannas; within it was lofty, domed and blessed with curling, majestic stairways. True, if you wanted to view the Pacific Ocean of the postcards you had to lift your gaze beyond a half-mile or so of black mud but the ocean was there alright; you could see it, glittering turquoise, and you could think of it stretching great distances to lap the shores of places like Tonga, Pitcairn, Kitibati, Tahiti and Australia. Looking inland there lay Albert Park, a vast playing field that could stage half-a-dozen rugby games at once. Set in the hill beyond the park, beyond acres of beautiful gardens, there glowed the pure white government house in front of whose splendidly imperial colonnades, catching the sunshine and the brisk sea-breeze, flew the flag of the heirs of Victoria. It was a far cry from the tumbledown shack above which Cakobau's ensign had flown at Levuka.

The heat, together with such other familiarities as hosts of geckos swarming all over the walls of my room, made me feel at home. From my balcony I could see the surf breaking in curtains of bubbles above the coral reefs seemingly miles away. I stood there marvelling at the turn of events whereby Stanley Hardy of 32 Garden Lane was now being paid to live in a tropical paradise. The pity of it was that that good feeling, at least not in its first powerful flush, didn't last long. The clear, crisp brilliance of those first few days soon gave way to what was soon established as the norm: weeks without end of cloud and rain interspersed with fleeting glimpses of what the travel agents promised was the eternal verity of Fiji – unbroken golden sunshine.

Fiji isn't a third-world country, more like a two-and-a-half one. First sandalwood, bêche-de-mer, cotton and copra and then sugar, bananas, timber, ginger and even gold, topped up since the 1950s with tourism, put it in the same league – or so the UN said – as Franco's Spain. Naturally its distant removal from trade routes jacked up the cost of all imported items; cars, cornflakes, cognac, chisels and cricket bats cost the earth. But co-operative-marketed local produce: tea, coffee, sugar, fruit, eggs, milk, vegetables and beer were cheap while a fat, happy, Buddha-like Chinese butcher named Wah Ley delivered excellent local meat at piggy-bank prices. From my predecessor we inherited a simple little wooden house on short stilts – No.15 Richard's Road; a nice, fat housekeeper, Mary Tokelau; and a personable cat, Homer, twinned with an enchanting puppy, Keke. DMF and I settled in for what promised to be an agreeable six years (two terms of two-and-a-half year contracts with two periods of five-monthly vacations).

It all began to go wrong, as I'd suspected it would, when the man I was replacing, a graceless Englishman, Jack Dodd, introduced me to the headquarters officers I was to command and when they in turn 'briefed' me on their individual portfolios. Like Dodd, most of them had come from Africa and their outlook, like his, reflected their impressions on, if not their direct experiences during, the Mao-Mao days in Kenya. And they, like Dodd, assumed that, even in 1968, any red-blooded colonialist – meaning the new boss – me – would share their uncomplicated, black-and-white outlook on race and politics.

They spoke of the 'riots' and the 'mayhem' that had afflicted Suva nine years earlier, an 'uprising' that had brought them hurrying to Fiji at the behest of a Governor who'd been panicked into believing that he was sitting on a powder-keg. They spoke darkly of 'subversives' like the local Indian political leader, A.D. Patel, and of 'rat-bag' anti colonialists such as the 'mulatto black-power advocate', James Anthony. And they rounded off their grim presentation by urging me to back Dodd's entreaties towards government to promote the status of the Special Branch through higher ranks, more generous expense accounts, more secret funds and many, many more electronic gadgets through which they could bug the homes and offices of anybody they didn't like the look of. Not a word had been uttered about how tranquil the country was and indeed – the 'riots' of 1959 apart – had been for almost a century, nor did anyone complain about being under-employed, which was plainly the position. I'd only walked Suva's streets for a day or two and I'd spent only an hour or so in Special Branch offices but it was enough for me to conclude that many Special Branch officers were either employed according to Parkinson's Law (and after all Parkinson had been a colonial official) meaning that they were filling in time uselessly.

But I kept quiet. I'd only been in the country for a week or two but I already suspected that I'd have too little to do myself. I'd already decided that I'd stay in Fiji for no longer than my first tour of 30 months. Anyway I saw Dodd off, did the calling-card rounds from Government House down to the home of the Museum curator, and made a quick dash around as much of the colony as I could reach without embarking on time-consuming sea-voyages to remote islands. Then I sat behind my desk and devised a plan, a subversive plan. I gave myself 18 months to get to the root of every little supposed 'threat to internal security', half a year to write an analysis of what I was already convinced I'd find out about them, and the last six months to refashion the Special Branch to fit the 'threats'. Even in those early days I had the idea that I'd be proposing drastic surgery.

Tracking the 600

Dodd had listed racial conflict as the first 'threat'. Given the bare demographic facts – the indigenous Fijians were in danger of being outnumbered on their own land by Indians who'd originally been brought in as migrant labourers – I had to agree that Dodd's assessment made sense. But there was no hard evidence to support the supposition that the country was suffering serious racial tension. To get a personal feel of the thing I asked to be taken, by random choice, to isolated Indian communities, typical of those that were said to be fearful of an outbreak of racial commotion. One such community, to which I was duly delivered, was a settlement of Sikhs which, ringed by Fijian koros, was perched high on a plateau above the ocean on the west coast, which, true to the tourist brochures, was sun-drenched for nine days out of every ten. There, in dreamlike, Arcadian surroundings I found a cattle-breeding community of Sikhs, which I knew at a glance to be one of the luckiest fellowships on God's earth.

The first white *turaga* (master) to have dropped in for many years, I was saluted and garlanded before being escorted by elders to sit beneath a magnificent banyan. About a hundred of the men folk shared its shade while their women and children lay scattered about under whatever mantle they could find elsewhere. Undaunted by being confronted by the principal spook in Fiji, the Sikh gentlemen began noisily to shout the odds. "You should be ashamed of yourself," they told me. "If you were a good secret police boss you'd be protecting us from cattle rustlers". There were neither expressions of fear of their Fijian neighbours nor any mention of political, religious, social or racial issues. And then we got down to it there wasn't much to be said about cattle rustling either. What evidence there was, was of bovine behavioural irregularities: the sometime inclination of a cow to wander from its owner's land to graze on somebody else's, its mistake being compounded by the regrettable tendency on the part of some herdsmen to open their fences on purpose.

Everybody was hot under the collar, well, overheated anyway. They were all shouting at once, all blaming in unison, "Matanito, Matanito, Matanito" (Government, Government, Government). My first thoughts were that they might be pulling my leg, then on second thoughts I felt like lecturing them on the wisdom of counting one's blessing. "Half a mo," I wanted to yell back at them, "Wait a minute; I've just come from Asia, a region your ancestors came from, a region in which people murdered each other over politics, places where they beheaded, napalmed, shot and gutted one another and even set fire to themselves over religious and racial differences. Do you think I'm going to lose any sleep over a few roaming cattle and chickens? Mend your fences, keep your gates and your mouths shut." That's what I wanted to say. As I saw it, those who lived in this heaven on earth and grumbled about it needed their turbaned heads knocked together. But I kept my peace, gradually catching up with the truth which, as I discovered to be the case throughout the islands, was that the lives of these people were so peaceful and easy that they were maddened by what to less fortunate folk elsewhere would be nothing worse than fleabites. Those followers of the Guru Nanak, sitting quietly and with full bellies above the blue-green Pacific, were among the most blessed and secure people in the world. The only thing was that, having no way of comparing their lot with that of others, they simply didn't know. That was all there was to it. I'd learned a lot. The Sikhs' problems, such as they were, had nothing to do with the Special Branch.

I visited Hindu settlements, Muslims, Buddhists and Sikhs. Wherever I went I gained the same impression: there was no anxiety about physical security; the only common concern was over the low rate paid for their sugar cane.

I began my next sampling by going into the Special Branch registry at HQ, there picking out, bran-tub style, the secret personal dossier of one of over 600 citizens who'd been fingered by the Special Branch as potential insurrectionists: rabble-rousers, lefties, trouble-makers, agitators, racists, anti-colonialists, would-be-revolutionaries and so on. My choice turned out to be an Indian – let's call him Nair – who tenant farmed (no Indian could own land in Fiji) a few acres (the average holding was ten) of sugar cane near to Labasa, the largest town on Fiji's second-largest island, Vanua Levu. Nair had come to have a personal dossier only because he happened to be a minor official of the Labasa branch of the National Federation Party, the Indian-run political party which, because it stood for 'liberation from colonialism', had been well and truly smeared not only by the colonial establishment but by the council of Fijian chiefs, the English-language press and the Special Branch as 'disloyal, subversive, ungrateful, destructive, serving only Delhi's interests and Moscow/Peking directed'. On that account, Nair, along with every other Federation party official in the colony, had been marked down as a public enemy, a red-at-heart who, given half a chance and the wherewithal, would throw bombs. It was to combat the threat posed by such 'devils' as Nair that my officers wanted higher ranks, high technology toys, more 'secret' money and more manpower.

There was nothing in Nair's file about his having spoken one single subversive word: his being assistant treasurer, or whatever he was, of his party branch was enough. Now, unlike my 'advisers' I'd actually talked with people who'd thrown real bombs, people who'd have welcomed Moscow/Peking direction; and I'd read my Guevara ('Ice in the heart steel in the hand'), Mao ('Power lies in the barrel of a gun') and Fanon ('Violence cleanses'). I didn't think, somehow, that Nair would turn out to be an aspirant real revolutionary. I went to see for myself; flying low over a hyacinth-coloured sea splattered with stunning little palm-fringed islets and spits of coral (how could anyone who lived down there have known or cared about Guevara and Molotov cocktails?) to Labasa where I picked up a translator and set out, unheralded, for Nair's place.

The man who came to the door of the pretty little house to greet us was a Gandhi look-alike – a black, skinny, bag-of-bones fellow who'd have been hard pushed to lift a hand-grenade let alone throw one. Judging by the number of religious artefacts that hung all over the house in honour of the great and colourful pantheon of Hindu gods, neither was he a Marxist. Nair voiced his displeasure at our sudden appearance at his door; it wasn't that he was put out by the presence on his threshold of an agent of imperialism, rather it was because, having had no warning, he'd nothing to offer us but tea and bananas.

As if to accentuate his synonymy with Gandhi, Nair spoke in the Mahatma's reedy little voice and with the great man's passion. He took fire as he grumbled about high rents and low cane prices. "That's colonial exploitation at both ends," said Nair, "surely even you, sir, can see that we'd be better off running our own affairs – we couldn't fail to make a better job of them than you have done?" Wagging a thing, brown finger at me, he lectured me on the way his party did everything out in the open. "We've nothing to hide. It was indeed your lot – you colonialists – who made us register our party so that we could openly and lawfully call upon you to depart." And so on. But he couldn't keep it up. He was very soon chuckling away to himself and owning up to being rather less a politician and more a farmer, husband, father and provider. Political agitation, he said, came a long way down his list of life's priorities. I liked Mr. Nair. I saw no menace in him at all. I flew back to Suva and ordered that his dossier be shredded.

I repeated the Nair test over and over again and though I wasn't as captivated by other Federation Party Officials as I'd been with Mr. Nair the results were always the same: files into the shredder. A big, muscular Irishman I'd known way back in Malaya, Dickie Craig turned up one day. Dickie was a bottle-a-day man and a conditioned anti-communist whose reward for writing a dry, artless and biased official synopsis of the Malayan emergency had been recruitment into MI6. He'd been sent to Fiji disguised as a diplomat to find out when Australian and American spooks said that the reds were stirring up anti-Western feeling in Fiji and forecasting an anti-colonial explosion, why the Fiji government, presumably reflecting the views of its new head Special Branch, had changed its tune and now predicted continuing tranquillity?

After drying him out (he'd spent several hours at 30,000 ft guzzling free Air India booze) I took Dickie on one of my fact-finding, Nair-type expeditions, this time to the home of a middle-ranking Federation Party Official living near to my favourite Fiji town – Lautoka. Dickie, for all his rabid right-wingism, got on with this brown, supposedly aspirant revolutionary, like a house on fire. They drank beer together, exchanged cheroots, 'slagged' off Marxism and violence and, with due deference to Dickie's Irishness, they ridiculed 'English colonialism'. They belched, farted and laughed together over their curry. Dickie was charmed. But, being the man he was, and his bosses being who they were, I don't suppose he went home with the idea of changing their minds over Fiji. But to me privately he avowed that Canberra and Washington had got it wrong.

A.D. Patel

The personal file marked 'SECRET: A.D. PATEL' ran into multiple fat volumes. Patel, you see, was the leader of the National Federation Party; ergo, the very first name on the Arrest Lists. An ascetic Gujarati, he was a lawyer who, it was said in the file (there was no evidence to substantiate it) had been sent to Fiji by Gandhi himself. What couldn't be gainsaid was that Patel was the first politically charged public figure in Fiji's history to stand in the open air to rail against colonialism. The Indians united in their worship of him; the Fijians suspecting him of wanting only to swap the British sahib for an Indian, heartily distrusted him; and the whites, goaded by their own newspaper, loathed him.

It would have been wrong to describe the *Fiji Times* as a gutter newspaper; Suva didn't have any gutters. More relevantly it could be said to have been an 'open drain' paper. The only English-language newspaper in the country, it gunned for Patel McCarthy-style, saddling him with the charge of being 'a tool of international communism'. While it was all very well for the *Fiji Times* to rant on about Patel being 'seditious, subversive, traitorous, an illegal immigrant' and so on – that was to be expected – it was a different kettle of fish altogether for a government department with the duties of objective assessment of security intelligence to copy every snippet of his drivel and read it into the record as gospel. Yet that is what had happened with Patel's personal dossier. True, Patel admired neither colonialism nor colonialists – and he said so – and he hadn't much of a sense of humour but he sure as hell had no plans to take to the jungle and all he'd have known about Marx was that Marx was a dead Western philosopher. But, just in case my thinking might have been as biased as I thought that of others was, I held my fire on Patel's file. His death in 1970 closed it for good anyway.

James Anthony

What about James Anthony, the man my deputy (a thick in the arm, thick in the head Yorkshire man) talked of as 'Public Enemy No.1'? Anthony, a young Eurasian, had gained fleeting notoriety during the 1959 'riots' when he was said to have inflamed mobs with anti-colonialist tirades. If his personal file was to be believed, he was at the East-West Centre in Hawaii in 1968 studying 'guerrilla warfare' and plotting to come home to practise it against the whites. At the risk of being tagged a 'fellow traveller' myself, I went in pursuit of Anthony's family, friends and former fellow students – anybody who could let me into James' individuality. I then turned back to a 'secret' paper commissioned by Dodd and finalised by his (then my) staff within a month or two of my arrival in Fiji. It lay on my desk, the covering letter awaiting only my signature to send copies to the Colonial Secretary (thence Governor) London (thence Washington), Wellington and Canberra. Its subject? James Anthony. Its conclusion? That Anthony was set on becoming the Castro of the South Seas. To howls of dismay, I withheld my signature and, in the end, the wretched document was put through the shredder.

The Myth and the Legacy from 1959

The 1959 'riots' had sparked such a panic that even nine years later the recollections were still sending shudders down the spines of colonial officials in all departments. Here we were, nine years on and the military and police-brass were still citing the events of 1959 in justification for their annual demands for expansion. Dodd, for example, making his case – submitted a few weeks before I arrived in Fiji – for the elevation of the post of head Special Branch to Senior Assistant Commissioner (with its promise of another few hundred dollars a year in salary) warned darkly of the necessity to be ever vigilant against a repetition of 1959. It seemed to me that a calmer reflection was now in order. Granted that it was easy to be complacent nine tranquil years after the events, even so at the end of my study I had it figured that back in 1959 the city of Suva (the rest of the colony had dozed all the way through it) had gone through two days of what most other cities in the world would have shrugged off as no more than your average Saturday night–Sunday morning rumpus. Nothing more than that: there hadn't, for instance, been a single serious casualty, let alone a dead body.

Excusable as excessive exaggeration might have been in the immediate aftermath of what had been for Fiji a unique happening, I couldn't see why it should be kept going in 1968. I told my people that from there on 1959 was a dead issue; indeed, all ideas of the branch's expansion or elevation in status was to be driven from their minds; instead they should prepare themselves for contraction.

The Cold Room

Situated between my office and that of my dipsomaniac deputy there was a windowless little 'ultra-secure' room pompously described to me by Dodd as 'our technical aids centre'. The only room in Police HQ to be air-conditioned, it housed what few bugging and surveillance devices Dodd and his predecessors had managed to scrounge out of London. Most of the place was taken up by bulky, old-fashioned machines made for tape-recording telephone calls intercepted by the ancient method of 'jumping' wires at the telephone exchange. We were also the proud possessors of a dummy briefcase, a rather bulky, black leather bag that concealed a camera whose lens peeked out of a tiny aperture drilled through one end of the case. Photographs could be taken either by pressing a button on the handle (by which means, provided always that you pointed the end with the hole in it at your target, you'd get a picture of somebody's knees) or by squeezing the two sides together while holding the case under your armpit (which method, since briefcases were as rare as snow-shoes in Fiji and, were in any case never carried under clammy armpits, would have made you stand out like an Eskimo – the very thing you'd have been seeking to avoid). And oh yes, we had an electric kettle for steaming letters open.

The very latest toy however was an 'activated telephone', an ordinary-looking handset, which, we were told, carried embedded within it a mini-microphone powerful enough to pick up anything said within a dozen yards of it and transmit same to a receiver miles away. All you had to do was get your tame telephone engineer to exchange it for the telephone used by your target (having first put his phone deliberately on the blink) and there you'd have it – you'd hear anything said within your enemy's living room! None of our few playthings was ever used; not a single phone call was ever bugged, not one letter was ever opened and not a single person was ever tailed. And, anyway, all of it quickly went out of whack when I ordered the air-conditioning to be switched off, allowing it quietly but speedily to rust away.

The Major Who Didn't Gallop

In view of the fact that the nearest British military establishment was in Hong Kong, I was surprised to find under my command a Military Intelligence Officer, a quiet, pleasant British army major whose job was to prepare the way for British Military assistance, should it ever be called for and, in the meantime, give me a hand with anything I could find for him to do. The major was unoccupied and bored. But so was everybody else in the branch. All I could do was advise him to stay in good cheer, cherish his family and treat his posting as a long, expenses-paid, South Pacific holiday. After a titanic struggle with the disbelieving ministry in London, I managed to talk the British army into not replacing the major when, at last, he packed his bags and left us.

The Goat Bag

Government doled out generous amounts of 'secret funds' – known to the old Kenyan hands for reasons I never asked – as 'the goat bag'. The account was never audited and if I wanted more I'd only to ask. The money was supposed to provide for spies' salaries, gadgets like our briefcase, and our detective's out-of-pocket expenses as they roamed the colony. A glimpse at the books showed however that thousands of dollars went annually on officers' club subscriptions. So, from July 1968 onwards, Special Branch officers, like everybody else, either paid their own club subscriptions or they left the clubs. There followed not the slightest decline in the flow of intelligence. And at the end of the year I refunded a thousand or two to an unbelieving treasury.

On the Boards

Our monthly intelligence reports said that all that stirred in Fiji were the palm trees; nonetheless a regular stream of Generalissimos, Rear

Admirals, Air Marshals, Ambassadors, Congressmen, high-flying spooks and other big-time trimmers from the Anglo-American-Australian world rushed regularly to Suva eager to be 'briefed' on the security situation but in reality to enjoy a taste of the South Pacific at somebody else's expense. We became so used to laying on the briefing session that the three stars of the shows: the Commissioner of Police, Roy Henry; the Commander of the Fiji Military Forces, a New Zealander Frank Rennie, and myself, needed but a minute's advance notice.

We had it down to pure theatre; all that was missing was an orchestra and a safety curtain. Seating our visiting worthies high above a huge scale-relief model of the colony picked out by spotlights from the ceiling of our playhouse – the army's gymnasium – the three of us would go through a routine as well honed as any West End smash hit on its 500th performance. The first act, always hammed-up and always to our visitors an encore item, was the *Kava* – welcome ceremony performed by Fijian soldiers dressed, or rather undressed, in cannibal-warrior costume. The next item was the appearance from the wings of a handsome young Lieutenant who, brasses gleaming in the spotlights, snapped into a smart salute and then set the scene for Act II by warning our bigwig visitors that they were about to hear secrets of enormous moment, secrets that they must in all circumstances keep to themselves.

Then it was my turn. Wearing a tie and trousers, raiment rarely worn in Fiji, I'd mount the podium and with the dapper Lieutenant following my address by motioning towards the relief map with a long-handled pointer ("Cane crushing is done at the mill at B, gold is mined at Vatukuola; there's a landing strip at Taveuni"; and so on). I spoke sonorously about Fiji's political history and about its present-day security problems, which were, I concluded, remarkable by their almost total absence.

The final act starred Henry and Rennie, a double-act as slick as Abbot and Costello. Bouncing gags off one another (both were natural comedians) they nonetheless contradicted the purport of my own soliloquy, which had been that Fiji needed neither an army nor armaments. Instead, they played the gallery for all they were worth, ending, like all the best comedy acts, in bathos: a heart-rending plea for more policemen, more soldiers, more guns and more money. And, it goes without saying, their pleas fell on receptive ears. While all three of us got curtain calls, the visiting nabobs never failed to side with Henry and Rennie. Without fail also they'd praise the show, saying that it had been worth coming all the way to Fiji to hear. What soured those occasions for me (besides having to wear a tie) was the realisation that none of our illustrious visitors ever learned anything they couldn't have learned at home for nothing more than a monthly glance at our intelligence summaries.

The Last Post

Because I was forever being out-voted, I should perhaps have felt more down-in-the-dumps than I did. But I reasoned to myself that since I had no expectation of ever winning the argument over excessive expeditions on security there was no point in getting uptight about it. Henry and Rennie shared identical vested interests in uniforms and ordnance – as did our VIP visitors. No matter how tranquil the colony was they'd always be on the same hawkish wavelength and, therefore, they'd never stop asking for ever-larger police and military forces. But on one autumn morning in 1970 I approached the gym with my hopes high. It was to be the last briefing of the colonial era; our audience on that morning wasn't to be any Western militarist but Fiji's very first Prime Minister-designate together with his entire Cabinet-to-be. I told myself, surely, given their untainted minds and the sincerity of their professed aim to improve their country's living standards, surely I stood a good chance of carrying the day and of getting them to see the opportunities that reductions in 'defence' expenditure would open up?

It began well enough. There being no need for me to tell my new listeners where Fiji's nerve centres were located or how peacefully inclined their political opponents were (for they knew better than I), I was able to spend my 20 minutes congratulating them on their almost uniquely happy position of being able to get down to their portfolios without having to lose a moment's sleep over the fear that anyone of evil eye might be plotting against them in the shadows. But, in direct contradiction to my outline of the security situation, the army commander spoke up for modernising the army, urging the provision of the sort of sophisticated weaponry that, he said, was the hallmark of the modern state – and so on. Then Roy Henry also got the nod of the PM's leonine head by calling for an armed, mobile police unit that would stand ever ready to deal with (non-existent) trouble-makers. To cap it all and to seal my chagrin, we'd no sooner rung down the curtain than the PM accepted an American offer of two clapped-out gunboats with which to start, for God's sake, a navy! I'd lost in an even bigger way than usual and when I left the gymnasium for the last time I was pleased that my second acting career was over.

The Windsors

The Fijians were besotted with the idea of regnancy. They'd long ago created and still maintained, a class system that by comparison made the British order seem balanced, egalitarian. They had *Tuis* (Kings), *Ratus* (Princes) and *Turagas* (Chiefs) of their own but they'd also become bewitched by the Windsors. Colourfully and reverentially as it was performed, the bowing and scraping with which they approached, and withdrew from, 'nobility' and, indeed to and from any superior was also the least appealing side of the Fijians' nature. Nonetheless, judged by the frequency with which they returned to be given the treatment, the Windsors couldn't get enough of it. Mercifully, the old gin-guzzler, the Queen's mother, stayed clear of us, as did Margaret, whose habit of using tropical islands to shack-up with pop singers might not have gone down very well with the prudish Fijians. But all the rest of the family, from the monarch down, came more than once while I was there. Their personal safety was my affair. Why, I even had to make sure that bouquets had no pins that might prick a royal thumb, that the ceremonial *kava* was made from sterilised water, that the royal aircraft was fuelled with the purest oil and so on.

Every government department milked the royal visits for what they were worth, a Windsor had only to drop in and the treasury opened up like a petal to the sun. The Special Branch for instance had been accustomed to using its 'goat bag' shamelessly to outfit officers in stylish new clothes on the excuse that bodyguards (or as Dodd preferred 'personal escorts') ought not to look out of place alongside the royals they were escorting. I put a stop to that but admit to having authorised lashing out secret funds to kit out Aseri Tagicakeravata with a jacket and *sulu* (the skirt worn by Fijian males) made from the finest English wool and tailored, expensively, to Saville Road standards so that he, Aseri, matched the Crown Prince at Fiji's independence celebrations. Other spin-offs for our people included expense accounts for entertaining the royal retinue: spending nights aboard the royal yacht supping its cellars dry and writing letters to all and sundry on the fine vellum 'Royal Yacht Brittania' crested notepaper provided for free in the cabins; scoffing succulent leftovers and half-empty bottles of Moselle from the royal table; and in joy-riding in the royal Rolls. Ardent anti-royalist that I was and remain, I was always glad to see the Windsors because they gave us something to do.

All the same, baby-sitting them was a bore; each visit followed the same old format: a grog-ceremony in which painted Fijians grovelled before their pale imperators; silent crowds lined the streets (silence, not uproar, was the Fijian way of displaying reverence); the tinsel; the frozen smiles; the kids marshalled to wave their flags; the over-dressing (oh! those big Fijian women wearing elbow-length gloves) and the tearful farewell hymn *I Sa Lei*, this latter event invariably and genuinely magnificent because Fijians en-masse singing anything at all always made a marvellous sound.

The monotony was twice broken by divine intervention. The first time was when the heir-to-the-throne came to Fiji and the great council of chiefs determined to add a 'Fish Drive' to the programme. A fish drive was a Fijian blood sport that made English fox-hunting look like a kid's three-leg race. A dozen or so strong Fijian males, armed with razor-sharp knives, would dive from canoes into a circle of sea boiling with fish that had been corralled beforehand within an ever-closing ring of nets from which they (the fish) couldn't escape. Once among their prey the men would slash about with their knives until the ocean was blood-red all around. Like fox-hunting it was bloodletting for the sake of bloodletting, a barbaric so-called 'sport'. But the fish swimming in the sea off Levuka were in luck because on the day of their planned mass murder the seas raged so furiously that the dragnets broke and the whole thing had to be called off. Ironically, Charles would have missed it in any case because the same seas that saved the fish also made the Crown Prince heave his lunch up all over his cabin in the New Zealand warship that was carrying him; he couldn't have made it to the open deck.

Then there was the day when Edinburgh dropped in, also alone. The council of chiefs voted to send him to the Yasawas there to be fed a monumental *magiti* (feast). The Yasawas were brain-numbingly beautiful little islands removed in those days from the tourist routes and, until then, uncontaminated by physical contact with the Windsors. I had no quarrel with the chiefs' choice; the only threat to the Duke's person on the Yasawas or anywhere else in Fiji for that matter was that of over-indulgence. Even in a country renowned for gluttony (just look at the size of Fijians) the Yasawans were notorious gourmandisers. Way back in 1789, rather than taking the risk of landing on the islands and literally of being eaten, Captain Bligh, set adrift on an open boat from the Bounty and being at death's door, nonetheless sailed right past them. Notwithstanding this, I entrusted Philip to a single, unarmed, Special Branch constable, one 'Eroni 63' (about whom more later). I despatched Eroni, a native Yasawan, a day in advance with orders to make sure that neither the champagne nor the charlotte mousse were swilled down before the Prince got there. He was also to see to it that the dancers were sober enough to perform their *mekes* and, when it came to the blowout he was to shield the Duke from offerings either too exotic (like water snake) or too bountiful.

The gods decided however upon a repetition of the weather that had blighted Charles' fish drive. While the islands themselves remained becalmed, the seas pounded Viti Levu with such force that Edinburgh could progress no further than the Governors' retreat in the hills overlooking Lautoka. Be that as it was, the Yasawans were in no mood to be denied their *magiti*. The clay-ovens had been at work for hours, the champagne was chilled to perfection and the lobsters were getting restless in their buckets. The local chiefs hit on a way out. Since Eroni was the only 'visitor' that had turned up, they elected him 'Duke' for the day and then they all sat down cross-legged on their mats and got stuck in. After welcoming 'Viscount Eroni' in proper style they proceeded to devour every last drumstick, caviar ball, lobster claw and bonbon and they knocked back every last drop of Chablis and ale. Having wolfed down about ten times as much as Edinburgh would have put away, Eroni decided to phone headquarters. He was anxious to hear the latest rugby scores. Never mind, for once, praise be, every dollar of the taxpayers money spent on that day had gone on entertaining the humblest of the humble; not a cent had been wasted on the nobs.

Thumb Twiddlers

Truth was, we were idlers. Never having been a workaholic, I wasn't too concerned about my own indolence which could have been put down to my (meritorious) ability to delegate authority and which in any case spelled only good for the country at large because it meant that Fiji was safe and secure enough for its security intelligence chief to twiddle his thumbs. Moreover, since DMF and I had decided early on that, good as our life was, we wouldn't be coming back to Fiji for the second-half of our five-year stint, I'd no need to stretch myself trying to create the impression of always being on the go. But on the other hand I was uncomfortably aware of condoning the idleness of a score of juniors, officers who, having loafed about for years, looked forward only to spending many more in the same lotus-eating way. We were all of us being paid for doing next-to-nothing yet the Treasury, so keen to cut the budgets of other departments, never asked the Special Branch to account for its salaries' bill and never questioned my officers' expense claims, for instance for weekends spent at Fiji's most exclusive resorts, or lunches at fancy restaurants; the words 'on security intelligence investigations' silenced the government's accountants and auditors as swiftly and as surely as guillotines would have done.

The Treatise

I called for, and immersed myself in, all the 'secret' assessments I could lay my hands on, some of them written ages ago in beautiful hand by Governors, Colonial Secretaries and other luminaries in Suva, London, Wellington, Melbourne, Canberra, Singapore and Hong Kong (to which latter two territories Fiji had once been subordinately linked and from which it was to have been militarily reinforced in case of need, hence the reason for exchanging political and security intelligence). I poured over the 'War Book', the strategic plan drawn up in London for the defence of Fiji in case of war, a tome that in itself weighed almost as much as a large bomb. I ploughed through histories, diaries, biographies, economic digests, catalogues, journals, novels, comics and newspapers. I wasted many an hour in the Indian Trade Commissioner's Office, going through English language newspapers from India, lingering, I admit, over the cricket and matrimonial agency pages.

To cut an 18-month story short, I eventually came to conclusions based on facts as opposed to supposition. For example, I started off with the greatest bogeyman of all – 'communism' – the 'threat' that was on top of every Western and Westward-leaning government's list of both internal and external dangers. I pointed to the facts that there wasn't a single communist party member within 2,000 miles of the islands and, apart from my own voice raised during my infrequent lectures on the subject, no single public utterance had ever been recorded in favour of communism.

Then I turned to the more understandable fears of racial conflict. Nothing in the late 1960s, I said, suggested that Indo-Fijian-European-part European relations were any different than they'd been for a century: uneasy but tranquil. What lay at the heart of this reassuring finding was the fact that much as Indian and Fijian political leaders openly reviled each other, the masses rubbed along together very well indeed.

Trade Unions holding the power to cripple a country's economy?

Western and Western-influenced establishments invariably in those days associated trade unions with 'communism' and with the creation of social disorder. The union movement in Fiji was a pitiful little creation boasting but a handful of mainly non-contributing members, led, within a society in which class-status meant everything, by persons of no consequence whatsoever. Ergo, it could safely have been ignored; no need to spend a Fiji dollar on watching over it.

Then there was 'New Leftism'. Associated with 'Black Power', it was a cause much in vogue among bourgeois youth in the 1960s. But it was one that, like all the others, had failed to awaken the slightest interest among Fiji's youthful intellectuals, who were too busy working their way into establishment favour to spare time for reading Marcuse or any of the other 'New Left' prophets or to get overheated by what was happening in Vietnam, America or South Africa.

And so it went on until I concluded by saying that the only serious threat facing Fiji for as long as it was possible to foresee was that, if provoked by the formation of a government perceived by Fijians to be dominated by non-indigenes, the Fijian military might stage a *coup d'état*. Refuting opposition from my own officers – particularly from the Kenyans who'd spent years presenting contrary opinions – I decided to deliver my analysis to government in the form of a Special Branch paper, to accompany which I presented a separate paper proposing a 50% cut in Special Branch strength and the closure of no fewer than seven of eight 'field' units. The result was that while changing their own tunes by not as much as a note, Rennie, Henry and the Secretariat all gave their blessings to both papers. Out went all but one of the Kenyans, up went the shutters on all Special Branch offices except those in Suva and Lautoka and into the shredder went hundreds of files. It was an exercise that justified my three years' employment by the Fiji government.

The South Seas Bubble

There were brief moments when, as the man said, Suva was like the world as God meant it to be. But, because of its execrable weather and because it was home to a small, hide-bound, colonialised, claustrophobic community, God himself would never have chosen to live there. The city was dotted about by bewitching *koros* (villages), each quite as pretty as they appeared on the picture-postcards but each hidden behind acres of the most awful urban shanties. Its few, tiny beaches were taken over by Western tourists, its hotel bars priced the locals away to squalid alehouses, and its young Fijians either hung around jobless or drudged as ill-paid menials in the service of tourists. For much of the time therefore Suva was a dispiriting place invoking a strong inducement to flee from it at every opportunity. But while I could escape easily whenever I felt like it, and with the knowledge that Government would pay for me to travel by road, sea or air and to stay in any hotel, poor DMF was stuck in what I began to curse as the arsehole of the country. Selfishly, I made good use of the Treasury's largesse (never once did it query any of my expense claims) drawing the line only at dunning the taxpayer for trips to faraway places like Rotuna, Lau, Pitcairn and 300 other islands none of which suffered in the slightest degree from my failure to drop in on them.

No.15 Richard's Road, Suva

Not having a growth industry, Fiji's civil service wasn't much of a problem when it came to housing its officials. Not only that but, agreeably, it was done equitably. Apart from one or two more spacious dwellings allocated to the very top brass, all our homes were identical: single-storey (a precaution against hurricanes) wooden bungalows with but the plainest of aspects. Structurally alike as they were however, by being set in large, separate, well-sited plots, they managed to look different. Our own abode was No.15 Richard's Road; it was just the same as Nos. 13, 14 and 16, but, being perched upon a spur of land running spine-like above the dirt road, it had a character all of its own. We had views on the one side, distantly, of the rolling Pacific, on the other of a verdant, uncultivated valley. No.15 stood on a meter-high concrete legs (a precaution against floods) and was topped by a roof of corrugated iron – a material that was not only cheap and practical but could easily be salvaged and replaced following hurricanes.

The design itself was simple: a shoebox with sloping lid. At one end a veranda, at the other the kitchen. On either side of the passageway running right down its centre – a sitting room, a dining room, three bedrooms, a bathroom and a boiler-room-cum-airing-cupboard-cum-store room. A small extension from the kitchen was meant for a housekeeper.

A good third of the exterior walls, all the way round, was open window space, screened on the inside by anti-mosquito wire mesh and equipped on the outside with wooden shutters. There wasn't a pane of glass in the whole house. With the shutters opened the bungalow took on the air of a tent with its sides raised. While keeping out most flying insects, the anti-mosquito netting also blocked off the clear passage of desperately needed breezes. And, since inevitably a few mosquitoes gained admission whenever a door was opened, it seemed doubtful if the netting was all that much of an improvement on the old practices after sundown of wearing trousers and long-sleeved shirts or floor-length dresses together with knee-length 'mosquito boots' and long-sleeved blouses and sleeping under nets.

Given that driving rain howled across Suva for most of the time – or at least that's what it seemed like our window shutters were closed more than they were open. For long, long hours and sometimes for days on end, No.15 Richard's Road was a steamship afloat on a dark sea, incendiary as heat arising from its boiler room. Even though we slept with not so much as a sheet to cover us, we'd still suffocate. A good, reliable, 24-hour electricity supply gave us light, hot water, refrigeration, a cooker and in the sitting room a ceiling fan that was our only mechanical means of stirring up the hot, muggy air. Air-conditioning was by no means unknown in those days but it was beyond the reach of a civil servant's pocket (not even Government House boasted of it) we simply had to sweat it out.

Just as each official house was externally the same as the next one, so internally did each have the very same prison-made furniture issued on a strictly utilitarian basis: eight straight-back chairs; a coir-padded sofa and two similarly upholstered armchairs: a plain, not to say rough-hewn, dining table; severe, unornamental sideboards; metal beds with sorbo-rubber mattresses; and the ubiquitous, colonial, wire-meshed 'meat safe'

I've already introduced you to. You'd have thought therefore that every house would have looked the very same inside as well as outside but it wasn't so, not by many a mile it wasn't. A glance round a colonial official's sitting room could show you where he'd been before coming to Fiji: there'd be Afghan rugs, camphor-wood chests, Selangor pewter ware, New Guinea masks, Ghanaian royal stools, Kenyan fly-whisks, bronze figures of Hindu deities and Zanzibar lockers.

DMF and Fiji

While I was lazing around reading all about Fiji, DMF, as always kept herself as busy as the proverbial long-tailed cat in a room full of rocking chairs. She ran No.15 Richard's Road where she bestowed love and lashings of food upon Mary Tokalao and where she wrote long letters to Jane, Christopher and a host of others half way across the world. Then for many a sweltering hour several times a week she sweated in hole-in-corner 'clinics' where she tried to teach disbelieving black women how to use contraceptives. From other equally clammy closets she helped dish out alms to the urban poor. She argued theology at Anglican church-gatherings and once expounded her non-conformist doctrine from the pulpit of the cathedral. In sum, just as she'd always done, she contributed to the common good more than I did and by many times over at that. It was that feature of our colonial life – DMF's unsentimental yet fervent and sincere service to the indigenous poor – that salved my conscience when I banked my salary at the end of each month. Just as sure as I hadn't earned it, DMF had.

Barney's Boat

I'd read in the books I'd studied before setting out for Fiji that because of complex conditions from its location, Suva suffered the worst possible weather. But I'd preferred instead to believe the Fiji Tourist Bureau's picture of a capital that reposed in almost endless sunshine. Hence my dismay at discovering the academics, not the salesmen, had told the truth. For an example, under the heading 'What to Do on a Rainy Day in Suva', one of the bureau's many glossy brochures glorified such adventures as taking in the public library (which would have occupied the visitor no more than half an hour at the outside) and the museum (ditto), shopping for Scotch grouse soup (a delicacy sold in only one store in town and presumably picked on by the bureau because it reasoned that visiting Yanks and Aussies would think a can of soup from Scotland would make an exotic present for the folks back home) and going to the cinema (only one movie house in town showed English-language films, the rest stuck to Bollywood). Had it been honest the bureau would have warned visitors to be prepared for not just one but for as many as 20 or even 30 days of rain at a time. There was one good thing to be said about Suva's weather: just as rare sunny days in an English summer are to be treasured, so Suva's occasional sunshine came as an almighty blessing.

The great coral reef lay a couple of miles off Suva's black beaches, beckoning yet out of easy reach. That is until we got use of Barney's boat. Barney was a fat, cheerful Fijian, the police armourer, a position that, given that the whole force owned less than a few dozen old Lee-Enfield's, wasn't too demanding. I came across Barney one brilliant morning (once outside the Suva basin and Fiji's weather was everything the tourist bureau claimed for it) on a beach at Natewa on the east coast of the island of Vanua Levu. Natewa was little more than a Catholic church that with its attached school gave the impression of arising, miraculously, straight out of an otherwise empty mile of perfect, palm-fringed beach. Barney was at Natewa because he was taking a rifle – just one and shorn of ammunition at that – to the police post on the island of Taveuni. Meeting him on the beach by accident I cadged a lift from him.

We zipped across the Somosomo Straits as if we'd been on a life-saving mission (every motor-boat in Fiji waters was seemingly driven by a suicide). Poor Barney, he heaved his mother's good food over the side, losing all his interest in his precious cargo. Green in the gills as I was myself, I took the rifle from him and clung on to it until we moored, at last, in Taveuni. Thus did Barney and I become comrades-in-arms, and so it was that Barney offered me the use of his dugout fishing boat whenever I wanted it back in Suva.

By that time, coincidentally, we'd become the proud, but nonplussed, owners of a second-hand 'lightweight' outboard motor that just happened to fit very snugly on the stern of the Barney boat, a crude but dependable craft that lay on the black mud flats near the armourer's Suva house. Thus equipped we were ready to explore the reef that lay tantalisingly on the horizon. All we needed was a low tide, day light and one of Barney's many sons to guide us to the landward edge of the reef and then for him to stand guard over the boat while Jane and I (Jane came out, courtesy of the Foreign and Commonwealth office, twice a year) wandered over the shoals. I judged the boy's guard to be a matter of life and death because had we been stranded or lost on the reef before an oncoming tide we'd either have been drowned or slashed to ribbons by razor-sharp coral, probably both. It was vital therefore that the sentinel made himself highly visible by tying a piece of white-cloth to his pole (no oars were used) and holding it aloft.

Walking the uneven surface of the reef was exhausting and tiresome; each stumble meant cuts that could turn (but, luckily for us, never did) into ulcers. But the rewards were worth a thousand ulcers. You walked across a seemingly never-ending, multi-patterned, polychromatic carpet into which had been woven bright festoons of yellow, heliotrope, pink and blue coral into which again holes had been irregularly created, holes filled with bright, clear, sparkling water: swimming pools for myriads of fish, some with streaming ribbon like tail fins, some streaked and coloured like butterflies, others flying what looked like Durham miners' banners or wearing football jerseys; minnows so small that in order to be seen at all they grouped in millions to resemble pale blue clouds in the water; clams with scarlet and cerulean lips; *bêche-de-mer*; puff-balls that emitted ink when touched; starfish as big as dinner-plates and far more colourful than any you'd ever eat off; and stone-fish (creatures disguised, thankfully imperfectly, as stones) if trodden on bare-footed they'd inject enough venom into you to cripple you for weeks. And then there was lichen and grasses both whisper soft and granite hard, pliant and silvery, brittle and menacing. We'd seen many a wonder in Asia and Africa but we'd seen nothing to touch that of the reef off Suva.

One day, determined at doing it, Jane and I left Barney's dugout and made off as fast as we could go across the reef, aiming for the outer ocean shelf upon which we eventually stood, congratulating ourselves as if we'd crossed to the South Pole or climbed Everest. Frightened out of our skins we looked over the verge just below and into the ocean, black and fathomless. The sea lapped clear, cold and unthreatening around our ankles yet that same sea plunged dark and dangerous a foot or so away from our toes. And there came up to us then, as if on cue, to swim before our very eyes, as if on display only for Jane and I in that whole wide world, there swam by a shoal of glorious parrot fish, big and incandescent in their rainbow glory, moving beautifully, peacefully and safely within an environment that would have finished off Jane and I within half-an-hour.

The Indian Lodge

Back in No.15 Richard's Road, much as we tossed and turned in the combustive Suva nights and while marvelling that we were not sprouting fungi from our perpetually damp skins, we nonetheless kept remarkably healthy. The local food was wholesome, good and cheap. We ate the country's rice, fruit, meat (coming from cattle whose hides glistened from a diet of sugar-cane residue) milk and tea. You could drink the water straight from the tap, 'Fiji Bitter' came in litre-size bottles, tasted good and gave you a kick, and a lone Chinese way up on Nadrivatu baked really great bread.

Eating out however, wasn't so easy, mainly because restaurants catered for tourists and were, consequently pricey. But we discovered the 'Indian Lodges'. No 'Lodge' was ever listed in the tourist bureau's handouts; they were meant to serve only hungry Indian manual labourers: dustmen, road-sweepers, sanitation wallahs and ditch diggers.

Entering a 'Lodge' before it opened for business (they only did tiffins) was like going into the mess hall of one of Stalin's gulags. They were plain wooden sheds with floors made up of dirt mixed with millions of cigarette buts and the powdered bones of dead goats. They were furnished with two or three long, metal-topped tables each with plank benches to either side. A metalled serving counter that ran at a right angle to the tables carried piles of large tin plates, scores of big tin mugs, two whopping great metal bowls full of curry – one of tiny slivers of goat meat and lots of little bones, the other of brinjal (aubergine), together with a mountain of chapatti (baked unleavened bread pancake). Positioned behind the counter was a mammoth vat of white rice cooked to perfection. They didn't go in for knives, forks, spoons or like refinements; no tissues, no condiments, no menus (the fare never, ever varied) no wine lists (the tin beakers were strictly for water which came free of charge) no background music, no waiters and no toilets (or if there was one just around the corner you'd rather not have known about it). There was a washbasin and there was soap – every 'coolie', knowing he'd eat with his fingers, used both punctiliously. Hanging above the hand basin there'd be a small smelly towel you'd touch only at your peril. In short, every 'Lodge' threatened you with the flux; one mouthful of the food however and you'd have given any one of them top Egon Ronay billing.

Victoria School, Pride and Joy

It was easy to escape Suva's wetness; you'd only to drive 30 miles north. There, at Tailevu, the sun shone almost daily. Under it browsed an academy set up long years ago for the education, along English boarding-school lines, of the sons of Fijian chiefs and, latterly of any Fijian male whose parents could afford the fees. Victoria School (it couldn't have had any other name) had a reputation as a good seat of learning but what made it stand above any other school I'd ever clapped eyes on was the sheer grandeur of its setting. The headmaster's house (coincidentally occupied at that time by a man I'd know as head of the Sao Hill private school near Mbeya in Tanganyika) stood at the top of a hill overlooking the school, a hill from whose summit flowed a square half mile of flawless, deep-green playing fields running into copses of casuarinas and palms and thence into an impeccable, white beach and, lastly, into the emerald ocean from which, a couple of miles distant to the south there arose the needle sharp point of Tailevu Point.

Small wonder the place graduated rugby players who dazzled the world – Victoria was a rugby college whose grounds could stage half-a-dozen games at any one time. But I loved it best during the cricket season. Pretty postcards may tell of havens of cricketing bliss in the English countryside but to see white-clothed black boys at gracious play on Victoria's green from which a six might sail into the Pacific Ocean was to view, surely, Nirvana.

Cricket Overture

Talking of cricket, I was inveigled into playing for the police eleven. Eleven? More often than not – amazing for a supposedly disciplined force – only seven or eight turned up – and they the less talented – leaving us to rope-in passers-by. Cricket was played Saturday afternoons between October and April, meaning that we almost always played in rain and with mud up to our ankles. Because of that we played on matting but the carpet was so badly worn that it'd have been less dangerous to have played on the uncovered, damp turf. Playing the army one day, for instance, our fastest bowler (Fijians were all fast, spin bowling was regarding as prissy) broke the Colonel's nose with a ball that reared up straight from a hole in the mat; 20 years later the Colonel's face stared at me out of the world's newspaper – he was by then a Brigadier but he'd been ousted in a coup staged by his fellow officers. His nose, I could see, was still crooked. He, Epeli Hailakitau, later became Fiji's ambassador to London.

Our cricket team was blighted by the curse of alcohol, the agent (outside of the *koros*) of much undoing of the Fijian way of life. It was a sad tradition – one copied from their white rulers – that Saturday noontimes were celebrated with booze-ups. Which was bad for Saturday afternoon sports. The best of our cricketers were 'Fiji Bitter' addicts, who turned to the *yangona* (grog bowl) when the money ran out. We had a left-handed Sergeant Major, for example, who, even though he was past his best years was, on his day, a black David Gower. But our Sergeant Major would play only on our home ground at the police depot because, since his house was just beyond the boundary rope, he could drink and play cricket at the same time. This meant a ritual whereby we'd drag him to his feet, bleary-eyed and foul-breathed and propel him to the crease when, half-stoned as he was, he'd still strike the ball with a certainty and a sweetness that was beyond the fittest and most sober among us.

Then there was Malele, a shambling fellow who seemed to bowl better the more sizzled he was. Our captain was Aseri Tagicakaverata, a handsome fellow who flashed his bat as if it'd been one of his tribe's ancient war clubs; every ball bowled at him he'd try to smash out of the ground. He adopted a most interesting mode of captaincy: simply, he never fielded; when he wasn't trying to hit sixes he'd sit beneath the shade of a tree outside the boundary rope guzzling grog and shouting instructions on bowling and fielding changes.

Our star performer though was a young giant from the faraway Lau group of islands, one Jonni, as slow of wit as he was fleet of foot. It was Jonni, sporting the frizzy mop of hair beloved of Fijians of yore, who'd laid the Colonel low and it was Jonni who nearly won us a famous victory. We'd drawn in a cup game against the most formidable side in Suva – the all-conquering gentlemen of the New Zealand Bank, a team that took itself very seriously indeed. White Kiwis to the last man, they turned out in pukka, spotless gear with blancoed pads, studded white boots over snow-white socks, mauve caps, batting and wicket-keeping gloves, shiny new balls, properly oiled bats, stumps and bails.

Our side on that day mustered only seven – six Fijians and an ageing white (me) wearing a variety of costume: sulus, shorts, vests and either sandals or plimsolls. We carried a battered old cricket bag containing a couple of bats made serviceable only with the aid of lashings of adhesive tape; three brownish leg-pads broken at the knees; a stump or two, a bail or two; a pair of wicket-keeping gloves as thin as washing-up mittens; a variety of batting gloves all so rotten that they were never worn; and four or five badly scuffed balls we'd bought second-hand from wealthier sides like the New Zealand Bank team which, for obvious reasons, had no money troubles. Anyway, we won the toss and perforce (because we hoped that by the time we came to bat, we'd have recruited one or two reinforcements) we chose to bat first. Leaving the other six to get on with it, I took off on my familiar Saturday afternoon trawl of Suva's speak-easies, roping in Captain Aseri, Malele, a shoe-shine boy who turned out to be a wicket-keeper a la Jeffrey Dujon and, finally, a passer-by.

By the time I got back to the ground with my haul, our score stood at 15 for 5. Aseri, high as a kite, decided that it was time for a captain's knock and in he went. To add to our woes, the Commissioner, Roy Henry, had chosen this day of all others to give up his post-Saturday lunch brandies, cigars and snoozes to cheer his cricket team on at Albert Park. Predictably, by the time I got back, Roy, who understood little about cricket but who could nevertheless see that things were near disastrous, was looking decidedly pilli-walli. The New Zealanders on the other hand looked as if they'd been given the freedom of their own bank vaults. Aseri, wearing only one grubby pad and that one flopping at the knee like a post-coital penis, was not a reassuring sight. He opened up, as he always did, but trying to hit his very first ball as far as the outlying coral reef. He missed and over went his middle stump. Luckily, the umpire happened to be one of Aseri's drinking chums; to the New Zealanders' chagrin he yelled, belatedly, "No ball!" thereby giving our hero the chance to flag a swift 20 or 30 runs before we were all out for a score of 60 or thereabouts. Aseri settled down with a bowl of grog and directed further proceedings from the boundary.

Because we always took longer over an innings than we should have done (being short of pads our incoming batsmen had to wait for the outgoing players' gear) by the time the New Zealanders went in to bat the light was poor and it was drizzling. But, of course, in Suva there was no such rule as stopping play for bad light or rain; to have done so would have killed almost every cricket game stone dead. In the murky conditions of that memorable evening our young colossus from the Lau, Jonni, must have presented a most fearsome sight to our opponents. All that their batsmen could have seen coming at them through the gloom was a huge, ebony black figure made all the taller by a crop of hair about a foot high, a physique around whose massive thighs flew, like the skirt of a speeding hovercraft, a white sulu. That apparition hurtled towards them to throw steel-hard projectiles straight at them. The bankers were unmanned and we damn nearly won; their umpires called close of play when they were 50 for 9. And whom did the *Fiji Times* hail as the hero of the hour? None other than Aseri for his 'cool yet spirited leadership'.

Tennis Wizard

Tennis was played all the year round and I looked for a place to use my new racquet bought at Honolulu on my way out to Fiji. I joined the 'Indian Reform League', an organisation which, despite its name, at least as far as I could see, never set out to reform Indians or anybody else. The League leased a piece of land just big enough for two tennis courts and a Club House large enough only for storing a couple of nets and a drum of whitewash but declined to finance their upkeep, leaving the rolling and marking to those who played the game. Half an hour of dragging a heavy roller in 29.5°C with 90% humidity took more out of us than the tennis did, but afterwards we got a couple of hours of uninterrupted tennis and we could then go straight home without having to 'mix' at a bar. It suited me fine.

The doyen of my fellow 'reformers', all lower-middle-class Indians born in Fiji, was George Subramaniam, a well-to-do builder who wasn't too bright, who didn't play to the standard of the rest of us (thereby upsetting the balance) and who had a few un-Indian habits the others didn't care for (like drinking beer, the addiction to which had given him the tell-tale belly). But George was a generous, even-tempered fellow, always ready to pay for the samosas and lemonade whenever we staged a tournament. For sure he was a nicer chap than Karunananda.

Karunananda ('Call me 'K'), a Singhalese gnome, was all that George wasn't: vegetarian, teetotaller, non-smoker and know-all. A professor at the South Pacific Polytechnic, he was a walking Encyclopaedia Britannica. In a flash he'd give you the name of the Lord Buddha's 13th cousin, the precise weight of the handful of salt picked up by Gandhi at Dandi beach in 1930, an analysis of Marx's theory of value, the titles of all Verdi's operas, and the birth date of every single British royal. He'd perform like a master on piano, tabla, lute, sitar, mouth organ, trombone or Jew's harp; he was an algebraist in the Einstein class; and he cooked like the master chef at the Paris Ritz. But nobody ever looked less athletic than he did on the day he first showed up at our tennis courts. He looked just like one of those deliberately starved, skeletal waifs you see begging in Bombay, hardly able, it seemed, to bear the weight of his racquet let alone use it.

George Subramaniam disliked 'K' on sight (it took the rest of us a wee bit longer). He drooled as he anticipated taking the professor, down a peg or two. He admitted that he'd smaller brain cells (well, we all owned up to that) but given their respective physiques he was sure he could give him a right shellacking on the tennis court. We all shared his self-confidence on that score. Hence his Cheshire-cat grin when he informed Karunananda of the League's rule (it was the first any of the rest of us had ever heard about rules) that new player-members had to be graded, like golfers, according to their prowess on the court. Predictably 'K' piped up that it wasn't necessary in his case because he was famed throughout Sri Lanka as a tennis wizard. But he didn't make a lot of fuss and showed no alarm when, lots having been drawn, it fell to me to put the professor to the test.

"Run him into the ground," said George, "don't let him have a single point." And with 'K' tottering on to the court like a ruptured duckling I figured on doing exactly that – six-love, six-love. We all thought the professor was about to be humbled and it wasn't before time either. We should have known better. No sooner did 'K's toes touch the chalk-mark than he was transformed into a shortened, sun-tanned Bjorn Borg. It went six-love, six-love alright but with me, not 'K' on the love end of it. He went on to skin the rest of the reformers just as comprehensively. The Indian Reform League having failed to reform him, it was left to the Polytechnic to give him the sack for, incredibly, incompetence. When I last saw Karunananda, he was full of his old cocksureness planning to take the world's emporiums by storm through marketing cutout cardboard models of its greatest monuments.

Nananu i Ra

Just off the northwest tip of Viti Levu, close by a large Fijian koro, Raki-Raki, there lay Nananu i Ra – one of Fiji's hundreds of miniscule islands. No more than a small, dazzling sliver of land, it was the personal property of a Suva hotelier, a part-European (a horrid appellation for a small but influential clan in Fiji, the issue, initially, of Melanesian/Polynesian mothers and Caucasian fathers but by the 1960s inter-bred). The island had come down to the hotelier from his great-grandfather who a hundred years or so ago had purchased it from an easily deluded local chieftain in return for a broken watch and a shotgun.

Seen from the mainland Nananu i Ra shimmered in the sun but promised cool winds off the sea and deep shade beneath its palms. Yet because of its almost total lack of fresh water (the shortcoming of hundreds of other Fiji islands) only two human beings lived there: the owner's elderly brother and his comely young Fijian *marama*. An incongruous but seemingly devoted couple, they lived a Robinson Crusoe sort of existence in a crude but spacious and comfortable palm-roofed hut on a beach at the island's western tip. Two much more stylish, modern cabins, built for the landlord and his family to holiday in, lay to the east. They were empty for most of the time, the hotelier's ancient brother being responsible for seeing that people were kept away. The owner was nevertheless always on the look-out for a few trusted folk who, in return for free holiday accommodation, would give the cabin an occasional airing and cleaning and in this way we were twice invited to holiday on Nananu i Ra.

It was a tropical paradise. There wasn't a wheel on the island. There wasn't a metre of road, not even an inch of paved footpath; if you wanted to walk round the island you had to wait for a low tide. No crop had ever been grown on its earth. Water, collected from roofs and stored in steel drums, was used only for drinking and cooking. There were no pull-chain lavatories, only holes in the ground. For bathing there lay but a couple of steps away a trillion gallons of crystal-clear water. But, like all tropical islands, at dusk each day the Gods of Nananu i Ra set off signals pitched beyond the range of the human ear – tocsins signalling into action great multitudes of winged creatures each single one equipped with razor-sharp teeth or needle-sharp bayonet and each single one bent on maiming other, particularly human, creatures. Thus Nananu i Ra spelled early dinners and early dives beneath mosquito netting.

You'd only to walk out of the cabin, cross a few metres of fine, white sand and you could plunge headfirst into a deep, deep basin formed by a ring of coral. The basin was always filled to the brim with clean salt-water always kept by nature at a perfect temperature for bathing. It was an outsized bathtub-cum-swimming pool-cum-aquarium. It was so paradisiacal that it might have been fashioned by some mighty Melanesian deity commissioned by even mightier gods to design a lagoon within which privileged humans could float around goggling at myriads of phenomenally colourful fish without their having to risk diving into the depths of the open sea. And what's more that thoughtful, divine architect had stocked every cubic inch of the water in his pool with creatures that he'd had painted, varnished, lacquered, shellacked, gilded and silvered to a hundred thousand different designs.

Meanwhile the elderly watchman in his hut half a mile away was host or guardian or, better still maybe, doyen to a great shoal of large garoupa that lived in an ocean pool which dropped many, many feet straight from the edge of the old man's beach. So clear was the water that viewed from the shore the garoupa appeared to be captive, on display in an enormous, glass aquarium.

They were tame fish which'd become domesticated years ago when the old man had learned so much about fish, while angling always above the same spot on the reef that he'd befriended a female garoupa which, having mated on the reef, had chosen to follow him home there to gestate, rear her family and then to raise it in the ancient's front-door lagoon. Ever since then, her progeny had multiplied right there beneath her old friend's protective gaze. It was a beautiful thing to behold, unbelievable but there it was. The snag was that the garoupas, outside their habitat on the reef, had become dependent upon their guardian for food and the old man found himself fishing more for his marine school than for himself and his *marama*. The fish were totally without fear of human beings. You could swim among them as I did myself and stroke their silky sides while feeding them live sprats they'd take from your fingers.

The world, doubtless by this time including Nananu i Ra, has changed so greatly in the past 20 years that I can't see how youngsters who read this can ever visualise a true picture. How can you conjure up an ocean into which neither nitrates nor detergents had ever been littered (decorated would be more appropriate) with weirdly, beautifully coloured, sensuously shaped seeds washed down hillsides by acid-free rain – seeds that Jane and I collected by the hundreds as though they were jewels? How can you picture earth that had never been disturbed by the turn of a wheel?

Here We Go Again!

Most of the Empire had been dismantled long before the year 1968 yet in Fiji the imperial idea was still going strong. Believe it or not, it was claimed with every justification that the majority of native Fijians actually rejoiced in their colonial status. The blame, or according to how you looked at it, the credit, for their political indolence could be attributed to a sustained campaign waged by a powerful coalition of purblind colonial officials together with Fiji-domiciled Europeans and part-Europeans; foreign merchants (bankers, hoteliers, tradesmen, sugar-barons etc) and, most tellingly, by paramount Fijian chiefs who'd been made 'Sirs', CBEs, OBEs and so on by 'their Queen' for 'services to the crown'.

That blimpish junta continually warned Fiji's Great Council of Chiefs that without the crown's protection the weak, 'backward' Fijians would fall under the domination of Indian 'immigrants', resulting in the liquidation of the system of chieftainships and the end of Fijian culture. By nature conservative in the first place, the chiefs weren't hard to convince. Indeed, the blimps' propaganda scared them witless. Moreover, they were discomfited by young Fijians going about whispering that a hundred years ago the chiefs' ancestors had humiliated their race by ceding their country to the 'Great Queen across the water... to be a possession and dependency of the British crown'. Small wonder then that the Great Council favoured the status quo.

But in the end neither the chiefs nor the imperialists could stand against the winds of change that had already felled colonialists almost everywhere else. Come the late 1960s and those same breezes could be heard rustling through the palms on Viti Levu. Slowly for a time then with the force of a typhoon the chiefs were won over by the case put forward by a group of their own offspring, a gathering of Fijian intellectuals known as the 'Young Turks' and who cried shame on the status quo. According to the 'Young Turks', by tolerating, let alone wallowing in, their state of subservience, their Fijian brethren were debasing their own race; to rely on outsiders for 'protection' within their very own islands and to plead that Fijians lacked the skills necessary to take care of their own society was humiliating. And lo! Before you could say 'Independence' in Fijian and before the colonial troglodytes could fix the blame on 'communists', the Fijians, who only yesterday had been docile and obedient to the crown, were today shouting louder than the Indians for 'Freedom'.

The (Labour) Cabinet in London, eager as the 'Young Turks', though for different reasons (they wanted to be shot of the burden) to see Fiji independent, despatched post-haste to Suva its colonial trouble-shooter, the amiable Lord Shepherd. The good Shepherd, a bright, approachable, down-to-earth chap, went all over the colony asking everybody he met – with particular attention to Fijians – the same question: "No kidding now, do you really want independence?" Then, sitting at his final tête-à-tête with the Governor, he summoned me to his presence in Government House.

There, in a splendid room-cum-office high up in the house, yet still with the feel of a Turkish bath about it, we sat, three of us: Minister of State, Governor, and lowly fake police officer. Our view through enormous open windows (no need for anti-bomb netting in those days and no money for central-heating either) was of the lovely sweep of the fabulous gardens. Beyond them we could see the sparkling ocean and, in the far distance, the froth made by the sea breaking upon the reef and the gap in the reef, that very same opening through which adventurers had first sailed into Suva harbour. The Minister opened by saying that from all he'd heard from chiefs and commoners alike, from Indian Brahmins and *khidmatgars*, and from the Governor and the Governor's gardeners, we could start hauling the flag down right away. "All right then," said Shepherd, "forget the Indians – we know they're all for it – just answer this question yes or no: Do most of the Fijians want to run their own show – really want to?" And I answered "Yes my lord, they do."

And so it was done. Shepherd flew home and within a matter of weeks I found myself engaged in an exercise I'd become familiar with: sub-committees dealing with diverse matters such as designing a national flag; composing a national anthem, ordering the bunting for Independence Day celebrations; making arrangements to house, entertain and transport scores of visiting dignitaries; planning the ceremonies (including the state banquet) creating and naming new government departments, localising the civil service; and, this being a place where such things were taken very seriously indeed, designing coats of arms, medallions, ribbons and sashes.

Then there was my own sub-committee: security. The Windsors, who always had a crush on Fiji, bestowed pre-independence knighthoods and CBEs, etc right and left, signed up their No.2 mega-star, Charles, for the job of lowering the imperial flag. The security business was ratcheted up a notch or two and it went up one or two more when lists were compiled showing that 50 or more Ambassadors Extraordinary, Ministers Plenipotentiary, Emissaries, Imams and Nuncios had declared their intention of travelling from far afield to get the freebies that went with independence celebrations and to see that Charles did the job properly.

But in those days their security wasn't all that much of a headache. If you think of what such a gathering of notables would mean today you'd be into armour-plating, steel-vests, mace, screening, vetting, machine-guns, plastic bullets, bodyguards, ambulances, quadrupling your manpower, computing the costs of overtime pay and God knows what else. But this being Fiji in 1970, all I needed in extras was a few hundred dollars to provide my people with clothing to give them a twice-a-day change. I called neither for a single reinforcement nor for a single firearm of any sort. My fears weren't of assassins but of the mayhem that might be sparked by events of pure chance. Hence I thought about what might happen if a 'Gujerati fellow' (to the 'Fijians, all Indians were 'Gujerati fellows') turned his back to say something to his auntie behind him just as Charles passed by in the procession and the Fijians nearby got the idea that he was turning his back on a Windsor. Or if a 'Gujerati fellow' half asleep among a mass of Fijians, was slow to rise to his feet to the national anthem. But such things couldn't be prepared for and, in the end, didn't happen.

Independence Day – 10 October 1970 – 96 years to the day since Cakobau ceded his kingdom to Victoria, was, unbelievably for Suva, fine and dry. And even though right up until the last minute diehard whites predicted mayhem, the city was as tranquil as a city in festive mood could ever be. Thronging Albert Park hours before the carnival was due to begin, huge crowds of Fijian Protestants and Catholics mixed in good humour with Hindus and Muslims. To perform the religious rites at the centre of the ceremony there gathered on the dais magnificently costumed Hindu *pujaris, mullahs,* Roman and Anglican bishops, Methodist ministers, Mormon deacons, rabbis, bonzes and Mother Superiors. The clerics were however outshone by the corps diplomatique, which, topped off by the megastar, Charles Windsor who was made up as an Admiral in dazzling white with a chest full of stars and crosses and a flashy sword, was robed in all its stagy splendour. Masses and masters alike, the great multitude was entertained by a fine musical extravaganza (musical because wherever two or more Fijians are gathered together you've got a high-class chorus). I may have missed the pomp and pageantry on stage but I had a great view of the auditorium filled to the brim with 30,000 exuberant browns and blacks. All of them, dressed to the nines, made whoopee while the new pale-blue flag with a small Union Jack in the left-hand corner and a shield in the fly, flew with a cheerful, youthful heart above them.

Homeward Bound

Independence gave us a way out of our five-year contract with the Fiji government. For all its bewitchery, Fiji for us was just too far removed from mainstream human vitality; even for philistines like myself Fiji was a cultural desert, or it felt like one. And, of course, we were far too far away from the children. The most decisive factor in our leaving though was my inability to justify to myself the taking of a salary – no matter how modest it was – from a 'poorish' treasury, for doing next to nothing. Hence, we leapt at the chance of cutting short our time in Fiji without having to suffer financial penalty.

We were due for mid-contract home leave in November 1970, only a few days after the declaration of independence and of course the worst time of the year to go on holiday to the UK. It wasn't difficult for me to argue that the timing was bad; it would be more sensible for me to stay on post for the first six months of the new regime's life and then retire.

And so it came to pass that three years to the day after we'd flown into Nadi, DMF and I flew above the same blue lagoons, this time on our way out. As the Canadian Pacific aeroplane banked, we wept at the thought that we were seeing that superb panorama for the last time; we cursed our brainlessness in having ever volunteered to leave Fiji and, finally, we thanked whatever deity it was that had blessed us with the gift of Fiji as our home for three whole years of our lives.

1971–1982
Hong Kong

The Perfumed Harbour and Dirty Tricks

After fretting over the chances of our finding another overseas job after Fiji, we were flattered to find that we were wanted all over the place. We chose Hong Kong because after over 20 years I could forsake the charade of being a policeman. I was employed as a civilian to make sense of all the 'intelligence' coming into the Special Branch and to compose reports to Government and other intelligence agencies. Come 1971, you needed to hold a magnifying glass over a map of the world if you wanted to locate the tiny pink dots that showed all that remained of an empire that had once covered one-third of the world's surface. The most important, though not the largest, of these remnants was the colony of Hong Kong. Once one of the least promising of British possessions, by 1971 it was home to more souls than inhabited all the rest of the dots put together.

The island of Hong Kong came into British hands in 1841 by way of one of the murkiest episodes in an already dark imperial history. In the same manner in which the Sicilian mafia was later to run the drug trade in America, the British strong-armed the Chinese Emperor into giving up his attempts to protect his people against the devastating effects of opium addiction. Grown in British India, the drug was, in effect, force-fed to the Chinese masses in return for tea and silver. The Emperor tried using arms to stop the trade, but he was bullied not only into allowing its continuation, and also, at pistol-point, into giving up the island of Hong Kong 'in perpetuity'.

Home is Where You Make it

For all the massive environmental atrocities committed against Hong Kong since it was colonised, particularly since the end of the Japanese occupation, we could still see how wonderful Hong Kong must have looked to the first colonisers. Approaching the island from Macao as the pioneer colonialist would have done, you'd have sailed past little islets lying green and tranquil in the sun while junks quite as picturesque close-up as they were on the old postcards would have been sailing serenely in and out of sleepy little bays, and you'd have entered that 'perfumed harbour', intoxicatingly beautiful if not anywhere near as sweet smelling as it had been when it earned its name. Arising out of it stood Hong Kong island, like a massive ocean liner being serviced by fleets of ferry-boats, oil-tankers, merchant ships, hydrofoils, junks, lighters, tugs, yachts, schooners, houseboats, sailboats, skiffs, packets, warships and sampans in unbelievable numbers.

Once ashore though, it was welcome to the perpetual blare and blast of a million engines combusting within a very small space. In short, Hong Kong was further removed from Fiji than several thousand miles of sea; it was, in fact, one of the world's most heavily industrialised cities, a hothouse dedicated to one overriding purpose: making money – fast.

Repulse Bay

A few miles from the city proper and facing a palm-lined flight of graceful steps that gave way to the finest beach on the island, the venerable Repulse Bay Hotel, our home for several months, sat elegantly against a backdrop of modest hills. At one end of its beach stood 'Eucliff', a tasteless parody of an English castle built by a Chinese merchant possibly in the expectation that his imperial masters might reward his philanthropy by giving him a knighthood to go with his citadel. As if to emphasise his point, or perhaps in the hope of getting two knighthoods, the same merchant built a copy on the other side of the island and called it 'Euston'.

Burrowed into the hill at the other end of the beach there was a temple dedicated to the Chinese Queen of Heaven, Goddess of Seafarers, Tin Hao, she of the tall hat with its prison-bars style veil. A colossal statue of the Goddess stood gazing out to sea. On Sundays she attracted great throngs of Chinese worshippers. The spectacle made a cameo of Hong Kong: overpopulated, boisterous, clamorous, turbulent and rich.

The Junta

The 11 years we spent in Hong Kong added up to a third of our overseas life. I almost said 'colonial' life but, no matter that Hong Kong had a plumed-hatted governor, a legislative council, stuffy clubs, statues of Victoria and all the other associated regalia of Empire, I never felt it to be a colony, it just hadn't that feel about it: it lacked the sort of governmental disorder we'd felt comfortable with elsewhere. The place was, in fact, run not so much by colonial officials as by an all-powerful cabal of bankers, jobbers, accountants, merchants, lawyers and retired military brass and it showed: its governance was harsh, brash, soulless, hard disciplined and clinically efficient.

Made up of loan-sharks and retired generals, by way of lineal wealth and privilege, the controlling junta remained the true heirs of these giant 19th century British drug-traffickers who'd won the cession of Hong Kong from China in the first place. Indeed in 1972 it was still resonant with the very names of some of those old gentlemen-gangsters: Jardine Matheson, Butterfield, Swire and more. Those early titans spawned, or at least inspired generations of spivs from whence sprang the then current indaba: quick, clever, unscrupulous men (and a female or two), few of whom really believed in the notion that they were working for the good of Empire. Still less did they dream that they were taking up the white man's burden. They nevertheless perfected imperious, if not imperial, postures. They both dazzled and overawed outsiders by their arrogance, self-control, and extravagant lifestyles and by their self-conviction that they had the right to rule the territory and that it was the Chinese, not they, who were the interlopers.

A gratifying note is necessary at this stage because in the mid-1970s the portent of an – albeit distant – Chinese government takeover of the whole shebang began to darken the horizon, the ruling bankers' soviet consented to quite dramatic changes. It encouraged a wider Chinese participation in the financial institutions and in industrial control and politics. It had a sincere go at cleaning up the markets, approved of the installation of a thorough-going anti-corruption agency, and of anti-pollution measures, and gave the nod to enormous improvements in public housing.

The Line of Work

No matter what Hong Kong was like, the job I'd taken (report writing for the Special Branch) meant that I was supposed to help defend her from encroachment by 'the reds', meaning the billion Chinese to whom she actually belonged. As our plane nosed down during its approach into Kai Tak, we could see the Chinese mainland but, according to our propagandists, what we were looking at was a mean, unjust and joyless country: 'Red China'. No matter, it remained a fact that since I shared the same paymaster as the propagandists, I was constrained, at least on official paper, to toe the same line. Suffice to say that deprived of the opportunity I'd enjoyed in every other colony I'd worked in to escape from my desk by leaping aboard a *sampan*, launch, bus, automobile, aeroplane or bicycle, I found the hours of work confining and extremely stressful. Out-of-office hours weren't free from stress either; how could they have been when the very anatomy of Hong Kong suffered from chronic high-blood pressure? But they held many rewards as well, some of them enduring.

We learned to take advantage of the elements and, to our amazement, to discover rolling plains, sharp peaks, rugged shorelines, sandy beaches, walled-villages ancestral halls, shuttered temples, centuries old flag-stone pathways, burial sites, reservoirs, streams, ponds and the innumerable oceans of peasants bent low over rice fields. We'd swim in the sea only to climb once more and then scramble down again. Most of our walks were completed in sunshine but quite often we faced deluges of rain and, sometimes, cold, biting sleet and numbing winds blowing straight down from Siberia. We'd come to Hong Kong totally unprepared for its concealed, magnificent rural hinterland. One thing's certain: had we not discovered it, we'd never have stayed there for 11 whole years. The difference between town and country was sharp. Instead of breathing poisonous machine-age wastes you drew in the keen, rancid, overpowering odour of the earth together with a mix of human leavings, rotting fish and chemical fertilisers.

Like any Chinese with a sense of his country's history the urban Hong Kong Chinese would count his blessings. "My God!" he'd say, "Vegetables,

meat, fruit and tea, as much rice as I can eat twice a day – this is paradise."
He preferred the factory floor to his home, he never dreamt of going on
strike, never wanted a holiday and worked all the overtime he could get.

He could also have spent time in one of several excellent sports
stadia, swimming pools or, if he'd a dollar or two to spare, racecourses;
all of them second-to-none in the world. But he'd have been prepared
also to push and shove, elbow and kick his way in and out, the truth
was that just about anywhere was better than home, a sad fact that sent
thousands to add to the already appalling street congestion by pushing
wheelbarrows piled high with 'bargains'. These itinerant hawkers
peddled not only in the hope of making money but also because
peddling kept them usefully out of their homes at times when it wasn't
their turn to use one of the bunks (many a bed space in public housing
in those days was occupied by three people taking eight-hour turns).
You'd see people squatting on the five-foot way selling cigarettes from
a stock of as little as four or five packets or you'd have seen men sitting
behind tiny shoe-cleaning boxes who'd polish, at best, three or four
pairs of shoes a day; these people couldn't possibly have made enough
to live on but that wasn't the point – the objective was to stay clear of
home and if you could do that and turn a few cents into the bargain,
so much the better.

Those privileged few (by no means most of them white) whose
homes gave them enough space, comfort and privacy to entice them to
spend a lot of their free time in them could also – again unlike the masses
– repair whenever they felt like it to clubs, golf-courses and marinas,
playgrounds of such opulence (*lapis lazuli* restrooms, onyx staircases and
silent, leather-chaired, and well-stocked libraries) that they had to be seen
to be believed. On top of all that for the same favoured few (though
not in this matter due to the size of their wallets but because of their
Western cultural disposition), there were theatricals performed under the
patronage of the same mafia of power brokers and influence peddlers who
held the reins over the ruling junta. Keen to promote their city-state to
cultural as well as commercial prominence, they ordained and supervised

the staging of arts and film festivals, operas and ballets and they endowed a Philharmonic Orchestra.

The Anglican cathedral staged lunchtime concerts. Apart from its great doors and windows being flung wide open and the scores of ceiling-fans that whirred as if the rafters were full of little helicopters, on these musical occasions the church resembled nothing so much as an English Priory. But wait: a Chinese baritone sings Schubert in German, a Filipino soprano sings Rossini's 'O Mio Balbino Cara' in Italian and the concert ends with the two of them singing a Sullivan duet in English.

DMF and I often shared the Lamma Island ferryboat with a couple of hundred factory workers or students taking a rare day off. Even to other Chinese, the Cantonese are notoriously the loudest-mouthed people on earth. Put 200 of them together in a confined space, get them in a holiday mood and distribute one ghetto-blaster to every third holiday-maker and you have added mightily to Hong Kong's noise pollution problems. Adding to noise defilement, every single one of the 200 would happily spend the hour's crossing in tossing garbage into the ocean. Angelic-looking young females, so scrubbed and fastidious that they would never touch their sugared buns with their delicate, bare fingers, but would instead hold them carefully within their plastic wrappers right up until the last crumb had been consumed, when without giving the matter another thought they'd cheerfully fling the wrappers straight overboard. The ferry's litterbins stayed empty while the abused ocean heaved beneath a carpet of refuse; just about the only things not thrown over the sides were the 'Keep Hong Kong Clean' posters. The same prim girls, oblivious to what there was in front of their eyes, would queue patiently in long lines waiting their turn to use one of the two unspeakably filthy lavatories, latrines awash with faeces that had missed the hole that was meant to carry them into the sea. Individually spotless, shy, quiet and beautifully mannered, our 200 companions were collectively, although they themselves would never have believed it, raucous, rude and unclean.

Once ashore, graceful, sweet, clean-looking young things, gossamer girls charming in their bikinis and pretty as pictures, laughed in the sunshine and, as if they were gliding into the purest salt-waters in the world, walked into what had been turned into a wet garbage dump.

Old colonials from the furthest corners of the dying Empire finished up in Hong Kong: a former colonial secretary from Fiji; policeman from Lesotho; a magistrate from Tanganyika; an Arabian classicist from Aden; a surgeon from Nigeria; a forester from Ghana and so on. Meeting for the first time in their lives in Hong Kong however they behaved as if they'd been friends forever; they immediately established social and professional cohesion, remembered mutual acquaintances, shared jokes and stories about PWD furniture in Sierra Leone and the Solomon Islands, shipping lines, clubs, scandals, exams, pay and oddball characters.

You'd find identical drugstores in every town in every country that housed a Chinese community, at the counter you could order a bewildering array of exotic nostrums: tiger-bone wine; antler juice; dried sea-horse (from a display of a variety from which you'd take your pick); pressed bumble-bees; pearls (for sucking, not for adornment); miniature pyramids that you'd place above a contusion and then set them alight; rhino horn for impotency, lassitude and fevers; the powder from crushed, dried sparrows for defective eyesight; anything between an inch and a metre of grotesquely shaped ginseng root, again, for frigidity. Essence of snake! The dust of pulverised cicadas! A cocktail of frog's spawn! Jellied antelopes' heels to put a spring in your step! Serpent's blood! Dog's broth for hypothermia! Bear's paws (delicacies that for just one banquet serving would set you back tens of thousands – they had to be soaked in ice-cold water until the flesh could be eased from the bone without losing the hairs)! Monkey's brains!

Mount Stenhouse

Curious as I was I never got around to finding who Stenhouse was – or had been – when he'd lived in Hong Kong. He must have been a somebody though to have had a hill named after him. Mount Stenhouse rose to 1,500 ft above Lamma Island, not much of a mountain and not much of an island but a hill that was easy to climb and from whose summit you could drink in a heart-stopping vista. DMF and I, regular climbers of Mount Stenhouse, never once came across another human visitor but we never missed sighting two of its more conspicuous permanent inhabitants – a pair of 'Benotti's' eagles. I never found out who Benotti was either. Given its close proximity to nerve-wrecking Hong Kong island, Stenhouse's golden silence was uncanny as was the vision of those two spectacular birds circling high over their territory – above the ocean above the sweep of wild, tangled scrub, flying within their own generous space of empty sky. Oh fortunate Benottis!

Alone on top of Stenhouse one hot brilliant day, I lay for hours on a warm slab of stone looking in vain for the Benottis. Then, just when I'd given them up I spotted one hovering above the sea, a speck in the distance. The next moment, as if from nowhere its mate was hanging but a metre above me, all of its one metre wing span aflutter as it turned first one eye then the other to inspect me, trying perhaps to figure out whether or not I promised food. I could have reached up and touched it, it was that close, but I held my breath instead, hoping to detain it. Then, as suddenly as it had appeared it banked and swooped away to join its mate out at sea.

There were restaurants bearing comparison with the smartest in New York, offering menus that would have graced any bistro in Paris. Yet within a few metres of these centres of excellence there'd be sidewalk stalls displaying, among many other unspeakable delicacies, strings of what looked like upside-down, mottled-pink, wax candles but which were in fact sausages made from pork fat compounded with substances whose origins were best not enquired into, the result being tubes of meat speckled with knots of creamy, unhealthy-looking fat. Whole streets were given over to eating houses offering specialities such as noodles, dim-sum, raw-fish, salads, T-bone steaks, roast beef, snake soup, crumpets, goulash, pastries, gizzards, fried chicken and some, under the counter, stewed dog. There was a commonly held conviction among the Chinese that the less money the management spent on hygiene, the more he'd have left over to spend on its food; ergo, the darker, grimier and smellier the place, the tastier its dishes.

Colonies and Constables

No comparison can be drawn between the homeland police force and those in protectorates, dependencies mandated territories, or what we'll call the colonies. On the one hand the home forces were answerable to elected local councillors who exercised little political influence nationally and who bore no intelligence responsibility whatsoever. Hence their Special Branches enjoyed only a limited, provincial competency and performed but a poor second-fiddle role to the national intelligence agencies: M15, MI6 and GCHQ.

Colonial police forces on the other hand were centralised and clothed with authority sufficient for them to apply the will of colonial administrators empowered to run countries often larger than the imperial homeland itself. Unfettered by obligations to electorates, colonial governments were charged exclusively to promote the imperial interest. Their need for armed support and security intelligence, such as it was pre-war, was met almost wholly by small constabularies. These were compelled to strengthen and exalt urgently as the anti-colonialist gale blew across the post-war world.

And so it was that from 1947 onwards, colonial police forces found once-niggardly treasuries offering them blank cheques. With their pockets full and their motivation coarsened by Cold War polemics, colonial Special Branches bought up all the esoteric, high-tech merchandise they could get their hands on.

Never mind that many parts of Empire lacked reliable electricity, fancy electronic gadgetry was nevertheless rushed to its farthest corners. In colonies whose telephone lines were tied to coconut trees and whose telephone directories had fewer pages than their parish magazines it became *de rigueur* to tap telephones. Big, costly, wasteful and sometimes baleful Special Branches became fashionable parts of the machinery of colonial governments. They were supposed to help abate if not halt the growth of anti-colonialist movements but, given the speed with which the Empire came to an end, big as they grew to be, they quite clearly failed. One or two examples apart, colonial Special Branches grew too quickly; they became expensive legacies with which outgoing colonialists saddled incoming nationalists.

One colonial Special Branch remained very much alive into the 1990s and even expanded all the time; such was the nature of the beast. That was the one in Hong Kong, a colony that way back in 1949 had appeared to be the most threatened of all but one that outlasted all the others. Hong Kong in 1949 was set about by anti-imperialism: to the east lay 'Red China'; to the west the Philippines were wrecked with 'communist' insurgency; to the south the French were embattled in Indo-China, Malaya had declared a state of emergency, while Indonesia was being taken over by revolutionaries. Lastly, to the north, was Stalin's Soviet Union. Feeling besieged, Hong Kong's alarmed governor sought insurance by allocating a hefty slice of his colony's revenue to the police force. A good share of that bonus went to the Special Branch, which, in turn, spent it on inflation of manpower and on shopping around for electronic bits and pieces.

The Hong Kong Police Service, more than 25,000 strong, was a para-military organisation controlled through a regimental-style chain-of-command designed to ensure instant, blind obedience of orders. Nine out of ten of those who graduated through its training course found life to be exactly what they'd hoped for, the square-bashing, the uniform-wearing and the foul language suited them just fine. Far from questioning what they were told by superiors who'd graduated through the same procedures years before, they themselves ended up ramming down their equally unquestioning juniors' throats the same vulgar credo they'd had drilled into them: they were proud to be yeomen of the international capitalist fraternity – 'defenders of the free world', they would steadfastly keep guard over a system of economics and of governance whose every critic was, to them, malevolent.

The Special Branch's manpower came from within that herd-culture. In uniform one day, policemen would on the next find themselves in mufti attending a course of introduction to the Special Branch, a course wherein the 'instructors' were fellow policemen who, probably, only weeks before had themselves been supervising traffic flows but who, having been, perhaps in charge of the Special Branch's 'Russian desk' for a week or two, were judged to be qualified to lecture on the evils of the Soviet system. All the lecturer had to do was read aloud from notes prepared by MI6 during the iciest of the Cold War years. It counted in his favour, however, if he were to speak his anti-'red' lines with venom.

As for the students, having been programmed in advance to believe in the righteousness of the cause to which the Special Branch was sworn, they hardly needed a training course to convince them that 'Marxists' were to blame for all the world's troubles. Far above the novices there stood the Director, a Deputy Commissioner of Police who ran the special branch through a pompously named 'Directorate' made up of himself and his four most senior subordinates. His 'directorate' ruled over several hundred policeman supported by a couple of hundred 'civilians', all of whom directly, or indirectly, were spooks.

From the director down to the lowest detective no single policeman in the Special Branch was ever allowed to forget that first and foremost they belonged to a uniformed, disciplined service. Already subject to countless ukase like colonial regulations, civil service rules and routine police orders, he was in addition called upon to obey scores of internal directives known as 'Special Branch Standing Orders', compliance with which closed the bureaucratic ring already tightly drawn around his professional and private lives.

On top of all that the CIA was present in powerful force, the FBI also stuck its nose in and of course the various consulates carried the usual quota of spooks. But whatever they were called separately: MI5, MI6, CIA, FBI, military intelligence, GCHQ, Special Branch; all of them were cloaked with some charlatan mystique crafted to portray them as good guys fighting bad guys. The myth was meant to cover their indiscriminate use of dirty tricks and their hole-and-corner style of work. The 'free world' was forever being told that the mainly anonymous figures who ran the nations' underground services were God-fearing paragons appointed in secret maybe, but with all due propriety, by democratic governments. It was put about that they were fearless – albeit faceless – defenders of freedom who shared their secrets one with the other. Their judgements therefore, the story went on, were based, finally, on the broadest available wealth of intelligence. Ergo, it continued, their advice could be ignored only at the 'free world's' peril. The denouement, buttressed in mass-produced, best-selling, romantic spy novels, was that the 'free world's' secret heroes were masters of their art; both morally and professionally more than a match for enemy outfits such as the KGB which, conversely, were led by thugs and manned by mobsters.

Double-speak and Double Glazing

One of the world's leading manufacturing and financial centres, Hong Kong was home to a monstrously top-sided, over-populated society ruled over by foreigners appointed by an alien, unloved, far-removed monarch. Far from being in turmoil, apart from World Wars and the knock-on effect of China's Cultural Revolution in 1967, Hong Kong reposed in more than a century of tranquillity. Critics of the colonial regime just couldn't make their voices heard above the clatter of cash registers.

Given, however, that the ruling junta was teeming with hawks and abounding in riches the Special Branch was overstaffed with officers following the dictat that 'the threats' ('threat' was a much overworked buzz-word within Hong Kong's law-and-order circles) were many and diverse but that the overriding 'threat' came, of course, from 'communism'. The truth was however that the communists (and there were indeed many of them), were the least likely of any anti-colonial group to do anything to disturb the status quo. No amount of re-writing the script could alter the fact that the communists needed only to wait until 1997 for the entire glittering caboodle to fall into their lap without having to raise a finger. It was indeed to China's enormous advantage, actually to help the British keep the peace.

Neither was it a secret calling for undercover scrutiny that the leading positions in these organisations would always be filled by party cadres. Hence, from a glance at the staff lists published openly by 'left wing' or 'patriotic' institutions you could keep score of party members in strict order of seniority; there was no call for Special Branch to spend more than a few dollars a year on identifying and categorising the 'enemy order of battle'.

To counter the threat the directorate was influenced by the fact that two-legged spies had gone out of fashion internationally. Electronic espionage was all the rage. It being no longer disreputable therefore for intelligence agencies to be without human agents, the directorate was under no pressure to improve its abysmal record in that area. Instead, it pinned its faith in electronic eavesdropping, the mechanical opening of people's mail and telescopic surveillance.

'Techops' promised instant intelligence but their electronic gadgetry could be nerve-wreckingly difficult to instal and devilishly unreliable when in place. Among its many problems in this regard, the directorate always faced the ghastly prospect of policemen being discovered *in flagrante delicto* as they tried to break into one of the buildings owned by the Chinese state. As any reader of spy-fiction knows – and the directorate were avid readers of the genre – the chances of being caught in the act of bugging were high. Small wonder then that hardly a week passed by without some techop idea being scrapped.

The hazards were legion; there was simply no guaranteed safe and sound way of planting electronic devices. A power drill, for instance, muffled or not, always gave off a whine; a hammer could easily slip from fingers with a crash or it could bring forth an involuntary scream as it crushed a thumb; a passer-by falling over an unexpected, outstretched foot would yell out in surprise; torches went on the blink; the toughest of tough guys would hiccough or sneeze; what was thought to be merely plaster would turn out to be concrete; doors wouldn't lead where they were supposed to lead; concealed pipes and cables would turn out to be encountered in places they'd no right to be; the catalogue of possible pitfalls was endless.

For all that however some microphones were indeed triumphantly pushed home but the festive spirit was usually dampened by the first sober analysis of what the microphones were actually picking up, leaving both operators and directorate feeling sorry that they'd chosen to rely on electronic, not flesh-and-blood spies. Time and time again for example the lesson was rammed home that gadgets couldn't respond to pleas for the target to speak slowly and clearly, to stick to the point, refrain from exaggeration, avoid prejudice, tell the truth, cut the cackle or be punctual. Nor could anything be gained by threatening to cut an electronic circuit's pay if it didn't do any better. Nor yet could it be switched to a different target sent on a training course, spurred on by praise or by an extra thousand dollars, blacklisted, intimidated or made to feel ashamed of itself.

Finally, to anybody who had reason to have been taught a few rudimentary rules (and they included every single Chinese Communist Party member), prophylactic action against techops was child's play. If you feared being bugged all you had to do to be safe was regularly move your furniture around, play background music, swap telephones, hang curtains, paint the walls, cover your floors with lino or rugs, never talk business over the phone and/or – a sure-fire way of silencing an 'activator' – place your telephone in a cardboard box. And, if you were really determined, there was any amount of anti-gadget gadgetry on sale in the local market place.

Blunders, Bungles and Bumbles

In all the 33 years between the end of the war and 1982 (the year I left Hong Kong) the Special Branch, MI5, MI6 and the CIA working in concert in the colony, managed to recruit just two flesh-and-blood spies who had any chance at all of ever promising anything that might truthfully have been described as 'intelligence' about this principal, mutual target; the Chinese Communist Party. Neither lived up to their billing. One of the two was Lee Cheeming a member of the CCP who'd been recruited – albeit by a fluke – by the Special Branch in the late 1960s. He seldom produced intelligence that wasn't available from weekly 50-cent copies of the *Ta Kung Pao*. The other was one Luo Chungxun, a party member and editor of the Beijing-controlled newspaper, *New Evening Post*. He was recruited in the early 1970s by a CIA team which, together with the Special Branch, paid him vast sums of money for nothing worth more than a few dollars a month.

All things considered, the wonder of it was that Luo wasn't 'blown' years before he was. In the spring of 1992 he was summoned to Beijing for 'consultations'. He never came back. According to later releases by the New China News Agency he'd been 'detained for investigation into alleged spying for the US, tried, convicted and sentenced to ten years imprisonment'. Unexpectedly, in a land where people are shot for a lot less than spying, after serving only a few months in custody, Luo was released 'on parole'.

Greenhouse

"Thank heaven," it was always being said in Special Branch headquarters, "thank heaven for 'Greenhouse', he's the one who never let us down." 'Greenhouse' was the code name for a techop that began in the late 1960s when a miniature microphone was pushed into a room that served as the headquarters of Tang Wei, the CCP cadre responsible for the party-controlled trade unions in Hong Kong. Positioned but a stone's throw from police headquarters, that little device worked well, confining its tantrums to the summer months when an air-conditioner, crying out in vain for urgent attention, rattled away in the background to deafen the microphone.

That's how it came about that a team of people at police headquarters worked full-time, year in, year out, repeatedly recording the same extraordinarily uncomplicated message: The 'communist' trade unions, enacting a strategy directed from Beijing, were going out of their way to help the colonial administration preserve industrial peace and social good order in the colony.

Mutiny and Misdirection

The operations briefly touched upon were those of which the Special Branch was most proud – a fact that will give you a good idea about the standard of the rest of them. Fortunately, it didn't matter a damn because Hong Kong's security situation was so sound that it could have done without a Special Branch altogether. Indeed, the colony would have been better off without the Special Branch because the millions it cost annually could have been better spent on social measures thus reducing social discontent and by that act improving security at the same time.

Even so, on a November morning in 1977 the populace nearly paid a very high price indeed for having an incompetent intelligence service. On that momentous day hundreds of rank-and-file policemen marched, unlawfully, upon police headquarters where they formed ranks in smart military-cum-police-depot fashion. Paraded thus beneath their very own Commissioner's window they bellowed on command demanding that Government's newly formed anti-corruption agency be dragged off their backs, or else.

The Commissioner was shell-shocked. And within minutes the alarm bells were ringing also in Government House. Aides rushed in to warn His Excellency that he faced the immediate prospect of 20,000 policemen breaking the peace they were paid and, more alarmingly, were armed to keep. Confronted out of the blue with a threat that could hardly have been more dire, the Governor had no choice but to give way to the mutineers. The classic colonial option of deploying locally-based imperial soldiers against recalcitrant native policemen was closed to the Governor of Hong Kong because of the fear that the rebellious Chinese police officers might call for 'patriotic' support from the 'motherland', where units of the People's Liberation Army stood but a few hours march away. But for the particular Governor in 1977 the hurried backdown was made all the more painful because he was the very same Governor whom on taking office years earlier, had pledged himself to cleansing the colony of its life-long curse of corruption. Now, embarrassed and humbled, he was compelled to declare an amnesty for hundreds of allegedly corrupt policemen. As the *South China Morning Post* put it on the 6 February 1978: '5 Nov 1977 will long be remembered as a black day in the history of Hong Kong. That day the government succumbed to blackmail by policemen and declared an amnesty for the corrupt'.

But even more discomposed than the Governor was the Director of Special Branch for the first thing he knew about the mutiny was hearing the roar of angry voices rising from the throats of policemen massed in the courtyard beneath his very own eyes and ears. He'd given government not the slightest hint that the most serious threat to the colony's well-being in its history (bar World War II) was to come not from the communist enemy he was always going on about but from its own police force – a service in which he, the Director of Special Branch himself, was a Deputy Commissioner. Not one of his awesome array of bugs, taps, moles, spies, laser-beams, hidden cameras, snares, double-dealers, interrogators, agents provocateurs, bully boys, lounge lizards and assorted swindlers, paid to keep him informed about all manner of goings-on, had picked up even the feeblest warning about the serious discontent raging amongst his very own men. Like the infamous great howitzers of Singapore, when the crucial moment came for them to be of value, all of the Director's costly 'sources' faced, immovably, in the wrong direction. They were listening out for whispers about trouble that might arise in just about every quarter except the one in which it did in fact break out.

The intelligence failure was so total and so nearly catastrophic that even some of the Branch's staunchest law-and-order allies shook their heads. But not for long. No sooner was it being put about in the corridors of power that a secret, high-level enquiry might be on the cards than the old, self-serving, incestuous alliance of policemen, soldiers, firemen, prison officials, bankers, MI5, MI6, GCHQ, Legislative Councillors and Secretaries of Security closed ranks around the beleaguered director. Within a day or two it was business as usual; the only change being that yet more government money was poured into Special Branch to enable the Director to set up yet another section, this one to spy on his own police force.

Endpiece

Every state in the world is entitled to employ espionage in its own defence. That entitlement applied no less to colonies. But, unlike sovereign states, colonies had to trust their police forces to do the job. In nine colonies out of ten it was a trust well-placed. Hong Kong, however, was not among the nine; she relied for her security and for much of her political intelligence on a Special Branch officered, with many honourable exceptions, by men who ought instead to have been patrolling the terraces of British soccer grounds. They comprised an unprincipled, artless, inefficient and wasteful secret society that, to its shame, the Hong Kong government was too craven to bring to heel.

Having lived for 11 years in Hong Kong we headed for Shropshire with no regrets apart from the sadness of leaving behind her magnificent hills and valleys and her buoyant, irrepressible people. By not so strange alchemy, the last of our imperialist days roughly coincided with the end of the Empire itself. We shall always live with the sweet memories of the languor and the sensuousness of Malaya, the endless sweep of the superb steppes of Tanzania, the multiple charms of Sarawak, the glory and robustness of Fiji and the grandeur of Hong Kong's hilltops. I remain a socialist, as I was back in Sutton-in-Ashfield, and a convinced opponent of colonialism.

And so ended our colonial life. We had experienced the lowering of the flag in four different territories while watching the ensign flutter its last gasps in a fifth. As a boy I had been repelled by the very concept of Empire; in my 60s I was elated to have seen the end of it. If there is one chapter of imperialism we British can be proud of it is the seemly manner in which we withdrew from it.2

Tim loathe wearing the uniform but when duty calls...